RUTGERS UNIVERSITY STUDIES IN PHILOSOPHY

NUMBER ONE

BISHOP BUTLER

MORALIST & DIVINE

BISHOP BUTLER

MORALIST & DIVINE

By

WILLIAM J. NORTON, Jr.

NEW BRUNSWICK

RUTGERS UNIVERSITY PRESS

1940

COPYRIGHT 1940 BY THE TRUSTEES OF RUTGERS COLLEGE

IN NEW JERSEY

PRINTED IN THE UNITED STATES OF AMERICA

To the Memory of My Brother

FRANCIS J. NORTON

this book is affectionately
dedicated

CONTENTS

CONTENTS

ƒ

PREFACE

THE PRESENT *work has grown out of an interest in fathoming, to the fullest extent possible, Butler's views on morality. In its present form it represents a comprehensive survey of his philosophy.*

One aspect of it, namely the moral, represents an attempt to discover from the totality of Butler's writings his answer to the question "What is virtue"; and to understand his answer when he tells us that virtue consists in man's following nature. In my treatment of this phase of Butler's philosophy I have viewed all of his writings with this particular interest in mind. I have regarded his public sermons and his religious writings as sources of information, capable of affording us further insight into his ethical point of view.

One result of surveying his religious and public writings from the point of view of morality has been a restatement of his doctrine of conscience that has taken us away from the usual orthodox interpretation that so many readers of Butler have believed in. We can no longer regard conscience in exclusion from man's wider interests. Morality no longer stands apart, but becomes a lesser aspect of a wider order. Within that wider scheme conscience assumes a definite status; in other words conscience leads us into politics, metaphysics and religion for its completed understanding. In terms of them it must be informed, if it is to be legitimately expressed, or relied upon as a guide to life.

Yet, I have not regarded Butler's writings merely as issues that contribute to the problem of morality. Although they can be so regarded, yet they refuse to remain so narrowly interpreted. Religion may be regarded as affording an insight as to my course of action here on earth; I may have in relation to it a problem as to how far I should believe in its tenets, or how far I should obey its teachings, yet, besides regarding it so, I am compelled to recognize that it has something to say on its own behalf, and that it aims to present a view as to the scheme of things. In recognition of this fact I have at the same time tried to view Butler's public and religious writings in the setting that he was

ix

interested in their having; I have sought, e.g., to view his thoughts on religion from the standpoint of its polemical relation to the Deists, as well as from the standpoint of its metaphysical implications. The latter point of view has, however, engaged my attention more than the former.

Towards this end I have interested myself in piecing together Butler's system of metaphysics. Most of this task has required a persistent effort to view as one piece Butler's implications and innuendoes on this subject; it has been necessary to scan rather closely his ethical and public writings so as to draw out from his obiter dicta his pertinent remarks and allusions to metaphysics and religion. I have felt, however, the task to be worth while, though the extent to which I have succeeded in its fulfilment, rests with the judgment of the reader. This aspect of my book represents in its statement a system of metaphysics that can be fairly called a Christian and Protestant one, in contrast to those of the Greeks, or of the Church fathers. How typically true it is of all Protestant creeds and sects au fond is not for me to say; nevertheless it can respectfully take its place along with systems of other metaphysical expression.

In reviewing Butler's writings I have become all too conscious of his dependence upon his contemporaries, namely Shaftesbury and Locke, but I have refrained to make this dependence explicit at the various stages of my exposition. To have done so would have taken me beyond my present aim, i.e., the interpretation of Butler's philosophy as a whole, viewed internally. But realizing the importance of making clear Butler's philosophical heritage together with my own inadequacy for such a task, I shall have to ask the meticulous reader to make good this deficiency for himself. I shall spare myself all the blame for this neglect in the hope that I have tried to supply him with one half of his labor. . . . It may also be objected by some that my exposition would have been heightened had I proceeded along more critical and evaluating lines, but here again, my defence is simply that I prefer the reader to do this for himself. After all, evaluation ab extra is so often a matter of individual attitude; and an insistence by an author of his own competence to do so is no guaranty that such criticism is valid. All too often, mastery of a particular subject matter is marred by the exhibited belief that such mastery renders one competent to judge its value in terms of alien materials and external standards. Against this intrusion *of evaluation upon exposition my objective presentation must be regarded as a protest.*

At this point I would like to acknowledge my indebtedness to those whose assistance has proved invaluable. Towards this end I would like to express my sincere thanks to Dr. John Storck under whose guidance this work originally progressed; also to Professors John Coss, Herbert Schneider, and John H. Randall, Jr., for help afforded. But particularly I owe a deep debt of gratitude to my wife whose constant assistance, encouragement and patience have made possible every word of my manuscript. To Professors W. D. Ross of Oriel College, Oxford, and Charles Hendel of McGill University, I am gratefully indebted for their close reading and helpful criticisms, many of which have saved me from inexcusable errors and hasty interpretations. And lastly to my mother and father I am thankful for their encouragement which has been a constant incentive to complete and publish this manuscript in its present form.

W. J. N.

BISHOP BUTLER

MORALIST & DIVINE

PART ONE

THE MORAL QUEST

1

INTRODUCTION

WHAT is the rule of life? What should we do, how should we conduct ourselves in life? This is the problem of morality, which is man's problem, the most important one he can raise for himself; and also the most difficult to answer. It is the problem that Butler sets himself to solve. Although he couched the problem in different terms by asking: What is virtue? the issue is the same as that which was raised before him by Plato, Aristotle, and after him by Kant and many others in their moral treatises.

One's failure to understand Butler's views on morality lies in the fact that too many of his readers have narrowed themselves exclusively to the study of the Ethical Sermons—to the neglect of his Public Sermons and *Analogy*—for an answer to their quest. The *Analogy* especially has been regarded merely as a controversial work in religion.

For the sake of convenience I shall refer to Butler's *Fifteen Sermons* as his Ethical Sermons, or Sermons; *Six Sermons Preached upon Public Occasions* as his Public Sermons; and his *Analogy of Religion Natural and Revealed to the Constitution and Course of Nature*, as his Analogy.

All references to Butler's writings will be made to the Gladstone Edition, Oxford, 1897, in my text simply by volume and page. Elaboration of arguments from the same edition, as well as references to other sources will be entered in as footnotes at the bottom of the page. For complete titles, see Appendix.

The belief that Butler's Ethical Sermons afford all that he had to say on the subject of morality has obscured from the ordinary reader the wider realms of positive content that are to be found in his other writings. It has been the main cause of misconceptions as to Butler's fundamental position on moral issues. The nature of conscience, for instance, has been misconceived. Its claims to supremacy have been contested by some; they

1

have maintained self-love and benevolence to be rival principles. Does conscience evolve for man the ideals of correct conduct, or does it discover these in the nature of the universe? Upon what authority does conscience deliver its dictates; are they infallible or not? On all of these issues there have been evidenced indecision and contradictory points of view. But if we take the self in its larger context and view it in reference to Butler's views on metaphysics and religion, many of these misconceptions are cleared up, and a higher degree of unanimity on these mooted issues is attained. To do this successfully we must take into account all of Butler's views and trace their bearing upon the fundamental issues of morality.

The nucleus of Butler's ethical theory is to be found in his *Fifteen Sermons*, first published in 1726. Of these the most important are the first three, for they contain the theoretical framework of his moral system. The remaining twelve sermons represent an expansion of his theoretical position applied to particular issues. In the preface to his Ethical Sermons we find a summary of his extensive statements, and in his *Dissertation on Virtue*, published in 1736, as an appendix to the *Analogy*, we find re-expounded his views on "conscience" especially since Hutcheson's moral sense theory was beginning to attract attention.

We know that Butler's printed Sermons do not contain all that he had to say on the subject of morals—for in the first edition of the Sermons, he tells us himself that they were selected from among many others "preached in the same place throughout a course of eight years." Furthermore, it is quite plausible to believe that the papers Butler had burnt by the arrangements of his will contained many other sermons.[1] To what extent these would have thrown further light on Butler's ethical position, had they been preserved and published, remains of course a matter of interesting conjecture.[2]

[1] Clause two of his will: "lastly, it is my positive and express will, that all my sermons, letters and papers, whatever, which are in a deal box, locked, directed to Dr. Forster, and now standing in the little room within my library at Hampstead, be burnt without being read by anyone, as soon as may be after my decease." Bartlett, pp. 275-6.

[2] In Chalmers' Lectures on Butler's Analogy—Posthumous Works, edited by the Rev. W. Hanna, Vol. IX, Edinburgh, by Thos. Constable and Co., MDCCCLII, on p. XLIV, we have offered for our consideration the following surmise. ". . . the best conjecture we can form may be, that the remaining sermons at the Rolls, (for the future publication of which that sentence in the preface seems designed to prepare,) were afterwards worked into the *Analogy*."

A second edition of the Sermons was published four years later than the first on September 16, 1729, while Butler was still at Stanhope. The reason for the appearance of this second edition is to be found in Butler's attempt to meet the charge of obscurity that was raised against the Sermons when they first appeared. No essential changes were made, however, other than those of punctuation. In regard to the charge of obscurity he defended himself in his preface by saying that the alleged difficulty of the subject matter was due to the uninformed intellectual state of his readers.[3] He was supported in this respect by Dr. Samuel Clarke who in comparing Butler's Sermons to Euclid's Elements said: "Difficulties they may have, but difficulties soon mastered by the degree of attention which such subjects require." [4]

It is only when we come for consideration to Butler's *Analogy* published in 1736 and his Public Sermons delivered between the years 1738 to 1748 that we are introduced to supplementary material. Through the *Analogy* we become acquainted with Butler's cosmological views; and learn for the first time the wider references of the self, the sanctions of the moral life, and in the accounts of rational thought we gather the justification for Butler's moral theory. In the Public Sermons are afforded us Butler's philosophical views of society and the consequent duties incumbent upon man to follow. Taken together these two sources, i.e., the *Analogy* and the Public Sermons, complete Butler's theoretical structure of ethics, first presented in 1726.

The conjecture is strongly supported by our finding that the germ or leading principle of the *Analogy* had already been recognized, as when, in his sixth sermon, Butler says, "that there is a much more exact correspondence between the natural and moral world than we are apt to take notice of." "If when arranging his sermons at the Rolls, taking out fifteen from amongst them for present publication, there were others which, on account of their containing the great principles of his future work, Butler carefully reserved, and if he took these sermons with him to the country to be slowly reconstructed and condensed during the long period of his seclusion at Stanhope, the *Analogy*, which was at last given to the world in 1736, might fairly enough be said to have been 'carefully and closely packed up' out of at least eighteen years' hard thinking."

[3] *Vide* Vol. II, p. 4. "Thus a subject may be treated in a manner, which all along supposes the reader acquainted with what has been said upon it, both by ancient and modern writers; and with what is the present state of opinion in the world concerning such subject. This will create a difficulty of a very peculiar kind, and even throw an obscurity over the whole before those who are not thus informed; but those who are will be disposed to excuse such a manner, and other things of the like kind, as a saving of their patience."

[4] Bartlett, *Vide opus cit.*, p. 34.

In his Ethical Sermons Butler announces the method of enquiry he intends to follow. The subject matter of morality, he holds, can be treated in one of two ways: either from the abstract relations of things, i.e., the discovery by reason of virtue, its meanings, kinds and interrelations, carried on independently of their specific exemplification in human affairs; or from a study of moral facts themselves in which human nature is directly seen to be the central figure and accordingly the locus of one's investigation. Concerning the first type of investigation Butler presumably had in mind such treatments as those of Clarke and Wollaston; whereas Shaftesbury as his contemporary was undoubtedly the chief representative of the second view.

Each method has its advantages, and both, Butler maintains, may lead to the practice of virtue. Whereas the former method of treatment shows vice to be contrary to the nature and reason of things, the second shows vice to be a breaking in upon *human* nature. Neither is to be considered, however, as exclusive of the other point of view; but each must be looked upon as reinforcing and strengthening the other. The abstract method has this in its favor, namely, that it can discuss the subject of morality and establish its truths in a direct, certain and formal manner; but the empirical method of investigating morality has the advantage of discussing the problem in its more specific and concrete embodiments, namely as reflected in the observed circumstances of human relationships and affairs. In this respect it can make a wider appeal (Vol. II, p. 5). It is presumably for this reason that Butler announces his intention of pursuing the particularistic and empirical method of approach, and not because the rationalistic method is in any way inadequate to encompass the problem of morals.

The announcement of the empirical method allies Butler to the school of Locke that was beginning to make its influence felt. In his later writings Butler develops for his reader his views on epistemology and inductive logic; the former rather scantily in his Sermons on Human Ignorance and Chapter One of the *Analogy*, the latter in the Introduction to the *Analogy* and briefly in the second footnote to Sermon One of the Ethical Sermons. I have discussed in full Butler's methodology in my chapter on Reason in the Moral Life. He disclaims all *a priori* assumptions, though he speaks so fervently of reason at times that the reader is apt to believe that he has fallen into the ranks of rationalism (Vol. I, pp. 172, 183). But his position is consistently empirical, in that reason discovers through the reported evidence of the senses all that man is capable of finding out and all that he needs to discover for practical living. This is no less true of man's religious knowledge, which is the highest kind he can gather; even one's knowledge of God, the Universe as his creation, and the progressive development characteristic of all created things, comes to man only as he persistently applies himself to a study of extant facts and gives himself up to the discovery of their causes. In this task reason is limited to what the senses report.

2

BUTLER AND HIS TIMES

IT IS surprising that so little should be known about a man whose contribution to ethics is extravagantly hailed as a "plummet dropped into depths before unsounded," [1] and whose work on the philosophy of religion Mackintosh calls, "the most original and profound work extant in any language." [2] Outside of a few remains discovered since the writing of Bartlett's *Memoirs*—published in 1839—our chief source of material concerning the life of Butler is still Bartlett's work. And even this comprehensive study was made some eighty-five years after Butler's death, so that the more minute details which the work furnishes must be accepted with a wary caution. In Egglestone's *Stanhope Memorials*, one seeks in vain to learn further about the life, habits and intimate thoughts of Butler during the time when he published his Sermons and wrote his *Analogy;* one is rewarded only by lists of petty expenditures made during Butler's rectorship, or chronologies of the tradesmen who were his contemporaries— and the incidental fact that Butler attended to mortar as well as to metaphysics . . . Whatever papers might have thrown more light upon the details of his life were requested by Butler himself, in his last will, to be burnt,[3] and the few actual remains of writings other than the known published works that have survived are most trivial in nature.

Although a great deal is known about the times that Butler lived through, yet we possess no information as to how he reacted to them; or indeed whether he was spiritually a part of them. Whether Butler was heir to a philosophic tradition that passed on to him its unsolved difficulties, we have no precise means of knowing. Pattison suggests that Butler's *Analogy* was an answer to the arguments of the Deists, that Butler had carefully formulated during his metaphysical evenings with Queen Caroline and her coterie. If so, Butler's relation to his age was of an academic nature. Both in Butler's Ethical Sermons and in his Public Sermons we find indicated no close rapport between him and the events of his time. His Sermons are actuated largely by theoretic

---

[1] *Vide* Whyte, A., *Bishop Butler, An Appreciation;* Eager, p. 31.
[2] Mackintosh, *Dissertation on the Progress of Ethical Philosophy*, p. 135.
[3] Cp. Bartlett, *opus cit.*, pp. 275-6.

interests, or based upon Biblical texts, chosen at random; in his Public Sermons he commemorates historical occasions, or elicits support for charitable and educational institutions.

Our knowledge of Butler in relation to his time must be gathered from a perusal of his writings. Even there the direct references are few. They make clear, however, that he regarded the age in which he labored as one in which both morals and religion were at a low ebb; he held that the two dominant vices of the period were the decline of religious belief and the inordinate prevalence of a narrow self-regard. In his Sermons on Public Occasions, notably the first and the second, he mentions that irreligion is at present the chief danger of the age (Vol. II, p. 248), and that the scorn of religion generally abounds (Vol. II, p. 267). Nor does Butler change his mind in his other writings. The advertisement to the *Analogy* comments upon the prevailing attitude of disbelief, and animadverts on the mirth with which religious tenets are received. "It is come," he says, "I know not how, to be taken for granted, by many persons, that Christianity is not so much a subject of inquiry; but that it is, now at length, discovered to be fictitious. And accordingly they treat it, as if, in the present age, this were an agreed point among all people of discernment; and nothing remained, but to set it up as a principal subject of mirth and ridicule, as it were by way of reprisals, for its having so long interrupted the pleasures of the world" (Vol. I, pp. 1, 2).

The growing seriousness of the situation led Butler at the time of his translation to Durham to make the laxity and decline of religion his main theme in his initial address to his clergy. He laments the general decay of religion as well as the increase in the number of professed disbelievers; he again declares the scorn of religion and the growing disregard of it to be the chief characteristics of his age (Vol. II, pp. 334, 335). Likewise with the current moral practices. Concerning these he says in his Sermon Upon the Love of Our Neighbour, "it may be spoken of as very much the distinction of the present to profess a contracted spirit, and greater regards to self-interest, than appears to have been done formerly" (Vol. II, p. 156).[4]

[4] Cp. also Vol. II, p. 16: "I am persuaded, that a very great part of the wickedness of the world is, one way or other, owing to the self-partiality, self-flattery, and self-deceit, endeavoured there to be laid open and explained. It is to be observed amongst persons of the lowest rank, in proportion to their compass of thought, as much as amongst men of education and improvement."

Apart from these random references to the times, such as those that have been quoted, there is little indication that Butler's references ever explicitly illustrate the current moral practices; they are always incidental to his discussion of a theory or a belief that has for him a more absorbing interest than the reform of his age. We can say that his interests are more largely academic and speculative than purposively practical—though this is not to commit ourselves to the statement that his theory of morals has no practical application. There is no particular evidence to afford us insight into the motives he had in mind when he delivered his ethical Sermons, whether they were to meet actual conditions of the day and combat current vicious moral practices, or whether his intentions were largely speculative and controversial. The latter, as we have mentioned, seems to be the proper interpretation; for in his discussion of fallacious moral doctrines he does not confine himself to his contemporaries, but includes within his survey the views of the classical moralists as well.

The sermons on morals were delivered in the chapel of the Rolls Court, but no material is extant that would inform us as to the number or nature of his parishioners or Butler's specific relations to them. His reading public was presumably drawn from the upper circles of London, and in addressing himself to them he deplores their indifference and mental sluggishness, their failure to exercise their judgments in seeking the truth of the principles which they follow in their conduct of life (Vol. II, p. 1; Cp. Pub. Sermons, I, II, IV, VI). In fact the age as Butler saw it was neither skeptical nor discriminating. Not only did the people take many things for granted, but they likewise whiled away their time in the idleness of light reading, and gave themselves over completely to books and papers of amusement. The result for the mind of this dissipation was that it led to an intellectual apathy, to an indifference to important and fundamental issues, and to a disregard of arguments, especially when their presentation appeared to be difficult.

All of this, Butler considers, is most genuinely reflected in the attitude of the people towards the problems of morals. Here is a subject of undoubted difficulty, one that requires assiduous attention, for the ideas of which it treats are never clear and suf-

(*Vide* also references made in his Sermons on Public Occasions; pp. 254, 259, 267, 275.)

ficiently determinate in themselves. We must see the moral ideas we are to discuss in a variety of contexts; for even in the same author they frequently undergo a change of meaning. Even the exact manner in which moral ideas are expounded may vary with the writers; all of which adds to the difficulty of understanding.

Our attitude towards Butler's writings has been influenced largely by the fact that in their essential thought they are so little a product of their times. We do not disclaim that they are controversial in their manner of presentation, or that the language is the language of the 18th century. There is traceable in many parts of his positive views the influence of Locke and Shaftesbury. Likewise he explicitly opposes his views to Hobbes, and often has Hutcheson in mind. But there is likewise traceable in his positively held views the influence of Plato, Aristotle, the Stoics and Origen. It will be pointed out by some that Butler's *Analogy* is wholly a product of the age, and that its failure to grip the modern reader is owing to the fact that it is an extended controversy against 18th century Deism, a line of thought that has long since been superseded. The statement is undeniably true, but it is only a half truth that obscures the unique contributions of his own that Butler advanced. My own attitude towards the *Analogy* is one that sees in its more positive side the substance of man's moral ideas, and a well-thought-out metaphysics in which the rational explanation of these ideas can be found.

The following chapters will be concerned with the systematic exposition of Butler's moral philosophy; an attempt to present his fundamental views as they are implicit in and grow out of his statement that virtue is living in accordance with nature.

3

RIVAL THEORIES OF VIRTUE

TO FOLLOW nature is the meaning of virtue, but this phrase is by no means clear; it has been interpreted in a variety of ways that according to Butler do violence to the original intentions of the classical writers on morality. Unfortunately Butler does not state in any one part of his writings for the benefit of his reader the substance of these rival views. He touches upon them here and there, and unconsciously assumes his readers' familiarity with them.

Butler had in mind no one antagonist that he was eager to controvert. The issues and views to which he was opposed are not wholly representative of one individual or age, and his Ethical Sermons must be looked upon as an answer to a variety of fallacious moral tenets that have survived throughout the ages in the literature of morals, rather than views that were extant in any current moral practices. His controversial mind, eager in the search of truth, enables us to appreciate the wherefore of his arguments, and thus to avoid falling victims to confusion, or embracing as his positive doctrine what is only an answer to one rival position. We experience this uncertainty of meaning or stability in Butler's views as we try to grasp his attitude on self-love and benevolence or on happiness and virtue, for his method of treatment causes in the mind of the reader an uncertainty of judgment as to the drift of Butler's own professed beliefs. When he argues for instance that duty and interest are coincident, or that happiness and misery are of the greatest importance to us; or again "that fidelity, honour, strict justice, are approved or disapproved by mankind in general, in quite another view than as conducive to the happiness or misery of the world," he seems in these remarks plainly to be affirming contradictory views, and to challenge the patience of the reader who is intent on gaining access to his moral position. But when we recall that his intention in these various instances is polemical, i.e., merely to emphasize for the moment the elements of moral truth that he sees to be threatened, our difficulties are only partly solved for us, for there still devolves upon us the need of gathering Butler's ideas as he meant them to be known.

I do not wish to maintain that Butler himself is free from

overt contradictory statements, for he is not. One would have little difficulty in showing that his remarks on the principle of benevolence are far from unwavering. What I do maintain is that most of these views are not as inconsistent as they at first sight appear. I have found that the number of diverse interpretations that center about Butler's writings—and their number is legion—is owing largely to the fact that the interpreters seize upon some of these statements and ignore others. They take no trouble to collate these contradictory passages and strive for consistency. To render Butler consistent—i.e., to see his writings as all of one piece is no easy task, but only in doing this can one gain access to his thought, that otherwise stands foreign and obscure.

The polemical method is not without its ill effect; for his desultory way of handling controversy Butler pays the penalty by being a very difficult writer to read and understand. Whether interested in it or not, Butler was prevented from expounding his ethical views in any systematic manner. If he were conscious of his underlying systematic principles, he never made them explicitly clear to his reader, nor did he formulate them in any detail. The formulation of this ethical system we shall make our special task after we have first considered the moral beliefs that Butler thought were destructive of a genuine theory of morality. We shall now proceed to state the sum and substance of these beliefs.

EGOISTIC INDIVIDUALISM

First is the view that maintains all actions to be inherently selfish, motivated by a narrow self-interest on the part of the individual. Butler sees Epicureanism especially as represented in Torquatus's account given by Cicero in his *De Finibus*, to be a typical instance. In the more modern systems he sees the writings of Hobbes to be vitiated by the same error. According to Butler both these ethical positions denied the possibility of disinterested acts, and held that what one chooses to call benevolence turns out upon deeper investigation to be egoistic acts in disguise. "The desire of praise, and of being beloved," says Butler, paraphrasing the account of Torquatus, "he explains to be no other than desire of safety: regard to our country, even in the most virtuous character, to be nothing but regard to ourselves" (Vol. II, p. 18).

The moral theory that would follow from the blind and uncritical acceptance of man's nature as so depicted would be an individualism in which each act was morally sanctioned only as it served to portray the progressive establishment of self-love; one that was narrowly divorced from the consideration of others. We can expect in Butler's Sermons a reply to this position, based upon a reconsideration of man's psychological nature, within which the reality of disinterested acts is affirmed and given its proper moral setting. Hobbes, for Butler, is one of the chief offenders in his denial of disinterested acts (Vol. II, p. 356). Butler's answer to Hobbes's position, stated in his First Sermon on Human Nature, is an attempt to win recognition for the existence of benevolence as an original tendency in the nature of man; later on, i.e., in his Fifth Sermon, Butler again takes up arms to affirm man's natural tendency towards compassion. The denial that all acts spring from motives of self-love does not commit Butler to the view that no acts of self-love are virtuous, for he never wearies of telling us that self-love in its due degree forms an integral part of the virtuous man. One thing that we can expect to find in Butler's sermons is a detailed analysis of self-love in which its moral value and its relations to the other tendencies in human nature are made clear.

MORALISTIC ALTRUISM

Secondly, Butler is equally averse to those moral teachings that go to the other extreme, that insist upon benevolence as the highest virtue, and that appraise all moral acts only in terms of their approximation to this benevolent ideal. In reply to such views, Butler asserts: "The goodness or badness of actions does not arise from hence, that the epithet, interested or disinterested, may be applied to them, any more than any other indifferent epithet, suppose inquisitive or jealous, may or may not be applied to them" (Vol. II, p. 21). And then further on: "we may judge and determine, that an action is morally good or evil, before we so much as consider, whether it be interested or disinterested." Indeed, "disinterestedness is so far from being in itself commendable, that the utmost possible depravity which we can in imagination conceive, is that of disinterested cruelty" (Vol. II, p. 22).

We must be cautious here against embracing an extreme position in our search for Butler's own moral position. To affirm as Butler does that disinterestedness unguarded can often lead to cruelty and depravity should not result in the categorical rejection or discrediting of benevolent actions. In its proper setting and under the guidance of reason disinterested benevolence constitutes a specific attribute of the moral man. Accordingly we can expect from Butler a consideration of benevolence, a discussion of its origin as a natural tendency within the nature of man and an evaluation from the standpoint of morality of its virtuous aspect in relation to the admitted virtue of self-love.

While Butler does not refer specifically to any one writer as upholding the view that all virtues are resolvable into benevolence, according to Dr. Angus he probably had in mind the ethical views of Leibniz; and to this we can add the names of his contemporaries, Shaftesbury and Hutcheson—especially the latter. Butler's Dissertation on Virtue, which appeared in 1736 as an appendix to Part One, Chapter Three, of the *Analogy*, makes a special plea for the rejection of the claim of benevolence as the highest virtue. "Some (authors) of great and distinguished merit have, I think, expressed themselves in a manner, which may occasion some danger, to careless readers, of imagining the whole of virtue to consist in singly aiming, according to the best of their judgment, at promoting the happiness of mankind in the present state; and the whole of vice, in doing what they foresee, or might foresee, is likely to produce an overbalance of unhappiness in it; than which mistakes, none can be conceived more terrible" (Vol. I, pp. 336, 7). Since the first of Hutcheson's writings had appeared in 1725, the year before the Sermons of Butler were collectively published, and the other writings of Hutcheson had appeared before the publication of the *Analogy*, it is probable that Butler had in mind the intention of considering those aspects of Hutcheson which laid so much emphasis upon the nature of benevolence as the supreme virtue. The footnote to his Twelfth Sermon would indicate that Butler was concerned with not assigning too great a value to benevolence, and one can account for its appearance as a way of meeting controversially current statements that had appeared only after the Sermons had been delivered and been arranged for publication.

MORALISTIC NATURALISM

Finally, we can cite another moral position which Butler considered as ethically fallacious: the point of view that denied to man a moral sense or conscience, or which in admitting the existence of such a faculty within man's nature denied to it the supremacy that Butler would like to see assigned to it. As to those who denied to man the presence of a moral sense, Butler is directing his attacks against individuals who declare the morality of man to consist in following nature, but who construe the word "nature" to mean the instinct or tendency that happens at the moment of action to be the strongest within him. Such an interpretation of man would reduce him to the level of brute existence, and would declare his self-expression to lie mechanically in the blind pursuit of instinctive satisfaction. This view Butler sees to be destructive of the very groundwork of morality, for if we concede that the purpose of virtue and religion requires "that the *whole* character be formed upon thought and reflection; that *every* action be directed by some determinate rule, some other rule than the strength and prevalency of any principle or passion" (Vol. II, p. 47), it is necessary that we grant to man the presence of a moral sense or conscience that can determine this rule in advance of the moral act. Accordingly, we can expect that Butler will be interested in the establishment for man of the principle of conscience, that he will investigate its nature, seek its origin and evaluate it in its relations to his other moral and non-moral principles.

There are some moral theorists who admit that man is endowed with a moral sense, but who refuse to grant to it the highest degree of sovereignty for the moral determination of his actions. Such a deficiency of treatment can be detected, according to Butler, in Lord Shaftesbury's account of conscience in his Inquiry Concerning Virtue. The position, as Butler sees it, is that if the dictates of conscience were at any time to run counter to the happiness of the individual as he foresees it, then in the absence of the recognition that conscience should be absolutely supreme, there would be nothing for the individual to do but to follow his own happiness, which is a manifest obligation. And in extreme cases his own self-interest may prompt him to act viciously. The remedy of this lies, for Butler, in an analysis of conscience which will enable us once and for all to determine its degree of sovereignty and sphere of influence. It will show us at the same time that if we wish to take morality seriously we must accord to conscience supreme command and authority as its essential characteristics.

4

STATEMENT OF THE PROBLEM

WE ARE now in a better position to appreciate the purpose and drift of Butler's moral sermons. We can discern first a controversial element and secondly an attempt to establish a particular theory of morals.

There is scarcely a sermon of Butler's in which the controversial element is not markedly present; indeed this is outstandingly true even of the *Analogy* itself, which is a long reasoned reply to the Deists. As to the Sermons, compare, for instance, the First on Human Nature which disputes the reduction of benevolence to self-love and animadverts on the extension of self-love to those provinces that belong to the particular propensions; also in the same sermon, the denial of malevolent tendencies in man's nature. Likewise in Sermons Two and Three we find that the main discussion is centered upon those who define "nature" in such a way as to discredit its value for morals, while particularly in the latter sermon, Butler strives to defend the superiority of conscience against those who would look askance upon its *de jure* sovereignty. In the Fifth and Sixth Sermons on Compassion there again appears the element of controversy, which in this instance seeks against Hobbes to defend compassion as a fundamental tendency in the nature of man, and advances arguments against its reduction to pity and self-regard; in a like manner exception is taken to those who, while admitting the existence of compassion, proclaim that its encouraged use would endanger the impartiality of judgment, and thus obscure true moral insight. The Sermon on Resentment presents an argued defence for the place of resentment within the moral life against those who see in it no more than a source of evil. The polemical element is so outstanding in his Eleventh and Twelfth Sermons, On The Love of Our Neighbour, that the reader at first glance is at a loss to gather the intended drift of Butler's discussion and what he is actually committing himself to. His first thought is that Butler is contradicting himself, or establishing a position that is at variance with the statements in the earlier sermons. In these sermons, On The Love of Our Neighbour, he strives so much to secure recognition for benevolence as a fundamental tendency in man's nature that one is led to believe that Butler is discrediting self-love; but towards the end of the former sermon, i.e., the Eleventh, Butler is so eager not to underestimate the importance of self-love that his statements become emphatic enough to lead the reader unwarily to believe that benevolence is of secondary importance, and that here Butler is establishing an ethical hedonism. And as another instance we can point to the Dissertation Upon Virtue as an attempt to show that all virtue is not resolvable into benevolence, as some contemporaries of Butler upheld. . . . To state that the elements of controversy rage high in Butler's Sermons must not blind us to the fact that he was also concerned with the formulation of a constructive theory. Our intention is only to state that Butler made his disagreement with certain current ethical doctrines the occasion for the statement of his own constructive moral theory. It is their consideration and rejection that form for Butler the opportunity for advancing his own reflections and developing his own theory. And primarily it is the intruding presence of Butler's polemical interests that obscures for the reader Butler's own position. But upon an examination of his writings we can say that the systematic aspect of Butler's ethics lies implicit in the background of his thought, directing his weapons of attack and guiding their thrusts.

We can expect to find in Butler's Sermons a large part of the discussion given over to the determination of the relative positions of self-love, benevolence and conscience. But in order to arrive at a fair apportionment from the standpoint of virtue of these contending moral ideals, there must be some way in which their relative merits for the moral life can be discovered, and their places accordingly assigned. We have mentioned above that of the two possible ways in which the subject of morality can be pursued, the empirical—as I have chosen to call it—is the one to which Butler allies himself. Its mode of treatment must show that virtue is the expression of *human* nature, and that its contrary, i.e., vice, is the failure to express this nature. But to pursue this empirical method successfully, the nature of man must be investigated; we must apprise ourselves of man's structure and the parts that compose it; we must seek the relations of these parts to each other so that we can inform ourselves of those aspects of his nature which are truly representative of him and of those which are not; of the differences between him and the brutes. When we have informed ourselves of what it means to be a man, then we can indicate the course that he should follow if he wishes truly to live the moral life. We should also consider the sanctions for this moral prescription, natural or otherwise, the advantages internal to himself and the results in the way of happiness and satisfaction of that course of living. Lastly, we should know whether the moral life is a free self-expression or a submission of the self to elements or orders higher than its nature, i.e., to God. Upon all of these issues, Butler has something to say.

When Butler states that the problem of virtue can be settled by a determination of man's nature, and that virtue consists in the expression of that nature, he believes himself to be walking in the footsteps of the ancients,—notably the Stoics.[1] He maintains that this view is but a restatement of the classical position. His excuse for repeating it is his contention that in modern times the phrase 'to follow nature' has not been sufficiently understood; and that by some writers it has been grossly misrepresented. Butler had in mind here the statement of Wollaston in his Religion of Nature. Turning to it for a moment, we can better appreciate the force of Butler's contentions. Wollaston says in his first section on Moral Good and Evil,[2] "they who place all *in following nature,* if they mean by that phrase acting according to the natures of things (*that is,* treating things as being what they in nature are, or according to truth) say what is right. But this does not seem to be their meaning. And if it is only that a Man must follow his own nature, since his nature is not purely rational, but there is a part of him, which he has in common with brutes, they appoint him a guide which I fear will mislead him, this being commonly more likely to prevail,

---

[1] Professor Hendel has pointed out in this connection that Butler was probably influenced in his views on nature by Aristotle more than by the Stoics. While this much can be conceded, I have refrained from including any explicit reference to either Aristotle or Plato in the course of my exposition, largely because Butler himself does not refer to them openly, whereas he does to the Stoics. Also, I have been interested in presenting what Butler himself states about the nature of man, and how he uses the term 'nature,' as a working principle for his ethics more than I have been concerned with his intellectual inheritance or indebtedness. It is doubtful to my mind whether further light would have been thrown upon Butler's views, had I undertaken this additional task. Had his own use of the term been inconsistent or obscure, some sort of reference to the implicit sources would have been necessary, but the conception of nature, as Butler uses it, affords the reader no particular difficulty, as far as I can see.

[2] Wollaston, *The Religion of Nature Delineated,* p. 36.

than the rational part. At best this talk is loose." Wollaston has in mind here, according to his own references, the views of both Diogenes Laertius and Cicero. His disagreement with their view is defended in a footnote by saying that morality implies that man's nature is actually imperfect, hence in seeking the perfection that religion approves of (i.e., truth), human nature cannot be urged to follow itself; for were the nature of man already perfect, the dictates of a moral religion urging him to follow his nature would be meaningless, and since it is not perfect one cannot urge man to follow it.

Wollaston's attitude towards the adjuration to follow nature is but one of many misrepresentations. To be clear as to the meaning of following nature as the essence of morality—for in one sense Butler builds his system of ethics upon it—we must first be on our guard as to the many actual false interpretations that he sees may be put upon it. We shall proceed to consider for a few moments some of these constructions.

First. Nature is sometimes spoken of as meaning to act as we please (Vol. II, p. 48). But as Butler says in reply to this, "If by following nature were meant only acting as we please, it would indeed be ridiculous to speak of nature as any guide in morals: nay the very mention of deviating from nature would be absurd; and the mention of following it, when spoken by way of distinction, would absolutely have no meaning. For did ever any one act otherwise than as he pleased?"

Secondly, another meaning ascribed to "nature" is the expression of any principle in man without regard either to the kind or degree of it (Vol. II, p. 49). Butler sees that to take this meaning as a serious guide for morals would furnish us with no assistance. As he observes: "the same person hath often contrary principles, which at the same time draw contrary ways, he may by the same action both follow and contradict his nature in this sense of the word; he may follow one passion and contradict another" (Vol. II, p. 49).

Thirdly, a further interpretation often put upon nature is that which takes it to consist of those passions that are the strongest, and, in being such, influence actions more than the others. But since the strongest passions are often the most vicious, to follow nature in this sense of the term would be to pursue vice.

Fourthly, according to St. Paul, the Gentiles *do by Nature the things contained in the law.* This is apparently another sense in which the term can be used. The reference here must be to those tendencies in human nature that make for good, such as man's natural disposition to compassion and kindness, which lead him to act in the interest of society. But there prevail in human nature in a greater degree other tendencies that carry him on in the direction of his private interests, and to a certain extent these tendencies are likewise natural. But neither these good elements, nor those that in excess lead to vice, can be those by which man is a law to himself. Hence another meaning of "nature" must be intended, indicating a faculty which decrees the morality of acts, and decides the proper proportion or stress to be laid upon his other natural tendencies.

Of the various interpretations that Butler sees may be put upon the term, he finds that the view last mentioned comes nearest to his meaning. Nature, according to this construction, means the self as a constitution—today we should use the word system—in which the parts, i.e., the instinctive tendencies to action, stand in an intimate relation to the moral faculty, and by following which man truly expresses himself. But this view, Butler maintains, is the view of the ancients, and is what they had in mind when they spoke of man's being born to virtue, and of vice as the destruction of this nature. As Butler says, "I have no doubt, but that this is the true account of the ground of that conviction which they referred to, when they said, vice was contrary to nature" (Vol. II, p. 9). It is with this statement that Butler finds himself to be in complete agreement; it is this which leads him to say that he is but re-expounding their views. "Upon the whole, this is a fair and true account of what was the ground of their conviction; of what they intended to refer to, when they said, virtue consisted in following nature: *a manner of speaking not loose and undeterminate, but clear and distinct, strictly just and true*" (Vol. II, p. 10; italics, mine).

We have just gathered that the nature of man presupposed by a sound system of ethics is a system of parts regulated by the highest of its inner principles; that this principle adjudicates on the morality of our acts, and determines the release of those tendencies that are self-regarding or other-regarding.

How can we be assured of the truth of a system of morals based upon human nature; or that man's nature is what Butler declares it to be? Many authors dispute the reality of benevolent

acts, others minimize the importance of self-regarding tendencies, while again there are those who see in man's nature no
genuinely moral principle such as Butler affirms him to have.
Surely all this needs a justification. To justify his position,
Butler must now substantiate the statement he makes in the
preface to his Sermons that virtue consists in the pursuit of
nature.[3]

The assertion will require a minute analysis of human nature,
the enumeration of its parts, the interrelation of these parts to
each other, and their reference to conscience, within which they
find their unity. Then we shall be in a position to know how
morality consists in self-expression. Our order of procedure will
be as follows. First we shall present Butler's general views on
the psychology of human nature, and then we shall successively
examine in detail each of its constituent parts. Our aim shall
be to show how the unity of the self is present within all of its
parts, and how the moral self is evolved as each part takes its
naturally allotted place within the self's systematic structure.

[3] Vol. II, p. 5. The following discourses "were intended to explain what is
meant by the nature of man, when it is said that virtue consists in following,
and vice in deviating from it; *and by explaining to shew that the assertion is
true.*" (Italics mine.)

PART TWO

THE PSYCHOLOGY OF THE MORAL SELF

5

ANALYSIS OF HUMAN NATURE

A PSYCHOLOGICAL examination of man shows us that he is pre-eminently active or dynamic, being composed of innumerable springs to action, seeking their outward expression in objects; and in the process of self-construction.

In the interest of intelligible reference I shall indifferently call these springs to action by the name of "affections." [1] One chief distinction between them is the presence in some of self-consciousness, whereas in others this characteristic is absent. For precision in the use of terms I shall refer to the conscious affections as "principles"; the remaining affections, whose drives to activity are unconsciously directed towards set and established ends, I shall call "propensions." [2] Their distinctive characteristics are discoverable in the ends they normally strike out towards, and within which they receive satisfaction. We shall refer to this latter aspect of the affections as their 'objective course.'

AFFECTIONS, PROPENSIONS AND PRINCIPLES

If we view man's impulses in terms of their objective course, we shall see that they fall naturally into one of four types, ac-

[1] I should like to make clear at this point of my inquiry that the analysis and description that follows is nowhere worked out by Butler with the degree of detail and argument here presented, but is only suggested by him in its most general outlines. Only by dint of working over his arguments and collating his statements have I succeeded in developing from the many references scattered throughout his writings a consistent mosaic of his position as it is reflected in his psychological assumptions. I may point out that the difficulty of gathering his point of view is largely owing to the love of controversy that intrudes itself upon the reader.

[2] This terminology is taken from Butler directly, but he is careless and incon-sistent in the use of his terms. He often refers to man's psychological drives as principles of action, propensions, particular affections, instincts, appetites, passions, and desires. Yet throughout this careless usage there are indications of a settled doctrine, especially when he refers to, and distinguishes principles of action and propensions.

cording to the object that they seek. One of these types is ego-istic. Its objective course is the agent's own individual nature; to seek consciously its preservation, happiness and enhancement. This self-conscious affection, whose aim is the interest of the agent within whom it is embedded, Butler calls "self-love." It is none other than the urge within the individual self-consciously to seek his own good. When uninformed and unenlightened, it is reprehensible, for its activities may often lead its agent to blun-ders and even to disaster. But when informed and enlightened, it is a principle of the highest worth and leads its possessor along the paths of virtue. It is the principle that makes for the self-conscious unification of the agent, that drives him on into the outer world, that views the realm of objects, things and ideals, as so much material for his expansive growth and appropriation.[3]

A second impulse in man is altruistic. It is the tendency within his nature that urges him to pay attention to other individuals, to regard them as ends in themselves. Butler calls it "benevo-lence." Like self-love it is conscious. By calling it conscious, Butler is pointing out that the individual is aware of this affec-tion and knows that its concern is directed towards the interest of his fellow-beings. Properly exercised and intelligently guided it seeks for his fellow-beings what self-love seeks for himself; namely, the greatest good. It offers him assistance for his self-development and self-expression. Each agent normally seeks his own good, and is assisted in his search by his companions. By virtue of benevolence, society is consciously developed.[4]

But the nature of man is not exhausted by the principles of self-love and benevolence. There are many actions which he performs that are not the result of a labored reflection, but which are mechanical in their expression. He eats because he is

[3] For Butler's description of self-love, consider especially his sermons on the Love of Our Neighbour. He describes it throughout his writings in different ways. The following are some of the characteristics specifically ascribed to it: (a) reflectiveness (Vol. II, p. 158), (b) tendency towards the self's private good (Vol. II, p. 163), (c) tendency to preserve the health and life of the individual (Vol. II, p. 34), (d) search for the interest and happiness of the individual (Vol. II, p. 23; Sermon XI, pp. 157, 159).

[4] For precise description of this principle, refer especially to Vol. II, Ser-mons XI and XII. (a) Contrasted with self-love it is termed disinterested (Vol. II, p. 18); (b) it seeks the good and happiness of society (Vol. II, Sermons I, p. 30; XIII, p. 198). (c) More specifically it is a disposition to friendship, com-passion, and to paternal and filial affection (Vol. II, Sermon I, p. 31). In Sermon VI, p. 98, it is spoken of as a principle, and more specifically in Vol. II, Sermon XI, p. 169.

hungry and drinks because he is thirsty, he loves applause and approbation, and instinctively turns away from acts of vengeance. In these acts we witness the mechanical aspect of human nature which gives itself up to its instincts and appetites. An uneasiness occurs in his nature and grows in intensity; it seeks its object, and vents itself eagerly upon it. After its satisfaction it subsides, only to bestir itself again in the presence of its stimulus; or urged from within it seeks again the object by which it can be quieted. This entire class of impulses Butler calls "particular propensions," and one main point of difference between them and the principles of self-love and benevolence is their entire lack of reflection. Their objective course is towards objects more varied and more specific than those of the principles. Thus in reference to myself, I can say that I am often vague about what my own good consists in, or what would be the best I could do for my neighbor, but I am never in doubt what to do in the felt presence of hunger or thirst.[5]

Lastly, the behavior of men indicates that their lives are often under the guidance of another principle. Their performance of an act may often suggest to them such questions as: is this act right or wrong, valuable, desirable or good? Likewise their behavior may suggest to the observer a sense of regret at what they have done, a reprobation of acts committed. These attitudes towards right and wrong considered as ends in themselves and not as means are preconditioned by a tendency to reflect morally. It is not a tendency which is devoted to the expediency of acts, or a consideration of acts instrumental to the good of others; to self-expression, or to particular concrete objects, but it is a genuine yearning for an object different in kind from those that satisfy these other tendencies. It is a search for virtue, and the principle of the search is called "conscience" (Vol. II, Sermon III, especially; also Second Diss., Vol. I). These constitute for Butler the fundamental ways in which man expresses his nature.

[5] Instances of particular propensions are the appetites of hunger; desire of esteem (Vol. II, p. 33); love of society, indignation against successful vice (Vol. II, p. 35); appetites of sense, resentment, compassion, curiosity and ambition; honor, power, harm or good of another (Vol. II, p. 19). Their characteristics are (a) tendency towards particular external objects (Vol. II, p. 19; also Sermon XI, pp. 157, 158), and not towards pleasure arising from attaining these objects, for this is presumably the aim of self-love; (b) disinterestedness (Vol. II, p. 19).

I will now indicate certain elements that all of these acts have in common. All outward expression is preconditioned by an impulse or tendency within man's nature. Man seeks his own good because of a prior disposition to do so; the same is true when he seeks the good of others. He acts benevolently because in a definite sense he possesses the tendency to act in this way. Also, man seeks the good as an end in itself because, again, his nature is so constituted that it demands the good for its satisfaction. We are to believe that the structure of human nature preconditions every act committed and guides every moral act reflected upon.

I shall at this place introduce a digression by way of satisfying certain questions that might naturally be raised at this stage. It might very well be asked: Do these four types of activity represent a complete enumeration of man's fundamental tendencies? If so, what of speculative reason? Has no man a tendency that drives him on to the pursuit of truth as well as to action? Also: are we justified in ascribing to man *as many* as four fundamental affections, especially when there are not wanting individual moralists who assert that man is primarily governed by fewer? We shall briefly consider each issue in turn.

As far as observation informs us, we can discover no more than these four main types of affection within ourselves or within our fellowmen. In other words, Butler was satisfied that his enumeration was logically exhaustive. We are led to believe that if future observation yields us further types of actions, these actions can be reduced to one of the four that we have mentioned as being fundamental. In calling these affections fundamental, it is our intention to point out that Butler conceived them as being distinctive in the sense that they cannot be reduced to each other, and explanatory of all other types of human actions.

But in what respect can we speak of these affections as representing an exhaustive classification of man's spurs to action? Only in this sense, that both self-love and the particular propensions are "open classes"; owing to the broad nature of both, every conceivable type of action can be ascribed to one of them. If a tendency of man be discovered that is self-conscious, it will presumably fall under self-love; if it is of the blind mechanical instinctive sort, its place belongs within the class of the particular propensions. This does not hold of the principle of benevolence, which, since it has a single aim, we can call an affection of single content. Regarding it we can conceive of no further additions to its aim. But with the propensions and self-love, as we have seen, it is otherwise. Their contents are indefinite, and it is conceivable that any newly discovered tendencies in man's nature must fall within either group. By this means Butler has allowed himself a flexible mode of classification and has guarded himself against the eventualities of a self-imposed restriction. That it leads him into palpable difficulties we shall see later, for it forces him to characterize the principle of self-love in such broad and expansive terms that it breaks the bounds of its initially ascribed meaning. Being forced to include all self-conscious actions, self-love is unable strictly to account for any.

We may at this stage of our investigation of man's nature be startled by the apparent absence of speculative reason as a fundamental characteristic. It may be asked: is not man a creature who seeks disinterested truth as well as disinterested good? Concerning the claim of speculative reason as a fundamental principle in man's nature whose objective course is the pursuit of truth or ideal objects as ends in themselves, Butler would deny to it a status equal in kind with that of the principles or affections. Not that he denies its existence or minimizes its importance, but he sees it bound up with the principles in too intimate a way to justify its claim as an independent affection. In accounting for speculative reason, Butler accords to it only an instrumental value. We reason to achieve an end, but the end is never ultimate. The objects achieved are always subservient to the more ultimate aims of self-love, benevolence or conscience, within whose service reason works.[6]

Butler does not maintain that reason cannot set as its special task the pursuit of knowledge as an end in itself, but he sees in the pursuit of such an aim the very perversion of reason. We shall see later on when we discuss its place within the moral life his reasons for this position. We shall content ourselves at present with remarking that the natural function of reason, as revealed to us by an impartial observation, is to further the happiness of ourselves and others, as well as the establishment of the good as an end in itself. The full activity of self-love, benevolence and conscience entails a degree of speculation as to how self-love, benevolence and conscience are to be expressed. To exist under the active dominion of a principle means specula-

6 *Vide infra*, Ch. *31*.

tively to consider the best way the principle can achieve the actualization of its aim. The means of attaining this end are to be determined by reason. Hence reason exists as a handmaid to the principles, and to live under the guidance of a principle entails an active application of reason.

We have just seen that there are no more than four fundamental tendencies in man's nature. But such a consideration leads us to foresee a difficulty of another kind that may be raised. May there not be fewer than four fundamental types of impulses in man? May it not be possible to reduce benevolence to self-love, or self-love to benevolence, or even conscience to self-love? Such a reduction had been attempted by Hobbes and the Epicureans. But the way in which they set about explaining disinterested acts as expressions of self-love was tantamount to the negation of benevolence and conscience. Their very nature, according to Butler, had been explained away, and what Butler saw to be their essential characteristic was blatantly denied. Since Hobbes and the Epicurean had denied the existence of benevolence it was incumbent upon Butler to justify the presence of benevolence as a fundamental tendency in man's nature. Compassion too had been called into question by Hobbes. Likewise with conscience; to many its real existence was dubious. For them man had no moral urges; he did not reflect approvingly or disapprovingly upon his acts, except as they established some design or plan of action he had already decided upon. This principle too had to be defended against those who would undermine it or deny its existence altogether. We shall state the reasoned defense that Butler makes for the respective claims of benevolence and conscience to existence as fundamental affections in man's nature.

Classifying all acts other than those of self-love as disinterested, we shall now see in a general way the reasons why Butler holds the existence within man of disinterested actions.

Hobbes and the Epicureans, among many others, had declared, according to Butler, that the expression of man's self was the continued exercise of self-love. All actions, they held, were done primarily for the interest of the agent conceiving them. For the Epicureans man's motive in any act was the pursuit of pleasure; for Hobbes his motives were love of power, and the delight in the exercise of it (Vol. II, p. 31). Butler sees these statements to be a too narrow account of man's nature, especially in their assertion that no act of ours can have as its end the good of our fellow being. They do not deny that we can seek the good of another, but insist that this good is achieved only indirectly when we foresee advantages to ourselves. We are incapable of acting unless our own pleasure of self-enhancement is directly aimed at. A benevolent act *in se* is impossible, and what we call a benevolent act is but an egoistic act in disguise. This may mean one of two things: either that we cannot seek the good of our fellow being, or that we can seek his good only incidentally, i.e., by way of seeking our own good. Both of these statements amount to the same thing, namely that man cannot act disinterestedly. If Hobbes and the Epicureans are right, then the existence of particular propensions as well as those of benevolence and conscience are denied. We should for instance be incapable of genuinely expressing indignation, resentment or compassion. It was Butler's aim not to deny self-love but to show that the claim to existence of the particular propensions and of benevolence and conscience was as convincing as the claim of the former.

What would follow, asks Butler, were we to admit that all of man's actions were strictly egoistic? In doing so, we should gain nothing, for all distinction between acts would be forfeited. As far as their origin is concerned, all acts are rooted in the self ". . . no one can act but from a desire, or choice, or preference of his own" (Vol. II, p. 19; cp. also p. 158). But if we were to classify these acts in terms of the end that they strive towards, we should be forced to note a distinction between their objective courses. This is what common sense does, and Butler holds that its point of view is right. It recognizes that some of the affections have the good of the self as their object, whereas others seek the satisfaction of the appetites, the expression of resentment and of compassion, or the display of curiosity and ambition. Common sense calls our attention to the fact that these latter are not one and the same with self-enhancement. If the former acts are termed interested, then the latter by contrast may be termed disinterested. As Butler says: "We should want words to express the difference, between the principle of an action, proceeding from cool consideration that it will be to my own advantage; and an action, suppose of revenge, or of friendship, by which a man runs upon a certain ruin, to do evil or good to another. It is manifest the principles of these actions are totally different, and so want different words to be distinguished by" (Vol. II, pp. 158-9).

To summarize the substance of this retort, which shows the teleological bent of Butler's mind: all actions are preconditioned by natural tendencies within the self to which they owe their source or origin. From the standpoint of their origin all actions can be spoken of as selfish. But this would not tell us how one selfish act differs from another. To state this, we must trace the overt expression of these tendencies in activity. We then see that they are directed towards different goals. Some affections seek food and drink, another seeks the good of the agent within which it is embedded, while a third is interested in the welfare of other selves. But if we now classify these tendencies from the standpoint of the objects they seek, only one of them could be properly called selfish or interested; the others would be disinterested. We have on our hands for consideration a twofold means of classifying the tendencies in man's nature, the genetic or the teleological, and we are asked to choose between them. To classify our actions genetically would be to ignore the reality of their completed aspect as they overtly express themselves. But such a classification would be faulty because it would be incomplete. It would say that the ends of the impulses make no difference to the nature of the impulses. The teleological classification would remedy this deficiency. It is to be preferred because it takes into account the objective course of the tendencies, while at the same time it admits their subjective source. But the teleological classification says that affections are known in terms of their objective course, and this reveals to us the existence of disinterested acts. If by the same method of observation, we affirm the existence of an egoistic tendency, we cannot deny the existence of disinterested tendencies, which means the existence of particular propensions and of benevolence and conscience. Hence, these latter can neither be denied nor identified with self-love.

By way of anticipation we may call attention to the use that Butler makes of the principle of self-love. It is the most indeterminate in his system, and his references to it give the reader no end of trouble. Let us point out in the first place that it primarily represents the self-conscious nature of the individual, and is consistent with every act of the individual that is sanctioned as good. This is its broader meaning. But it is also used in contrast to other activities in man such as benevolence and particular propensions and conscience. This constitutes its narrower meaning, and is the use that Butler has in mind when he asks whether all activity can be explained in terms of it. While his answer to his question is no, it appears that he himself is open to the same charge when he subordinates all self-conscious activities to its keeping. But by this time, self-love has taken on a meaning much broader than Butler allowed either Hobbes or the Epicureans to entertain when he denounced them as subjugating all tendencies in man to self-love.

HABIT IN THE MORAL SELF

Self-conscious life implies a state of growth and development, in which the experiences of the past are stored up and lie in readiness for future situations. This is readily observable in the case of our bodily actions, and explains, e.g., the skill that is acquired by us in the ordinary course of using our limbs. It is no less true of our mental experience. The repetition of visual sensations enables us to estimate the distance and size of an object, and to make corrections concerning its reported magnitude. The constant hearing of a language familiarizes us with its meaning, and the sense of its words. In these quoted instances it can be appreciated that habit cuts across the life of the individual; it is neither a propension nor a principle, nor a capacity for the attainment of knowledge. It is however an aspect that our propensions and capacities can assume through repetition and practice.

Butler distinguishes between two kinds of habits: passive and active. By passive habits he means the association of ideas, thoughts, principles, precepts, etc., that never break into overt activity themselves, but remain within the mind as something to be contemplated, but not acted upon. Active habits, on the contrary, are those that emerge into outer activity, and that carry the individual into his environment. Each of these types of habits obeys laws of its own. Passive impressions grow weaker through repetition. To dwell upon a theory of virtue, and yet to do nothing about it, will lead to a moral indifference. As Butler says: "thoughts, by often passing through the mind, are felt less sensibly: being accustomed to danger, begets intrepidity, i.e., lessens fear; to distress, lessens the passion of pity; to instances of others' mortality, lessens the sensible apprehension of our own" (Vol. I, p. 92). This is different from active habits. Repetition strengthens them. Through the practice of virtue, man becomes more readily virtuous. Constantly to pursue the principles of justice is to become just. Butler contrasts these two kinds of habit in reference to our feeling and exercise of compassion. Merely to pity people, but to do nothing about their relief, leads in time to a callousness and a growing unwillingness actively to relieve. But on the other hand, actively to aid the distressed will result in a greater aptitude to assist and befriend them, although it will also mean that he passively compassionates the distressed less (Vol. I, p. 93).

These two types of habits are not unrelated. The sphere of passive habits corresponds to our motives or causes of action; active habits are equivalent to the consequences of these motives as they overtly emerge and play into man's environment. Active habits cannot stand alone; to be self-conscious about them, we must presuppose an inner desire in the direction of their activity. Yet to emphasize the inner aspect of one's thoughts is not in itself sufficient. To achieve the growth of character, we must consciously exercise it in our experience. As Butler tells us: "passive impressions made upon our minds by admonition, experience, example, though they may have a remote efficacy, and a very great one, towards forming active habits, yet, can have this efficacy no otherwise than by inducing us to such a course of action: and that it is not being affected so and so, but acting, which forms those habits . . ." (Vol. I, p. 93).

A self in which habits have been thoroughly wrought is one in which the motive towards action becomes responsive, and flows into the environment effortlessly and freely. It is a self which acquires aptitude and facility as well as pleasure in what it performs. Accustoming itself to the performance of its actions, the individual becomes increasingly free from the thwarting influence of counter motives; and less given over to the need of enforcing his motives when he consciously undertakes a devised course of action.

SUMMARY AND TRANSITION

Let us now briefly restate the conclusions that we have arrived at in order to make clear our transition to the next stage of the argument. Butler is interested in showing that morality consists for man in the expression of his nature. This led him to ask: what is man's nature, what does it consist of? Until we know this we cannot apply our dictum, or put it into practice. An analysis of man's nature revealed him to be motivated by no fewer than four fundamental tendencies: self-love, benevolence, particular propensions, and conscience. Furthermore these four fundamental tendencies are held to account for the infinite variety of man's individual acts. But at this stage of our argument we are presumably no better off as agents in search of a criterion for morality than we were at first; for we have on our hands four distinct motives to action instead of one. Which of these affections are we to follow? We must either show that these four tendencies are intimately related in such a way that one is superior to the other three, so that the expression of that one enables us at the same time to express the inferior tendency; or we must deny as original drives three of the tendencies in favor of one, and thereby preserve the unity of man's moral nature. But we cannot follow the latter course because to deny some aspects of man's nature, especially when a careful observation has shown them to be as fundamental as the drive we arbitrarily favor, would result in a mutilated self, the consequence of which would be the denial of our fundamental moral precept, and the compulsion to build a moral theory upon some other basis than the one Butler claims. What remains for us to show is that the variety of affections that we have selected as fundamental and representative in our nature are not mutually self-exclusive. We shall proceed to show that they are so intimately related to each other that the comprehension of one leads us to accept all of the others in a unity of implication.

Man as systematically viewed will show an interrelation of parts in an arrangement of hierarchical status and function. After we have made clear the fact that man's nature is a disposition of parts systematically arranged we shall then be in a position to see that there is one part of man's nature, namely conscience, that stands superior. For man to express himself in terms of it is to live as nature intended; to apply himself to its commands is at the same time to take into account all the other constituent aspects of his nature such as benevolence, self-love and the particular propensions. These latter affections not only imply conscience, but become expressed through its rational direction in a way more true to themselves than if they were to ignore its voice.

6

PARTICULAR PROPENSIONS

GENERAL CHARACTERISTICS

IN HIS moments of unreflection man is a creature of many activities. His attention seems to be scattered over a multitude of pursuits that apparently have no connection with each other. If we examine these activities more closely we find that they dominate man more than man masters them. In their presence and expression man feels himself to be the passive medium of their activities, and his consciousness reports to him—if attentive to what takes place within him—a restless search, an uncontrollable urge that carries him to the experience of the objects that surround him. This type of activity Butler classifies as the particular propensions. It is our aim in the present chapter to examine their nature in detail, and to see in what respect they tell us about the nature of the self.

The particular propensions form the substance of man's nature. They are basic activities and are prior to all others. Forming the *sine quâ non* of man's conscious life, they are the materials upon which all of his higher processes depend, such as his deliberation or moral propensities. They are also fundamental in the sense that they form the minimum amount of activity upon which man can subsist. To understand their nature and importance, let us first mention a few of them.

Man's nature requires food, drink and companionship; he is likewise normally curious about his surroundings (Vol. II, p. 19). Many individuals manifest a love of power, and exert themselves to attain it. These instinctive activities are some of the instances that Butler has in mind when he speaks of man's particular propensions. But they are not all. In our desire for esteem (Vol. II, p. 33), and social approval, Butler sees other instances of the particular propensions. Even the more elevated sentiments such as compassion, which has a moral flavor, resentment against wrongdoing and indignation against successful vice (Vol. II, p. 35), come under this label. The ordinary routine of daily habit would likewise be included.

It is natural for us to ask at this point why these activities, so diverse in kind, should be classified under one heading as belonging to the same *genus?* At first sight there appears to be confusion in classifying impulses, instinct, habits and sentiments as being fundamentally the same.[1] What has Butler in mind in doing so?

The answer can be best stated by pointing out that all of these activities are essentially non-conscious, i.e., they occur without the explicit consent of man's consciousness. If it is pointed out in objection to this, that the regulated life of the mature individual controls these activities instead of being controlled by them, the objection does not carry the force of conviction. For this control by the maturer individual comes about later in time when he discovers within his nature this class of mechanical actions. In other words it is only because man experiences within himself an outward surgence towards definite objects within his environment, that he can control, regulate and release them.

When we call the propensions "non-conscious," we wish to emphasize, not the fact that they cannot be consciously managed or regulated, but that in the dawn of their expression, they appear before man ever regards them with conscious intention to regulate or control them. In other words man's consciousness may be regarded as a supervention upon what is already a working part of his nature; *a posteriori* to the propensions which are *a priori.*

The particular propensions are also mechanical. In the presence of their stimulus they respond by breaking into activity. They are provoked into activity without forethought or deliberation. The locus of the stimulus makes no difference to their mechanical aspect. We may be unaware that we are hungry until we see the food before us; or we may actively seek food because of the inner craving of the pangs of hunger. In either case we respond to the cause without being conscious of the meaning, or of the implications involved.

The aspects of being non-conscious and mechanical are what

---

[1] *Vide* Vol. II, p. 46, where Butler speaks of the "several propensions or instincts." Likewise in the preface, the same identifying of the propensions with instincts is made (Vol. II, pp. 10, 11). In the former citation, mankind is spoken of as having "various instincts and principles of actions, as brute creatures have." The use of 'principles' here is careless, for the reference is undoubtedly, as is shown by the allusion to brutes, to the particular propensions, and not to any principles implying reflection, which is specifically denied to brutes.

these propensions all have in common. They are alike in the point of origin, being centers of energy, differentiated in respect to the objects they seek, and carrying the individual to the encompassing of these objects in the environment. This feature of outward movement, whereby the propensions seek external objects, constitutes another characteristic of their nature.[2]

The particular propensions are not blind explosions of energy that strike out indifferently; they indicate a rational structure. Hunger seeks food, thirst requires water, the desire of companionship is directed towards men. These objects seem, by some inner contrivance and arrangement of our nature, to be sought long before they are actually discovered by us; and presumably, before the propensions are bestirred into activity. In them the propensions find their satisfaction; and through them man is carried over and linked inevitably with his environment. No one of the propensions is concerned with itself alone, for they find their completion in the enjoyment of objects; not one of them is directed towards the self. All of the propensions are alike in that they are the means whereby the self, quite apart from its own initiative, is interknitted with its environment and made dependent upon it.

We have ascertained that the particular propensions are drives centered in man's nature that carry him in a disinterested way to the enjoyment of the objects in his environment. Can we read any further meaning into them than that? Butler maintains that we can, for the acknowledgment of dynamic urges within man's nature exposes the errors of a false psychology, and points the way to a constructive morality.

Accepting as true Butler's account of the particular propensions, we are led to define the self in a new way, as that which is actively disposed towards the search of outer objects and things. It is to be defined in terms of this activity, and as characterized by the objects sought. But none of the objects sought pertains subjectively to the active agent *quâ* source. Quite the contrary: man's self is what it is because of the objects he experiences. In other words the conscious self is later in time and experience than the activities that compose it. Since the self can be known

---

2 See Vol. II, p. 19; also *ibid.*, pp. 157, 158: ". . . particular affections rest in the external things themselves" and "all particular appetites and passions are towards *external things themselves,* distinct from the *pleasure arising from them* . . ."

only in terms of its experiences which make it what it is, the self cannot be spoken of as a core of individual feelings that privately seeks to appropriate its surrounding objects. Granting that these activities are disinterested and other-regarding, we must likewise concede that man's nature is so. Thus the conscious self instead of being the cause of its experiences, or the substance that enjoys them, must now be regarded as the resultant and construction of processes that are fundamentally non-conscious in nature.

The recognition of the self as active informs us that the self is incomplete, for it is in the process of growth and construction. Constituted essentially by its dynamic drives, the self is constructed by its experiences. But its experiences are never completed at any one time. The satisfaction of its dynamic longings is temporary. Hunger, although once satisfied, expresses itself anew. Our thirst is only temporarily quenched. Our desire for companionship is never permanently satisfied. New objects to satisfy our instinctive longings are sought; likewise old friendships are renewed, and new associations are formed. Each experience is in a sense unique. None is a duplication of the old, and the self which is the repository of these changing experiences is added to, enriched and modified by these successive excursions of its drives.

Butler's account of the self thus shows the dependence of the self upon its physical and social environment. The objects that are sought by its drives are parts of the physical world, such as food and drink; or they are represented in the personalities of other individuals, living in groups and societies. Through the expression of its drives the self is carried over to the experience of other selves and objects.

A further instance of how the particular propensions carry man beyond the sphere of his own narrow realm of exclusively individual actions, i.e., those based upon a narrow self-love, can be seen in what Butler calls the 'natural principle of attraction' (Vol. II, pp. 38, 39). It is spoken of as a "previous bent and bias," as the "attraction in man towards man, that having trod the same tract of land, having breathed in the same climate, barely having been born in the same artificial district or division, becomes the occasion of contracting acquaintances and familiarities many years after" (*ibid.*). By reason of its activity man is drawn to his fellow-beings and the foundations of society are at first unconsciously laid. It furthermore enables us to explain how "men are so much one body, that in a peculiar manner they feel for each other, shame, sudden danger, resentment, honour, prosperity (and) distress" (*ibid.*).

The place in Butler's sermons where this affection is described leads to a confusion. Introduced as it is after the presentation of man's other constituent parts, it readily suggests to the mind of the reader that it is an affection distinct in kind from the other four types, i.e., from the particular propensions, self-love, benevolence and conscience. But Butler had no such intention in view. Like the nature of the propensions, for example, its exercise takes place in an unconscious way; like them it is teleological; having as its aim the establishment and growth of an organic society. Neither does it properly belong under the principle of benevolence which also has the interest of one's fellow beings in view; for whereas benevolence strives consciously for the consolidation of men in society, the principle of consolidation *unconsciously* works for the same end. We are justified in treating the latter not as a separate affection or as a principle, but as a particular propension.

Since objects and persons are sought by the drives that constitute us, they are necessary to their fulfilment and satisfaction. But no less are they necessary for the self which is represented in its drives. No self is solitary, nor can it live as such. In its process of expression it not only grows, but assimilates to itself the environment of persons and things that it finds necessary for its fulfilment.

Let us now consider in further detail the nature of one particular propension, i.e., compassion, to see how the self is characterized by its presence, and modified in the course of its expression.

PROPENSIONS AS MORAL EXPRESSION: COMPASSION

I have not discussed the place of all the particular propensions in the moral self, because the principle of their moral expression is the same in all cases, namely, the submission of each interest to conscience for its surveyance and approval. In the present section we shall be concerned only with compassion. One reason for not considering the other particular propensions is that Butler himself fails to do so; yet in his treatment of compassion we can appreciate the manner in which he would have discussed them, had he found it necessary.

The virtue of compassion was assailed by Hobbes (Vol. II, pp. 79-82) who tried to reduce it to a form of self-regard. We shall now try to rescue it from the wreckage of his assaults by first considering briefly Butler's type of reply. Hobbes's line of attacks runs as follows: "Pity (is) imagination, or fiction of future calamity to ourselves, proceeding from the sense of another man's calamity . . ." (Vol. II, p. 79). The degree of compassion that we individually show to others varies in direct proportion as we are acquainted with the person who evokes our pity. We pity our friends more than our lighter acquaintances because we are in more intimate touch with their characters; hence we are better able to appreciate their calamity; and to fear in some vicarious way for ourselves the possibilities of a similar experience. Were it a certain thing that we ourselves could never become victims of disaster, we would be incapable of feeling for others or of responding to them in their times of grief. Such is Hobbes's view of the matter, according to Butler.

In this account of pity Butler sees an undermining of common justice and honesty (Vol. II, p. 81, footnote). If it can be shown that pity and fear are not identical, or that pity cannot be legitimately reduced to a species of fear, then it must follow that compassion is an independent affection of man's nature especially when we have empirical evidence of it. It is this that Butler proceeds to show.

His first argument against the position of Hobbes questions whether fear and compassion are in any sense synonymous. An examination of compassion shows it to involve much more than an element of fear for ourselves. According to Butler, when we compassionate, there are often discernible four distinct elements: (a) real sorrow and concern for the misery of our fellow creatures, (b) some degree of satisfaction that we are free from that misery ourselves, (c) a reflection upon our own liability to the same or other calamities (Vol. II, p. 81, footnote), and (d) an expectancy to be treated with kindness by our fellow beings if we ever perchance fall into similar circumstances of distress (Vol. II, p. 80, footnote). All of these states of mind are equally real.

We cannot deny the reality of "(a)," "(b)," and "(d)," as Hobbes would have us do; for we have the same guarantee for their existence as we have for the existence of "(c)," i.e., a discovery of them through self-examination. If we declare "(c)" to be a real state of mind, we must likewise declare "(a)," "(b)," and "(d)" to be real. If we evaluate and ascribe a superiority to "(c)," and in terms of it seek to explain "(a)," "(b)," and "(d)," we must be convinced that in such arrangement "(a)," "(b)" and "(d)" receive their truly essential expression.

Thus Butler's first charge against Hobbes's position on compassion is that he is guilty of an unwarranted synonymity (*ibid.*). You cannot identify pity with fear and expect after the substitution to have no remainder. Furthermore if we carry out the substitution, we are led to an absurdity. Let us instance a case of this. A person who feels sorrow for another individual in distress often expects a return of kindness when he is himself in a similar position. Now if fear is to be put in the place of pity, accepting as a matter of experiment that commiseration is but fear of future calamity befalling ourselves, we should have to say that when A feels compassion for B, he means no more than that when a similar disaster befalls him, he will expect B to fear for himself. In other words: that the expectancy of future kindness is A's wish that B shall look out for himself and fear for his own future when he (A) is in distress. But this interpretation falsifies the reports of inward perception; the sympathy that A exhibits towards B is distinct from the fear that he may himself some day be unfortunate.

Compassion, defended from the charge of self-regard, can now be regarded as a fundamental urge in human nature. By observing its expression in others and ourselves, we can acquaint ourselves with its nature. Compassion concerns itself primarily in the relief of others. There is no particular need for man to rejoice in the prosperity of others, for nothing would be gained, but there is a particular need to assist them in times of distress. Butler tells us that "when a man has obtained any particular advantage or felicity, his end is gained; and he does not in that particular want the assistance of another: there was therefore no need of a distinct affection towards that felicity of another already obtained; neither would such affection directly carry him on to do good to that person: whereas men in distress want assistance; and compassion leads us directly to assist them. The object of the former is the present felicity of another; the object of the latter is the present misery of another. It is easy to see that the latter wants a particular affection for its relief, and that the

former does not want one, because it does not want assistance"
(Vol. II, pp. 82, 83).

Natural compassion is further required to counterbalance
our innate tendency to cause unhappiness to others. Without the
checking influence of a contrary urge, such as compassion there
would be considerable danger in the outburst of resentment.
Butler sees compassion to be the advocate within ourselves that
urges us to do good to others. It keeps in check an inner tendency
to reprehend without mercy the misery of others, especially if
brought about by themselves.

One might ask at this point why reason itself is not a sufficient
safeguard against apathy; why is not benevolence, whose sole
aim consists in the good of others, itself adequate to the fulfilment of this need? In answer to this, Butler emphasizes the
ineffectualness of the "settled reasonable principle of benevolence
to mankind" (Vol. II, p. 88) to remedy this indifference by itself.
"Benevolence," he says, "though natural in man to man, yet is in
a very low degree kept down by interest and competitions; and
men, for the most part, are so engaged in the business and
pleasures of the world, as to overlook and turn away from objects
of misery; which are plainly considered as interruptions to them
in their way, as intruders upon their business, their gaiety and
mirth" (Vol. II, pp. 95, 96; cp. also p. 124). Hence in the weakness or apathy of the higher principles it is necessary in some
way to assure through an affection distinct in kind the remedy
of our natural defects.

Compassion works for the prevention and relief of misery.
In its prevention of misery, it counteracts resentment, envy and
unreasonable self-love (Vol. II, p. 94). In its latter use, it "is a
call, a demand of nature, to relieve the unhappy; as hunger is a
natural call for food" (Vol. II, p. 96).

In neither of its functions should compassion work independently of conscience. To be morally expressed, it should submit
itself to the speculative scrutiny of the moral sense and await
its approval. As a mere propension or tendency it is apt to become excessive, and become a parody of benevolence. Or if not,
the enthusiasm to assist others may deprive us of the very end we
have in view; so that we kill with kindness those whom we seek
to save (Vol. II, p. 99).

What are the consequences for ourselves and others, both in
the employment of compassion and in its absence? Concerning

others, we are told that they experience positive relief where compassion is directed towards them; and in its absence there would be the misery additional to their state of distress that no one commiserated their case (Vol. II, p. 86). Concerning ourselves: we should be put in mind of our own destination, we should learn that "the present world is not our home; that we are merely strangers and travellers in it, as all our fathers were . . ." (Vol. II, p. 101). The specific virtues that would accrue to us would be moderation, humility and soberness of mind (Vol. II, p. 100). The absence of this virtue would produce disaster for ourselves as well as for others. Unchecked and unrestrained, resentment and envy would break forth venting their cruelty in their inflicted injuries on others (Vol. II, p. 87).

The ultimate reason why men should live up to their compassionate nature, and express it in its due proportion arises from the fact that it is essentially part of their nature to do so. "To endeavour to get rid of the sorrow of compassion by turning from the wretched, when yet it is in our power to relieve them, is as unnatural, as to endeavour to get rid of the pain of hunger by keeping from the sight of food. That we can do one with greater success than we can the other, is no proof that one is less a violation of nature than the other. Compassion is a call, a demand of nature, to relieve the unhappy; as hunger is a natural call for food" (Vol. II, p. 96). Butler acknowledges that we store up future profit in our moments of assistance towards others, or run the risk of their resentment if we do not (Vol. II, p. 88). The defence of compassion is not however to be found in expectant happiness, or avoidance of pain, but in the fulfilment of man's self-advancement and expression.

TRANSITION

Let us now see how the particular propensions enter into and contribute to the unity of the growing self. At the level of the particular propensions the self is expressed through the multiplicity of its drives. Through them it is engrossed by many types of object, so that its attention is devoted first to one activity and then to another. In its aspect of self-awareness the individual becomes conscious of its inner longings, and now learns in time to know the objects that will satisfy them. Further than this: the self may actively engage in bringing about the objects that its nature requires. It may procure food to satisfy its

hunger, or consciously seek the companionship of others to overcome its loneliness. Conducting itself along this level, it may
never attempt to relate its activities to each other. It may perceive no relationship between the pursuit of, e.g., food and that
of drink; it may observe no connection between the desire of
companionship, and the longing to wield power. In other words
the entire duration of its life can be one of disjointed and disconnected acts, reflecting no unity of purpose in its pursuits,
and observing no common property or relation in the objects
sought. But close scrutiny will reveal that the particular propensions, diverse as their aims appear, give indications of a genuine
underlying unity. We shall now see how.

The satisfaction of hunger and the desire of human companionship contribute directly to the well-being of the agent. The
individual within whom these drives are embedded is profited by
their successful expression. His life is preserved and his happiness
secured. In both instances he experiences a degree of pleasure
arising primarily from the fact that these drives have expressed
themselves and been satisfied. The attendant pleasure is a sign
that they have met their object and have completed their temporary restlessness. This attendant pleasure is not directly or
consciously sought, but comes to the agent as a result that the
drive has been satisfied. When the individual reflects upon his
drives, he can discover, according to Butler, in some of them a
common aim in which they remotely meet.

If the individual examines other particular propensions, he
will notice a unity among them as well; one that is remotely
implied. Consider for instance one's indignation against cruelty,
and one's feeling for his fellow creatures. Taken by itself, each of
these drives is distinct; and apparently they have nothing in
common. Their objects are not the same, nor is the motive of
the agent who expresses them. But viewing them more remotely,
we can observe a common element. Both of them have in mind
the well-being or happiness of another agent. In this remoter end
these two distinctly different drives meet, and their atomic or
self-excluding nature is broken down as this remoter common
pursuit is acknowledged. Now, if we were to examine our complete array of particular propensions, we should observe, according to Butler, that they all tend to converge into one of two
common aims, implied in their original nature as propensions.
One group of particular propensions would be seen remotely to

imply the immediate well-being of the agent, i.e., his happiness, health, or own good; another group would be seen to imply the well-being of other agents, being disinterestedly devoted to their happiness and well-being.[3]

As conscious agents we can regard our particular propensions in one of two ways. We can either fasten our attention upon the immediate ends of the particular propensions, and live a life that knows no common unity or aim, or we can regard them from the standpoint of their remoter goal, and consciously seek to live in terms of them. In this latter case the original disunity of our conscious life will become organized about our own welfare or the welfare of others. If concerned exclusively with the former goal, i.e., ourselves, we set before ourselves the principle of self-love as our aim in life; if we live consciously for others, we build our lives about the pursuit of benevolence. In either case we have emerged from the unrelated multiplicity of the particular propensions into the more unified life of the principles, and have advanced our life beyond the level of the particular propensions to the plane of the conscious principles.

Viewing this situation from the standpoint of the self, we must admit, at this stage of the self's activity, the discovery of two new drives: self-love and benevolence. The tendency of the particular propensions to carry the agent beyond the immediate objects of these propensions, quite unconsciously at first, to a self-expression that is seen upon reflection to have these two new aims gives evidence that within the self are these unconscious urges or affections, ready to express themselves as did the particular propensions in the outer world of persons and things. There can be no definite drive of the self towards its environment without a corresponding cause or affection within the self's structure.

What these principles are, how they are related to the particular propensions, and how they contribute to the construction of the self will be answered in the next two chapters.

[3] Vol. II, p. 35, footnote: "The object and end of the former is merely food; the object and end of the latter is merely esteem: but the latter can no more be gratified, without contributing to the good of society; than the former can be gratified, without contributing to the preservation of the individual. . . . It may be added, that as persons without any conviction from reason of the desirableness of life, would yet of course preserve it merely from the appetite of hunger; so by acting merely from regard (suppose) to reputation, without any consideration of the good of others, men often contribute to public good." (See Vol. II, pp. 35, 87, 92, 127.)

7

PRINCIPLE OF BENEVOLENCE

THE results of our last chapter have informed us of some basic characteristics of the self. We have learned that it is composed of fundamental drives through which it is constructed, and carried over into a world of objects and persons. We have also seen that it is the immanent tendency of these drives to converge to the unity of their more remote aims. To live in terms of the immediate ends of the particular propensions is to live disjointedly and without any far-reaching plan or purpose; to conduct one's life according to the economy of our nature is to focus our attention upon the remoter goal. But in doing the latter, we have advanced beyond the level of the particular propensions to that of the conscious principles. How are these principles best to be understood: merely as remotely implied ends of the particular propensions, or as independent affections? If not to be regarded as the former, should we view them as definite characteristics of the self with psychological properties of their own? Butler regarded them as separate affections of the self, which contributed to the self properties different from those afforded to it by the particular propensions. We shall follow him here in his interpretation, but we shall see that these two contrasting views are not so alien to each other as they first appear.

Our discussion of benevolence—which will be our task in the present chapter—will fall under two headings; the first will consider its claims to existence, and the second its general characteristics. Under the first heading we shall discuss the legitimacy of the claims of this principle to the status of an independent affection within man's nature. Since the reality of this principle had been called in question by Hobbes (*Vide* Vol. II, pp. 31-33), Butler felt that recognition should be reaccorded to it, and that it should be reinstated with some degree of dignity in the rank of those fundamental affections that characterize man psychologically and lead him into the moral life. Under the second heading we shall proceed as we did with the particular propensions, namely, to an examination of benevolence in its various aspects and relationships.

IN DEFENCE OF BENEVOLENCE

The reasons why Butler takes particular pains to argue the existence of benevolence are largely polemical and center around the Hobbesian contention—as he understood it—that all actions are narrowly egoistic. To this claim, Butler has one type of reply.

The defence offered here for the independence of benevolence as one of the principles is to be found in the footnote to Butler's first Sermon (Vol. II, pp. 31-33). The argument as presented there by Butler is of the same variety as that with which he defended the existence of the disinterested tendencies. These arguments, it will be recalled, were treated at length when we sought to justify Butler's position that there exist within man's nature actions other than those emanating from self-love. Hence I shall mention the present argument somewhat briefly and without undue comment.

In defence of benevolence Butler proceeds to offer us what he believes to be a crucial instance of its existence. Genuine benevolence is represented in those cases where an individual rejoices in the prosperity or advancement of his fellow-beings even though he has had no share in it. Butler holds that a narrow self-love cannot account for the presence of this feeling; and, since the existence of this feeling cannot be denied, we must affirm that it proves the presence of a motive other than narrow self-love. Under what circumstances would benevolence be egoism in disguise? Only when one's pleasure at the good fortune of others is owing to the direct part he has had in bringing about the good of his fellow beings. To be envious when the good fortune of others was not brought about by one's self is an instance of egoism.

A second instance of genuine benevolence is seen when an agent directly works for the good of another person, for presumably if his desire had really been love of power, he would have devoted his time towards its direct expression.

Thirdly, if we assert that all acts spring from the desire to exercise power, we shall have to assert that acts of charity, friendship, good will, etc., are the same in kind as acts of mischief and cruelty; that the tendency of the former is not to promote happiness, this latter being merely incidental.

Lastly, Butler maintains that the existence of benevolent acts is to be determined as are all other types of activities by a direct observation of man's constituent parts and the objects that they seek. "If any person can in earnest doubt, whether there be such a thing as good-will in one man towards another; (for the question is not concerning either the degree or extensiveness of it, but concerning the affection itself:) let it be observed, that *whether man be thus, or otherwise constituted, what is the inward frame in this particular*, is a mere question of fact or natural history, not provable immediately by reason" (Vol. II, p. 32).[1] If we grant to Butler the soundness of his arguments, we can pass to the second task that we set ourselves: namely, a discussion of the characteristics of benevolence and its place within the human system.

NATURE OF BENEVOLENCE

Under the influence of benevolence, man's attention is drawn away from himself in the direction of his fellow beings (Vol. II, p. 31). He is urged from within to concern himself about their cares, their welfare and happiness. But so too is man at the level of the propensions. Is the principle of benevolence a mere reduplication of function or does it serve a purpose of its own, one that is distinct from the propensions? Butler sees no duplication of function between them. Although they both refer to the same goal, the principle of benevolence is more rational and less mechanical than the particular propensions.

Under the dominance of the particular propensions the individual is almost mechanically drawn to the assistance of his fellow being. He does not argue within himself the worthiness of his proffered assistance; he exhibits sympathy before he has questioned the good of that attitude, he condemns cruelty without knowing why; in exhibitions of that kind his behavior proceeds upon a level as fully mechanical as his craving for food and drink when the preservation of his own life is at stake. But under the sway of benevolence his entire approach to those individuals who are the goal of this affection has undergone a trans-

---

[1] I have neither attempted to classify these arguments nor evaluate them. That they do not represent distinct and separate arguments, is I think, fairly clear. The last argument, with its appeal to experience, is only a plea for the validity of an empirical methodology; of which the first three arguments are specific instances. I have reserved for a later chapter the complete exposition and examination of Butler's epistemology. Since a critical appreciation of the present arguments can be made by the reader in terms of the conclusions we have reached there, it would be unwise to interrupt the continuity of our exposition by an anticipatory examination here.

formation. Society becomes rationally accepted. There is less of
the coerciveness which is so outstandingly the stamp of the particular propensions. The benevolent attitude is one which is intelligibly sympathetic. There is less constraint in his relations to
other individuals. Under its influence he has taken on a program
of active sympathy in the interest of a moral or social good. It
is a stage of behavior which the individual feels himself to have
accepted freely, and which, when endorsed by a sweet reasonableness of his nature, becomes the conscious principle whereby the
agent can work for a disinterested moral good. In its possession
the agent feels himself to be less dominated by it than he does
when he is under the sway of the particular propensions; within
its influence he experiences the expansiveness of his nature as it
flows out beyond his own private wants to the needs and interests
of his fellow man. Such are the general characteristics of
benevolence.

Let us now examine this principle at closer range and for
its own sake. Whom does it affect, and what does it accomplish?
These questions will occupy our attention in our next section.

THE AIM OF BENEVOLENCE

In the presence of benevolence I am consciously drawn into
contact with my kind, or as Butler says, my neighbor. But who
is my neighbor? Where is he to be found?

Ideally, benevolence can be satisfied by nothing less than a
love for the entire universe. But such a degree of love belongs
properly to God alone; and for mortals with their finite capacities
the scope of its range must be considerably narrowed if we wish
to make of this principle a practical instrument of behavior.
In seeking for the preciser restriction of its field of influence, we
must likewise reject in turn love of mankind and love of our
country (i.e., patriotism), as being too broad and ambitious for
it to be practically effectual. We are finally left with "that part
of the universe, that part of mankind, that part of our country,
which comes under our immediate notice, acquaintance, and influence, and with which we have to do" (Vol. II, p. 177). Within
this narrower area are found my neighbors, and to them the
principle of benevolence specifically refers.

Were one to point out here the deficiency of a principle that
is so narrowly interpreted, and one that would rule out all attempts to include humanity in its broadest sense as the more

fitting aim of benevolence, Butler would reply that the general care of others is God's province, for in scope it passes beyond all human skill. "The happiness of the world is the concern of him, who is the Lord and the Proprietor of it: nor do we know what we are about, when we endeavour to promote the good of mankind in any ways, but those which he has directed . . ." (Vol. I, p. 337).

What are my duties to my neighbors, how should I act in regard to them? Benevolence, properly interpreted, means no less than to love my neighbor as myself. But are the words 'as myself' sufficiently clear? Butler thinks not; for he sees in the uses of the phrase, three intended meanings, two of which he immediately accepts as moral precepts, while the third he accepts only with the most cautious of reservations.

To love my neighbor as myself might possibly mean (a) to show to him the same kind of affection as I show to myself; to employ in my relation to him the principle of benevolence in the same way as I employ the principle of self-love in regard to myself. If we interpret benevolence in this way, we can see involved at least two main paths of behavior; namely, to avoid all injurious behavior towards him, and secondly to advance his good and happiness in every conceivable way. But the command is to love him as I do myself. This requires me to think of *his* nature as I would my own, to appropriate to myself his acts, his feelings, so that they become, if possible, a part of my own being.

Through the medium of benevolence my human nature expands beyond its narrow confines to gather in the interest of others; it permits myself to transcend its private limits, to enter into the experiences of others, to live their lives as my own, to learn and respect their ambitions and to feel their sorrows and joys. It is the conscious means of escape for each of us to avoid the viciousness of an atomic individuality. Benevolence emphasizes the social aspects of man. In doing this, it fulfils its nature. It has nothing to say about self-love, which persistently sustains within each of us the felt privacy of our individuality throughout our social relationships. It cannot minimize the importance of the self-conscious unity, for this is not its province. Benevolence indicates for us that the completer nature of any one self cannot exclude the wider references to other individuals. It carries the self consciously beyond its narrow range to those places within a

social group within which it readily fits. Furthermore in the
absence of such suitable groups benevolence must consciously
modify the old, or create the new, so as to assure for any one self
the environment within which its individual nature can receive
its suitable expression, and to which it can make its unique
contributions.

(2)   The second meaning that can be given to the phrase, "as
myself," is "that we love our neighbour in some *proportion* or
other, *according as* we love ourselves" (Vol. II, p. 180). In its
outward display, when it is directed towards the happiness of
my neighbor, benevolence should be so exercised as to respect the
entire nature of that individual, to allow him to conduct his life
in accordance with the dictates of his felt nature. Hence my
display of benevolence towards him will primarily respect his
entire self. I cannot lay down in advance of experience the particular ways in which my assistance should be rendered. In a
general way only can my behavior be prescribed. In all of my
dealings with my neighbor I should allow him to express himself
as well as he can, I should understand his mind and his motives
and point out to him the path of virtue as far as we see it in
common. Intelligent direction and self-governing must come from
him. Whereas I may create for him the opportunity for his self-
expression in whatever capacity he finds himself, yet the fulfilment of his nature within that capacity must come from him.

(3)   The third sense in which the phrase "as myself" can be construed is mentioned only to be excluded. The interpretation says
that benevolence "should bear the particular proportion of
equality, that *it be in the same degree*" (Vol. II, p. 178). "Suppose a person to have the same settled regard to others, as to
himself; that in every deliberate scheme of pursuit he took their
interest into the account in the same degree as his own, so far as
an equality of affection would produce this: yet he would in
fact, and ought to be, much more taken up and employed about
himself, and his own concerns, than about others, and their
interests" (Vol. II, p. 183). The reason that Butler offers for
this statement is that "we are in a peculiar manner . . . . intrusted with ourselves; and therefore care of our own interests,
as well as of our conduct, particularly belongs to us" (Vol. II,
p. 184).

What influence can we expect from an applied course of
benevolent behavior? There is observable a general temper that

is common to all individuals who undertake to live seriously in accordance with this principle; it is to fulfil one's social capacities in the best degree possible. By virtue of benevolence each individual is drawn consciously into society. He finds himself within a host of various capacities and relationships: as a master, or servant, father, or son; each of which positions carries with it its peculiar obligations. To be a father entails the care of one's children and family; an obligation "committed to our charge by Nature and Providence" (Vol. II, p. 188). As a neighbor the benevolent individual will assist the poor, relieve the distressed, compassionate the suffering; as a master he will employ his wisdom and authority so as to be a blessing to his dependents; as a servant, he will pay respect, gratitude, and obedience, as due. The presence of benevolence in any walk of life engenders a spirit of emulation in which the agent asks himself, "Am I in reality a better master or servant, a better friend, a better neighbour, than such and such persons; whom, perhaps, I may think not to deserve the character of virtue and religion so much as myself?" (Vol. II, p. 186). Within the consciously benevolent agent one can expect a meekness and easiness of temper, a readiness to forego his right for the sake of peace, freedom from mistrust, and a disposition to believe well of his neighbor (Vol. II, p. 185). As Butler puts it: "A real good man had rather be deceived, than be suspicious; had rather forego his known right, than run the venture of doing even a hard thing" (ibid.).

In the presence of strife when dissension rages about differences of opinions held, and encourages a perpetuation of party spirit, benevolence should teach us firstly to make allowance for our fellow creatures, and secondly that the differences that separate us from each other are superficial differences only. It is not to be expected that benevolence taken by itself is sufficient to allay this strife, or to reduce these differences to a level of common understanding, for the presence of reason is not of a sufficient degree in all of us to allow for this, but what we can expect is that the continual exercise of benevolence will at least moderate and restrain us in the presence of each other (Vol. II, p. 187).

8

BENEVOLENCE AND VIRTUE

THE STATUS OF BENEVOLENCE

AT THIS point we shall find it necessary to consider and dispose of some objections that have been brought against the claims of benevolence by some of Butler's readers in the endeavor to appreciate the place that Butler himself accorded to it.

How does the principle of benevolence include within itself all the other virtues? To what extent can all the virtues be traced to it as a source? This is a question that Butler himself raises in his Twelfth Sermon (Vol. II, p. 176).

The framing of this question as stated here is of Butler's formulation, but is misleading none the less. Benevolence, he argues in this section at least, does not contain within itself all the virtues; conscience is manifestly superior. The principle of benevolence has been interpreted by Butler's readers in a variety of ways. Henry Sidgwick in his *Outline of the History of Ethics* denies to it the status of a principle. In his eyes it tends to drop out into the rank of the particular propensions. He was undoubtedly influenced in this interpretation by Butler's own references in the first sermon to its concrete instances. Compare for instance: "And if there be in mankind any disposition to friendship; if there be any such thing as compassion, for compassion is momentary love; if there be any such thing as the paternal or filial affections; if there be any affection in human nature, the object and end of which is the good of another; this is itself benevolence, or the love of another . . ." (Vol. II, pp. 31-33). Taken by itself this passage constitutes good evidence for the reduction of the principle of benevolence to the status of a particular propension. But such an interpretation can only be sustained provided that the later passage which speaks of benevolence as a *"virtuous principle* . . . gratified by a consciousness of *endeavouring* to promote the good of others . . ." (Vol. II, p. 169), be ignored.

There can be found in Butler passages that assign to benevolence a variety of contradictory statuses in the human self. Besides the one quoted that speaks of it as a propension, there are unguarded utterances throughout the Eleventh Sermon that tend to view it in the same light. For instance: "there is no peculiar contrariety between self-love and benevolence; no greater competition between these, than between *any other* particular affections and self-love" (Vol. II, p. 165). In the first sermon benevolence is allotted a standing *equal* to self-love. "To aim at public and private good are so far from being inconsistent, that they mutually promote each other" (Vol. II, p. 30). And for passages that appear to assign to benevolence a status superior to self-love, see Sermon XII, especially the passage that says: "Benevolence seems in the strictest sense to include in it all that is good and worthy" (Vol. II, p. 191). I shall not take up arguments for and against each separately stated position, but shall develop through the collating of various passages what I believe Butler's point of view to consist in.

In his sermons On the Love of Our Neighbour Butler wavers and is contradictory in his answers as to the status of benevolence. He says there: ". . . it is manifest that the common virtues, and the common vices of mankind, may be traced up to benevolence, or the want of it" (Vol. II, p. 190); that "in a higher and more general way of consideration, leaving out the particular nature of creatures, and the particular circumstances in which they are placed, benevolence seems in the strictest sense to include in it all that is good and worthy; all that is good, which we have any distinct particular notion of" (Vol. II, p. 191). And then: "If we consider a reasonable creature or moral agent, without regard to the particular relations and circumstances in which he is placed; we cannot conceive anything else to come in towards determining whether he is to be ranked in an higher or lower class of virtuous beings, but the higher or lower degree in which that principle, and what is manifestly connected with it, prevail in him" (Vol. II, p. 191).

If we take these passages by themselves, they manifestly run counter to Butler's previous statements that insist upon the superiority of self-love (Vol. II, p. 173). But the contradiction exists in appearance only. The statement that the common virtues and the common vices of mankind may be traced up to benevolence or the want of it, has already received its preliminary introduction in an immediately preceding passage. We are reminded there that man's love of others, "is not, any more than this regard to themselves, just, and in its due degree" (Vol. II, p. 190). To state that virtue can be viewed in its reference to benevolence does not mean the exclusion of self-love from virtue, but only that self-love is now being viewed in its particular aspect of benevolent activities. The virtues and vices that are spoken of as centering themselves in benevolence are the *common* ones; presumably not in the sense of ordinary or familiar, but as meaning social or public; i.e., as characterizing man in his relationship to others.

The second statement that we quoted, *viz.*: "benevolence seems in the strictest sense to include in it all that is good and worthy; all that is good, which we have any distinct particular notion of" is not so easy to explain. Taken apart from its context within Sermons XI and XII, it would appear to endorse benevolence as the supreme virtue; but recalling the arguments Butler had given to indicate its subordinateness to self-love, we can only say that the appearance of the present passage is well-nigh inexplicable. Butler himself seemed to be aware of the difficulty that such a statement would afford to his reader, for in his footnote to this passage, his thoughts swing extremely in the other direction in his endeavor to make some sort of amends.[1] He says there, "we are not competent judges, what is upon the whole for the good of the world, there may be other immediate ends appointed us to pursue, besides that of doing good, or producing happiness" (Footnote, p. 190, Vol. II). And further on: "There are certain dispositions of mind, and certain actions, which are in themselves approved or disapproved by mankind, abstracted from the consideration of their tendency to the happiness or misery of the world; approved or disapproved by reflection, by that principle within, which is the guide of life, the judge of right and wrong" (*ibid.*). And again: "thus much however is certain, that the things now instanced in, and numberless others, are approved or disapproved by mankind in general, in quite another view than as conducive to the happiness or misery of the world" (*ibid.*). If we can rely upon the second Dissertation on Virtue as the more certain pronouncement upon the status of benevolence within the moral life, we are left in no doubt. Butler says there: "Without inquiring how far, and in what sense, virtue is resolvable into benevolence, and vice into the

----

[1] In fact, his statements here are so extreme that he appears to be contradicting all that benevolence stands for. But the disinterested virtues that he mentions in this passage do not negate the virtue of benevolence, his aim is to show that the self is in touch with much more than benevolence can account for.

want of it; it may be proper to observe, that benevolence, and the want of it, singly considered, are in no sort the whole of virtue and vice" (Vol. I, p. 334).[2]

Having asserted that Butler's final point of view concerning the moral status of benevolence is one that assigns to it a sphere less inclusive than the highest virtue, we shall now proceed to offer in detail Butler's reasons for this assertion.

Suppose, says Butler, "that it were in the strictest sense true, without limitation, that benevolence includes in it all virtues; yet reason must come in as its guide and director, in order to attain its own end, the end of benevolence, the greatest public good" (Vol. II, pp. 188-9). These reasons are added to and illustrated for us in the Second Dissertation on Virtue, published some ten years later. Butler argues as follows. Suppose we were to grant that benevolence is the whole of virtue, and vice its absence, then it would naturally follow that we should be morally indifferent to everything but the degree to which benevolence prevailed. Falsehood and injustice would not be evaluated in themselves but would be disapproved of only to the extent that they failed to bring about happiness; their condemnation would consist in the amount of misery they would bring in their train. But this is not our attitude towards the disinterested virtues. "Fidelity, honour, strict justice, are themselves approved in the highest degree, abstracted from consideration of their tendency" (Vol. II, p. 191). What this illustration shows is that there are instances of moral repugnance not accountable for by the principle of benevolence. Hence as a moral criterion, it is clearly inadequate to the estimation of the disinterested virtues. Let us proceed to another illustration.

Suppose there are two competitors seeking the same advantages, which as far as we can tell, would be equal in both cases; let us further grant that the successful competitor is aided by a friend. The intervention of friendship, based perhaps upon gratitude, turns the scales, thus deciding upon the person who is to benefit. The causes determining the channels of benevolence here are surcharged with the elements of friendship; the factor of

---

[2] I have made no especial reference in my criticism of this passage i.e., footnote on p. 90, under consideration to the latter part of it, i.e., to lines 12 to 19, p. 191, from "If we consider a reasonable creature" . . . to "prevail in him." What we have said in our criticism of the second statement, holds in criticism of this. Both the footnote to Sermon XII and the remarks in the Second Dissertation on Virtue strike me as being sufficiently final.

decision is thus other than benevolence itself, for owing to its presence, the expression of benevolence has become a positive reality. And no one would deny that in such crucial circumstances, when it is possible to advance friendship, one should do so. This illustration further establishes that in those cases of conflicting benevolence, in which all the advantages to be gained are equal, the decision must rest upon a motive other than benevolence; and that this motive receives the endorsement of a reflective consciousness.

We can further conceive of a situation of the following kind. "Suppose one man should, by fraud or violence, take from another the fruit of his labour, with intent to give it to a third, who he thought would have as much pleasure from it as would balance the pleasure which the first possessor would have had in the enjoyment, and his vexation in the loss of it; suppose also that no bad consequence would follow: yet such an action would surely be vicious" (Vol. I, p. 335). This case is somewhat similar to the second; it is an instance of concretely realizing benevolence through means other than benevolence. The difference in this latter case is that the means of realizing benevolence are such as a moral sense would condemn as vicious. These three instances go plainly to show that "we are constituted so as to condemn falsehood, unprovoked violence, injustice, and to approve of benevolence to some preferably to others, abstracted from all consideration, which conduct is likeliest to produce an overbalance of happiness or misery" (Vol. I, p. 335).

Finally, were some people to argue that God's nature, which is primarily one of benevolence, should serve us as a model in our daily lives, Butler would hold "that this ought not to be asserted (i.e., that his nature is primarily one of benevolence), unless it can be proved; for we should speak with cautious reverence upon such a subject" (Vol. I, p. 55). Thus, "were the Author of nature to propose nothing to himself as an end but the production of happiness, were his moral character merely that of benevolence; yet ours is not so. Upon that supposition indeed the only reason of his giving us the above-mentioned approbation of benevolence to some persons rather than others, and disapprobation of falsehood, unprovoked violence, and injustice, must be, that he forsaw this constitution of our nature would produce more happiness, than forming us with a temper of mere general benevolence" (Vol. I, pp. 335-6).

BENEVOLENCE IN RELATION TO THE PROPENSIONS

At this stage of our discussion, we can more readily appreciate the relation between the principle of benevolence, and those particular propensions that in their remoter goal imply the same aim. At the beginning of our present chapter we touched, in a most general way, upon the differences between them. The purpose of the present section is more to emphasize their interrelation, and to appreciate how the nature of the self is more fully revealed through this relation.

Benevolence requires for its satisfactory expression some one type of general activity that it can find enjoyment in; it requires the presence of individual natures towards whom it can be compassionate; it seeks to assist individuals in times of distress, and to work constructively for their happiness. It is motivated by no one *definite* desire such as to aid them, or to rejoice with them in their prosperity, but comprises both of these capacities in its conscious aim to secure the happiness of others. Benevolence, to be effectively expressed, must have recourse to those particular drives that are conducive towards its conscious end. These drives can be none other than those particular propensions whose *remoter* aim is the good or interest of society.[3]

Let us illustrate in a particular way the significance of this interdependence of benevolence and the particular propensions. We shall consider an hypothetical individual who first lives under the dominance of his propensions and then later conducts his life on the level of conscious direction and control.

At the first stage of his mental activity the individual performs quite mechanically acts of compassion or sympathy, for in their intrinsic impulsive quality they override the individual and often take him by storm. Thus, through a prearrangement or natural disposition the sustenance of social groups is assured; the continued preservation of them is made possible through the constant exhibition and display of acts that are potentially disposed towards good, driving into expression independent of human will. But Butler reminds us that "notwithstanding all that has been said in recommendation of compassion, that it is

---

[3] *Vide* end of Ch. *6*. We stated there that the particular propensions implied remoter ends as well as immediate ends (Vol. II, p. 35). Taking desire of esteem as an instance, Butler tells as that the object of it is merely esteem, but it cannot be gratified without contributing to the good of society (*ibid.*, footnote).

most amiable, most becoming human nature, and most useful to the world; yet it must be owned, that every affection, as distinct from a principle of reason, may rise too high, and be beyond its just proportion. And by means of this one carried too far, a man throughout his life is subject to much more uneasiness than belongs to his share: and in particular instances, it may be in such a degree, as to incapacitate him from assisting the very person who is the object of it" (Vol. II, pp. 98-99).

Clearly then even though "the bare exercise of such affections would itself be for the good and happiness of the world" (Vol. II, p. 84), the uncritical practice of them would in the long run be inadequate and often highly unsatisfactory. This is equivalent to saying that a life conducted at the level of reasonable scrutiny is superior to one that is not. For whereas the life of particular propensions is one in which the rudimentary relationships of man to man are guaranteed and preserved, yet we can call it a life of barest moral subsistence. The automatic behavior which is the common characteristic of all the particular propensions would be restrained *eo ipso* in those of the other-regarding type. It is quite conceivable that occasions will arise in which the display of sympathy will be out of place, and where its exhibition will be unsolicited, or when it will exceed its mark and the purpose for which it has been originated. A little reasonableness in those cases would not be amiss. Since reflection would preserve the balance and proportion of compassion in those exceptional cases, guide its expression so that its objective activity will represent its inner intention or purposiveness, the constant presence of reflection in all sympathetic overtures would be our assurance that sympathy will always be expressed in a manner most adequate to its nature. But this exercise of reason working through those particular propensions whose native intention makes for the welfare of other individuals, and illuminating them is none other than an expression of the principle of benevolence.

We can exhaust our illustration by pointing out that any individual might be under the dominance of benevolence and yet weak in the expression of the particular propensions. He could have a reasonable longing to do good to other people, and be imbued with a love for humanity. But, were he fully conscious of this aim, he would see that the serious entertainment of an humanitarian feeling entails its outward expression. Benevolence to be of any value would have to be expressed in particular ways and concrete instances, thus calling forth potential drives within the nature of the individual. These potential drives could be no other than the particular propensions. Expressing the aim of the principle of benevolence, the particular propensions would at the same time do justice to themselves, and contribute value to a principle that would otherwise be ineffectual and merely formal.

It should be sufficiently clear by this time that the principle of benevolence and those particular propensions whose aim is other-regarding mutually imply each other in a very intimate way; that each taken by itself leads to the recognition of the others as its co-implicate; yet there is to be observed in Butler's explicit treatment of benevolence the tendency to keep the principles distinct from the particular propensions, influenced no doubt by the prevailing atomistic psychology. As a consequence he is led to overemphasize the separateness of these types of affections; while leaving it to the reader, in view of what he is told about man's nature as forming a system, to reconstruct for himself their systematic unity and intimate relatedness with the other drives of his nature.[4]

To break down the atomistic view as misrepresentative must not blind us to the difference between the particular propensions and the principle of benevolence. We can no longer say, as Butler incautiously does at times, that the difference between these two types of affection can be traced to the presence of a reasonable will, or speculative consciousness within the principle of benevolence, and its absence within the particular propensions which stand out as ultimate, hard, unyielding and unrational. For such

---

[4] Both in regard to self-love and benevolence this can be detected. Concerning the former, we are reminded in the first sermon that the principle of self-love and the particular propensions are *totally different*. *Vide* Sermon I, pp. 33-34, footnote: "every body makes a distinction between self-love, and the several particular passions, appetites, and affections; and yet they are often confounded again. That they are totally different, will be seen by any one who will distinguish between the passions and appetites *themselves, and endeavouring* after the means of their gratification. . . . Self-love and the several particular passions and appetites are in themselves totally different; so, that some actions proceed from one, and some from the other." Likewise with benevolence and the particular propensions; *vide,* Sermon XI, especially pp. 166 et seq., for the general position that distinguishes the particular propensions and the principle of benevolence. As we have been endeavoring to point out, this position cannot be taken as it stands, for the whole tenor of Butler's thought is towards their systematic interrelatedness.

a distinction if insisted upon as an ultimate one would be false
and destructive of Butler's deeper underlying intention to see
man as a system. A little observation of the kind that Butler
urges us to employ, would quickly reveal to us that a life carried
on in pursuance of a particular propension, e.g., desire of public
praise, would demand a rational activity, for it would require a
degree of consciousness focussed upon this aim, and a search for
the ways and means successfully to attain it; both of which are
aspects of reason.

How then does this particular propension differ from benevolence? When we speak of benevolence we do not mean the same as,
e.g., desire for public esteem as an end in itself, but this may be
included as part of the general purpose of that principle. We
should rather look upon benevolence as the more comprehensive
aim which truly represents the genuine goal of those particular
propensions that are recognized as other-regarding. Hence
benevolence as contrasted with the particular propensions is
more universal. At its level of completest activity it has taken
over the particular propensions of the social kind, which regarded
in themselves are unintelligible ends standing over against the
nature of man, and has through its aspect of inclusiveness
directed them towards a purpose that is at once intelligible and
unitary. Benevolence shares with the particular propensions an
element of awareness, that includes within itself a degree of
calculativeness to establish itself most effectively; it likewise possesses a voluntary endeavor to enforce its decision. The difference
between the principle and the particular propensions is one of
degree rather than of kind; a greater inclusiveness contrasted
with a less inclusiveness.

In the drive of a propension there is no universality that
carries us beyond the instinct, or beyond the object sought.
But with the principle it is otherwise. The insistence here that
the principle has no one definite or precise object means on its
positive side that it seeks the universal situation, one that is
common to all and which at the same time is its unity. It will
be recalled that the particular propensions mechanically making
for the preservation of the self complete their nature in their
discharge and in blind establishment of the results. But when the
propension becomes conscious of itself, it ceases strictly speaking to be a particular propension, and takes on the characteristic
of a principle. But the characteristic of a principle is the aware-

ness and appreciation that the particular propension has a significance beyond the particular end it expresses. At the stage of enlightenment, it is seen that the value of the definite object that satisfies the propensions lies in the fact that it is one concrete means of establishing an end more comprehensive than the propension, and an end to which the objective course of the particular propension is but partially contributory. Hence it can be seen that the universality of the principle makes it impossible that it ever have a concrete or definite object that is completely adequate and satisfactory to it. Although a principle can only be progressively established through particular concrete ends, availing itself in this respect of the appropriate propensions, yet in any one act of its self-expression a principle is much more comprehensive than the situation of the object of the moment. Contrasted with the object of the particular propensions, the end of a principle is comparatively elusive; it is ideal where that of the propension is particular.

We must be careful, in our contrast of the principles and the propensions, not to commit ourselves to the error of conceiving them as intrinsically distinct. Both are aspects of a continuous process; the principle is immanent within the propension, and the propension is carried on into the principle wherein it actively commands the conscious situation. The expression of the propension as such is the concentration of the agent upon the aspect of particularity of the drive or affection in question. It represents a state of mind in which the universal end is temporarily ignored and can be. But to pay attention to the element of universality whereby the situation becomes much more than a particularistic expression, is to emphasize the presence of the principle. Hence although the principle and the propensions are logically one and continuous, yet from the standpoint of the psychological agent, either can be emphasized to the exclusion of the other. The moral situation, as we have discussed it, would insist upon the expression of both the principle and the propensions; the latter being under the control of the former.

Ontologically considered, benevolence is no other than that stage in the life of an individual at which becoming enlightened as to the remoter end of the public affections, he seeks progressively to establish that end. We must no longer view the particular drives of man's nature as in any sense ultimate and discrete; all of these propensions whose activities are separately directed towards the welfare of others, really work for the establishment of a common public end. This common end, the guardianship of which is benevolence, rationally organizes the particular propensions and relates them to their intended goal so that they now become explicable and meaningful.

Although there is no ultimate separability of whole and parts, nevertheless to an analyzing consciousness each can be abstracted from the other, and made the focus of the mind's attention and activity. That is to say: an individual can become completely engrossed by the immediate objects of the particular propensions, giving his time and attention first to one, and then to another; treating each as a center of reference, and effecting no unity of aim in terms of which they can be organized; or he can emphasize benevolence in abstraction from the properties of its contributing parts. If he does the former, he treats the particular propensions as ends in themselves. Although the expression of them as such will undoubtedly tend to make for the activity of benevolence, nevertheless the degree to which benevolence will be expressive, if attention has not turned its eye expressly upon it, will be largely accidental. Failure to express the parts intelligently, in terms of the ultimate end that they involve, will likewise mean that these parts themselves will be inadequately expressed.

What we have said concerning the expression of the parts independently of the whole that they involve, applies *mutatis mutandi* to the expression of the whole in ignorance and neglect of the contributory parts. Calling our attention to the insufficiency of the principle of benevolence, taken in abstraction from the particular propensions, Butler assures us (Vol. II, p. 87) that without the assistance of suitable affections (speaking here specifically of the particular propension of compassion), it is absurd to imagine that an abstract calculation, drawing its inspiration *solely* from the values of right and wrong, i.e., benevolence as an end, would be a sufficient stimulus to urge us onward to perform the duties we owe to our fellow creatures. "Is it possible any can in earnest think," he says, "that a public spirit, i.e., a settled reasonable principle of benevolence to mankind, is so prevalent and strong in the species, as that we may venture to throw off the under-affections, which are its assistants, carry it forward and mark out particular courses for it; family, friends, neighbourhood, the distressed, our country?" (Vol. II, pp. 87-88). Concentrating upon benevolence as an end in abstraction from the particular propensions that really compose it, leads to its weak and often immoral expression. "Disinterestedness is so far from being in itself commendable, that the utmost possible depravity which we can in imagination conceive, is that of disinterested cruelty" (Vol. II, p. 22).

The remedy lies evidently in concretely grasping the parts in terms of the whole, and expressing the whole through the agency of the parts. When reason intelligently plays its part in the expression of the particular propensions, it illuminates them with a knowledge of their remotely implied ends; in doing this, it transforms them in terms of these ends, breaks down their apparent discreteness, and works towards their coordinated unity. A life intelligently centered about a particular propension would mean the forfeiture of that propension *quâ* ultimate; for man being drawn more and more to the *nisus* that such a propension involves would see that its goal implies many other parts upon which it is dependent, and which it at the same time assists; that the expressions of these co-implied parts check and restrain each other so intimately that the original propension has passed beyond its originally self-centered aims.

SUMMARY AND TRANSITION

We shall summarize briefly the results of our present chapter. The principle of benevolence represents a conscious disposition in the nature of man to seek the companionship of others and disinterestedly to promote their well-being. But the well-being of others is dictated by his particular dispositions, called propensions, such as the urge to compassionate others in distress, or to promote their prosperity. Benevolence is however the conscious interrelation of these particular drives, that expresses them in terms of the common aim that they remotely imply.

Through the exercise of benevolence the self achieves a degree of unity that would otherwise be denied it. This unity is forged self-consciously. It is not established at any one instant in time. Through its constant expression the self is made more intimate with its social environment; hence it is growing and progressive, as is the self by whose experiences it is affected.

Lastly, just as the nature of the self is reflected in its particular propensions, so is it represented in benevolence as its rational aim. This means that man's desire consciously to advance the well-being of his neighbor is at the same time an expression of his own nature, one that would be poorer were this benevolent principle to be thwarted or denied.

To describe still further the nature of the self, we are now led to investigate the principle of self-love, which we saw at the end of our last chapter was implied by those particular propensions whose remoter aim was self-regarding, i.e., having the good of the agent in mind. The complete description of this principle will occupy our attention in the next chapter.

9

PRINCIPLE OF SELF-LOVE

CRITICAL REMARKS

IN OUR classification of man's constituent parts we mentioned among them the principle of self-love, stating in regard to it that the objective aim of this principle was the conscious attainment of the happiness or welfare of the individual. In Butler's writings, however, there nowhere appears an explicit statement concerning this principle, and especially in the first three sermons which deal with the analysis of human nature, its exposition is only indirectly brought out in connection with the principle of benevolence (Vol. II, p. 31). In the later sermons, too, it is never distinctly formulated as a principle; reference to it occurs frequently and at such times as Butler feels it necessary in the demarcation of the human principles and propensions to keep them distinct.[1] But despite this fact we cannot underestimate its importance in Butler's system. When we recall that the age was one which paid homage to this principle in excess, and that Butler himself was concerned in the limitation of its sphere, we can quite easily see that for Butler there was no need of a specific formulation of a principle that every one assumed, but only a drastic need of showing its limited sphere of influence.

Of all the affections of human nature the principle of self-love is the most difficult for us to understand, and the variety of references to it in Butler's writings makes it easy for the reader to misinterpret the true meaning that Butler has in mind but never fully reveals to his reader. Of all the principles that Butler considers it is the only one which has thrown interpreters into hopeless confusion, and has led them to diverge widely in points of criticism. Some, like Broad, frankly admit an inconsistency in some of Butler's remarks, especially where he (Butler) states that self-love and virtue are coincident;[2] others directly an-

---

[1] *Vide* Vol. II, preface, pp. 11, 18; Sermon I, p. 30, note, p. 33; Sermon III, p. 63; Sermon V, p. 78; Sermon XI, pp. 157, 158, 159, 163, 165, 173; Vol. I, p. 110.

[2] See C. D. Broad: *Five Types of Ethical Theory,* pp. 79-81. H. Sidgwick coordinates self-love with conscience, seeing in both principles a parallel of authority. Cp. *Outline of the History of Ethics,* pp. 195-7. His reasons for the co-supremacy of self-love with conscience are based largely upon two passages taken from Butler's Sermons. "Reasonable self-love and conscience are the

nounce that it is the highest virtue for man, and classify Butler as some sort of an egoistic hedonist. But all of these interpretations are, as I shall endeavor to show, erroneous and ill-founded; the difficulty of determining the comparative status of the principles arises from attributing to Butler an atomistic logic, especially in his psychological treatment of the human mind. There is likewise the failure on the part of the reader to appreciate the close and intimate connection between Butler's psychological thory and its moral implications. The fault of misrepresenting the principle of self-love is not solely due to the reader; Butler himself, through a carelessness in his exposition and an uncertainty as to its implications, was not fully aware of the scope, limitation and internal determination of this principle of self-love.

Butler, as we have stated, was not indifferent to the importance of self-love, and the immediate sway that it exercises in its narrower aspects. He realized the drastic need there was for the controlling of it. In the opening words of his Sermon Upon the Love of Our Neighbour, he refers to it explicitly as one of the outstanding evils of the age. "It may be spoken of as very much the distinction of the present to profess a contracted spirit, and greater regards to self-interest, than appears to have been done formerly" (Vol. II, p. 156). We shall now consider its nature in detail, its place within man's systematic nature and finally its moral attributes.

This investigation first calls upon us to indicate the various ways in which Butler uses the term self-love. There is (a) a pejorative sense which Butler uses to designate within man the existence of a narrow selfishness or deprecable self-regard (Vol. II, pp. 18, 156, 7), (b) a usage that characterizes self-love in opposition to benevolence as a concern for man's private good (Vol. II, pp. 30, 159, 163), and finally (c) as characterizing man's general happiness, representing man's *entire* nature as it is known in terms of his many drives unitarily and systematically viewed (Vol. II, pp. 23, 158, 9). The first meaning of self-love does not indicate for Butler any original impulse in human nature, but rather a derivative drive whose origin is due to the

chief or superior principles in the nature of man . . ." etc., p. 64; and "Our ideas of happiness and misery are of all our ideas the nearest and most important to us" (S. XI, p. 173). For further interpretation, Cp. Lefevre, who sees self-love in coordination with benevolence, both being, however, subordinated to conscience.

perversion of self-love, viewed in the second or third sense. It will be our task to show that the second and third meanings of self-love are not in any sense opposed. When Butler speaks of self-love as a regard for our private interests as opposed to the interests and concerns of others, he is I believe, under the influence of an individualistic psychology and not quite clear as to its limitations, nor is this the position that a consistent development of his own position would lead him to accept.

GENERAL CHARACTERISTICS

In the initial exercise of its particular propensions the self is not unaware of their objective course; in its memory it can relive their history, trace their consequences and ascertain the ends that they normally tend to express. As it becomes cognizant of the objects sought by the particular propensions, the self learns that some of them tend indirectly to preserve the agent; to advance his happiness, life and general welfare. In this remoter aim the particular propensions, so divergent as hunger, thirst, or desire for approbation, meet. This self-regard constitutes their remoter goal, just as the regard for others is the remoter goal of compassion and resentment.[3]

In the awareness of this goal shared by the private propensions the self knows itself to be more of an entity, and less given over to the caprices of its instincts. It is now aware of its propensions not solely as drives blindly striking out, but also of an implicit order in their make-up that indicates the existence of a unitary end. In viewing its propensions in terms of this end, the self no longer feels strange in their presence and no longer looks upon them as alien to its nature. In a very important respect they have become most intimately and privately his own possession in whose successful expression and outcome he is now sympathetically concerned. This goal is none other than the appearance within the self of the principle of self-love. What in detail can we say about this principle?

Self-love makes us aware of ourselves as conscious, living agents. Through its influence we refer to ourselves actions that formerly struck us as being indifferently disposed. Seeing that

---

[3] We shall refer to those particular propensions whose remoter goal is the welfare of the agent as the private or self-regarding propensions, and to those particular propensions whose remoter goal is the welfare of others, as the public or other-regarding propensions.

many of our instincts and passions have a remoter bearing upon ourselves, we now strive consciously to bring them into an effective self-expression. We deliberate upon them; we seek to bring about the means of their gratification.[4]

Can we understand the nature of this principle further by asking what the agent sees his private good to consist in, or what he seeks to gratify? To a great extent this self-gratification depends upon the nature of the actual individual. Some seek it solely in health, others in pleasure. But to do so is falsely to see the nature of the self in too narrow a way. The enlightened self should aim at his general good (Vol. II, pp. 18, 19, 20). This will include private good and preservation of life, but will include much more besides. Mere existence is not satisfactory to the individual—to live well is also his aim. But to live well is to live happily, hence objects of self-love must in some degree assure the happiness of the individual.

Concerning the preservative tendency of self-love, Butler says: "There are as real and the same kind of indications in human nature, . . . that we were intended to take care of our own life and health and private good" (Vol. II, p. 30). Concerning its aim at the happiness of the individual, compare Vol. II, preface p. 23; also Sermon XI, p. 158: "The principle we call self-love never seeks anything external for the sake of the thing, but only as a means of happiness or good . . . (it) belongs to man as a reasonable creature reflecting upon his own interests or happiness." On the following page, i.e., p. 159, Butler again refers to it as the "cool principle of self-love, or general desire of our own happiness." Most explicit in this latter connection is: "private happiness or good is all which self-love can make us desire, or be concerned about: in having this consists its gratification: it is an affection to ourselves; a regard to our

---

[4] Butler contrasts self-love with the particular propensions, and warns us against confusing them with each other. He says: "that they are totally different, will be seen by any one who will distinguish between the passions and appetites *themselves,* and *endeavouring* after the means of their gratification." Likewise in the same passage, he says that "the coolest self-love . . . may put us upon making use of the *proper methods of obtaining* that pleasure" (Vol. I, pp. 33, 34)—(i.e., conceived good). That Butler conceived of self-love as intrinsically rational and deliberative is testified in his frequent references to it as reasonable, cool, and settled. Cp. Vol. II, pp. 64, 158, 19. Cp. also Vol. II, p. 157, where the principle of self-love is attributed to "all sensible creatures, who can reflect upon themselves and their own interest or happiness, so as to have that interest an object to their minds."

own interest, happiness, and private good: and in the proportion a man hath this, he is interested, or a lover of himself" (Vol. II, p. 159).

But how is this happiness to be secured? Only by taking into account the variety of tendencies in human nature, and directing them towards the objects they imply, so that satisfaction is afforded them. It follows then that for effective expression self-love must depend upon the particular propensions and avail itself of their inner and unconscious demands for outer objects. But it is a dependence in which self-love has the upper hand. The appreciation of the ends to be achieved, and of the best ways of securing them, rests upon the discretion of this principle.

In the preface (Vol. II, p. 20) this relationship is explicitly stated. "The very idea of an interested pursuit necessarily presupposes particular passions or appetites. . . . Take away these affections, and you leave self-love absolutely nothing at all to employ itself about; no end or object for it to pursue, excepting only that of avoiding pain . . . but the very idea of interest or happiness other than the absence of pain, implies particular appetites or passions; these being necessary to constitute that interest or happiness . . ." But the tendency in man that stands guardian for an interested pursuit is the principle of self-love. In his Sermon on Compassion, this is further developed where Butler says: "The private interest of the individual would not be sufficiently provided for by reasonable and cool self-love alone; therefore the appetites and passions are placed within as a guard and further security, without which it would not be taken due care of. It is manifest our life would be neglected, were it not for the calls of hunger, and thirst, and weariness; notwithstanding that without them reason would assure us, that the recruits of food and sleep are the necessary means of our preservation" (Vol. II, p. 87; cp. also pp. 160, 167, 169).

Both the principle of self-love and the particular propensions are checks upon the expression and activity of each other. Self-love through its rationality imposes a restraining influence upon the particular propensions, and the particular propensions in their role of furnishing themselves as contents to self-love keep self-love within a limited range of expression, force it to be concrete and determinate, and serve to inform self-love that its activity is best expressed only when it makes use of those particular propensions having the same aim as itself. The particular propensions and self-love regarded as separate affections, i.e., as independent of each other, may either be strong or weak; either in independence of the other may incautiously express itself and so exceed the aim that it tends naturally towards.

The absence from the particular propensions proper of the element of reflectiveness means the absence of restraint. Unguided by reason, they may discharge themselves so violently as to overreach their intended aim; on the other hand they may express themselves feebly when it would be to the advantage of the self were their activity more direct and forceful. This lack of self-measured control could be corrected by a reason dedicated to the interest of the self; one that would steadily keep the true and remoter aim of these drives before its mind. Self-love itself unsupported by the particular propensions would likewise fail to do entire justice to the self. Although possessed of a reflective element, yet if it unwisely deprived itself of the assistance of the particular propensions it would seek in vain for means of self-expression. It would either sink to the level of blind propensions, or remain altogether inert and inoperative.[5]

I will give a concrete illustration how the particular propensions enter into the expression of self-love. Hunger and thirst, e.g., by themselves are unmoral; they are the appetitive longings within any human being for food and drink. Let us grant that the individual becomes conscious of the objective courses of hunger and thirst. At first he is aware of their aim, but he is not content merely to note mentally that one course of action presupposes an instinct, and this instinct seeks water, and that another course of action presupposes an instinct for food. He proceeds further to reflect upon the ends of these instincts, to see whether or not they are interrelated. He finds that the tendencies

---

[5] In the preface to the Sermons (Vol. II, p. 23) Butler assures us that the passions have absolutely no bound or measure but what is set to them by self-love or moral consideration: and in his Sermon on Compassion, we are further told that "every affection, as distinct from a principle of reason, may rise too high, and be beyond its just proportion" (Vol. II, pp. 98-99). Also on the side of self-love can be detected a latitude of sway in which it can, more or less independently of the particular propensions, act on its own account disregarding those objects that it should take into consideration (Vol. II, p. 87). The possibility of self-love's acting independently of the particular propensions is also touched upon in the Sermon XI (Vol. II, p. 160), where Butler warns men against being wholly engrossed by self-love.

of hunger and thirst are directed towards the preservation of his private self; and that the significance of these drives lies in the furtherance of his life and happiness. He is now in a position to evaluate these instincts, and apply his knowledge to their activities and outcome. Since he knows that the true end of thirst is primarily the maintenance of life, he can become intelligent about its expression. Upon any particular occasion he can ask himself whether it is wise to satisfy the prompting of thirst, or to give way to his hunger. This type of deliberation shows the presence of self-love and the degree of authority it wields in reference to its own interests.

SUMMARY AND CONCLUSION

Before we advance our discussion further, let us state precisely what we have accomplished. We can then appreciate what there remains for us to do. The self whose psychological nature we undertook to analyse revealed a congeries of drives, each one of which sought unconsciously a specific kind of object for its satisfaction. Upon a scrutiny of these objects we noticed that the drives of our nature tended remotely at the same time to bring about or establish two other ends: namely, the welfare of the active agent himself, and the welfare of other individuals with whom he was brought into contact. The remoter ends of these particular propensions, Butler maintains, are their truer ends, for they represent more genuinely the objective course of the original drives. If this is so, we can no longer say that man's nature is composed of a multiplicity of drives, seeking in independence of each other their respective courses, but that the self is fundamentally urged on to seek its own good, as well as the good of other agents. And it seeks its own good by looking for happiness. At the level of self-love the expression of the self is dual, rather than multiple: dual, for at first it sees its interest in sharp contrast to the interests of others, but not multiple, for the self has now interrelated its multiplicity of demands in terms of the happiness they yield.

Self-expression no longer means the outward drive of a propension to its immediate object, but the expression of a propension so that it implies one or the other of these remoter goals. But can we rest satisfied with this account of the self? Apparently not, for if the self is a system, we must overcome the duality that is involved in these diverse ends of self-love and benevolence. Are they mutually exclusive? Or do they each imply more remotely, as did the particular propensions, a goal within which their apparent discreteness is broken down, and the harmony of the self achieved? It will be the purpose of our next chapter to answer this question.

10

SELF-LOVE AND BENEVOLENCE

THEIR CONFLICT

OUR psychological study of human nature has up to now informed us of the presence within man of organized impulses; one class being directed towards the well-being of the self, and the other towards the well-being of other selves. We have seen how the plurality of the particular propensions has given way to their remotely implied unities, so that at this stage of our exposition we have an apparent opposition of a concrete self-love, and a concrete benevolence.[1]

We are now interested in ascertaining whether these two types of organized drive, i.e., self-love and benevolence, really stand mutually opposed, or whether a closer observation will not reveal them to be intrinsically united in the same intimacy in which a closer observation revealed the particular propensions to be inseparably united with their remoter ends or principles? The first alternative we are forced to dismiss, for Butler's insistance upon the systematic structure of man's constituent parts precludes the possibility of any ultimate internal opposition of parts. It remains for us to consider precisely the relation discoverable between self-love and benevolence.

To common sense it appears as a self-evident truth that to be concerned with the interests of others entails a sacrifice of one's own; for how can one be attentive to one's neighbor without at the same time neglecting himself? The moral issue that is involved here may be restated as follows. Since the self can be expressed only through its partial aspects, which are always lesser in degree and importance than the self, how can the self avoid denying itself in some of its phases when it is expressing itself through others? When, for instance the agent undertakes a benevolent act, when he centers his attention around benevolence as a moral principle, to what extent must he purposely

---

[1] From now on, I shall refer to benevolence or self-love as "concrete," when I wish to imply their recognition of and expression through the particular propensions that are suitable to them. A "concrete self-love" will indicate the universality of self-enhancement within that plurality of particular propensions whose remoter aim is identical with it; and a "concrete benevolence" will stand for the universal aim of neighborly assistance as it takes account of the same.

neglect his own interests? This dilemma must be solved, for if morality consists in the proper expression of one's nature, it must take care that no mutilation is involved. If the pursuit of benevolence means the denial of that aspect of the self given over to self-love, then the agent who dedicates himself to the pursuit of benevolence is immoral. The same is true in a reversed situation. The pursuit of self-love must not preclude the interests of benevolence. In some way a co-ordination must be effected; or one principle must be organically related in such a way to another, that the expression of the higher serves the interests of the lower. Only under some such arrangement can the self remain unitary.

Butler asserts that there is no conflict between self-love and benevolence, offering as a reason for this assertion the fact that these principles have different objects towards which they are directed for satisfaction. Where there is a difference of aim, there can be no conflict of interests. Thirst can exclude hunger, but brings about no conflict where the aims are so diverse. No self feels that it is being cheated if in giving vent to its desire for food, it foregoes the opportunity to drink. Likewise with benevolence and self-love. To be attentive to the interests of my neighbor is an aim that is different from self-regard; that, in being different, may exclude without denying. So much is clear, but not convincing, for one feels the contrast of self-love with benevolence to involve an opposition that in crucial cases can and does verge upon the contradictory in a sense in which two instinctive acts do not. Were the aims of self-love and benevolence merely different, there would be no issue for the attention of morality. We must be shown that in those cases that appear to be crucially contradictory there is present no real conflict, no insoluble difficulty.

Butler's next argument is analogical. It shows that there are present in the principle of benevolence the same features that are present in the particular propensions, and points out that those features in the particular propensions that establish their intimate relationship to self-love should lead us to the same conclusion in regard to the principle of benevolence. We should affirm in this latter principle an organic conduciveness to the principle of self-love. This argument is reinforced *a fortiori*. The elements of actual conflict that can be observed between the particular propensions and the principle of self-love are not sufficient to deny the organic subservience of the former affections to the latter; yet between the principle of benevolence and the principle of self-love, the actually observed conflict is less than between the propensions and self-love, hence there is less reason to deny here the organic relationship that we affirm in the former.

In this analogical argument our attention is drawn to the relation that exists between the particular propensions and self-love. We have in this relationship an instance of affections that are different in aim, and that in being different are often in actual conflict. Swept off his feet by an inordinate desire for fame, or ambition, an individual may often be led into paths of behavior that run directly counter to his own interests. "Nothing is more common, than to see men give themselves up to a passion or an affection to their own prejudice and ruin, and in direct contradiction to manifest and real interest, and the loudest calls of self-love" (Vol. II, p. 171). But a deeper inspection will show us that "this competition or interfering is merely accidental" (*ibid.*). Being accidental between self-love and the particular propensions, between benevolence and self-love, the conflict is no less so. "It happens much oftener between pride, revenge, sensual gratifications, and private interest, than between private interest and benevolence" (*ibid.*). The resolution of this conflict that exists in appearance only was seen to lie in the subordination of the particular propensions to the rational control of self-love whose end these propensions remotely implied. We saw that a proper understanding of ambition, or desire for fame demanded the reference of these propensions to the principle of self-love, to which end they tended remotely to converge.

For Butler the solution of an apparent conflict between self-love and benevolence is of the same nature. The remoter expression of benevolence tends towards the interest of the self. When we perform an act of charity we experience the value of the act, and share in its results as much as the individual to whom it is purposively directed. We rejoice in an act, the nature of which we know to be good. "Does the benevolent man appear less easy with himself, from his love to his neighbour? Does he less relish his being? Is there any peculiar gloom seated on his face? Is his mind less open to entertainment, to any particular gratification? Nothing is more manifest, than that being in good humour, which is benevolence while it lasts, is itself the temper of satisfaction and enjoyment" (Vol. II, p. 167).

We can conclude this second argument by saying that since there is no conflict between self-love and the particular propensions, which latter are aspects of the self, there can be no genuine conflict between benevolence and self-love, for benevolence is as much an aspect of the self as are the particular propensions. The principle of benevolence may often lead to greater happiness of the self than the particular propensions. Being possessed of reason, and having it within its own power to advance its own interests, it can approximate to this end more satisfactorily than can the particular propensions that are blind and impulsive, and often achieve the happiness of the self through the barest element of chance. Hence if there is no conflict between self-love and the particular propensions that are unrational, there can be less possibility of a conflict between self-love and the principle of benevolence, especially when the latter is more highly organized than the particular propensions.

It should be clear to us now in what sense there is no conflict between self-love, and in what sense a conflict does exist. To consider this latter point first: In the actual life of man a conflict *does* exist. He sees himself as an entity distinct from his environment; and in his plans he accentuates each aspect, tending to make each one a focus about which can be built up definite interests. A conflict ensues just because he has accepted without question two loci of experience, whose nature has not been scrutinized, nor reduced to a common heading. But were the individual to encompass these two loci, he would see that the demand for their intelligibility would break down their opposition. Becoming amenable, they would give way to the nature of the self. In their new status private and public interests would merge as one. If we grant that this transcendence in the light of reason is a more faithful representation of the self, then there can be no conflict. The conflict that is an actual one breaks down through the intervention of a moral reason, that replaces the two ends by a higher one deemed more desirable. The self under moral reason is more genuinely itself than when it is not, and in this self (ideal at any one time to the actual self) there is and can be no conflict. The existence of conflict is owing to the partial exercise of reason that fails to see within these two affections the element of transcendence that proclaims a genuine unity. Taking as real their aspects of lesser completion, reason brings about a discord by accepting each affection as ultimate.

THEIR RESOLUTION

We have presented two of Butler's arguments that concern themselves with the supposed conflict between self-love and benevolence. They have informed us that no conflict exists. We shall now consider a further argument on this point, but one that differs from the others by bearing a positive character. Butler proceeds to tell us that the principle of benevolence, far from being in conflict with the self, is a necessary ingredient of its unity. Wherein, he asks, does happiness consist for us? Not in the pursuit of self-love alone. "Self-love may prevail and exert itself in a degree or manner which is not subservient to this end; then it will not follow, that our interest will be promoted in proportion to the degree in which that principle engrosses us, and prevails over others. Nay further, the private and contracted affection, when it is not subservient to this end, private good, may, for any thing that appears, have a direct contrary tendency and effect. And if we will consider the matter, we shall see that it often really has. *Disengagement* is absolutely necessary to enjoyment: and a person may have so steady and fixed an eye upon his own interest, whatever he places it in, as may hinder him from *attending* to many gratifications within his reach, which others have their minds *free* and *open* to" (Vol. II, pp. 160-1).[2]

We have already observed in our discussions of the particular propensions and the principle of self-love that the latter affection must be made concrete by including the former before it is expressed as nature intended it to be. The attendance of hap-

[2] Cp. also in the same section the illuminating passage: "Immoderate self-love does very ill consult its own interest: and, how much soever a paradox it may appear, it is certainly true, that even from self-love we should endeavour to get over all inordinate regard to, and consideration of ourselves. Every one of our passions and affections hath its natural stint and bound, which may easily be exceeded; whereas our enjoyments can possibly be but in a determinate measure and degree. Therefore such excess of the affection, since it cannot procure any enjoyment, must in all cases be useless; but is generally attended with inconveniences, and often is downright pain and misery. This holds as much with regard to self-love as to all other affections. The natural degree of it, so far as it sets us on work to gain and make use of the materials of satisfaction, may be to our real advantage; but beyond or besides this, it is in several respects an inconvenience and disadvantage. Thus it appears, that private interest is so far from being likely to be promoted in proportion to the degree in which self-love engrosses us, and prevails over all other principles; that *the contracted affection may be so prevalent as to disappoint itself, and even contradict its own end, private good*" (Vol. II, p. 161).

piness should be viewed as the emotional indication that the harmony of these two types of affections has been realized. But it is not the concrete expression of self-love viewed in its relationship to the unrational particular propensions that is now offered to us as the course within which the self can achieve its maximum happiness. Were this so, there would still be excluded from the nature of the self, and also from the happiness consequent to its natural exercise, the principle of benevolence viewed in its concrete relation to its subordinate particular propensions whose remoter aim is the same as its own. *It must follow that self-love must include in some way the concrete principle of benevolence.* An assurance of its maximum happiness can be maintained in no other way. The principle of self-love must expand so as rationally to include as part of its constituent nature the entire array of disinterested affections. Thus, it is in the actual stress between self-love and benevolence, which the self undertakes to allay and which it proceeds to expose as an unreal dichotomy, that the issue is solved by self-love's coming out the victor.

Strictly speaking, self-love is not co-ordinated with benevolence, neither does benevolence forfeit its disinterested character by being subordinated to the unity of the rational self. Benevolence neither loses its disinterestedness, nor does it become selfish. The growth takes place within the principle of self-love, the character of which is determined by the self's constituent parts. As representative of the self, viewed in its entirety of structure and singularity of aim, self-love definitely takes on the characteristics of the parts that compose it. Its fate in a sense rests in their hands, and its happiness is achieved through their proper expression.

Happiness of the agent, if not to be found in any one aspect of man's nature, must be centered in the expression of all his affections, of which one of the most important is the principle of benevolence.[3] Taken in independence of, or indifference to the

---

[3] *Vide* Vol. II, p. 160: "Happiness or satisfaction consists only in the enjoyment of those objects, which are by nature suited to our several particular appetites, passions, and affections. So that if self-love wholly engrossed us, and leaves no room for any other principle, there can be absolutely no such thing at all as happiness, or enjoyment of any kind whatever; since happiness consists in the gratification of particular passions, which supposes the having of them. Self-love then does not constitute *this* or *that* to be our interest or good; but, our interest or good being constituted by nature and supposed, self-love only puts us upon obtaining and securing it."

principle of benevolence, there can be no happiness for a self that is partially expressed; neither can such a self be moral.

Butler raises the question why the common belief prevails that there is of necessity a conflict between these two principles? In answer to this he finds that the belief owes its vitality largely to the pervasive influence that the idea of property plays, with its conceptions of quantity, within the sphere of our moral beliefs. To part with one's possessions, naturally means a lesser amount of goods for ourselves (Vol. II, p. 171). But this does not hold in regard to the principle of benevolence, for our attention to our neighbors is not a material possession that means a lesser enjoyment for ourselves in proportion to which they benefit. As we have pointed out above, the exercise of benevolence benefits the agent by virtue of its moral tone as well as the individual to whom it is directed. "So far as it is taken for granted, that barely having the means and materials of enjoyment is what constitutes interest and happiness; that our interest or good consists in possessions themselves, in having the property of riches, houses, lands, gardens, not in the enjoyment of them; so far it will even more strongly be taken for granted, in the way already explained, that an affection's conducing to the good of another, must even necessarily occasion it to conduce less to private good, if not to be positively detrimental to it. For, if property and happiness are one and the same thing, as by increasing the property of another, you lessen your own property, so by promoting the happiness of another, you must lessen your own happiness. But whatever occasioned the mistake, I hope it has been fully proved to be one . . ." (Vol. II, pp. 172-3).

It is only fitting that at this stage of our exposition we introduce for consideration our interpretation of the passage occurring towards the end of Butler's Eleventh Sermon, that has given to his readers no end of difficulty. I shall first quote it in full. "And to all of these things may be added, that religion, from whence arises our strongest obligation to benevolence, is

---

Vide, Vol. II, p. 167: ". . . This (i.e., happiness) can only consists in the enjoyment of those objects, which are by nature adapted to our several faculties. These particular enjoyments make up the sum total of our happiness."

Vide, Vol. II, p. 169: "Happiness consists in the gratification of certain affections, appetites, passions, with objects which are by nature adapted to them. Self-love may indeed set us on work to gratify these: but happiness or enjoyment has no immediate connection with self-love, but arises from such gratification alone. Love of our neighbour is one of those affections."

so far from disowning the principle of self-love, that it often addresses itself to that very principle, and always to the mind in that state when reason presides; and there can no access be had to the understanding, but by convincing men, that the course of life we would persuade them to is not contrary to their interest. It may be allowed, without any prejudice to the cause of virtue and religion, that our ideas of happiness and misery are of all our ideas the nearest and most important to us; that they will, nay, if you please, that they ought to prevail over those of order, and beauty, and harmony, and proportion, if there should ever be, as it is impossible there ever should be, any inconsistence between them: though these last too, as expressing the fitness of actions, are real as truth itself. Let it be allowed, though virtue or moral rectitude does indeed consist in affection to and pursuit of what is right and good, as such; yet, that when we sit down in a cool hour, we can neither justify to ourselves this or any other pursuit, till we are convinced that it will be for our happiness, or at least not contrary to it" (Vol. II, p. 173).

This entire passage is without doubt in eulogy of the principle of self-love, but the self-love to whose supremacy it deferentially bows is one that has undergone in the meantime a transformation that has carried it beyond the stage of an obstinate opposition to benevolence, to a level that has included its claims. Taken in this sense, the asperity of the passage weakens considerably, for the meaning of it is not that self-love should be pursued even though benevolence be neglected, but that no happiness can be forthcoming that does not take into account the entire self in its concrete possession of its disinterested affections. It is interesting for our purpose to note that the principle of benevolence is not mentioned in distinction from self-love. This fact, together with the drift of the entire sermon, should indicate to us that Butler had not in mind any intended opposition between the two principles.

Having settled the status of benevolence, and having reduced it to self-love, so that self-love now takes on its disinterested character, Butler sees no need here to make a further reference to their respective relationship. His concluding words before the introduction of this present passage, are reassuring and sufficiently final. "There is no peculiar rivalship or competition between self-love and benevolence." He further tells us: "that as there may be a competition between these two, so there may also between any particular affection whatever and self-love; that every particular affection, benevolence among the rest, is subservient to self-love by being the instrument of private enjoyment; and that in one respect benevolence contributes more to private interest, i.e. enjoyment or satisfaction, than any other of the particular common affections, as it is in a degree its own gratification" (Vol. II, p. 173).

But the reader, now having had his fears upon this point quieted, may suspect that there may be a possible rivalry between the self as so conceived, and the claims of religion. But religion to the extent that it is intimately tied up with the principle of benevolence can no more be at variance with self-love, than is benevolence. To those who perceive a conflict between self-love and the ideas of order, beauty, harmony, and proportion, comes the reassurance that even here, "it is impossible there ever should be any inconsistency between them." . . . It is the latter part of this passage that appears to me particularly significant, for it affords us in no unequivocal tones the criterion for moral acts that Butler has been constantly emphasizing. Any moral theory that fails to take account of the self for whom it has been originated cannot arrogate to itself the claims of moral sufficiency. Granted that virtue does consist in an objective good, yet there can be no assurance that we have discovered this good unless we can test it from the standpoint of our nature to see whether it measures up to our demands. Excluding this test, we can supply no others. "We are in a peculiar manner, as I may speak, intrusted with ourselves; and therefore care of our own interests, as well as of our conduct, particularly belongs to us. To these things must be added, that moral obligations can extend no further than to natural possibilities" (Vol. II, p. 184).

FINAL STATUS OF SELF-LOVE IN THE HUMAN SYSTEM

We shall now discuss how the term self-love has taken on quite unconsciously in Butler's hand a variety of meanings that appear at first view to be contradictory. I shall try to point out that I do not believe that they are.

In the examination of man's nature Butler's initial starting place is one that accepts the self as given complete in its totality of drives, and open to inspection by ourselves or others. Each individual is invited to examine himself or his neighbor and is asked to tabulate the contents revealed. The procedure, being through and through analytic, falsely presupposes a substantial self characterized by a multiplicity of drives. According to this account each drive would inhere within the self as an adjective; moreover, each drive would be less real or less important than the self whom it modified.

The atomism that is discernible in Butler's analysis of the self is an effect of the psychology current in his day, and more particularly of the point of view dominating Lockian procedure with its insistence upon ideas and faculties. Against this view Butler is unconsciously revolting, for he apprehends the inadequacy of this type of analysis for his more comprehensive view of the mind as organic, systematic and progressively constructive. Although he sees the self to consist in drives, and achieves thereby a dynamic psychology as opposed to the static psychology of a *tabula rasa*, Butler never completely frees himself from the atomistic metaphysics. While renouncing it in spirit, yet he never frees himself fully from its influence.[4] Butler's empirical analysis was philosophically acceptable since the writings of Locke had set the tone in philosophy for all subsequent analysis. To pay homage to Locke's thought meant to bring one's own thought into consonance not with the findings of one particular mind, but with the entire age which was epitomized in the methodology of Locke.[5]

What is important for use to observe in the individual nature viewed in this light is the status of self-love. It is at first represented as one drive among many; as such it would exclude benevolence and the particular propensions. In this nature self-love would have its province, while benevolence too would have its sphere of activity. The substantial self would be the passive bystander of their conflicts, powerless to amend the difficulty because of the inherent oppositions of the two principles. A diremption would be introduced into the moral life that would know no

[4] *Vide*, First Dissertation; also Ch. I, *Analogy*, arguments for immortality. Cp. also Whewell, *opus cit.*, p. 70, for acknowledgment of Locke's influence upon the empirical method.

[5] *Vide loc. cit.*, "Locke's office was not that of a discoverer but one which more commonly places a man at the head of a school of philosophers, the office of bringing together into a system, tenets which others have taught in a less connected form, and for which the time is ripe: of proposing safeguards by which their obvious dangerous consequences are seemingly averted; and of expounding them in a lucid and persuasive manner, generally intelligible to common readers" (*ibid.*).

solution. The question of the merits of self-love or benevolence as moral principles could receive no answer, for the expression of one would *ipso facto* mean the denial of the other, and a moral life would consist in a fragmentary expression of a mutilated self. Although this represents a possible phase of Butler's thought, we have had good reason to reject it as inexpressive of his deeper underlying intentions. The procedure and development of Butler's thought point to a radical transformation of this earlier position, and one that breaks definitely with his inherited views. Self-love which is at first contrasted with benevolence soon becomes viewed as that which is superior to it and inclusive of it. In the atomistic sense it is spoken of as a principle that is *less* than the entire nature of the self, as such excluding benevolence; in the sense of the later position, self-love indicates the *whole* self in which both the public and private interests are transformed into a common end: one that is potentially anterior to its actual expressions, and more complete than its outward acts reveal it to be.

This view represents, as we have been upholding, Butler's more genuine point of view. According to it the self is a progressive and developing thing, whose characteristics are discoverable in form, but never in any degree of complete expressiveness. Within its structure self-love holds a peculiarly sacred and important place. It is no longer one aspect of the self out of many, exclusive of propensions or inconsistent with benevolence, but is in a most important respect the guardian of the self in its whole array of principles and propensions. The actual phases of self-love are as numerous as are the various unified expressions of the self. What is this self and how does it manifest its activities? The self is known as a continuous expression in time of an expansive self-consciousness. It possesses a host of native endowments that lie latent within its nature, all of which exhibit an inner stress towards a definite outward display. Both in its knowledge of these tendencies, and in their overt activities, the self is continuously present, feeling itself part of their nature, outcome, and destiny.

In one important respect the self is no more than the contents of which it is conscious and of which it feels itself to be possessed. As they develop from latency to overt activity, its nature is created and grows; as their restless nature seeks constantly to discharge into objective courses, the self is consciously existent, and its being is sustained. During the various stages of its growth it can represent different ideals, i.e., goals of the pre-existent affections brought into consciousness and intellectualized. At the level of instinctive behavior its unity is conceivably a dull awareness of stimuli, responses and corresponding satisfactions; it knows no unity as such, it is urged by no attempt to organize its instincts or to relate them to a common end. Self-love as a conscious principle is as yet unborn.

But the inner urgencies that led in the first place to the expression of instincts, contain within themselves, in the same insistently dynamic way and prior to any conscious willing, elements of their own transcendence. A supervention of consciousness evolves, the tendencies now become cognizant of a remoter goal in terms of which they can become unified, which unity would allow for their more satisfactory self-expression. From a feeling of dull awareness, the individual conceivably passes into a stage of critical self-scrutiny in which he recognizes himself as himself, i.e., as possessing these drives and tendencies, and at the same time knows of the existence of other individual natures. Self-knowledge implies at the same time a privacy that excludes from itself the nature of other individual selves. At this stage of critical self-awareness self-love has become completely emergent, but not completely expressed. As a principle it stands for the progressive unification of its native equipment, the direction of the affections towards the goals that they remotely imply. The individual who lives under the dominance of self-love knows that his happiness, i.e., self-expression, consists in the rational exercise of his native tendencies, co-ordinating them towards the unities they imply. He must be at once individual and social. As individual, he is privately aware of his self in distinction from other selves, and he knows himself as the center of reference of his activities and degrees of happiness; as social, he knows that his private nature must have its relations towards his fellow beings in which his own nature is enriched but is never transcended. It remains constantly individual, for it carries with it the knowledge and feeling of private self-identity in all of its activities. We can appreciate now that there is no inner contradiction of the self, even though it is possessed of a diversity of aims.

The position of self-love in Butler's system should apprise us of the fact that the self is present in all of its acts and undertakings. There are no conscious acts to which the self can remain completely indifferent. But since the self is constituted by a variety of tendencies directed towards a common end, its nature at any one time of its expression can only be known in terms of the objects it seeks; its moral qualities can be determined largely through its sphere of activity. But since benevolence is one of the tendencies of the self, it stands in no way opposed to the self's nature. At the level when benevolence arises as a conscious principle, self-love expands to that extent. Self-love includes benevolence, in such a way that it now becomes expressive of the self's social qualities and implications. The self is put into society but not engulfed by it. We cannot say then that benevolence becomes "selfish," for the self can only be characterized in terms of benevolence and the particular propensions. The self is what they decree it to be; its nature is constructed by their existence, and sustained by their unitary activity.

Just as the remoter and more genuine ends of the particular propensions are self-redounding, so with benevolence; just as the self that they point towards is one that is constructed out of themselves, and by their very presence, likewise is it constructed out of benevolence. The latter principle in its most remote sense implies in its ultimate aim the self-interest and welfare of the agent which it advances and promotes. The self is formed and fashioned out of all of its subservient parts, taking in their characteristics whose ultimate unity it represents. Partly determined in its nature by the particular propensions of the more narrow self-regarding sort, self-love, we now witness, has in the presence of benevolence transcended the purely selfish level of activity, for it is now further developed and matured through the special contributions of benevolence, and of the particular propensions that have constructed it.

11

CONSCIENCE

LET us pause for a minute and restate briefly what we have accomplished in our analysis of the self. Our problem, it will be
recalled, asked for the nature of virtue. What is the good life?
Wherein does it consist? Many answers had been offered to these
questions, but, according to Butler, all of them failed to satisfy,
or to do justice to the questions raised. For Butler, morality is
a human affair; it is concerned with living men, not animals or
inanimate objects. Furthermore it is intimately an affair of the
thinking man more than of the child or the idiot. The answer
to the problem of morality must be sought—for it can be found
nowhere else—within the nature of man. But what aspect of
man's nature was his moral aspect? Investigation revealed to us
that man was composed of several parts. Which of these parts
furnished us the key to the moral life? And here we were confronted at once with a possible frustration of our problem.

If we were to admit that morality was to be found within one
aspect rather than another, our devotion to the moral life would
necessarily imply a denial of the other parts of our nature. And
for this denial, there could be offered no good reason. Butler
assures us that human nature despite the multiplicity of its parts
forms a system, so harmonious and so precise that each part leads
beyond itself to every other part. It would then appear that if
we voluntarily centered our efforts about the expression of any
one part in such a way that we should include all of its relations, the problem of morality would be solved for us. In a certain
sense this is true. There is however the prior task, to discover
the variety of parts of which human nature is composed; to see
through which part we are most effectively led into the moral
life. And this is what we proceeded to do.

The innumerable expressions of man's nature were discussed
as the particular propensions, and the principles of self-love and
benevolence. Through an immanent tendency the particular propensions carried man over into the self-conscious expression of
his principles. And from the principle of benevolence, we were
carried over into the realm of the principle of self-love as the
more inclusive of the two. Under the dominance of self-love it
was seen that the individual was more unified than when he was

under the control of the particular propensions; for under the dominance of the latter the self was divided in its interests, whereas under the more rational rule of self-love it had gathered itself together, brought order into the ranks of the propensions, and related them to self-interest as their remoter end. Self-expression is best instanced when, possessed of a unity of purpose, the self regulates its life so as to bring harmoniously under this unity all of its implied interests. It must neither thwart its fundamental affections, as represented in its propensions or in the principle of benevolence, nor openly deny their expression. Thus through the principle of self-love we were led into the moral life.

The enlightened expression of the self implies a scale of interests, from the simple demands of bodily satisfaction to the approval of a deed for its own sake. Just as the former expression presupposes in man's nature a fixity of interest that seeks its satisfaction, so does the latter. His persistence, when enlightened, in evincing an interest in moral evaluation, points to a basic drive within man's nature as the condition of its possibility. This drive is conscience, the most important of man's affections. But many people today are sceptical about the reality of conscience, and demand a proof for its existence. To them it is necessary to establish, as we did in the disputed cases of disinterested actions and benevolence, its claim to existence. After that, we shall discuss its characteristics and its expressions as it is reflected in the activities of the self. These questions will concern us for the rest of the chapter.

EXISTENCE OF CONSCIENCE

To many individuals, Butler would probably be unconvincing in his proof of the existence of conscience. But this would be so, only because for him conscience was far different from what we conceive it to be today—presuming that a consensus of opinion could be established. It is not until we reach the works of Shaftesbury and Hutcheson, that we encounter the moral sense which is recognized by them as a faculty in the mind of man. Butler taxes Hobbes with the absence of it in his writings. As Butler interprets him, life is conducted in the narrow pursuit of self-love, that exclusively dominates his interests. According to this view there is concern for nothing but the pursuit of happiness, or the avoidance of pain. Life is bound to this regime as a slave, and the freedom of expression which is man's highest and most natural possession is denied him. All types of action are turned to this end; compassion and benevolence become self-love in disguise. But there is, according to Butler, no justification for this way of speaking. Empirical analysis and observation expose to our eyes much more than a dominance of self-love. Man's nature impartially viewed, and accepted for what it is worth, reveals to us a genuine tendency within him that has regard for other individuals, and by means of which he is transported beyond a narrow self-circumscription to take in the interests of other agents.

A further observation informs us of much more than benevolent motives and man's honest desire to achieve them. It tells us that man is an agent for good, that his actions indicate that he is interested in the pursuit of pure virtue, the disinterested establishment of justice, veracity and common good. More than that, it tells us that by nature he is concerned primarily with these virtuous pursuits, that if he were aware of his true nature, he would be satisfied with nothing less.[1]

Can we doubt the moral tendency of man? If we are inclined to doubt that man is bent upon good works, Butler would urge in support of his statement that an impartial observation reveals that he is. He would bring against our doubts the fact that in the long run it was observation that established for Hobbes the fact that man was selfish. Using the same instrument of observation that commended itself to Hobbes, Butler claims that perception abundantly discloses the moral nature of man.

What can establish for us the existence of conscience within human nature? In defence of conscience as an affection within human nature the same support can be brought as was brought in the defence of benevolence. *"Whether man be thus, or otherwise constituted, what is the inward frame in this particular,* is a mere question of fact or natural history, not provable immediately by reason. It is therefore to be judged of and determined in the same way other facts or matters of natural history are:

---

[1] Vol. I, p. 335: "The fact then appears to be, that we are constituted so as to condemn falsehood, unprovoked violence, injustice, and to approve of benevolence to some preferably to others, abstracted from all consideration, which conduct is likeliest to produce an overbalance of happiness or misery." Cp. also *ante,* p. 329: "Acting, conduct, behaviour, abstracted from all regard to what is, in fact and event, the consequences of it, is itself the natural object of the moral discernment."

by appealing to the external senses, or inward perception"(Vol. II, p. 32).

Empirical observation must have its say. Both within ourselves and within the nature of others, the existence of conscience can be known. Within ourselves, it is immediately experienced; through an inner inspection it is known to us directly. But it is also known as a characteristic of others, for their actions can be interpreted in no other way than by our assuming that they possess it. Do we not continually pass judgment upon their actions, and do we not employ continually in regard to their behavior such terms as right and wrong, odious, etc., does not this usage indicate to us that we hold them responsible for their deeds, and ascribe to them a faculty similar to the one we have observed in ourselves, that approves and disapproves of acts? But besides this, evidence is furnished in abundance through indirect channels.

Literature also affords us overwhelming evidence of moral evaluation, since literary characters likewise meet with disapproval of their villainy and treachery; of approval of their righteousness, in the minds of their readers. "It cannot be imagined, that all these authors, throughout all these treatises, had absolutely no meaning at all to their words, or a meaning merely chimerical" (Vol. I, p. 327).

GENERAL CHARACTERISTICS

Granted the existence of conscience as an affection within man's nature that predisposes him towards the performance of good acts, let us now examine its nature still further. For Butler no individual is unpossessed of conscience. All human agents exhibit its nature in varying degrees of completeness. Where it is not fully expressed, we can be certain that it is latent, and that under the influence necessary to call it forth it will emerge. It may elude us because its presence is so multiform. There is no one type of expression within man's nature that fully reveals it; it is exhausted in no one of his acts, nor fully present in any one course of his behavior. It can be captured under no one guise, nor labelled by any one word. References to it appear under a bewildering assortment of names. For this reason there is no attempt upon the part of Butler to pin himself down to any one term or any one definition; furthermore he has not the slightest interest in doing so. Recognition of the existence of conscience is sufficient; and if we are clear about its nature, we can be indifferent to its nomenclature. "It is manifest great part of common language, and of common behaviour over the world, is formed upon supposition of such a moral faculty; whether called conscience, moral reason, moral sense, or divine reason; whether considered as a sentiment of the understanding, or as a perception of the heart; or, which seems the truth, as including both" (Vol. I, p. 328).[2]

How can conscience be best defined? The employment of so many terms is at first confusing, for the reader confronted with such a variety is at a loss to know whether Butler is playing fast and loose, or is suggesting through the medium of a varying vocabulary one central idea which the multiplicity of his terms is trying to bring out. An attempt sympathetically to understand this affection, and to see its place within the system of man's nature, soon informs us that Butler is trying to make clear its multiform character. Not to fasten this affection down with any one name, but to recognize it throughout its manifold activities for what it is worth, is the task of the moralist (Vol. II, p. 3).

No one term is adequate to cover the multiple aspects under which this principle reveals itself. Butler in his reference to it is trying to give expression to the quintessential unity of man's nature, as it exhibits itself throughout the array of his constituent parts, and as it actively fashions from their chaotic manifold an individuality expressing itself freely and harmoniously throughout the parts. He is trying to show us that this weaving unity has its many sides and many aspects. Examine as we will any one of its protean forms, and we are insensibly led to recognize the reality of the others. In one important sense conscience is the focal point of man's unity, the place towards which all other affections ideally converge and through the influence of which they become reorganized and redirected.

To speak of this principle as either conscience or reflection is not sufficient, for the use of one of these terms seems to exclude the other. For Butler, conscience implies much more. Its exercise indicates an intuition into the nature of what is good, but the term moral sense obscures from us the integral aspect

---

[2] It is not surprising then that Butler refers to it in various ways, such as: reflex approbation, conscience, reflection, conscience or reflection, the principle of rationality, and reflex sense of action. (Cp. Vol. II, pp. 13, 14, 36, 47, 51, 54, 57, 78, 79, 180, 181, 190 *et. ali.*)

of reason necessary for this insight. Yet the term reason while implying speculation, is too much allied to the discovery of truth and falsity to suffice alone, for the realm of moral values, without which there could be no virtuous living, is excluded. To emphasize that both the moral and the speculative aspect are essential to the moral life, Butler more often refers to man's virtuous tendency as conscience or reflection. Even now the full nature of conscience is not captured by these terms used singly or in combination. In his Second Dissertation on Virtue Butler refers to it as a perception of the heart or sentiment of the understanding, "or, which seems to be the truth, as including both" (Vol. I, p. 328), emphasizing thereby its aspect of feeling. But these terms fail to indicate its dynamic quality. Expressing the affective side only of this principle, they are inadequate to its equally conative aspect. The deficiency here is partly repaired by speaking of it as the reflex sense of action.

Discoverable within its integral nature is reason that permeates the parts of the self and gathers them into one mosaic of intellectual purpose. The urge to do so comes from within the self, and indicates the activity of a drive persistently commanding this exercise of reason. This constitutes the hortatory aspect of conscience, or its commands to self-expression.

Attendant upon the self's activities, and indeed so closely a part of them that the line of distinction cannot be drawn, is its emotional tone (*Vide* Analogy, Pt. I, ch. IV). It is experienced as the feeling of satisfaction that consummates the outcome of the self's expression; it informs the agent emotionally that the drive has met its object and rests completed in its attainment. This unity of feeling unbrokenly accompanies the multiple expressions of the agent.

Further observable within man's nature is his search for moral ideals. This aspect of conscience is closely allied to the rational activity of the self whose task of unifying the self depends upon them. In every contemplated act that we undertake, it is possible for us to say: is this act most to be desired; is it good, worthy, right, or wrong? Both question and answer are testimonies to the presence within us of a moral principle.

All of these aspects which we have briefly enumerated above are integral to human nature. They are essential to the moral life and it is difficult for us to retain individuality in the supposed absence of any of them. Not all of these aspects are done justice to by Butler in his portrayal of the moral individual. Greater prominence is laid upon its speculative and moral qualities. Only indirectly does he emphasize the feeling tone of the moral life; but his many references to happiness and virtue make clear the degree of importance that it holds. The dynamic quality of conscience is never distinctly formulated by him as an ingredient, but to recognize its presence within conscience is to allow to it no less than the urgency to outer activity that we have seen to be an integral part of the particular propensions. Its denial would mean the exclusion from the moral life of one's self-command to choose the better and to reject the worse.

In our next section we shall come to closer grips with the nature of conscience as it is revealed under three of these aspects. We shall take up in turn the rational, axiological and hortatory characteristics; reserving for a separate chapter the role of feeling in the moral life.[3]

INTRINSIC ASPECTS OF CONSCIENCE

Rational Aspect of Conscience. In calling conscience rational, i.e., as a principle of reflection, Butler wished to call attention to at least two of its important aspects. Firstly, he wanted to avoid the confusion of seeing in conscience no more than a moral sense, the pronouncements of which are based upon emotional qualities of pleasure or pain. Secondly, he wished to emphasize that the pronouncements of conscience imply an objective order of equal certainty and universality to that which is to be found in the sphere of theoretical truth.[4]

In calling attention to the rational aspect of conscience we must be careful to assure ourselves precisely what such a term covers or implies and what it does not. In the first place the

[3] Butler's doctrine of feeling is so bound up with his metaphysics, and his theory of the reign of natural law, that I have reserved a separate chapter for this topic in Part Five of my present work. *Vide infra* Ch. 26.

[4] Butler would hold that as far as man is concerned, there was no speculative pronouncement that had a validity equal to that of conscience. He takes no pains to conceal his disparagement of reason, and says in his Sermon upon the Ignorance of Man: "Knowledge is not our proper happiness . . . Indeed, if the proper happiness of man consisted in knowledge considered as a possession or treasure, men who are possessed of the largest share would have a very ill time of it; as they would be infinitely more sensible than others of their poverty in this respect" (Vol. II, pp. 227, 228). Living in an age of reason rather than faith,—for Deism in religion, and natural law in science were still in their own,— —Butler admitted the authority of science, although at the same time he acknowledged its limitations.

rationality of conscience is empirical and particularistic. Conscience neither works abstractly apart from the deeds and motives of actual men, nor does it think out in advance of experience any *a priori* schemes of the good life. Its pronouncements are made *ad hoc* upon concrete situations of men in their relationships to each other, society and God; thus they are confined to the situation at hand and limited to the particular case. In its rational aspects, conscience takes over the inductive procedure of speculative reason. It surveys proposed actions to view their outcome. By comparing them with previous actions committed, it hazards a prediction as to their consequences upon the agent himself and others.[5]

Conscience as Moral Insight. We shall now see that the rational aspect of conscience demands, still further, a realm of moral values as its inseparable aspect, for taking it strictly as rational it is a meaningless activity unless further completed by ideals of moral worth.

Reason consists in supplying means to ends; it observes the outcome of actions or traces them as effects of prior causes (*Vide* Vol. II, pp. 36, 51, 190 footnote). In its role as conscience it discriminates between actions proposed to its survey, and finally decides in favor of one, after laying upon it its moral approval. Thus in the workings of conscience there is evident more than its discursive activity. Its judgments evaluate and appraise the deed it surveys; not only does it note its causes and consequences but it pronounces them good or bad.

To admit so much of the exercise of conscience forces one to admit also its moral perceptiveness to which are revealed standards or criteria of moral correctness. For how can one discriminate at the discursive level between actions proposed unless there be presupposed a realm of moral principles in terms of which the discrimination takes place and becomes meaningful? And likewise with its aspect of approbation. This activity also implies a standard of some sort either known to conscience or created by it in terms of which significant approval ensues. It is for this reason that Butler refers to it as a law of man's nature (Vol. II, pp. 15, 51, 59). "*From his make, constitution, or nature, he is*

[5] As to the psychology of its operations, *Vide* references in Vol. I, pp. 326, 327; Vol. II, pp. 36, 51, 55. We are told that it makes actions objects to the mind, seeing what such actions would entail; it views alternate possibilities, distinguishes between them, evaluates in favour of one, and then in the full knowledge of data and consequences passes final judgment upon its worth.

in the strictest and most proper sense a law to himself. He hath
the rule of right within: what is wanting is only that he honestly
attend to it" (Vol. II, p. 59). The activity of conscience accepts
the unquestioned validity of no end, whether it be benevolence
or self-love, until its place within the scheme of things is seen.
These lesser principles are not accepted by it as impenetrable
ultimates. At no stage does conscience make its final pronouncement; it "always of course goes on to anticipate a higher and
more effectual sentence, which shall hereafter second and affirm
its own" (Vol. II, p. 51).[6]

The Hortatory Aspect of Conscience. If we examine conscience more closely we shall see that there is included an element
of command, without which it would be ineffectual. This constitutes its hortatory aspect.[7] Our approval of an act implies a
command that we realize it concretely to the fullest of our moral
ability. "The very constitution of our nature requires," says
Butler, "that we bring our whole conduct before this superior
faculty; wait its determination; enforce upon ourselves its authority, make it the business of our lives, as it is absolutely the
whole business of a moral agent, to conform ourselves to it" (Vol.
II, pp. 12-13). Unless we were urged from within to act upon
our judgments, by carrying them into overt activity, our life

---

[6] Although objective to man and qualifying a universe not of his making, yet
these ultimate ends are known to him and established *pari passu* in the act of
reasoning. It is highly improbable that in the absence of reason the significant
ends that discursive reason reveals would ever be known.

All the judgments of the completely self-conscious individual are moral judgments, no matter what particular contents or colouring these judgments bear. All
departments of human interests possess their moral aspects, and are moral
because in the last analysis they originate in human minds and refer to a perfect universe which is the product of a divine mind.

[7] *Vide* Vol. II, p. 13. Butler's disagreement with Shaftesbury arises from the
failure of the latter to take this aspect of conscience into account. "The not
taking into consideration this authority, which is implied in the idea of reflex
approbation or disapprobation, seems a material deficiency or omission in Lord
Shaftesbury's *Inquiry concerning Virtue.* He has shown beyond all contradiction,
that virtue is naturally the interest or happiness, and vice the misery, of such a
creature as man, placed in the circumstances which we are in this world. But
suppose there are particular exceptions; a case which this author was unwilling
to put, and yet surely it is to be put: or suppose a case which he has put and
determined, that of a sceptic not convinced of this happy tendency of virtue,
or being of a contrary opinion. His determination is, that it would be *without
remedy.* One may say more explicitly, that leaving out the authority of reflex
approbation or disapprobation, such as one would be under an obligation to act
viciously; since interest, one's own happiness, is a manifest obligation, and there
is not supposed to be any other obligation in the case."

would be spent in idle fancy or moral imaginings from which neither ourselves nor others would receive the slightest benefit.

In concluding our account of the characteristics of conscience we must draw attention more particularly to man for whom it legislates, for when conscience commands the fulfillment of a deed upon which it has previously passed its endorsement, it meets within the nature of man itself tendencies that run contrary to the proposed course of moral action. Standing out against the performance of a righteous deed is the exclusive yearning for narrow self-interest; or the outward play of appetites or passions, that in their unbridled strength know no bounds or measures. Only as man becomes conscious of their activity, does he see that they thwart the expression of his moral life. He sees that to realize his moral aims, he must restrain his impulses and lessen their propensity blindly to explode in outward activity. This requires the presence of a cool and rational conscience to keep down the irrational desires and to check the more violent of man's passions and instincts. Pervading the self, it tends to entrench itself more firmly than the desires it seeks to curb. Self-imposed, it knows that man's better interests lie in a quiet restraint and a virtuous control; that his truer self is to be found in submission to its voice and performance of its commands.

In subduing man's cruder passions, the work of conscience is not completed, for the active performance of virtuous deeds still remains to be done. How can this be accomplished, except through the release of those tendencies that favor this performance? Man's moral life is essentially and privately his own. To establish the inner disposition for the love and exercise of virtue is the task of conscience. This may be done simply by encouraging existent propensities towards good, and forming them into an habitual instrument of ready responsiveness. Or it may be accomplished in another way. By playing off one tendency against another, e.g., by curbing a narrow self-regard, but at the same time allowing one's tendency towards benevolent actions to have full sway, conscience can achieve its purposes. This mutual interplay of tendencies in which one offsets the other, illustrates the organizing control of conscience. Resentment tends to keep down the over-inclination for unreasoned sympathy; likewise our love for others counteracts the tendency to judge others without mercy. Thus in its restraining influence, as well as in its role of measured control, conscience coolly and deliberately but with imposing force reacts upon the refractory tendencies, and organizes them into the service of the moral life wherein it sees man's highest interests to lie.

We shall complete our present chapter by considering the alleged infallibility of conscience.

IS CONSCIENCE INFALLIBLE?

Butler never speaks of conscience as infallible, but his constant references to its absolute authority and absolute direction point towards this intention (Vol. II, pp. 12, 13). Actually the authority of conscience can be overridden by the other affections of man's nature. In his Sermon upon Self-Deceit, he says: "There are, you see, two things, which may thus prejudice and darken the understanding itself: that over-fondness for ourselves, which we are all so liable to; and also being under the power of any particular passion or appetite, or engaged in any particular pursuit.[8]

If this is admitted, what does he mean in speaking of conscience as the highest tribunal of appeal in man's nature? Only that if we allow it to express its judgments in complete freedom from prejudices, and govern constantly in our practical life, there is no higher principle to which we can appeal for guidance or advice. Actually conscience does not have its full say; nevertheless it should. Its authority is *de jure* but not *de facto*. Conscience can never forfeit its right to make moral pronouncements even though it may be actually overridden. To adduce instances in which the authority of conscience is prevented from having its full say, cannot be used as an argument that it does not possess this authority.

We must call attention to the absolute *de jure* authority of conscience to adjudicate on the morality of one's acts, and its errancy in the actual exercise of that authority. Even when we allow conscience complete freedom of expression, by keeping in abeyance all the conflicting forces of contrary opinions, such as false beliefs, and incompatible emotions, we must still deny that

[8] Vol. II, p. 147. Cp. also "Nothing is more manifest, than that affection and passion of all kinds influence the judgment" (Vol. II, p. 152). Butler allows then (1) that conscience is vulnerable in the sense that it may be influenced by strong outbursts of emotion and self-interest, and (11) that a life of habit formed along undesirable lines may rob it of its right and freedom to function. (Cp. as an instance, Vol. II, SS. IV, p. 290.)

its actual utterances are infallible, final or complete. That conscience recasts and remakes its former decisions is quite plain, for it is constantly under the necessity of correcting its former decisions, and even denying subsequently the validity of what it previously affirmed.[9]

But actual errancy is compatible with ultimate authority. The correction of former decisions that had once been morally sanctioned and commanded is always made by conscience itself. The absolute supremacy of conscience is seen in this: there is no higher moral source to which we can appeal for the revision of our former judgments than to the pronouncements of conscience. We cannot afford to neglect its advice or commands, even though we suspect that it will deny tomorrow all that it pronounces upon today as fitting and morally correct. We cannot disavow its authority, because there is no higher source to which we can go for more correct moral guidance. Every attempt on our part to reject its decisions implies its active presence.

The actual fallibility of conscience in its particular pronouncements is paralleled in the instance of speculative reason.[10] We are aware that in our speculations we never attain final or complete truth. And yet we never reject the speculative method just because the judgments of men undergo constant revision, for when we later reject what we formerly believed to be true, the rejection is an expression of our reason. If there is no difficulty in admitting the supremacy of the purely speculative reason, there should be none in admitting that of conscience.

In drawing this comparison between the rational aspect of conscience and the exercise of reason in its speculative sphere, Butler does not intend that the analogy should go further. Each in its own capacity is ultimate, for there is no higher authority we can go to in either case. The pronouncements of both are not

---

9 In his Second Sermon on Human Nature (Vol. II, p. 51), Butler speaks of conscience moving on to higher and more effectual sentences. The only meaning which we can ascribe to this statement is that the earlier sentences of conscience are open to modification and improvement. But that in spite of its erroneous pronouncements, conscience can still be superior, is indicated for us when Butler in the passage just referred to, tells us that the higher and more effectual sentence that replaces the earlier ones, endorses and affirms its later judgment.

10 Butler points out in his Second Dissertation on Virtue (Vol. I, p. 37, footnote), that the two stand on an equal footing in regard to their *ad hoc* pronouncements.

of equal value. Speculative reason is unreliable even in its own sphere, but conscience is not.[11]

The canons of morality that conscience has recourse to in its particular pronouncements are not open to revision. Butler tells us that it is not "at all doubtful in the general, what course of action this faculty, or practical discerning power within us, approves, and what it disapproves. For, as much as it has been disputed wherein virtue consists, or whatever ground for doubt there may be about particulars; yet, in general, there is in reality an universally acknowledged standard of it. It is that, which all ages and all countries have made profession of in public: it is that, which every man you meet puts on the show of: it is that, which the primary and fundamental laws of all civil constitutions over the face of the earth make it their business and endeavour to enforce and practice of upon mankind: namely, justice, veracity, and regard to common good" (Vol. I, p. 328). The fallibility of conscience lies mainly in the *circumstances* that it morally evaluates, and the particular act that it interprets as right or wrong, and not in the rules to which the particular acts are referred. It does not doubt that benevolence or veracity is good, but it is uncertain whether or not this particular act upon which it is called to judge is, e.g., a benevolent one. In the rejection today of an alleged benevolent act that conscience approved yesterday, it does not renounce the virtue of benevolence *in se* but is only denying, in view of relevant details subsequently received, that yesterday's act illustrated truly a benevolent principle.

[11] *Vide infra*, Ch. *31*.

12

CONSCIENCE AND COMPLETED SELF

AS THE highest principle of man's nature conscience represents the common end to which all his individual affections lead. Being such, it must necessarily be present within each of these particular drives long before they have been consciously adjusted to this far-reaching end. For if conscience were not present in these drives, how could they surpass themselves; how could they ever consciously pass judgment upon their own moral worth? It will be our purpose in this present chapter to show how this relationship is implicit.

We will try to show how the principle of reflection pervades the entire self, and how the self in its multiplicity of parts is completed only as they tend to rest in conscience as their actual end. In our first section, we shall show how conscience is potentially present within the lesser affections of the self, and how at the same time, these lesser affections imply conscience as their remoter goal. Our second section will be a continuation of our first section. We shall show there, somewhat in detail, how conscience in its aspect of rationality and function of moral insight is present and operative in man's particular propensions and his lesser principles. Our third section will try to show in particular how the aspect of command or authority in conscience likewise finds its origin in the particular propensions and the lesser principles; and to trace within their activities the evolution of this aspect. Lastly, we shall conclude our chapter by showing how conscience in its active expression is the mouthpiece for the entire self, and what it accomplishes for the self when it is allowed free expression.

CONSCIENCE AND SELF-UNITY

What does conscience judge when it is active? The deeds of other individuals or myself as an agent are its objects. It evaluates them in terms of its objective standards. But the deeds of other individuals or myself are deeds that emanate from the principle of self-love, or of benevolence. If my deeds are directed towards myself, I have my own interests in view; if they are directed towards my neighbor, my single aim is that of benevo-

lence. But likewise with my neighbor. He can have his own interests in mind or my own. But in either case he likewise is under
the dominance of one principle or the other.

Let us suppose that he has become conscious of his intimate
associations with other individuals or with society so that he sees
their interest to be a part of his own; even in this case, which
illustrates the rational subordination of benevolence to self-love,
his deeds of self-love would fall under the scrutiny of conscience.[1]

The judgments of conscience must be made with caution.
They cannot morally evaluate the motives or deeds of any non-
moral, i.e., non-rational, being. If conscience pronounces upon
the actions of brutes, children, or idiots, it must take their inca-
pacities into account. It should make a due allowance for the
moral capacity of the agent. Concerning this, Butler says: "It
does not appear, that brutes have the least reflex sense of actions,
as distinguished from events: or that will and design, which constitute the very nature of actions as such, are at all an object
to their perception. But to ours they are: and they are the object, and the only one, of the approving and disapproving faculty" (Vol. I, p. 329). Again, concerning those individuals in
whom reason is defective, due allowance must be made. Were an
individual to be deprived of the use of reflection in himself, owing
to natural deficiency, or because of moral disease,[2] the disapproving conscience of others at least would act towards him with a
certain amount of forbearance, and would before its judgment
"make a comparison of actions with the nature and capacities of
the agent" (Vol. I, p. 331). The more individuals were deprived
of rational insight, the nearer they would approach the level of
brute existence and cease to be an object of censure.

It may happen that an individual has not become clear as
to the ultimate direction of his impulses; he may not observe that
his actions tend to converge to the common end of self-love, or
of benevolence. His life may be conducted along the level of the
propensions wherein no unifying principle is at work. In cases

[1] Cp. respectively Diss. II, Vol. I, pp. 326 *et seq.;* Vol. II, pp. 51, 55; Diss.
II, Vol. I, pp. 326, 329, Vol. II, p. 51; Diss. II. Vol. I, pp. 326, 327, 330;
Vol. II, p. 51.

[2] Vol. I, p. 331: "For, every one has a different sense of harm done by an
idiot, madman, or child, and by one of mature and common understanding . . ."
Cp. Vol. II, p. 147, where Butler speaks of how the judgment is often
undermined from a blind excess of passion and habitual practice of vice. Cp. also
p. 152: "Nothing is more manifest, than that affection and passion of all kinds
influence the judgment"; also p. 110.

like these, conscience would concern itself directly with the particular propensions themselves, and would estimate the morality of each intended act, as the agent became conscious of it.

No part of man's nature remains foreign to the province of conscience, but likewise no part of man's nature is complete unless conscience openly operates. Each propension implies it for its own completion, and each principle requires its presence for its satisfactory expression. Let us consider the principles first.

Let us grant that an individual becomes conscious of his demands so that he sees in immediate reference to his own happiness the outcome of all his actions; also that he becomes interested in the acts of other agents for the same reason. Further, let us grant that he attempts to live solely in terms of this principle of self-love. If he believes his own interests to exclude the interests of others, he will soon become forced to take these agents into account, as he tries consistently to apply this principle. He must soon view them as individuals with claims of their own, protesting the importance of their own happiness with a claim as strong as his own. To judge in crucial instances whether he should be narrowly concerned with himself, or whether in temporary self-forgetfulness he should assist his neighbor, requires the scrutiny of both proposed acts in terms of a standard that stands objective to them. The situation imposes upon him the need of discovering which act is better; one of self-interest, or one of neighborly assistance. But this constraint of further scrutiny indicates the presence of conscience.

And the consequent act will neither be an act of self-love nor one of benevolence, but one of conscience; even though the answer given must favor one or the other of the lesser principles. If he aids himself, the moral reason for it will be known and appreciated; self-interest will not be a goal opaque to his understanding but will be known in the light of moral consciousness to be good, and ultimately in the service of a good principle. Or if he devotes himself to his neighbor, it will not be in this case the practice of an alien virtue, but the constant giving of assistance, the nature of which will be seen to embody a higher virtue. Taking either principle into conscious consideration means that the apparent ultimacy of each will be broken down. In this act of conscious surveillance the individual will be master of these principles instead of being mastered by them.

Consider his dilemma, were conscience temporarily to suspend its activity. So completely would he be tyrannized over by the ideal of, e.g., benevolence, that the insistent demands of self-love would remain unheeded.[3]

The reverse situation of his being tyrannized over by self-love is also possible and more frequently happens. Self-love narrowly conceived as independent of benevolence might descend upon the individual with all the dominating mastery of an instinct, becoming the conscious motive from which all of one's actions spring. There is also the further possibility, presumably the more rare, that the individual might blindly accept both self-love and benevolence, which he would never relate to each other. He thus becomes a victim to both ideals, for he possesses no single rule or principle which will determine the occasions for their proper and suitable expression. Whatever morality his acts might have would be largely accidental and despite his ignorance. We can now appreciate the importance of conscience; for it prevents these difficulties, and avoids the dilemma of a dual mastery, by supplying to the individual the rules of conduct that will unify his life and make clear to him that self-love and benevolence imply a common virtue.

Just as each principle when it comes into contact with another calls into activity the decrees of conscience, so does the principle of rational self-love, even when this principle has already arrogated to itself the contributions of benevolence. In this latter case an individual would be forced to question whether this act or that act of self-love would lead to his greater happiness. Is it to my own advantage to ignore, e.g., the warnings of medical advice, in my attendance upon others or not? Putting this question from the standpoint of enlightened self-love, we should be under the constraint of comparing the consequences of my self-sacrifice with the outcome of my neighbor's restoration to health. My health may be inevitably undermined, and my value to society may be considerably impaired as a consequence.

---

[3] The moral perversity of social reformers is an instance at hand and would represent for Butler the pathology of the moral life. In *Bleak House*, Dickens furnishes us with two admirable instances of the extremes into which an uncriticized benevolence can run. Mrs Jellyby and Mrs Pardiggle, whose total energies are devoted to social causes, grossly neglect the more immediate pressing claims of their personal requirements. A complete and impartial view of such a situation, Butler would hold to be a sufficient means for its correction, for reason would demand a justification for the extolling of benevolence, and an equally satisfying account of the right to neglect the demands of self-love that are equally pressing and urgent.

My neighbor may be a ne'er-do-well, and at the best a burden to those around him. Such are, let us suppose, the factors of the case. But although the factors of both alternatives are laid before me, I am impotent to judge or to act, until I have brought them together, compared them, and judged them in terms of a common standard, by asking: which outcome is more desirable and more worthy in and by itself? To reply means the invocation of conscience and the ultimate breaking down of each proposed act separately conceived. And even here, as in the case above-mentioned, the decision we fasten upon and follow will be an instance of an enlightened self-love that has turned into conscience; for the interest of the self is best served by following out and acting upon the decrees of conscience.

HOW CONSCIENCE PERVADES THE SELF

Being organic to the self, conscience must necessarily pervade all of its parts. Its rational aspect and its moral perceptiveness both have their glimmerings in man's various levels of conscious activity long before man actually orders his life according to conscience.

The rational and moral aspects of conscience are not present in man's lesser affections in the same degree as they are when man is fully conscious and expresses himself through the decisions of conscience; but they are none the less present, and their activity is discoverable. At the level of the particular propensions reason is active; for, consciously to express their nature, we must choose our occasions, discover the ways and means, and the opportunities for their best expression. To do this requires the presence and activity of reason. My instinct of hunger, e.g., can be best satisfied only as I am conscious of the object it seeks, and the occasions when this instinct is apt to be most pressing. Knowledge of this sort is the outcome of comparison and the discovery of causal relationships; it represents the early presence of a moral reason in its discursive activity. But conscience, in its completely rational aspect, is not yet present, for it is mainly instrumental in its expression. Accepting as ends the outward drives of the particular propensions, it does not question their value; it may not even see them in their remoter relationship either to self-love, or benevolence. Acknowledging these instinctive drives as affections to be expressed, reason proceeds to establish the means for their most efficient expression.

Likewise, the axiological aspect of conscience is present and active at the level of the particular propensions. When it assents to the means of best expressing its instinctive drives, the assent is more than logical. It must endorse these means as being suitable, fitting and proper to the ends they will express. Not only are these means regarded as conducive, but they are accepted as being good and desirable. To regard them as such is to view them as possessing value.

At the level of conscience reason has become more completely axiological without losing its instrumental function. As axiological, reason will accept no end of human behavior without first understanding it. Every course of action or ideal that it committed itself to would first be penetrated, explored, and evaluated for its own sake; it would be bound to no ideal that it had not at first fully understood and approved. But in its exercise reason at the level of conscience would be no less instrumental, for to vote for an ideal is to vote for the means of expressing that ideal. The instruments of the ideal impose upon reason the task of discovery. This discovery demands anew the search for the ways and means that are harmonious to the end and fitting to its moral temper.

At the higher levels of self-expression, when the agent governs his life in terms of self-love, or benevolence, the rational and axiological aspects of conscience are also in evidence; but more fully so than when he lives according to his instinctive drives. For an agent to organize his life consciously about his self-interest, or the happiness of others, imposes upon himself the discovery of ways and means most conducive to its concrete expression. But greater intellectual exercise is required, for he must not only relate his particular propensions to his ideal of self-love or benevolence, but he must likewise compare the particular propensions with themselves, to ascertain which will most effectively bring his conscious ideal to concrete fulfillment.

Also, the axiological aspect of conscience is in greater evidence than it was on the level of the particular propensions. For to adopt self-love or benevolence as one's guiding ideal for practical action means that the particular propensions are no longer opaque to human understanding. No longer are they merely accepted as mere instinctive drives of human nature to be expressed. They are now understood as conducive to ends beyond themselves, in terms of which they have become evaluated.

CONSCIENCE: ITS EVOLUTION OF AUTHORITY

There is another aspect of conscience, besides that of rational and axiological expression: namely, its aspect of command and authority which we have already referred to as its hortatory aspect. Just as the rational and axiological aspects of conscience permeate the entire nature of the self by being present within its lesser affections, so is the hortatory aspect of conscience evidenced at the lower stages of man's conscious activities. To see how, will be the purpose of this present section.

This element of command finds its source in the dynamic constitution of the self; in each one of its affections that seeks in the external world objects to satisfy its nature. In the lowest level of human behavior the dynamic quality of the propensions is instinctive and mechanical. The command that is later explicit in conscience is now at the lowest stage of self-expression undifferentiated from the activity or discharge itself. It is reflected there as a feeling of tense urgency, blindly to break into action and discover an object that will satisfy its restlessness. When the self is stirred into wakefulness and reflects upon its instincts, it observes that they should be rationally organized in terms of the lesser principles. When, for instance, the instinctive drive of hunger becomes aware of itself, seeing its purpose to lie in the direction of self-preservation, then the self becomes bound *ipso facto* to the fulfilment of this drive. In other words the dynamic quality has become vocalized and articulated. The duty to eat, so that the self is properly and adequately preserved, descends upon it as a command. But this command is of the nature of an hypothetical imperative, for it enjoins the fulfilment of the means whereby self-love, or benevolence are concretely satisfied.

When the self becomes aware of its principles, it is urged from within to express them. This desire to express self-love or benevolence is at bottom impulsive, revealing as yet no rational ground; even the assistance of reason that seeks a means of expression springs from this propulsive basis. When the self is under the dominance of benevolence, or self-love, there still exists the same urgency to outward behavior, as in the case of the propensions, but it has now become articulated into the search for the means adequate to their expression. There is as yet no appearance of absolute authority within the self that demands the exercise of benevolence or narrow self-love, for the self does not require a delivered command for their expression and realization, any more than it needed one in the impulsive discharge of its instincts. The attitude of the self towards these ends of self-love or benevolence is very much what it was towards its instincts before it had organized them as ideals. The presence of these lesser principles is felt as a vivid appetency for expression. No other special fiat is required here for their self-establishment. At this level of self-expression, the dynamic tendency towards expression has become articulated but only as an hypothetical imperative.

At the level of conscience the propulsive basis of the self becomes completely articulated, and emerges as a command and seat of absolute authority. We are still possessed by the same dynamic urge to expression that we had at the level of instinctive behavior. But this dynamic urge adapting itself to the medium of expression is expressed in a different manner. It has now taken on a further differentia—that of self-knowledge. It knows itself for what it is. The self is completely aware of its own nature. In the knowledge of its inner structure it appreciates its springs to action, it is apprised of its dynamic structure. It knows that to be a self is to strike out actively in the direction of objects that have been virtuously evaluated; that a completed self is one that is unified in terms of a virtuous end. It is furthermore aware that this unification is a progressive affair that requires enlightenment and constant guidance. Such, it knows to be the truth of its nature. It knows itself to be structural, ordered and determined; possessing a nature formed according to a plan or purpose, it learns in its moments of highest self-consciousness that it cannot be other than what it is, and that it cannot rationally will what runs counter to it. The recognition of its nature for what it is, implies at the same time the need to foster and preserve its internal economy. The commands that it issues to itself are both necessary and wise, for in obedience to them the self is actively unifying its own nature.

The individual is completely self-conscious only when he recognizes the various demands of his nature as instanced in his affections. To be conscious is to give utterance to these drives and to articulate their ends in imagination; but likewise it is to recognize their inner tendency towards activity and to release them towards the discovery of suitable objects. When the agent commands himself to live benevolently, he knows that this command is the self-awareness of an affection whose nature is intrinsically dynamic. The individual now recognizes in consciousness what he blindly feels when he uncritically pursues a benevolent course of action. He is expressing in an intelligible way what the principle of benevolence would express for itself, were it to become self-conscious. What appears as an imposition of alien authority to the individual when he lives under the uncritical dominance, e.g., of a benevolent idea, becomes now in the light of self-consciousness a rational understanding of this natural tendency to serve other people.

The element of command is not solely confined to any one principle or propension. It extends in equal measure to all. It is the conscious awareness of the agent that his constitution as a human being is dependent upon the outward play of his impulses and drives, properly organized and integrated.

The injunction of conscience is thus conditioned by the propulsive basis that underlies the expression both of the propension and of the principles. It must now be regarded as the way in which the dynamic characteristic of the self operates and functions at the highest level of self-consciousness. To put the same thought another way: the "ought" of conscience is none other than the arrival of the self's dynamic affections at the level of self-awareness; at which level they are cognizant of their individual nature, the aims they were blindly directed towards and the one common aim they most remotely imply.

Nothing materially different has been added to the nature of these drives. They have gained nothing but self-knowledge, and self-knowledge means awareness of the ends that these have been destined for by a natural predisposition. It does not mean that in this aspect of self-awareness, the individual can avoid the achievement of the end that he now knows himself to be directed towards, but it does mean that his wisdom lies in the conscious and economic fulfilment of a destiny that he cannot conveniently avoid without going against his active nature. The individual possesses at the stage of highest consciousness the freedom to acknowledge the natural patterns of his constitution and to further their concrete aims. He can if he wishes refuse to heed his conscience (i.e., the voice of his entire nature), but he does so at the risk of unhappiness and self-violation.

The commands of conscience are the voices of the affections that have arisen to self-consciousness of their nature and aims.

The nature of the command, in contradistinction to the commands of conscious self-love or benevolence, is a categorical imperative; but not a bare ultimate self-injunction that this or that affection be expressed. It is through and through rational, and expresses the teleological nature of the self whose mouthpiece it is. It requires that the expression of the various affections be made in strict fidelity to the ends that they are directed towards. In the absence of the command, i.e., in the absence of the knowledge of one's affections, their nature and end, the affections would undoubtedly be expressed, but would be expressed as instincts are expressed, i.e., explosively and extravagantly. If the affections met their ends it would be the merest chance of haphazard occurrence. More often than not, the affections would over-shoot their mark, or perhaps fall too low. The purpose for which the affections had been designed would contain the knowledge of the affection in point of activity and end. The command to live in terms of it is a self-injunction to express it with due propriety so that the function for which it has been designed will be fulfilled with the precision and delicacy that is adequate to man's economy.

CONSCIENCE AND SELF-CONSCIOUS LIVING

To live in accordance with conscience means to conduct one's life in a self-conscious manner; to be aware of every deed and action performed, and to ask of each, whether or not it is the best act possible; whether it is in conformance with one's nature and whether in its proposed expression it will violate any other of one's fundamental demands. A life conducted according to the decrees of conscience will accept as its final motive no type of activity that has not been fully explored, penetrated and finally accepted for the moral worth it reveals.

In the pursuit of benevolence or self-love the individual feels restricted beforehand by an end that he takes for granted and which he never questions as an end worthy or unworthy of pursuit. In the case of conscience, the individual feels himself bound down to no such restraint. In the exercise of conscience he faces objects that he can comprehend, and feels free to accept. He now questions the ultimate desirability of being benevolent or narrowly egoistic, either as a consistent aim or as a temporary measure. It may be irksome for him to pursue an existence of moral righteousness, but it is never unintelligible. But when the individual centers his life around self-love or benevolence as governing principles, he never achieves complete emancipation, and is consequently never a perfect self. For in this proposed path of pursuit he is always faced by ends that appear impenetrable, the meanings of which he cannot fathom; neither can he understand fully the reason why he should pursue them when he does. If he did, he would *ipso facto* govern his life in terms of conscience.

When conscience evaluates the proposed ends of self-love and benevolence, it does not discard them merely as unworthy ends; it sees in them for the first time their proper *rationale*, and accepts them as necessary principles and ingredients of the moral life. The individual now, understanding self-love and benevolence, sees implied within them their own transcendence. He sees that the genuine expression of either must be moral in the sense that the one he proposes to make his principle of action must first be justified as such before a standard. In possession of this moral standard he is now enabled to determine between the propriety of their conflicting claims in any given instance. Further, he is now in a position to appreciate better the realization of one or the other; and in the fuller knowledge of the ends that these means are to serve, he can decide upon the economy of the means necessary to bring them about.

In his evaluation and appreciation of self-love and benevolence the individual reduces these two principles to instances within a common range of virtue. He sees now that these principles can complete their nature only within the common ideal of what is good and right. He has known that each principle reigns over a different province, but now learns that these differences are not deep-seated, and that they meet in the domain of conscience. In this sense conscience is superior to self-love and benevolence. Its greater comprehensiveness lies then in the explicit expression that it gives to the one end of virtue implied by each of these lesser principles.

No act of the self is too mean or unimportant to come under its scrutiny, and no act should evade its searchlight of criticism. In its alliance with the particular propensions it seeks to understand the purpose of instinctive expression, not to deny it *ab initio*, but to express it, as nature intended it. Drink and food, to take these as instances, must be used in moderation to sustain the self in its healthfulness and to foster its preservation. Compassion must not exceed its aim. Its sole purpose is to alleviate the misery of other individuals. To live abstemiously, or to be intelligent in our overtures to others, demands a knowledge of the situation at hand and an evaluation of its claim. It is therefore to live self-consciously, or in the light of one's conscience.

Living according to one's conscience, means more than moral endorsement, or evaluation of the act to be performed; it means more than its approval in ourselves or others; besides all of this it means a life of integration. The actual self is a scattered self, it is one of dispersed consciousness. Attracted first in this direction and then in that, its attention is seldom engaged upon both at once. If urged from within to seek food, to quench one's thirst, or to assist others, it acts upon one to the exclusion of the other, seeing in none of them any remoter implication. A life of conscience leads to this correction of multiple aim and intention. It sees within the actions of the self an implicit unity the concrete nature of which it seeks to discover and to put into activity. Through its working the self becomes one agent, aware of its many interests and activities. The variety of affections becomes directly expressed in terms of the one end of virtue that they all remotely imply.

Lastly, this leads us to see that the integration of the self as it is achieved through conscience is constantly in the making; the unity of the self is never achieved in any one instant of time, but is progressively established as the self interrelates its aims and purposes. Out of the accomplishments of its expressed acts grow new plans and actions which add to and enrich our past experiences. Together they manifest a more illuminated purpose whose collective nature leads still further into future plans, their formation and execution.

13

CONSCIENCE AND SELF-LOVE

IN HIS earlier sermons on Human Nature, Butler informs us that "reasonable self-love and conscience are the chief or superior principles in the nature of man" . . . that . . . "conscience and self-love, if we understand our true happiness, always leads us the same way" (Vol. II, pp. 64-65). These quotations would indicate that Butler held these principles to share a supremacy of authority, and for some individuals would point to an inconsistency in Butler's system. We ourselves have laid emphasis upon self-love as man's highest principle, and have shown in our treatment of that principle how it took on ascendency over all of man's affections, not excepting benevolence itself. Yet in our last two chapters we have discussed the characteristics of conscience as if this principle were man's most supreme principle and source of authority. To understand the true status of self-love and conscience in their respective claims, it will be necessary to consider them in reference to one another. Our position in this present chapter will show that each of these principles is supreme in its individual claims, yet perfectly consistent with the other; that taken singly as a principle of practical living, each is incomplete until the other is taken into account.

That there is an obvious danger in insisting upon the supremacy of either principle to the exclusion of the other cannot be denied. For if we assert self-love to be unconditionally superior, we run the risk of thwarting the very nature of conscience itself. Under the guidance of self-love conscience would be a slavish subservient to self-advancement; and all virtue would be a reduction to an unsympathetic egoism. But since this interpretation would force Butler into the same category as he believes Hobbes to rest in, we cannot believe that Butler would unwittingly accept a position that favors this outlook. Hence the view that fosters this interpretation must be rejected.

But on the other hand, if we ascribe to conscience an unconditional supremacy, overriding in its rational pronouncements the fundamental claims of the self, we might witness the tyranny of virtue over the self's own interests. And if this were so, to what avail would be our psychological analysis of the self: one that aimed to see in its fundamental drives a key to the understanding of the moral life? For if their claims could be summarily ignored in one's deference to conscience, the urgent claim of virtue, that it consists in our following nature and not one of its parts, would now become a travesty of its original intention. Hence we cannot accept this position as intelligible or final, any more than the former which would ascribe to self-love the complete supremacy of direction. What is the solution?

We must grant that self-love is the highest principle of human nature, for its sole concern is our own happiness, and what can be of greater importance to us than this? Even morality must recognize the importance of happiness, for the individual whom it exhorts to act morally is the center and source of expression with capacities for action and limitations in ability; in his sensibilities he feels the result of virtuous acts and experiences the natural punishment entailed by unvirtuous ones. Religion too cannot ignore the self, for its appeals can be effective only as they take into account the capacities of the individual for pleasure and pain. Apart from this its calls and exhortations would be in vain. An indifferent and insentient self cannot be reached. But the guardian of the self in its pursuit of happiness is, as we have had occasion to repeat, the principle of self-love.

Since conscience is the source of moral distinctions and morality is the concern of the self, conscience is at the same time the mouthpiece of the self whom it serves and whose capacities for experience it takes into account. Hence, conscience is subordinated to self-love, for it cannot forget the self whose instrument of moral expression it is. Without the self there would be no need of conscience; its announcements of moral truths would be in vain, serving and aiding no agent. But conscience not only implies the self, but in a very genuine sense must continually bear it in mind as the being whose nature it is interested in exalting. Let us expand this point of ours further.

Self-love is that principle within the individual that urges him on to the complete expression of his nature. The contents of that nature are the affections that we have already enumerated and classified, all of which we have seen terminate in objects that run beyond the individual within which they originate. Self-expression is achieved only as the various affections in man's nature seek the objects that they are directed towards. The self retains the memory of those experiences, and is presumably self-conscious of them, referring them to itself as a possessor. They form its contents. Not only do they qualify the self but they add intrinsically to its nature. As these objects are, such presumably is the temper of the self. Apart from its experiences of them the self can neither be characterized, nor be real.

But the self is not a passive recipient of objective experiences. It does not indiscriminately absorb experiences without first coming to grips with them. It selects them according to its desires, evaluates them according to their perceived worth, and unifies them in terms of its own purpose. The self sees in the outer order objects that more fully satisfy it than others. The highest of these objects to be experienced are moral ends which are made known to it by conscience or the principle of reflection. Conscience supplies to self-love what it really seeks, and gives to it what it fundamentally needs in order that the self may be completely and most really expressed, i.e., moral values and standards.

The deliverances of moral ideals that conscience commands the self to act upon are stored up by it, worked into its fabric, and assist in its process of self-construction. Conscience, like benevolence and the particular propensions, makes its unique contribution to the self. In the practice of its moral decrees, the self grows so as to include them; as a result of this experience the self has become further enriched. Under its influence the self has expanded and taken over as part of itself the moral contributions of conscience. As a result, the self is no longer satisfied with a life that ignores moral ideals or that evaluates its actions only as they are instrumental to its narrow self-advance or the welfare of others; it can no longer tolerate a life that never investigates beforehand the value of either undertaking. With anything less than virtuous living it is no longer satisfied.

Although self-love takes over the unique contributions of the self's affections, which it incorporates, it does not forfeit its own unity, which is a feeling of private consciousness. Throughout its experience of self-expansion, the agent has not forgotten his private personality, which stands distinct from other individuals but not in any antagonism to them. And this is particularly true in his exercise of conscience. Selfhood of which self-love is the guardian principle has undergone no delimitation. On the contrary it has become further enriched by the contributions of conscience, and further determined by its pronouncements. In his activity of conscience, the individual is no less aware of himself, he is in no sense transcended in its exercise. On the contrary he now knows himself to be more than he formerly thought, and knows that his selfhood is essentially moral because the sought-for unity can be satisfied by nothing less.

Yet we cannot minimize the supreme importance of conscience nor fail to see in what respect self-love must be beholden to it. Upon it the self depends for its further enlightenment, and without it the self is condemned to wander in moral obliquity, falling into ignorance as to its destiny and into confusion as to its aims. In its intelligent expression self-love must look upon conscience as the means of its completion, without which the self would be less real as a self. In its appreciation it must see that through conscience the self bears a wider range and reference than it originally thought. For whereas it formerly believed the self to be primarily concerned with other agents, it now learns that the self is essentially concerned with virtue, and that to its discovery and practice each individual is unconsciously adapted.

Although conscience is an instrument of moral determination that transcends the self in its announcements, commanding the courses of behavior that the self must follow if it is to realize its selfhood, nevertheless in its activities conscience is interested because it has in mind the advantage of the self. In this role it is the instrument of the self's advancement, issuing to it commands that it must heed if it wishes to realize its nature fully and achieve its own happiness. If observant of its advice, the self can expand its borders of self-consciousness into a realm of moral values that rigidly determine for it the extent to which its proposed deeds are right or wrong.

To call conscience interested must not imply that it is narrowly concerned with a private good or happiness that in any *a priori* way excludes the private good or happiness of other individuals. It is interested only in the sense that the self it refers to and for whom it prescribes, points to a socially objective sphere, for it is characterized by tendencies that carry it beyond a narrow and self-circumscribed barrier. And in the widest sense it embraces potentially at least in a unity of expansive self-consciousness the whole gamut of human relations both public and private. To speak of conscience in subjective terms as the self's highest principle indicates that ultimately conscience has its individual reference in personal centers. The psychological investigation that runs preparatory to Butler's theory of morals necessarily dictates this usage and recognition.[1]

Both self-love and conscience, if taken as single aims for human living, lead into one another, for neither is complete unless it takes the other into account. Rational self-love is *ipso facto* moral. We cannot attain our happiness unless we see the immediate value of conscience, and act upon its commands. A completed principle of self-love is at once an instrument of moral advance. There can be no conflict between self-love and conscience, for to understand our self-interest and happiness is to see that it can be achieved only through moral living. As Butler says: "Conscience and self-love, if we understand our true happiness, always lead us the same way" (Vol. II, p. 65; also pp. 63-65).

Neither can conscience be adhered to unless it takes self-love into account. To be rational, conscience must understand the nature of the individual and the order of the world. To do so, it must observe that the fundamental drives of human nature are bent upon self-expression. It must prescribe for them, and see that they achieve in proper measure the ends they are intent upon finding. To ignore the claims of the self would result in disaster, for it might prescribe courses of action which the self was incapable of following, and command the pursuit of an ideal behavior which the self saw no advantage in following.

Both self-love and conscience must now be regarded as limitations upon the activities of each other. One is not supreme in its divorce from the other. Both together constitute the self. When we are urged to follow self-love, we are urged to follow our nature, but since our nature is primarily to be found in the virtuous activity of conscience, it turns out that self-love and

[1] If we ask why our ideas of happiness and misery are of all our ideas the nearest and most important to us (Vol. II, p. 173), and why man should be concerned especially with his own self-expression, we are told: "That moral obligations can extend no further than to natural possibilities" (Vol. II, p. 184); and these possibilities created by and limited to a "perception of our own interests, like consciousness of our own existence, which we always carry about with us; and which, in its continuation, kind, and degree, seems impossible to be felt in respect to the interests of others." But a full recognition of this does not mean that our natural capabilities are less social, or that the self is exclusively atomic. Limited to a consciousness of ourselves in terms of our own interests, "we are in a peculiar manner . . . intrusted with ourselves; and therefore care of our own interests, as well as of our conduct, particularly belongs to us" (Vol. II, p. 184; cp. also pp. 182, 183).

conscience are perfectly coincident, as Butler has been maintaining right along. The happiness for any self lies in the fulfilment of its nature. As such, it can stop short of nothing less than the commands of conscience which show it the way. Likewise we can say that if we follow our conscience we are expressing our nature and incidentally that we are following self-love; conscience being no more than the self-consciousness of man's drives as they are directed to a common unifying goal.

14

VICE IN THE MORAL SELF

NATURE OF VICE

A COMPLETE description of the moral self must allow for an explanation of vice; and Butler's theory of virtue must account for vice in such a way that it will stand in no contradiction to his repeated exhortation that men should follow their nature. Shaftesbury's analysis of human nature admitted the original existence within man of unnatural tendencies, i.e., the malevolent or superstitious; which tendencies it was the task of the moral sense to uproot and destroy.[1] To Butler an analysis of human nature revealed no such independent affections, and what appeared as such in human activity must be viewed in some way as derivatives of natural impulses (Vol. II, p. 116). Owing to his religious beliefs, Butler could not grant that God had endowed man with passions in themselves evil (Vol. II, p. 116); and it was probably this deeper religious insight that dictated to him his theory of virtue.

If we accept with Butler that the good is essentially self-development, we can appreciate at once the difficulties that would be involved if the unnatural tendencies of Shaftesbury were allowed entrance into the rank of man's psychological principles. From the standpoint of his moral life, man would be forced to admit as part of his virtuous activity the expression of elements that he had previously stamped as vicious. But in doing so he would be caught in a contradiction; for if the sanction of conscience constitutes moral approval, and this because its expression is the voice of the self-conscious individual in his aspect of complete integrality of aim, then these malevolent impulses are not really vicious, and should not be termed so in the course of any psychological investigation. On the other hand, if we acknowledge the independent existence of these unnatural tendencies, there are two possible attitudes that could be taken in regard to them. We could deny them their place within man's moral life; or we could admit them only after a radical transformation. In both cases we should be deserting Butler's banner.

In denying them a place within man's moral life, we should

---

[1] *Vide* H. Sidgwick, *opus cit.,* circa p. 187.

be advocating the *partial* expression of man's nature; the rejection of the unrepresented parts having been previously made on the ground of the assumed truth of a rationalistic standard. We should be evaluating beforehand the entire array of impulses and desires, when we have already agreed that moral pronouncement comes only after the parts have been accepted and woven into the nature of the whole self. We cannot construct a moral self upon the accepted worth of all the constituent parts and then proceed to reject in terms of its articulate expression some of the parts that contributed towards its determination; for in doing so, we should be attempting an illicit use of our criterion. Persistent efforts to succeed would result in the negation of our criterion, or would remind us of the impossibility of the rejection. Likewise the thorough farce of erecting a theory of morals upon a prior psychological examination would be speedily exposed in such an attempt. Why presume to base ethics on psychology if the reports of the latter are to be carefully gauged by an *a priori* theory of the former?

Nor could one admit the independent existence of irascible tendencies and hold that in the greater interest of the self they should be radically transformed; in taking this position, we should again be renouncing Butler's theory of virtue; for the exhortation to follow one's nature must in disguise assume here some standard exterior to the nature of the self in terms of which the transformation would occur.

When we mentioned above that the analysis of man's nature revealed no original malevolent tendencies, we did not intend to imply a non-existence of evil acts; but only that such acts could be traced to sources themself innocent of vicious aims. But if we seek precisely for the tendencies that in some sense become diverted into channels of vice, we are limited in our search to man's array of principles and propensions. Each affection, from conscience as the highest to the particular propensions as the lowest, is capable of becoming diverted into a particular type of vicious expression.

We can now proceed to ask ourselves two questions both of which will throw further light on our discussion. What constitutes evil acts for Butler? How are they brought about? To answer the first: a good act is one that expresses a tendency in such a way as to achieve for that tendency the due and proportionate expression of its intended aim. Hence an evil act is one in which the natural impulse exceeds its due proportion or falls below its intended aim. But just as a good act is one that is determined by the nature of the whole self within which it forms an harmonious factor contributing to the ideal proportion of the self as naturally implied, an evil act is one that in its excess overreaches itself; claims for itself more than is due to it from the standpoint of the complete self; and so directly prevents the establishment of the ideal unitary self, making for the destruction of the unity that it has already achieved. Each virtue then implies its corresponding vices. The virtuous activity of conscience may easily degenerate into over-conscientiousness or unscrupulousness, depending upon its unintelligent excess or indifference to moral reflective scrutiny. Likewise with self-love, its improper expression can lead to a narrow self-regard, or a vicious indifference to one's immediate and necessary concerns. And in benevolence we note the possibility of pampering others, or ignoring what is humanly due to them from us, consequent upon the misexpression of that impulse. Similarly with the particular propensions: each has its intended aim and corresponding virtue, and falling short of their aims or exceeding them will result in vicious behavior.

To state that a vicious act is one that makes for the disproportion of the entire self is not however to tell the whole story. It is not solely because the unity of the self is weakened that we characterize as vicious those acts that bring about its disunity, though this does enter into the nature of vicious acts; it is because the self within which the act originates is directly responsible for the growth, development and release of the tendency, the objective expression of which it sees to be excessive and ultimately disuniting to its own interests.

The root of evil can be traced to the imperfect expression of moral consciousness, the same factor that in its complete state of self-establishment is the factor making for unity and good. In its limitation of vision and in its exercise of narrow interests it stands opposed to the self's development. Being the incomplete expression of conscience, vice can be an attribute only of human beings; brutes being incapable of vicious actions (Vol. I, p. 331). In the absence of reason, man would not cease to be a system, but he would cease being vicious or virtuous.

We are now led to inquire still further for the causes within the nature of conscience that allow for the expression of evil, or in other words, for the incomplete expression and exercise of moral reflectiveness. We are told by Butler in his Dissertation on Virtue (Vol. I, p. 331) that vice in human creatures consists chiefly in the absence or want of a virtuous principle. But to guard against the possible charge that man cannot be held morally responsible for that in which he is deficient, Butler asserts concerning this virtuous principle that man "had it not in such a degree, as to prevail over the temptation: but possibly he had it in a degree, which would have rendered him proof against common temptations" (*ibid.*).

Then too, the failure on the part of the self to legislate in terms of its own advantage may lie in the perversion of that principle by an habitual and uncriticized employment of the lesser affections. Whether through ignorance, or intellectual carelessness, the self becomes incapable of seeing clearly the virtues of an act, certain it is, that conscience can become corrupt (Vol. II, pp. 146, 7, 150), or totally insensible (Vol. II, p. 110). And here the viciousness lies not so much in the detrimental effect that the acts exert upon oneself or upon others, but in the fact that the legislativeness of conscience has ceased to function according to the rights of its own nature, and what might originally have been otherwise and in the interests of the self is now contributory to its one-sided expression and ultimate disruption.

NATURE OF RESENTMENT

As opposed to Butler's statement that human beings are not naturally malevolent, it might be pointed out that of the various propensions whose aims are external objects, there may be discerned resentment whose direct aim is the misery of our fellow beings. But even here a closer scrutiny reveals that the natural end towards which this tendency is directed is one that is morally justified in the light of the entire self.

An analysis of resentment reveals it to be of two kinds: hasty and sudden, or settled and deliberative (Vol. II, p. 117, *et seq.*). The first kind, in its absence of reflectiveness, cannot properly be termed vicious, although under the control of a perverted reason it could easily become so. The purpose of sudden anger can be appreciated in the ends for which man was liable to it: namely that "he might be better qualified to prevent, and likewise (or perhaps chiefly) to resist and defeat, sudden force, violence, and opposition, considered merely as such, and without

regard to the fault or demerit of him who is the author of them"
(Vol. II, p. 118). But concerning deliberate resentment, "it
seems *in us* plainly connected with a sense of virtue and vice, of
moral good and evil" (Vol. II, p. 119). The object is always
seen to be some injury or wrong inflicted upon our fellow beings
against whom we become indignant. Although resentment appears to be directed against other individuals, it is not; directed
against the vicious actions of which we feel them to be the conscious authors, its purpose is the deprecation of those acts and,
through the medium of inflicted punishment, the prevention of
similar future acts (Vol. II, p. 134).

Resentment, morally considered, is a means whereby "society
is held together; (in) a fellow-feeling, which each individual
has in behalf of the whole species, as well as of himself" (Vol. II,
pp. 119, 129, 130). Like every other passion in human nature it
is open to abuse; unlike the other passions whose direct aim may
be gratified without entailing any contradiction of the remoter
aim towards which they are ultimately subservient, resentment,
if not carefully expressed in terms of its explicit end under the
strict surveillance of an enlightened conscience, is capable of
producing far more misery than the other propensions (Vol. II,
pp. 132, 133).

Some instances of its abuse are seen in those cases when we
resent wrongs to ourselves and others that are purely imaginary,
very slight injuries or those that have been grossly exaggerated,
or lastly persons who have innocently been the cause of evil. Its
abuse is most reprehensible when it becomes an end in itself (Vol.
II, pp. 123, 132). If we seek the justification within us of an
affection so easily open to misuse as is resentment, we see that
its presence is necessary to check and offset the lenience of compassion towards others, that would render the administration of
justice difficult (Vol. II, p. 124). It should be observed however
that the guard in human nature which acts against the abusive
employment of resentment is the fear that men have of becoming
the object of the resentment of others to whom they have been
unfair.[2]

Were we to trace out in detail the misuse of the remaining
particular propensions and principles, we should discover that

[2] See. Vol. II, pp. 88, 125; Cp. also p. 129: "Malice or resentment towards any
man hath plainly a tendency to beget the same passion in him who is the object
of it; and this again increases it in the other." Also Vol. II, p. 136.

the cause which stamps these acts as vicious is fundamentally the same as we have seen in our instance of resentment. Taken by themselves, these affections are morally indifferent; in their direct activity towards the end for which they have been designed, they are good; in their failure to achieve this end, because inadequately expressed through the incomplete presence of reflective conscience, they are evil. To complete our illustration, we shall consider briefly the two sermons in which Butler develops the origin of vice and its influence upon our nature: namely, Upon the Character of Balaam, and Upon Self-Deceit.

In the former, we are shown an individual who in the full light of his reason, under the influence of divine authority, convinced of the path of his duty, voluntarily chooses to follow the worse course. This contradiction of character, which Butler holds not to be uncommon, is one in which is witnessed not the prevalence of the stronger passions over the principle of rationality, but the apparent voluntary selection of the worse in the full knowledge of the better. But he shows that the imposition upon conscience to make it sanction the worse follows only when the worse has been made to appear the better, when what we want to do is first made to appear to us as our duty.

We can see in this sermon that the habitual performance of vicious acts in which conscience has been continually ignored, leads eventually to its utter corruption so that in subsequent pronouncements it becomes an unreliable authority, and ultimately indifferent to the development and reign of wickedness.

The sermon Upon Self-Deceit shows likewise the undermining of one's reflective conscience, but in this case as arising from an habitual over-regard for one's self. The self towards which we are partially disposed is one that sees its interests to lie in exclusion from the interests of others; it is that aspect of the self that narrowly conceives its own advantages to lie not in the expression of its whole nature as directed by conscience, but in the more circumscribed aspect of a narrow self-regard to which conscience is made subservient. It is instanced in "persons having so fixed and steady an eye upon their own interest, whatever they place it in, and the interest of these whom they consider as themselves, as in a manner to regard nothing else; their views are almost confined to this alone" (Vol. II, p. 145).

In one's practical life, this narrow self-regard, i.e., the concern for the partial self, is instanced in many ways. One is apt to set himself apart from others and reason differently concerning himself. The vices that he discerns in others, he condones in himself. Some individuals may be unaware of this self-partiality; others may protest loudly that their behavior leaves nothing to be desired. Self-partiality has many degrees. There are those individuals who are so ignorant of their true nature that they are biased in all judgments which refer to themselves directly. Yet in regard to other individuals, they can reason correctly and soundly (Vol. II, p. 146). This is the most perverse form of narrow self-love.

In other individuals this vice is less widespread; for bias and prejudice do not extend to their entire self. But it is present none the less. Self-partiality in them is confined narrowly to one particular interest. About this interest their reasoning is prejudiced and their views are distorted. Yet this type of partiality is not so reprehensible as the other; for the self remains clear in all judgments that concern itself except its one particular interest.

The evils that follow from all instances of self-partiality are many. Inattention to the needs of others is most outstanding. No particular evil or wrong is committed here, but a purblindness to the needs of others is formed. About this particular consequence of exclusive self-interest, Butler informs us: "Whoever will consider the whole commerce of human life, will see that a great part, perhaps the greatest part, of the intercourse amongst mankind, cannot be reduced to fixed determinate rules. Yet in these cases there is a right and a wrong: a merciful, a liberal, a kind and compassionate behaviour, which surely is our duty; and an unmerciful contracted spirit, an hard and oppressive course of behaviour, which is most certainly immoral and vicious" (Vol. II, p. 148).

More serious than this apathy to the needs of others, or the want of positive benevolence, is the direct injustice wrought when the mind's eye is fastened upon a set interest. In these cases the individual never stops to evaluate morally the consequences of attaining his end; he seldom foresees its effects upon others. From attitudes of hardheartedness and injustice the individual is soon led to the committing of crimes such as robbery and murder. These latter deeds are never committed for their own sake— for no individual embraces evil *in se*—but as a means towards some one narrowly exclusive end.

The greatest harm that eventually arises from a narrow self-regard is the corruption of the entire self; the corruption of the whole moral character in its principle of conscience. At this stage the entire self is degraded; moral distinctions are lost, and the self is no longer able to think soundly or correctly upon any subject whether it touches itself or not (Vol. II, p. 150).

Such are the evils of a narrow self-regard. What is its cure, or at least its prevention? These can be effected only as the self rigorously takes a survey of its character from time to time. One's general attitude, asserts Butler, should be one of self-suspicion. One should suspect the presence of this tendency to overrate the importance of all that concerns one. Butler suggests the following means for the discovery of our faults. "Suppose then an enemy were to set about defaming you, what part of your character would he single out? What particular scandal, think you, would he be most likely to fix upon you? And what would the world be most ready to believe? . . . What is that ill thing, that faulty behaviour, which I am apprehensive an enemy, who was thoroughly acquainted with me, would be most likely to lay to my charge, and which the world would be most apt to believe? It is indeed possible that a man may not be guilty in that respect. All that I say is, let him in plainness and honesty fix upon that part of his character for a particular survey and reflection; and by this he will come to be acquainted, whether he be guilty or innocent in that respect, and how far he is one or the other" (Vol. II, p. 153). The continual practice of the golden rule will insure us of a fairer treatment towards others and less of a regard for ourselves.

PART THREE

SOME METAPHYSICAL ASPECTS OF THE MORAL SELF

15

SELF-IDENTITY

OUR leading idea in the course of the present work has been the discovery of virtue. Having been initially told that it consists in man's following nature, we have explored the various affections of his nature, and discovered their mutual interrelatedness to conscience and to self-love. We must now ask ourselves whether man's nature is completely known in the psychological account we have advanced; or whether there remain for exposition aspects of his nature that we have not as yet discussed, but which enter as factors into man's moral life. The present chapter will concern itself with two problems that are closely related. First, it will show that man's constitution has other aspects than we have presented, and secondly that man's self in his completed array of characteristics is a single, indivisible self, continuous with his own acts.

THE METAPHYSICAL SELF

Man's self comprises much more than his various affections as they stand organically related to conscience. All of these are aspects of his conscious life, but they do not exhaust the area of his conscious possessions. His mind contains faculties for action, capacities for perceiving and powers for exercise. Moreover there is the feature of memory. Besides, his mind is sensitive to enjoyment, with its phases of pleasure and pain. All of these enter into his conscious life. At times, man is consciously aware of them; at other times he is not, especially when in a faint or a swoon he lapses from consciousness as we ordinarily conceive it. Of some of these mental possessions he may be completely unaware. Before they mature and enter into his conscious life, man's adaptabilities may lie latent like hidden instincts awaiting their time and their place. Other features of his mind are not of the nature of consciousness, and do not enter directly into the conscious life. Man's capacities for perceiving, to take this as an instance, are the means whereby he is able to know physical objects. Being other than the act of knowing, which is consciously experienced, this capacity represents from the standpoint of the mind the cause and the possibility of all perceptual knowledge. Added to all of these features, man possesses a free will and imagination. Through the latter he can conceive plans of his own, through the former he can execute them. In the exercise of his free will he can assiduously apply himself to the practice of virtue as he understands it. Such are some of the characteristics of man's self as Butler sees them. For our own advantage let us view this situation more closely.

When we speak of man's self, we do not intend to include under this term his body, physical possessions or social relationships. Although all of these may prove to be indispensable to self-expression and self-advancement, yet none of them can be properly viewed as man's inner frame or constitution. Man's self is an entity that is distinct from his body or social groups; and like them it has laws of its own. As such we shall consider it.

Let us first point out how little of our nature is really accessible to us, how much more it contains than we can ever know. We may recognize the fact that we have a memory, or that an unconscious cause must be postulated to account for our ability to perceive and recognize, but about these instances we cannot tell how or why (Vol. I, p. 22; Vol. II, p. 219). "How we were made, how our being is continued and preserved, what the faculties of our minds are, and upon what the power of exercising them depends"—these and many more besides elude our most persistent search. They indicate the presence of laws and purposes that we cannot find out.

We admit our ignorance upon this score; yet there is much that we do know, and that we are aware of through observation. We have mentioned above some of these mental characteristics; we shall now consider some of them at closer range, such as the capacity of perception and the faculty of reasoning. In taking these issues up for closer consideration, we shall be able to draw more distinctly the line of demarcation between the self and its body, and at the same time to illustrate some intrinsic characteristics of the agent himself. First as to sensation or perception.

Our sensations and perceptions show us to be in close union

with our bodies. Upon the senses themselves we seem to be directly dependent for our mental data such as colors, sounds, etc. Yet the conscious experience of sensations belongs to the mind and not to the senses, which are physical. These latter must be regarded only as the physical conditions or instruments whereby the conscious powers of the mind are enabled to exert themselves, and not as the conscious percipients. Let us expand this point further by illustrating it in regard to vision.

Optical experiments show us how sight is aided by the use of glasses; these latter are the means or instruments of vision, but not the conscious perception itself. But our actual senses although attached to our bodies are to be regarded as instruments in the same way as those mechanical devices that are foreign to our bodies. As instruments they prepare the way for the reception of ideas from the outer world. We see with our eyes in the same way as we see with glasses. The retina and the optic nerves are merely the physiological instruments through which we perceive. "Nor is there any reason to believe," Butler assures us, "that we see with them in any other sense; any other I mean, which would lead us to think the eye itself a percipient" (Vol. I, p. 29). "Our organs of sense prepare and convey on objects, in order to their being perceived, in like manner as foreign matter does, without affording any shadow of appearance, that they themselves perceive" (*ibid.*, p. 30).

Undoubtedly there exists between the sense organs of the body, and the mind's capacity to perceive, a most intimate relation. Without the use of our sensory organs we would be considerably impoverished as to the stock of our ideas. And in the present state at least there would be no means of supplying the deficiency.

The powers of reflection are even less dependent upon bodily assistance than sensations. Sensations presuppose the material sense organs, as their physical condition, but reflection, as far as we can see, does not presuppose that. In speaking thus about reason, Butler does not mean that reason can operate *in vacuo*. He admits that our external organs of sense are necessary as the conveyancers of ideas to our reasoning faculties. But once the ideas have gained admittance into our mind, we are independent of the means through which they have gained entrance. Butler tells us "when these ideas are brought in, we are capable of reflecting in the most intense degree, and of enjoying the greatest pleasure, and feeling the greatest pain, by means of that reflection, without any assistance from our senses" (Vol. I, p. 34).

In this independence the power of reason appears to be superior to the capacities of sensation. There can be no immediate vision without the organ of sense, but there is no evidence that there can be no reflection apart from sense. Furthermore, all that which is seen depends upon the state of health of the sensory organs, but with the powers of reflection such is not the case. There is no presumption in this latter instance that the power to think is impaired by mortal disease. On the contrary there is abundant evidence to show that the mental power is often in its highest vigor when the body is most attenuated. Persons on the point of death "discover apprehension, memory, reason, all entire; with the utmost force of affection; sense of a character, of shame and honour; and the highest mental enjoyments and sufferings, even to the last gasp: and these surely prove even greater vigour of life than bodily strength does" (Vol. I, p. 35).

We have selected as illustrations of the mind's broader compass two of its important aspects. In showing how sensation and reflection directly qualify the mind, we have also shown how the mind is conceivable as an entity distinct in kind from the body. We shall now advance our discussion of the nature of the mind one step further, by asking whether the various aspects of the mind that we have enumerated in this section, are related to each other. Do the powers of reflection, capacities of sensation, abilities of memory, etc., betoken a unitary individual, or do they merely hang together loosely in some empirical way, so that the mind is a nominalistic term for this variety of particular aspects? Living in an age when the thought of Descartes and Locke was currently predominant, Butler allies himself to the belief that each agent is a single individual entity in which his mental attributes inhere. How is he assured of his position here? He reaches it in two ways.

Man knows himself as being self-conscious. In his act of self-awareness he is assured of being one and indivisible, for his exercise of consciousness proclaims its nature as such. "It is a contradiction to suppose one part of it should be here and the other there . . ." (Vol. I, p. 25). Likewise the conditions upon which an indivisible consciousness depends are one and indivisible.

But these conditions point to a single subject as the cause, that is unitary because its effect, i.e., conscious exercise, is unitary.

Butler's second argument is scholastic in thought. Every thing must be a substance or a property of a substance, and this is no less true of a person. "If he, if person, be a substance; then consciousness that he is the same person is consciousness that he is the same substance. If the person, or he, be the property of a substance, still consciousness that he is the same property is as certain a proof that his substance remains the same, as consciousness that he remains the same substance would be: since the same property cannot be transferred from one substance to another" (Vol. I, p. 324).

We should by this time have arrived at a clearer understanding of Butler's conception of a self. We have pointed out that man's own inner self is not to be identified with his body, but is a distinct entity with laws of its own. Although the self is in intimate union with its body, it is not subject to the same laws of change or the mutilations of the latter. Butler points out that "persons can trace up the existence of themselves to a time, when the bulk of their bodies were extremely small, in comparison of what it is in mature age" (Vol. I, p. 27). But there is no reason for us to believe that in this increase or diminution of physical substance we are any less of a self or a living being. "We have already several times over lost a great part or perhaps the whole of our body, according to certain common established laws of nature; yet we remain the same living agents . . ." (Vol. I, p. 28). The laws of the body (i.e., its growth, identity and change) are such that they have no influence over the mind.

The loss of bodily parts might be in the nature of mutilations, where we suffer the dismemberment of an arm or leg. And yet we are none the less living agents because of this loss, nor does the unity of our consciousness appear to be affected at all (*ibid.*). Also the self can be acted upon by physical bodies and yet retain its distinctive nature. . . . Likewise the self can act upon physical objects and not forfeit its self-identity.

While there is much that we do not know about the self, there is sufficient evidence, both empirical and rational, that it contains more than we shall ever know. But what we do know is that its characteristics, such as its varieties of powers and capacities, are aspects of a single and indivisible subject, being inseparably related to it as properties to substance. Some of these characteristics, we have reason to believe, are more truly representative of the mature of mind than others. Although the mind has its perceptual quality, this is less essential to it than its rational aspect, for under favorable conditions the self, being unhindered by its sensory exercise, tends to express itself more in the light of reason.

PROBLEM OF SELF-IDENTITY

In the above section we have been mainly concerned with the characteristics of the self from the standpoint of its wider compass and in reference to its aspect of being a unitary subject. In the present section we are concerned more directly with the unity of the self as it survives and lives throughout its active states. Am I the same subject of experience as I was some time ago? Shall I be the same self tomorrow as I am today?

My self-identity is a particular instance of self-identity in general. What do I mean when I apply the term to other objects such as trees or plants? I can speak of a tree as being the same as it was years ago, even though I know that during the period that has elapsed since my earliest experience of it, every physical particular of its nature has been replaced, so that strictly speaking it is no longer the same tree. In calling it the same, however, I am, according to Butler, conforming to a common usage. In respect to its relation to surrounding objects it bears a constant ratio of distance, etc. Philosophically speaking, the use of the term "same" here is not justifiable, that "being evidently a contradiction in terms, to say they are, when no part of their substance, and no one of their properties is the same . . . because it is allowed, that the same property cannot be transferred from one substance to another" (Vol. I, pp. 319, 320).

There is another sense in which I can refer to this tree as the same with its earlier stages of growth, and that is when I have in mind its aspect of life or organization. It is this aspect of sameness that I have in mind when I speak of persons. In the latter case the principle of organization is reason, whereas in the former case it is the particular law of its own nature.[1]

---

[1] In the passage of which the above is an attempted paraphrase, Butler is unusually obscure, and I have presented what I believe to be an interpretation that is consistent with his views of a system. (*Vide* Vol. II, pp. 58, 59.) Butler's use of the teleological principle commits him to the designation of an object in terms of its system and organization. Man differs from plants and animals in being self-conscious, but all three are similar in respect to their form of organization. It is this latter that constitutes their thinghood. "Every work both of

This experiencing of self-consciousness in ourselves is an indubitable fact, and the recognition of it in others is equally open to evidence. In both instances experience guarantees that we are essentially the same today as we were yesterday. Through the examination of our present and past ideas we know our present selves to be the same as our past selves. Although my ideas of the past, when examined, exist in the present, yet they bear upon their face the guarantee of a past experience together with the fact that they are my own. Just as we can compare two triangles and grasp their similarity, we can compare our present self with our past self and know that they are the same. Yet when we come intellectually to examine the meaning implied by the term personal identity, we are apt to fall into an initial confusion. We cannot define clearly what personal identity consists in, or the conditions that make for its being an actual fact. As a consequence many men have been unwisely led to renounce the reality of personal identity instead of seeing that the difficulty lies only in their own cognitive approach. Let us present and examine some of their views, and state in turn Butler's replies to them.

Butler proceeds first to consider the statements of Locke concerning self-identity. He finds that Locke has given a clear answer to the question whether a person is the same identical substance. For Locke defines a person as a thinking being. The identity of self would be the sameness of rationality. But since rational being and substance stand for the same idea there can be no difficulty for us; but neither are we afforded any enlightenment. To put this question and answer in this form does not touch the heart of the issue; for it is still left open for us to decide whether there is a continuity within the rational being,

nature and art is a system" says Butler (Vol. II, p. 7). According to this, the material aspects or parts as such are irrelevant to the nature of the system and to its continuance as such. But in his Dissertation on Virtue, Butler says: "In a loose and popular sense, then, the life and the organization and the plant are justly said to be the same, notwithstanding the perpetual change of the parts" (Vol. I, p. 320). Taking this sentence by itself with an emphasis upon the word "justly," there would be no inconsistency of meaning, for it would indicate that the popular meaning was justified. But then comes the following sentence: "But in a strict and philosophical manner of speech, no man, no being, no mode of being, no anything, can be the same with that, with which it hath indeed nothing the same." Now sameness is used in this latter sense (meaning life and organization?) when applied to persons. The identity of these (i.e., persons), therefore, cannot subsist with the diversity of substance (i.e., change of physical or material parts?).

or if we please, within the personal substance (Vol. I, pp. 320).
Merely to state their one-to-one identity does not advance the
issue for us or solve it.

If we now ask Locke whether the self is identical in or during
any of its successive states, we get a different answer. The term
self covers for Locke—according to Butler—a series or a succession of conscious acts or events taking place necessarily in
different portions of time. Represented by the succession of
states to which it is reducible without remainder, the self is as
different from itself during any two moments as the moments
of time which separate our mental states. But, for Butler, this
can be offered as no disproof of personal identity or continuous
selfhood. We can admit with Locke that the successive moments
of consciousness are different from each other, and that, occurring in different periods of time they can no more be the same
than the moments of time in which they are present. But to admit
so much does not prevent our seeing that these states of consciousness are aspects of the one person or self differently expressed, and as such provide no refutation of self-identity.

The difficulty, according to Butler, of Locke's argument is
that it confuses the object as it is, with the object as it is known.
Butler says: "it is surely conceivable, that a person may have a
capacity of knowing some object or other to be the same now,
which it was when he contemplated it formerly: yet in this case,
where, by the supposition, the object is perceived to be the same,
the perception of it in any two moments cannot be one and the
same perception" (Vol. I, p. 321). In the case of ourselves the
act of knowing is directed towards us as objects. We can grant
that our acts of consciousness are different from each other, but
we can at the same time affirm the continuity of the same self.
I can know my present self to be the same as my past by recalling
my past, and yet I can know that the consciousness of the past
differs from the consciousness of the present, seeing them to be
two aspects of the same thing. Admitted then that consciousness
of the various stages or moments of our existence is not the same,
but what it reveals is the same, we must not confuse the act of
perception with the thing perceived. In other words, the similarity or sameness is revealed by successive acts of consciousness
but not constituted by it.

In this attempt to reduce the self to a plurality of conscious
acts, Butler sees grave moral consequences. My present life, ac-

cording to this view, can have no vital concern for my past self, nor can I be essentially interested in what is to happen to me tomorrow. From the standpoint of moral consequences, I can disavow the acts of my past self and disclaim all results that are believed to be the outcome of my deeds. It is true that the opponents of Butler admit that my present self is much more than a momentary aspect limited to the narrowest bands of self-consciousness. For them it extends as far as memory can discover. But in claiming even this much for the continuity or sameness of the self, they are, according to Butler, at odds with themselves. They are verbally maintaining a continuity which their asserted doctrine has led them to deny. "For it is self-evident, that the personality cannot be really the same, if, as they expressly assert, that in which it consists is not the same" (Vol. I, p. 322).

Against this stated position of Locke and his disciples, Butler maintains that the belief in the discreteness of our individual self is a notion that runs counter to our convictions, that memory is not an infallible criterion to rely upon in the settlement of the issue, and lastly that self-identity is guaranteed by our conscious experience. We shall state each in turn.

That we are continuous with our past states and future states is a conviction borne in upon us by the nature of things. To prove that this is so, let us assume it to be established that we shall be actually different tomorrow from what we are today. Even if this were the case, it would make no actual difference to us or to our plans. In other words the conviction that tomorrow we shall be continuous with ourselves today is so strong with us that we should not alter our conduct with regard to our health or our affairs (Vol. I, p. 323). Hence it is reasonable to act as if we were the same, and to assume such a belief as the basis for the future as well as for our present actions.

Can we rely solely upon the reports of memory? For Butler, "remembering or forgetting can make no alteration in the truth of past matter of fact" (Vol. I, p. 324). The continuity of a person is brought home to him by an inner conviction that what he now enjoys and suffers, he enjoyed and suffered in the past. This may not be guaranteed by memory, but the failure to recall it does not deny for us the fact that it is so. If memory fails to report the fact, it means that we cannot grant it a superior insight, or endow it with an infallibility of recall, for it is ad-

mitted that people forget actions of the past that they themselves originated at that time, just as they forget the existence
of inanimate objects. An individual can be defective in regard
to the memory of his past self, just as he is in regard to other
things.

This retort of Butler's brings out the truth that our present
forgetfulness of our past existence is no sign that we did not
exist, for if we did exist in the past we might very well have forgotten the fact now. In stating this much, Butler's argument is
fair. But Butler goes beyond the assertion that the self might
have existed contrary to all reports of memory; he maintains
our prior existence to be an indubitable fact. As to those who
would maintain that memory did reveal our past states, but did
not reveal them to indicate the sameness of the agent, Butler
replies that "there is no more difficulty in conceiving it to have
a power of knowing itself to be the same living being which it
was some time ago, of remembering some of its actions, sufferings, and enjoyments, and forgetting others, than in conceiving
it to know or remember or forget any thing else" (Vol. I,
p. 324).

The second argument, we have seen, is largely negative in its
results. Its value lies in Butler's pointing out that personal
identity is not disproved by our failure to recall. Likewise, personal identity is not disproved even in the cases when we do
recall, for whereas the actual states of consciousness that are
recalled are manifestly different from each other, that does not
exclude the possibility of a permanent self to which they are
relative. In his third argument that we are about to consider,
Butler's point of view concerning the continuity of the self
takes on a more positive character. It runs as follows.

In my present act of consciousness, I can recall a past state
or a past event. But I likewise recall as essential to that past
state the fact that it belongs to me. The ownership of the past
act is recalled with the act itself. I must either accept the latter
with the former, or deny the reality of the past event recalled.
The guarantee of consciousness is the same in both instances.
It often happens that the belief in past events rises largely from
the feeling that I myself originated the act. In this case the
evidence of personal identity is directly given. I have every
reason to accept its being what it proclaims itself to be, and
none to reject it as spurious.

There are not wanting those readers who will declare that we might be mistaken about our past experiences and so easily become dupes of illusory memory experience. To this Butler replies that this question can be raised at the end of any demonstration whatever (Vol. I, p. 325). He says: "And he who can doubt, whether perception by memory can in this case be depended upon, may doubt also, whether perception by deduction and reasoning, which also include memory, or indeed whether intuitive perception can" (*ibid.*). To adopt such an attitude would lead us to a universal skepticism or a complete denial of any truth. "For it is ridiculous to attempt to prove the truth of those perceptions, whose truth we can no otherwise prove, than by other perceptions of exactly the same kind with them, and which there is just the same ground to suspect; or to attempt to prove the truth of our faculties, which can no otherwise be proved, than by the use or means of those very suspected faculties themselves" (*ibid.*).

SUMMARY AND TRANSITION

According to Butler, the belief in personal identity is one that is necessary to the moral life. If there were no self-continuity it would be impossible for us to profit from our past experiences; to base upon them plans for future action. Self-construction could not advance in its work if it had nothing to build upon, nor could the progressive achievement of the moral life take place in its absence.

Our present chapter has brought out in regard to the self many features which are necessary to the moral life, for there can be no morality where there is no single agent prosecuting his plans, or where the agent's identity is dispersed completely over his acts. Yet we have not learned all that there is to learn about the self until we show that the self is immortal. The discussion of this issue will occupy us in the next chapter.

16

PROBLEM OF IMMORTALITY

IN ONE of his ethical Sermons Butler reminds us that "the present world is not our home; that we are merely strangers and travellers in it, as all our fathers were" (Vol. II, p. 101). The belief in a future life he held to be essential to the cause of religion. In his *Analogy* he remarks that "as religion implies a future state, any presumption against such a state, is a presumption against religion" (Vol. I, p. 40). Should it turn out that religion furnishes to conscience the ideals of which it can advisedly approve, then likewise it must turn out that the belief in a future life is a fundamental principle of morality. Whatever may be the present opinion about the necessary connection of morality and immortality, for Butler at any rate there was no doubt of their intimate interconnection. A sound morality meant the belief in a future life: to question the latter meant the unsettling of the former.

For Butler survival was indicated as an intrinsic aspect of man's nature, and its verifiability was open to one's observation. Our plans to live morally must recognize this feature of our nature, taking into account the fact that we possess an infinite amount of time in which this conscious principle can gain ascendency, and organize our nature. What arguments does Butler offer as a proof of man's immortality; what is the nature of the self that survives? We shall try to do justice to these questions in our present chapter.

Our chapter on Personal Identity revealed to us the permanence that Butler held to be inseparable from the nature of the self. It held that the self was not to be identified solely with its states; that over and above its powers, capacities and activities, though not separable from it, was the "underlying" self that was identical in its past and present states. The present issue raises the question whether this self-identity will not continue; not merely during our immediate future states, but beyond them into our post-temporal future. The issue of immortality presupposes that the self is self-identical, but the question that it raises cannot be answered by the issue of self-identity. This latter issue brings out the fact that permanence is necessary as a prerequisite for immortal life, but it proves no more. At the best it leaves the issue open.

Butler's arguments for the immortality of the self are of two kinds, the rationalistic and the empirical. The former arguments follow as a consequence from the nature of the self as we know it to be. The latter arguments are based more directly upon experience itself. The rationalistic arguments are not original, but show the influence of Samuel Clarke, under whose philosophical dominance Butler came early in his life. The empirical arguments represent Butler's original cast of mind that is reflected at large in his Analogy of Religion.

RATIONALISTIC ARGUMENTS FOR IMMORTALITY

The self has been shown to be different from the body. Whereas the body is composed of many material parts, the self is single and indivisible. Death, which means the destruction of the body, cannot affect the self, for since the self is uncompounded, it cannot be destroyed. What cannot be destroyed is immortal. But since the self is immortal, so are its innumerable aspects: its capacities and powers, its affections and reasoning.

Intimately connected with its body, the self is unaffected by the laws of bodily change and growth. Now it happens that the body may change its parts so completely that over a course of years no part of the original body-substance remains—yet the self inhabiting the body knows itself as continuous and as the same. But since the self is known to survive changes in matter, what difficulty is there in conceiving that it can survive all matter, particularly the complete destruction of its body?

We should carefully remark that when we speak of death in reference to the self, we have in mind only the destruction of the body, i.e., its so called outward bodily form and can have nothing more. We know nothing of the intrinsic self, which is hidden from our view. The mind and its capacities are invisible, and we have no means of tracing their existence to see what becomes of them. These capacities are known to us only through their effects in the body to which they are united. We cannot ascribe to the causes what we only know to apply to the bodily effects. A man becomes paralyzed, let us say. This means that he cannot move his leg, which is material and a means through which the inner capacity for self-motion works. It does not mean that the cause responsible for the motion of the limb is itself paralyzed; it may be merely inactive. Awaiting more favorable physical conditions, it will re-exert itself in the presence of a healthy and responsive limb.

Certain bodily effects show the presence of mental causes, but the cessation of these effects does not indicate the cessation of the causes. The capacities of the mind must remain intact, and like it must be indestructible. Butler informs us on this point: "that we have these powers and capacities before death, is a presumption that we shall retain them through and after death; indeed a probability of it abundantly sufficient to act upon, unless there be some positive reason to think that death is the destruction of those living powers; because there is in every case a probability, that all things will continue as we experience they are, in all respects, except those in which we have some reason to think they will be altered" (Vol. I, p. 20).[1]

Nor do we possess any evidence to the contrary. Let us see why. The suspense of the mental faculties of persons in a swoon, or of ourselves in our dream life, does not justify one in concluding that the mental powers, i.e., the capacities to act, have in any way been impaired. As Butler comments here: ". . . the suspension of a power and the destruction of it, are effects so totally different in kind, as we experience from sleep and a swoon, that we cannot in any wise argue from one to the other; or conclude even to the lowest degree of probability, that the same kind of force which is sufficient to suspend our faculties, though it be increased ever so much, will be sufficient to destroy them" (Vol. I, p. 37).

In the second place we can admit the total impairment of the bodily equipment, such as the loss of our eyes and our limbs; yet we should not be justified in assuming that the mental capacity to perceive or act had been destroyed or even touched. Concerning this aspect, Butler tells us: "So with regard to our power of moving, or directing motion by will and choice: upon the destruction of a limb, this active power remains, as it evidently seems, unlessened; so as that the living being, who has suffered this loss, would be capable of moving as before, if it had another limb to move with. It can walk by the help of an artificial leg; just as it can make use of a pole or a lever, to

---

[1] "We have no more reason to think a being endued with living powers, ever loses them during its whole existence, than to believe that a stone ever acquires them" (Vol. I, p. 21).

reach towards itself and to move things, beyond the length and power of its natural arm: and this last it does in the same manner as it reaches and moves, with its natural arm, things nearer and of less weight" (Vol. I, pp. 30-1). Nor is there any other relationship subsistent between the sensory organs and the mind than we have outlined. The power of sight lies no more in the sensory organs than in the glasses it uses, nor does the power of walking lie more in the limb than in the staff that aids it.

Since the mind is known to be indestructible (destruction being a term applicable only to the physical body), it can survive many systems of matter, and form union with many physical bodies, all of which it can successively animate. The sensory life of the mind can be different in each case, for the sensory organs, as we have seen in our last chapter, are the property of the body and presumably take on the characteristics of the individual body. But the capacity of perceiving, i.e., of the conscious act of appreciation, remains a property of the mind itself. Likewise with the mind's power of reflection. Less dependent upon the body for its incoming ideas than the sensory capacity of the mind, the powers of reflection manifest themselves with a less degree of variance. So independent does Butler conceive the essential nature of the mind to be in its higher aspects of reasoning and memory, that he maintains that "our post-humous life, whatever there may be in it additional to our present, yet may not be entirely beginning anew; but going on" (Vol. I, p. 36). And he suggests that the senses "may be the only natural hindrance to our existing, immediately and of course, in a higher state of reflection" (Vol. I, p. 37).

Butler's remaining argument for the immortality of the self is based upon the "analogy of nature." This argument is undoubtedly Butler's own contribution to the issue of immortality. The first argument that we have just discussed was a common metaphysical doctrine of his day, as old as Plato's in its origin, but brought again into prominence through the efforts of Samuel Clarke. Its underlying attempt was to show that mind in being different from body was not a victim of dissolution as was body, and hence must be immortal. But all that Butler has succeeded in showing here is that mind is not conclusively mortal. His services consisted in freeing the mind from the dogmatism of any foregone conclusions as to the perishability of the self. In doing this he left the positive question of its immortal state an open one. We shall see in our next section Butler's unique contribution in the advancement of a more positive type of proof.

EMPIRICAL PROOFS FOR IMMORTALITY

Individual life endures throughout a variety of changes; from its earliest to its latest stages it assumes forms of great diversity. All living things are able to survive great changes of temperature, and adapt themselves to most unusual conditions. To take the case of an insect. What can be of greater contrast with each other than the successive stages of a caterpillar? At one time it is a cocoon, and at a later time it emerges as a butter-fly. And yet we refer to it as the same thing that exists in a variety of changes. Unusual as these stages are, yet they are not so different as to warrant their being called two distinct forms of life. The phases of human life are likewise remarkable in their degrees of contrast. "The states of life in which we ourselves existed formerly in the womb and in our infancy, are almost as different from our present in mature age, as it is possible to conceive any two states or degrees of life can be" (Vol. I, p. 19). Throughout this extraordinary change within our own life, we remain the same individual just as throughout the various stages of its existence, the insect remains the same creature. Such is the general law of nature in our own species "that the same creatures, the same individuals, should exist in degrees of life and perception, with capacities of action, of enjoyment and suffering, in one period of their being, greatly different from those appointed them in another period of it. And in other creatures the same law holds" (Vol. I, p. 19).

What bearing has this upon the problem of immortality? Death may be a different stage of man's continuous existence; a state that we as observers may be unable to trace. Yet the mere fact that it is different cannot be used as an argument that man does not survive.

Butler advances his argument one step further. He states that unless we have good reason for believing that death means the destruction of our minds as it does mean the dissolution of our physical bodies, we are bound to believe in a posthumous life. But every evidence is afforded us that life continues; for within the life span of any individual, nothing is destroyed; at the most, capacities are suspended and become inactive. Nor are we afforded any evidence to the contrary. We have no right to say at the dissolution of an individual's body, that his mind has perished or that he has completely ceased to be, for all of our observations are against this; probability assures us that the individual lives on. We cannot readily dispense with the reports of probability in this case when we accept its evidence in all other cases. If we reject the reports of probability for his continuance, we must reject our beliefs concerning everything, for all of them rest upon the same criterion. Our only reason for "believing the course of the world will continue to-morrow," is that "it has done so far as our experience or knowledge of history can carry us back. Nay, it seems our only reason for believing, that any one substance now existing will continue to exist a moment longer . . ." (Vol. I, p. 21).

In his insistence upon the respectable evidence of probability Butler is maintaining that the basis for any belief must be a positive one, founded upon an observable experience. He is under no illusion that experience is an infallible guide to truth, but it is the only support we can rely upon; consequently, we must accept what it reveals. Nor does he blindly believe that one or two reports of experience are sufficient to induce us to believe. The certainty of any truth is dependent upon the number of times it has been observed to hold; the greater the number of observations we make, the sounder our judgments are apt to be. And our final reasons for believing in any one thing more convincedly than in any other is that the former has more steadily and progressively revealed itself in the consistency of its nature.

A high degree of probability then confirms our belief in immortality; for we discover no one instant in a man's life time up to the moment of his physical death to warrant our asserting the destruction of his mental powers or capacities. Throughout this time we have observed innumerable examples of his mental activities; or in the absence of his overt activities we have noted the suspension of his faculties. Are we not assured in the highest degree possible that his life will continue? Should we not reject as irrelevant the fact of his bodily death, since bodily decomposition is a physical and not a mental phenomenon? The unequivocal statement that man will not survive must be based upon experience, as must all similar statements—in regard to immortality, no counter-evidence exists. Furthermore this experience must offer a weightier evidence than the more plausible evidence for man's continuance. We have every indication that man will survive but none that he will not. Are there any reasons for believing that man will not survive, other than the probable evidence of experience? According to Butler, belief in the extinction of man must rest upon the nature of the thing, or upon analogy, and neither of these assures us that man will not survive.

First as to the nature of the thing: We know nothing about the nature of death except that it involves a change in the appearance of the body. But since the mind with its capacities to act is not the same as the body, we possess no positive evidence that death will affect the mind. Likewise "we know not at all upon what the existence of our living powers depends, this shows further, there can no probability be collected from the reason of the thing, that death will be their destruction" (Vol. I, p. 22). Neither can we argue from the analogy of nature. For until the moment of the individual's death, we have positive and sufficient evidence that he is in possession of his living powers. At the moment of death, i.e., of dissolution of the physical body, we are deprived of further or sensible evidence, i.e., outward signs or effects, of his having them. But not possessing this latter evidence is no reason for us to conclude that the individual is destroyed; he could still be in possession of his faculties, but in such a way that their existence would now be unknown to us. We cannot affirm that absence of sensible evidence is positive conclusion that they are destroyed, for an individual might possess what we as observers are ignorant of; the fault lies with us and not with them. If we dogmatically say that absence of sensible evidence is conclusive proof of their destruction, we should create an impassable screen between ourselves and our ever knowing individual minds in their capacities and powers.

There are some readers who are apt unfairly to reason from the lower orders of life, i.e., vegetables, to that of man, seeing an analogy where none exists (Vol. I, p. 37). Assuming that vegetables are not immortal, may we not say that human beings are not either? This comparison would be plausible if the similarity between man and vegetable life were greater. But as a matter of fact, no analogy between them exists. Vegetables have no power or capacity of perception, and none of reason; man admittedly has. And it is the continuance of man in so far as he is possessed of them, that we are concerned with in respect to his immortality.

In my opinion this empirical argument of Butler's is his most remarkable and original. It brings out quite clearly the need for positive basic evidence on the issue of immortality, and goes a considerable way in supplying it. It fails however in being ultimately convincing, because of the possibility for suspense in one's judgment concerning the evidence. In other words: I may have no positive evidence against the acceptance of immortality, but likewise I may have no conclusive evidence for it. Not to have evidence for immortality does not mean its denial, any more than not to have evidence against it means its categorical acceptance. Yet we must not belittle what he has done. To some, it will seem that Butler's argument reduces itself to this: that the life of the individual as far as we have observed indicates no dissolution, hence its death is not likely to happen. As Eliot tells us "the older a man gets, the more difficult it is to him to retain a believing conception of his own death." To them it will seem that all that Butler has said is that within the physical life-span of the individual there has been observed no instance of death, hence this one solitary instance of his final collapse and demise is insufficient to convince him. But we shall have occasion to observe later the sense of continuity and system was so strong in Butler's mind that he refused to recognize any one domain of existence as more fundamental or more natural than any other. To his mind the natural did not consist merely and only of the visible. "It would be a shortness of thought scarce credible," he warns us, "to imagine, that no system or course of things can be so, but only what we see at present" (Vol. I, p. 39). If we take as our conclusion that immortality is possible, then it is not difficult to believe in the posthumous life, for as Butler points out, it may very well be that life continues but is no longer in communication with us. And we cannot say that absence of communication is an indubitable proof of spiritual non-existence.

PART FOUR

SOCIAL AND POLITICAL PHILOSOPHY

17

NATURE OF SOCIETY

NO SELF can live alone. It requires the presence of its fellow beings for the fulfilment of its nature. But these fellow beings exist in societies, banded together by their laws and institutions. Conscience, we have seen, is the mouthpiece of the self, proclaiming for the individual within whom it resides as a principle of reflection the paths of behavior it must pursue if it wishes to live virtuously. In its moral pronouncements conscience must take account of society, within which man finds himself. It must ascertain its structure, study its laws, and adjust the individual to its nature. Only as conscience succeeds in availing itself of a knowledge of society, and only as it passes judgment upon the moral worth of its laws and institutions, can the individual be said to fulfil his nature and live virtuously.

The following account of society is a piecemeal construction from Butler's *Sermons Delivered on Public Occasions*, and the first part of the *Analogy*. He nowhere develops explicitly for us his views on society; nor does he treat as a special aspect of his philosophy man's place within society and the obligations he owes it. As a consequence, one cannot maintain with certainty that the account of society that follows would be endorsed by Butler as the ideal type for all individuals and for all times. It shows clearly the influence upon his thought of the prevailing English institutions with which he was intimately acquainted. Whether or not Butler was familiar with actual social conditions in other countries is not known. Certain it is that he never left England, and his cast of mind upon social conditions, their precise needs and problems, is clearly influenced by this fact. His views on society, which I have attempted to present here as a consistent piece, are scattered throughout his addresses, which were dedicated to particular problems and occasions such as appeals for funds for charitable, educational and religious institutions. The allusions are of necessity local and of his time.

Yet throughout all of this there is indicated the theoretical trend that implies a philosophical view and not merely an historical or contemporaneous point of view. It has been my endeavor in the present chapter to make clear these more fundamental outlooks. What seems to be permanent and universal in his social philosophy I have tried to indicate in the course of my exposition.

There may be little or no justification for arranging his social philosophy under the four headings that I have used, but in this respect I have been guided by the model of the psychological self. Correlated with the fundamental propensions is the economic aspect of society, answering in its own way to man's economic needs. Then comes the political, which indicates the laws under which man in his more immediate social bearing must take account of others. This aspect roughly corresponds to man's compassionate and benevolent nature. Lastly I have seen that man's moral principle of reflection makes its particular demands too without which his nature would be thwarted and unsatisfied, in no less a degree than his craving for food, drink, or the companionship of others. To satisfy this demand of conscience there must correspondingly exist in society both moral and religious interests. And upon them society must be based and unified, just as in the individual nature his array of affections meet within the unifying nature of conscience. In other words I have endeavored to see society as the individual writ large.

The emphasis, within Butler's social philosophy, on the economic, political, moral, and religious elements, I feel sure, he would hold to be a necessary and universal feature of human society. Likewise, he would undoubtedly grant to the religious and moral institutions a higher place than he would to the economic; higher in the sense of their being a later development for which the others prepare the way. Asked to choose between them, he could not; for man's livelihood and the means of earning it are biologically essential. But once they have been established their sole meaning consists in the furtherance of man's other institutions within which man's nature becomes satisfied, for these allow, as the economic institutions do not, the progressive fulfilment of his moral nature.

Admitting within society itself a gradation of institutions, some of which are admittedly higher than others, Butler would also have to grant that state functionaries hold a more exalted rank than civilians, or ministers of religion than lay folk; and this is what we discover. Society is hierarchically disposed, and manifests in its make-up ranks and orders that are superior to others. As a consequence the individuals of society fall more or less into their appointed places; class interests are preserved intact and perpetuated. Their element of good consists in their being neatly demarcated from other classes. Thus, classes and ranks of varying degrees of worth, Butler would hold to be essential features of society, although not precisely in the sense in which his illustrations are given.

Such are some of the main points of Butler's social philosophy that I have tried to develop in my fourfold treament. None of them are explicitly stated by Butler as topics with which he was directly concerned. All of his philosophical views of society, as here recounted, have been constructed out of sermons whose interests were largely practical, dealing with particular concrete problems. Hidden in the background of his public addresses, they require a painstaking search guided by a degree of conjecture, to be crystallized in the form in which I have presented them here.

ORIGINS OF SOCIETY

Man cannot live outside of society if he is to achieve the fullest expression of his nature. Supposing that he could exist outside of an ordered society, we must grant that he must have run wild (Vol. II, p. 305), and that he was the committer of fraud and violence. There can be in the uncivil state of nature no knowledge of order or security, and no insight into the realm of divine things. For their mutual protection, and for the assurance of peace and security men united, and in this way brought about the conditions of their preservation and the possibilities of their virtuous self-expression.

We cannot believe that this uniting of men into society was a conscious agreement or a compact made with a full sense of responsibility. The gradual formation of society as well as its earlier growth must have been largely an unconscious affair, being the objective expression of man's instinct for companionship. But the final reasons for the uniting of men into society were teleological: namely to prepare for the emergence of his moral sense, and to allow for the conditions under which it could express itself.

The emergence of society is clearly a function of human individuals; it appears as a result of their mutual needs and wants. To believe that it arose through any other agency is incredible. If we view society as an agency for human companionship, we can see this point more clearly. The occasions offered us there for the expression of companionship could not take place were it not for the previous bent and bias of our nature (Vol. II, p. 38). This previous bent and bias is instanced in innumerable ways, none of which is consciously planned, although they may later be consciously directed.

To view society from the point of its goal, we can see that its being an instrument of morality was implied in man's more primitive nature; it is not to say that man was conscious of it in the earlier days of herding, or that he had the least inkling of it. We must presuppose the existence within his nature of some sort of entelechy prearranged in such a way as to bring about this higher end of society. We must believe in the receptivity of external nature to accept its outward expressions; and furthermore in some harmonious prearrangement between man's inner frame and the external condition and circumstances of life in which he is placed (Vol. II, p. 92). In other words we are driven to accept the existence of final causes throughout, applied by the infinite wisdom of God (*ibid.*, cp. also *Analogy*, p. 53). We must likewise believe that man's nature was so contrived and so fashioned that it carries out the original intention of that design (Cp. *Analogy*, Ch. II, esp. pp. 42, 43, 44, 45) without any direct intervention from God, or conscious knowledge of its purpose on the part of man. The final cause of there being a society is God's will, the reason of there being a society is to allow for the moral expression of man's nature. But the *immediate causes* of the existence of society are to be found within man's nature of which it is an outgrowth, an objective counterpart.

We instinctively feel for our fellow creatures at large, but more particularly for those with whom we come into close and constant contact. For those who live in the same neighborhood, we form attachments that last us all our lives, and often of a degree of strength that is out of all proportion to the nature of the persons; and that cannot be explained by the division or district the boundaries of which are artificial. The feelings of one man become the feelings of another. Disgraces of one become the shame of another, whereas honor and prosperity become common joys. The bonds of society are to be found in the unconscious depths of human nature. As Butler tells us: "Men are so much one body, that in a peculiar manner they feel for each other, shame, sudden danger, resentment, honour, prosperity, distress; one or another, or all of these, from the social nature in general, from benevolence, upon the occasion of natural relation, acquaintance, protection, dependence; each of these being distinct cements of society" (Vol. II, p. 39).

We cannot dismiss the fact of society as illusory or as unimportant, as an external arrangement, an artificial supervention, or a tyrannical imposition made by those in power. It is based upon no external ties which men can sever and still retain the essence of their nature, for to deny society is to cut from our nature those particular propensions whose nature it is to carry us over into these relationships. To consider ourselves as single or independent "is the same absurdity, as to suppose a hand, or any part to have no natural respect to any other, or to the whole body" (*ibid.*). And neither is the fact of society unimportant; for, being implicit within the nature of man, society is the way man must travel if he is to achieve eternal salvation; it furnishes to man the scope for the exercise of his conscience, and the materials that make for the strengthening of the moral life.

Society is the direct outgrowth of man's nature and assuredly would not be, were there no men. It is an effect of human forces, working collectively and over a long period of time; transmitting to posterity the results of earlier efforts. But we must be on our guard against saying that it is *merely* an effect; that its reality is none other than the nature from which it springs. Once we admit its existence, no matter what its cause is, society is seen to have a nature of its own, and laws of its own being. This nature and these laws, while in the final scheme of things they are not at variance with man's nature as ideally implied, are none the less not the same as his individual and finite nature, to which they may appear as alien and externally imposing.

To say that man is organic to society does not make sufficiently clear to us the positions and classes within society that men occupy. Man does not owe to society at large an indiscriminate allegiance irrespective of the position and rank he holds. Man is always a particular man in a specific class of society; to understand this class as necessary is the precondition of many kinds of obligations. In other words: the phenomenon of society manifests its inner nature. It reveals itself as a living organism, with parts internally related, hierarchies of functionaries, and people who through their native vocational adaptability fall into economic ranks. Society has its strata of social color which differentiate the inferior from the superior. To be a participant of one class is to have obligations to another. But since the classes are hierarchically disposed these social relations are not reversible. Once, as I have said, we grant the existence of society, we must grant to it all that it essentially implies. From the standpoint of man, whose aim is to live in accordance with virtue, his task is to learn this social nature, recognize its inexorable law, and adapt himself to it.

What then are the specific inner aspects of society? As society develops, we note within its structure definite internal formations; its differentiation into ranks and classes, within which are to be found individuals of superior and inferior worth. Its expression requires the institution of governments with their hierarchy of officials to enforce its laws and to make manifest that government is nothing but the publication of natural law (Vol. II, p. 305). And then a consciousness of religion is required to point out to the subjects the divine aspect of society; to bring home to them the fact that "civil government is that part of God's government over the world, which he exercises by the instrumentality of men" (*ibid.*). In the complexity of social life arises the need for the lesser institutions of education, the endowment and support of hospitals and other charitable institutions. Such are instances of some of the aspects that society assumes when men become conscious of the multifarious bonds by which they are tied to one another.

To be a member of society is to be a participant in its institutions, and to recognize the position that one holds by necessity. The various classes of which one is a member determine for him the duties he owes. Virtuous behavior is dictated by rank; what is becoming in the attitude of the rich, is unseemly in the attitude of the poor; privileges of the superior class are not to be shared with the lower. In regard to education the poor are not to be trained beyond their class (Vol. II, p. 297), but "in such a manner, as has a tendency to make them good, and useful, and contented, whatever their particular station might be" (Vol. II, p. 297). "Everyone," says Butler, "should conform his behaviour to what his situation in life requires, without which the order of society must be broken in upon" (Vol. II, p. 329).

Society is developed according to a law of its own, working through the nature of man that has given rise to it. Its development is neither haphazard, nor mechanical; neither is it sustained through the arbitrariness of its members to be dissolved at their will. To admit society is to acknowledge a law of its nature, and such a law is transcendent to the particular whims and desires of its members. To recognize society is to recognize the scope of one's moral nature without which one is not completely one's self.

Discernible within the structure of society are the broader outlines of order. A full grown society will manifest its aspect of government backed by authority, and supported by religion, within which are to be found its members that have taken their places in various ranks according to their "natural" abilities. As a consequence we shall always find in any society a disposition of men in terms of superior and inferior classes. Within a mature society we can observe a respect for moral values, that find their source in the invisible government of God of which they are but a fragmentary part.

We shall now proceed to examine more fully and in greater detail the growth of society as instanced particularly in its economic activity. We shall next observe the place and function of government within society. Then we shall discuss its moral aspect, and lastly its religious implications. We shall try to see how each of these aspects represents for Butler the *sine quâ non* of any society, and furthermore how each aspect of society gives rise to duties and obligations that the moral nature of man must increasingly respect to the extent that he becomes conscious of himself and the rank he holds.

These aspects of society too are objective to man in the sense that they represent for him lines of conduct, or intimations of law that he must conform to. The nature of society, it will be seen, will furnish one answer to the question of man—what must I do to be moral. Its reply is: Conform to the objective laws of society so that your conduct reflects in each moment this wider scheme of things.

18

ECONOMIC ASPECT OF SOCIETY

MAN is so constructed that he is dependent upon others for the fulfilment of his economic demands (Vol. II, p. 255). In the earliest times the economic unit was the family, in which the greater part of the work was carried on by the servants, and managed by the masters. The duties of the former were numerous. To them were entrusted care of cattle, tillage of the fields, spinning, weaving and manufacture of furniture. The work of the masters was not merely that of an economic nature. With superiority in wealth usually went superiority in authority and understanding. The accumulation of wealth entailed a civic responsibility, so that economic development implied inevitably a leading share in the affairs of the government.

The underlying current of economic development in more recent times has been the same as in former times. The outward expression of the economic activity has taken different forms in modern times, but the guiding law of its growth is continuous and providential. Whatever differences there are are superficial. It is true that the laboring class is no longer under the direct supervision of the masters of households, for expansion in production has been attended by a division of labor that has removed the laboring class from the immediate influence of the wealthy classes who purchase their goods. The many things that were formerly made at home "now pass through a multitude of unknown poor hands successively, and are by them prepared, at a distance, for the use of the rich" (Vol. II, p. 258). Yet the early and fundamental relationship subsists between these two classes today, just the same as if they lived side by side on the one manor.[1]

The work of the laborer is not for himself alone, but also for those who supply him with the economic opportunities. Upon them the laborer is dependent for his opportunities. Although this economic dependence of the poor upon the rich is of early origin, it has not changed with differences in production. Part

[1] "In this state of the world, the relation between the rich and the poor could not but be universally seen and acknowledged. Now indeed it is less in sight, by means of artificial methods of carrying on business, but yet are not blamable. But the relation still subsists, and the obligations arising out of it . . ." (Vol. II, p. 258).

of the laborer's work is to supply the rich with the necessities or
luxuries of life, and it is owing to their demands for these that
he is enabled to rely upon them in turn for those goods of life
that he cannot get for himself. The seamen and manufacturers
of more recent times are an instance at hand; they are employed
in the immediate business of the rich. Butler tells us that "they
are servants of merchants, and other principal traders; as much
your servants as if they lived under your roof: though by their
not doing so, the relation is less in sight. . . . They are indeed
servants of the public; and so are all industrious poor people as
well as they" (Vol. II, p. 330).

We do not know how the rich achieved ascendancy. We must
accept their superior status in society as a fact. We must recognize that they control, and that furthermore it is their right to
rule over the poor. As he tells us: "And this their general intercourse, (i.e., of rich and poor,) with the superiority on one
hand, and dependence on the other, are in no sort accidental,
but arise necessarily from a settled providential disposition of
things, for their common good" (Vol. II, p. 255; cp. also pp.
257, 258, 259, 267, 281). We shall now confine our attention to
some of the social outcomes of this economic order. In terms of
it we can account for the growth of wealth and the formation of
classes.

GROWTH OF WEALTH

The immediate purpose of the economic unit is provision for
man's ordinary wants. The production of these necessary goods
constitutes its first stage. These wants are soon satisfied, for
man is so constituted that in a short time he produces more
goods than he has a direct need of.

After the distribution and exchange of goods have satisfied
the fundamental wants of all, production enters into its second
stage of activity, i.e., into the manufacture and output of superfluous goods. Thus arose the opportunity for the amassing of
riches. This amassing is the direct outgrowth of man's labor and
should be looked upon as a reward for his diligence, frugality
and prudent management. "Riches," according to Butler, "then
were first bestowed upon the world, as they are still continued
in it, by the blessing of God upon the industry of men, in the
use of their understanding and strength" (Vol. II, p. 252).
But just as some men are so fortunate as to accumulate more

than they can use, others are unfortunate enough to be in want of them. This latter class becomes dependent upon the former, to whom it contributes economically through its labor.

Wealth begins after the necessities of life are supplied. The satisfaction of one's bodily needs gives rise to a host of secondary wants. These latter consist largely in the love of the ornamental, and the desire for entertainment; they arise to gratify the imagination and the senses of men. Time and labor are now given over to the manufacture of these superfluous articles until the greater part of man's work is concerned with their output. To supply one with the necessities of mere subsistence would require far fewer hands than are at present engaged in the production of luxuries. Had production remained at this second stage of economic activity, a limit would soon have been set to commerce and trade, for these secondary wants would have been satiated. Man would soon be content with the accumulation of luxuries, and reach a level when more of the same luxuries would have been useless for him. Wealth of this kind would tend to become concentrated in the hands of the few. But just as sounds in language have been substituted for thoughts, so in economic activity money was substituted for real natural riches. And money had this advantage, that it was more portable than specific goods and more lasting in value. Thus the third stage of economic development was entered upon, with the consequence that this new type of riches had greater area over which to circulate, and many more hands to pass through. It now became the tendency of wealth to extend to more people.

To be carried over from the satisfaction of bodily wants to the amassing of wealth is a natural economic development. But immoderate desire and inordinate production lead to the perversion of the natural trend, bringing with it evil consequences. Luxury insensibly makes its inroad, it makes for misery and impoverishment in the lower classes as well as for the growth of covetousness in the upper. Unless the wealthy are constantly on their guard their possession of riches is apt to be their moral ruin, leading to the neglect of those who serve them. The third stage of the economic activity wherein money is substituted for goods likewise tends to become a perversion. In its abnormal expression it gives greater scope and encouragement to temptation and covetousness than ever before. To prevent this abnormal turn it is necessary for the rich to be alert, liberal to the necessitous, and abstemious to themselves.

FORMATION OF CLASSES

In the course of normal economic growth arises a variety of classes, each of which has its specific type of obligation to the other.[2] In the earliest stages of man's economic life, when production and distribution were carried on solely in the family, there existed only two distinct classes: the servant and the master. In the intimacy of their interrelation there was no poverty and no neglect. "The obvious humanity, which everyone feels, must have induced them to be kind to all whom they found under their roof, in sickness and old age" (Vol. II, p. 258). With the division of labor the simplicity of this economic system ceased. New classes were formed as commerce became extended, the family unity broke up, but the fundamental economic relation of master and servant continued as an underlying principle. Owing to this separation of personalities the moral tie of responsibility was lost sight of. With the complexities that arose in the means of production, there grew up a poor laboring class and a wealthy capitalist class, until in modern times society had its three classes of people instead of the former two classes; namely the rich, the middle class and the poor. Together they form one natural society. The middle class which emerged from this economic development brought with it felicitous virtues of its own; its members "are in good measure, free from the vices of the highest and lowest part of mankind" (Vol. II, p. 254).

We shall now view still further the natural conditions of these classes and the stated relationships they bear to each other. After we make clear to ourselves the relative positions of each we can proceed to pronounce upon the mutual duties and obligations of their members.[3]

[2] I have ascribed to economic activity the cause of the demarcation of classes; to what extent economic activity has made these classes Butler does not say. It is better to assume that economic activity brings out the vocational ability as well as the social status of man, rather than to believe that they are the direct outcome of the economic way of living, for Butler's general point of view favors the latter more than the former.

[3] The interest of the preacher is exhibited more in the direction of reform than of commendation of what is good. Hence in what follows the status of the middle class is largely neglected. They afford no difficult problems as do the higher and the lower classes, both of which according to Butler are deficient in the moral duties.

We have maintained that the growth of classes is a natural one.[4] The moral ties which bind these classes together are natural ones. To sustain the mutual interdependence of these classes requires that the individuals observe their relative values, by fostering in their own nature the characteristic of the class in which they find themselves. But the rich are the greatest offenders in their absence of conscious regard for the poor; the poor, being the necessitous, can make demands upon them.

Both rich and poor meet upon a footing of great inequality (Vol. II, p. 255).[5] The mental and material deficiencies of the lower classes lead them to repose simple confidence in their superiors. As Butler says: "Their opinions of persons and things they take upon trust. Their behaviour has very little in it original or of home-growth; very little which may not be traced up to the influence of others, and less which is not capable of being changed by such influence" (Vol. II, p. 256). "Accordingly Providence has made provision for this case of the poor: not, only by forming their minds peculiarly apt to be influenced by their superiors, and giving those superiors abilities to direct and relieve them; but also by putting the latter under the care and protection of the former: for this is plainly done, by means of that intercourse of various kinds between them, which, in the natural course of things, is unavoidably necessary" (Vol. II, p. 257).

A great trust falls consequently upon the shoulders of the rich. This obligation is of two sorts. First, there is the obligation that follows from the economic condition itself. Butler tells us that "the rich then are charged, by natural providence, as much as by revealed appointment, with the care of the poor: not to maintain them idle; which, were it possible they could be so maintained, would produce greater mischiefs than those

[4] In calling it natural Butler has in mind that the internal structure of society has been arranged for by God; and that his intentions are visibly instanced in its workings (Vol. II, p. 255). As Butler tells us: "In short, he who has distributed men into these different ranks, and at the same time united them into a society, in such sort as men are united, has, by this constitution of things, formally put the poor under the superintendency and patronage of the rich" (Vol. II, p. 258), and later on in his third Public Sermon, Butler speaks of "subordinations in life being a providential appointment of things."

[5] The word "inequality" is inadvisedly used here, for such inequality is a natural one, and what is natural should not be spoken of as unequal. Butler probably means that viewing the poor from the standpoint of the rich, the former are seen to be less fortunate, and more dependent; less sufficient and more reliant upon those who can supply.

which charity is to prevent; but to take care, that they maintain themselves by their labors, or in case they cannot, then to relieve them; to restrain their vices, and form their minds to virtue and religion. This is a trust, yet it is not a burden, but a privilege, annexed to riches" (Vol. II, pp. 258-9).

Secondly, there are the obligations of a more spiritual kind, which are more important than the first. The position of the rich has put them into a state of unusual influence. With a possession of riches goes a sense of superiority. Whether we admit or not that this superiority is a natural consequence of wealth, it is inevitably bound up with it. The wealth of those in power may not have been brought about by their superior wisdom; on the contrary they may possess only a paucity of native understanding, but none the less in their possession of money the wealthy classes have opportunities for improvement, and may command information that others do not have (Vol. II, p. 256). Their position in society is such that they influence the lower classes as a matter of course. Their thoughts and actions set the tone of good behavior, becoming for their inferiors, exemplars for them to follow. The rich should "instil instruction, and recommend it in a peculiar manner by their example, and enforce it still further with favour and discouragement of various kinds. And experience shows, that they do direct and change the course of the world as they please. Not only the civil welfare, but the morals and religion of their fellow-creatures, greatly depend upon them; much more indeed than they would, if the common people were not greatly wanting to their duty" (Vol. II, p. 256). Thus the wealthy have it in their power to instruct the poor in morals and in religion (Vol. II, p. 258); and the mere possession of this power makes it incumbent upon them to use it correctly.

Still more important than verbal instruction in morals and religion is the ability of the rich to impart to the poor a sense of virtuous life by conducting themselves as virtuous beings. The poor classes turn to the upper classes for guidance in their affairs of conduct. "If, upon their coming abroad into the world, they find the principles of virtue and religion recommended by the example of their superiors, and vice and irreligion really discountenanced, this will confirm them in the good principles in which they have been brought up, and give the best ground to hope they will never depart from them" (Vol. II, p. 266).

In the normal course of wealth accumulation luxury insensibly makes its inroads, bringing with it a train of evil consequences within their ranks (Vol. II, p. 259). Among the more grave is the prevalence of irreligion (Vol. II, p. 248; cp. also p. 295), covetousness and debauchery (Vol. II, p. 259). Until these vices and many others disappear from the ranks of the rich, there can be little hope for the reform of the lower classes (Vol. II, p. 254). Yet every man's behavior is his own concern; the poor as well as the rich must account for their own deeds (Vol. II, p. 260). The poor cannot offer as sole explanation for their vices the fact that they have had bad examples set them, but still they are partly justified in this. The rich have had the benefits of education, and their failure to set a good example to the poor may be reckoned as worse than the failure of the poor to follow what they know to be right. Speaking of the important obligations that arise from the superior fortune of the superior classes, Butler informs us that "the fewer of them he neglects, and the less mischief he does, the less share of the vices and miseries of his inferiors will lie at his door; the less will be his guilt and punishment" (Vol. II, p. 259).

19

POLITICAL ASPECT OF SOCIETY

OUR previous chapter brought out the fact that no man is sufficient unto himself. There has always been the tendency for men to unite within a society, and this tendency was first instanced in the economic urge they had, to preserve their life and to provide materially for its continuance. The conditions of society are traceable to a self, but once society is established it affords to the self the opportunity for it better to express its nature. The earliest form of society was economic, but discernible within its structure was the semblance of order or government. This constitutes its political aspect, and it will be our purpose in the present chapter to present Butler's views concerning it.

Men cannot live out of society, nor can they live within society without government (Vol. II, p. 282). In earlier times the political unit was the family. "The instruction of these large families, and the oversight of their morals and religion, plainly belonged to the heads of them" (Vol. II, p. 258). The complexities of economic life changed the outward expression from the family as the center of production and consumption to the impersonal arrangement wherein the producer and consumer are separated by great distances from each other. A corresponding change was necessarily brought about in the political unit, but like the economic arrangement the political change was a superficial one; for the underlying purpose of the political system remained at one with itself.

What is the underlying purpose of the political system? Does it consist solely in the orderly arrangement of the economic life; is its function one that is dedicated only to the advancement of man's economic relationship, the adjustment of his ways and hours of employment? The existence of government is in the long run a moral and religious one. Government must represent, if it is true to its nature, the arrangement of means and conditions whereby man is free to express himself as nature intended he should. On one hand it exists as the *sine quâ non* of man's moral life (*Analogy*, p. 64); on the other hand it represents in its structural nature the manifestation of its inner law that man must respect and conform himself to if he is to express his nature most truly. "Civil government," says Butler, "has been instituted over the world, both by the light of nature and by revelation, to instruct men in the duties of fidelity, justice, and regard to common good, and enforce the practice of these virtues, without which there could have been no peace or quiet among mankind; and to preserve, in different ways a sense of religion as well as virtue, and of God's authority over us" (Vol. II, p. 305).

To view the function of government solely from the standpoint of its authority would make it appear as a meaningless tyranny, exerting its authority by reason of its superior power to enforce what it believes to be right. Only when viewed from the standpoint of the citizen does the purpose of government become more intelligible, and its impositions less harsh and less arbitrary. The destiny of man is best expressed in the words of the apostle (*sic*) to lead a quiet and peaceable life in all godliness and honesty, to which Butler further adds, "*a quiet and peaceable life*, by way of distinction, surely, from eager, tumultuary pursuits in our private capacity, as well as in opposition both to our making insurrections in the state, and to our suffering oppression from it. . . . In aid to this general appointment of Providence, civil government has been instituted over the world" (Vol. II, p. 304). Of these two views of government Butler is directly concerned with the first rather than the second. He does not deny the importance of the second view, but being more interested in duties and obligations, he finds that to treat the nature of government from the first viewpoint is more useful to his purposes.

Our discussion of the state will be arranged for the sake of convenience under the following headings: 1, its nature and 2, the duties implied in such an arrangement. Under 1, we shall consider (a) the organization of the state, (b) its monistic tendency, (c) its expression through a system of laws, (d) its aspect of legal and religious equality, (e) the meaning of liberty and freedom within the state, (f) the nature and place of punishment within the state, and (g) the sanction of political obligation.

NATURE OF THE STATE

State Organization. The existence of government requires some sort of administration. Butler does not make clear to us in the course of his writings the precise nature of governmental management, nor the relative position of the officials. His various allusions in the *Analogy* when speaking of the nature of God as being analogous to that of officials on earth would indicate that he held some sort of hierarchy of officialdom, with a prince or king at the head as being divinely appointed. We find Butler saying in the *Analogy*, when speaking of the meaning that we can attach to the government of God: "It implies government of the very same kind with that, which a master exercises over his servants, or a civil magistrate over his subjects" (Vol. I, p. 54; cp. also p. 337). Throughout his Public Sermons there is the insistence upon class, rank, inferior and superior people, and the duties that are owed by the lower ranks to the higher.[1]

Likewise in the duties of men we are told that the subjects of any government should respect its subordinations and ranks; that it is in the nature of their obligations to honor in their behavior all the magistrates and people in authority. We obtain a sense of their proportionate ranks when we consider the immorality of disrespect and vilification towards their persons. According to Butler the degree of immorality "increases in proportion to the integrity and superior rank of the persons thus treated" (Vol. II, p. 284). And he goes on to say: "It is therefore in the highest degree immoral, when it extends to the supreme authority in the person of a prince . . ." (*ibid.*).

Construing these statements together with many others of their kind (*Vide*, e.g., Vol. II, pp. 271, 279, 280), we are left to fashion a conception of civil government under the will and design of God (Vol. II, p. 305), who works through the instrumentality of men to whom he has delegated degrees of authority. In basing the justification of government upon the sanction of God, Butler is a proponent and defender of the divine right of kings. There is no doubt in his mind that the British government illustrates this to the best degree. He is sensible that it is in no degree perfect (Vol. II, p. 278), but goes on to say that "we are certainly a freer nation than any other we have an account of; and as free, it seems, as the very nature of government will permit. . . . In some other countries the upper part of the world

---

[1] *Vide* Vol. II, pp. 255, 257, 258, 259, 267. The nearest that Butler comes to a definite description of civil constitution is in his third ethical sermon when he indirectly refers to it in order to illustrate the meaning of system or a natural constitution. He says there that "the idea of a civil constitution implies in it united strength, various subordinations, under one direction, that of supreme authority; the different strength of each particular member of the society not coming into the idea; whereas, if you leave out the subordination, the union, and the one direction, you destroy and lose it" (Vol. II, p. 57).

is free, but in Great Britain the whole body of people is free"
(Vol. II, p. 307).

Monistic Tendency of Government. We may ask without
prejudice whether Butler selects for his illustration the present
form of the British government because it approximates to what
he conceives to be the ideal of government. In all fairness to his
intentions it appears that Butler is not desirous either to defend
the actual or praise without criticism what falls immediately
under his eye. He sees in the workings of the British constitution
the approximation to an ideal; in his professed belief in the
ideal, i.e., of virtue, he is favorable to whatever concretely expresses it.

A point that is of more immediate concern to our issue is the
external appearance or machinery of government. Rulers, we
are told, are directly responsible to God from whom they derive
their authority; but are they beholden to each other? In other
words: is the tendency of God's will on earth, as expressed in
civil government, monistic or pluralistic? Are virtues exclusively
nationalistic, or in their alleged purity do they transcend nationalistic limits? We have maintained as our thesis that virtue
works through the nature of society and man, and partakes of
the nature of the social structure. In this sense virtue is not
transcendent to society or government in the sense of being
indifferent to their forms. Within any actual government there
is the constraining influence of the social medium to dictate to
its subjects the form or way in which the virtue is to be expressed, as for instance it is just for inferiors to submit; i.e.,
justice entails resignation and submissiveness; but it is likewise
incumbent on superiors to assist the inferiors in their rank of
servitude.

All this can be admitted, but still virtue tends to expand,
and to unite the pluralities of similar ranks under the dominion
of the highest of civil authorities. Still working through the
forms of government, virtue would tend to bring about their
coalescence, still preserving the internal divisions of rank with
their consequent obligations of respect and deference. "In such
a state . . . men of the greatest capacity would of course, all
along, have the chief direction of their affairs willingly yielded
to them. . . . Each of these would have the part assigned to
him, to which his genius was peculiarly adapted: and others,
who had not any distinguished genius, would be safe, and think

themselves very happy by being under the protection and guidance of those who had . . ." (*Analogy*, pp. 72, 73).

As the state grew it would undoubtedly retain its inner divisions. But existing under the law of virtue it would grow beyond its immediate boundaries. "It would plainly be superior to all others, and the world must gradually come under its empire: not by means of lawless violence; but partly by what must be allowed to be just conquest; and partly by other kingdoms submitting themselves voluntarily to it, throughout a course of ages, and claiming its protection, one after another, in successive exigencies. The head of it would be an universal monarch, in another sense than any mortal has yet been; and the eastern style would be literally applicable to him, that *all people, nations, and languages should serve* him" (*Analogy*, p. 73). The ideal government would be a world state under the virtuous influence of Christian ideals.

Legislative Aspect of Government. No organized society can express itself except through the medium of laws the fundamental purpose of which is to make known the moral character upon which the state rests, and to make clear that the freedom of the individual citizen is to be found in conformance to them. Besides this, the state should aim at bringing about the conditions conducive to man's moral life, punishing those who interfere with others or who fail to achieve virtue for themselves. In fulfilment of this purpose laws must define what is right and wrong, so that individual actions can be evaluated. But these laws must be general ones (Vol. II, p. 282). They cannot provide for every possible case or situation; nor can they always guarantee that all virtuous actions are exactly defined and legally protected. Law makers must recognize that there will arise innumerable opportunities for evasion.

Imperfections in governmental machinery must be expected, as in the delays that occur in the attempts to redress justice. These delays arise chiefly out of the fact that the civil government can allow of no redress except through legal means. Individual interference cannot be encouraged. "Perfection of justice," we are told, "cannot in any sort take place in this world, even under the very best governments; yet under the worst, men have been enabled to lead much more quiet and peaceable lives, as well as attend to and keep up a sense of religion much more, than they could possibly have done without any government at all" (Vol. II, p. 306).

Legal and Civil Equality. Civil government is God's government on earth, and it constitutes his will. We can expect to find within its prescriptions neither favoritism nor partiality. "I would observe," Butler says, "that our laws and whole constitution, civil and ecclesiastical, go more upon supposition of an equality amongst mankind, than the constitution and laws of other countries. . . . It is, I suppose, acknowledged, that they have greater liberty here, than they have anywhere else in the world" (Vol. II, p. 265). The sense in which all men are equal is that "every man is equally under the protection of the laws; may have equal justice against the most rich and powerful; and securely enjoy all the common blessings of life, with which the industry of his ancestors, or his own, has furnished him" (Vol. II, p. 307).

To admit the existence of equality within the state does not mean the disavowment of rank. Equality consists in the respect that the higher classes have for the lower classes; it means essentially the trust with which they accept their appointed commission. Stated from the standpoint of legislation it means "equal laws, by which the great are disabled from oppressing those below them" (Vol. II, p. 314). The equality of the poor and rich is not to be confused with an equality of position, rank, social standing or wealth. As recognized by the law it means that each person has the right to claim protection for himself and for the station of life in which he finds himself. The right for the poor is the freedom to continue in that walk of life without oppression from those in power. This is what the law according to Butler is ready to provide.

Besides the existence of just laws which allow to rich and poor alike the claims of each according to his nature and rank (without which the order of society must be broken in upon: p. 329), there are the religious privileges that likewise extend to all classes equally. All classes can benefit from the gifts of a pure reformed church, preserved by God through infinite dangers (Vol. II, p. 313). There is the freedom to accept its teachings, without the consequence of persecution, if one cares to live like a Christian, or to suffer dishonor if one fails to live in decency.[2]

2 Butler resents the claim that Catholicism makes to absolute authority in religion (Vol. II, p. 309), for in this role he sees the "open usurpation of all

Liberty and Freedom Within the State. What meaning can we give to the concept of liberty and its place in any governmental scheme? Absolute freedom consists in the entire coincidence of our wills with the will of God in the most literal and proper sense (Vol. II, p. 270). Hence liberty is a religious conception. But in a civil government it can only mean the submission of one's self to those in authority; and respect and obedience to their commands as representing the expressed will of God. To be free consists in the coincidence of ones will with the laws of one's country. It is not to exercise our humors and passions (Vol. II, p. 314), but to restrain ourselves in conformance to the fiat of civil authority.[3]

Butler refuses to believe in the right of rebellion or revolution. No government is perfect, he admits, but the "destruction of a free constitution of government, though men see or fancy many defects in it, and whatever they design or pretend, ought not to be thought of without horror" (Vol. II, p. 277). But this does not say that no redress is possible. Those in office are not infallible, but in virtue of their rank their position is necessarily authoritative. As actual men, officials make mistakes and many procrastinate unconscionably. All of this can be corrected and should be, but peacefully and gradually so as not to endanger the unity of the civil structure (Vol. II, p. 278).

Nowhere does Butler inform us of the means or persons whereby the proposed reforms are to be brought about. But the spirit of his sermons would point to the enlightened wisdom of the upper classes, i.e., the rich whose share in governmental affairs is a natural concomitant of their wealth. Those who are

human and divine authority" (*ibid.*). Besides this claim, it enforces belief of its tenets by the use of force instead of reasonable argument. Butler's reference here is to make clear the absence of enforced authority in the Church of England where the freedom to accept and believe is based on rational grounds. "Our religious establishment disclaims all principles of this kind, and desires not to keep persons in its communion, or gain proselytes to it, by any other methods than the Christian ones of argument and conviction" (Vol. II, p. 311).

[3] In contrast to his conception of freedom Butler draws a picture of licentiousness—which for him stands for the perversion of freedom. Licentiousness arises from an excess of liberty (Vol. II, p. 279), as when one claims for himself more than he is entitled to. This soon leads to the breakdown of civil constitution and individual morale. The long-aged customs that have grown up in human society are swept aside, with the result that human beings sink insensibly into a precivilized state (Vol. II, p. 278). The inevitable outcome of licentiousness is a deep-seated distrust in their minds of authority of all kinds, governmental and religious (Vol. II, p. 281)—leading to profligacy and fanaticism (*ibid.*, cp. also pp. 306-7; 313).

actually engaged in the work of the government should introduce
the needed measures of reform.[4]

Punishment by the State. Civil government has been instituted not only in the interest of virtue but likewise in its enforcement (Vol. II, p. 305). Some system of rewards and punishments
is needed. To punish for ill-doing is more important for society
than to reward individuals for doing well. Presumably doing well
is its own reward, but the punishment for vicious acts has the
protection of society in mind. Civil government is more competent too in ferreting out the evil and punishing it than it is in
judging what is good. Yet much escapes its surveillance, but
whatever fails to come directly under its authority shall meet
its reckoning in time to come, for *"God shall bring every work
into judgment, with every secret thing, whether it be good, or
whether it be evil"* (Vol. II, p. 285).

How should punishment be exacted, and on what principle
should it work? The purpose of punishment is to indicate that
civil and moral law has been violated; it should aim at preventing
these future violations.

Thus, civil punishment should preserve society and advance
it towards a more ideal state. In so doing it seeks to make
possible the conditions whereby man can win his greatest self-
expression, by living morally. In its exercise of punishment the
government must be viewed as the guardian of morality (Vol.
II, p. 285).

But the state is limited in its scope of function; also in what
it can punish for. Its laws are both moral and utilitarian. The
moral laws relate to the preservation of the state, or the happiness of the people within it. Its interests are largely benevolent;
hence individuals "are often punished, and sometimes rewarded
. . . in view of their being mischievous, or eminently beneficial
to society" (Vol. I, p. 59). There lies outside the control of

---

4 *Vide* Vol. II, p. 256: "In all governments, particularly in our own, a good
share of civil authority accompanies them." Butler's Sermons delivered on
Public Occasions are addressed without a doubt to an influential audience, for
his pleas are mainly on behalf of what is due to the inferior and the poor; his
admonitions are addressed to the rich, to the effect that an exemplary behaviour
on their part would have its salutary consequences on the lower classes. Also in
the two public sermons in which reform is made an explicit note, his audience
in both instances is the House of Lords (Vol. II, p. 267. Cp. also SSII, p. 256).
Speaking of the rich, he says: "And experience shows, that they do direct and
change the course of the world as they please."

the state an entire field of moral activity that belongs to the individual privately.[5]

But even in bringing a malefactor to justice the state is insensibly influenced by his moral state, i.e., his motives, his degree of purposive intention in doing what he did; it holds the individual less responsible if he is morally without vicious intention. As Butler says: "That, though civil government be supposed to take cognizance of actions in no other view than as prejudicial to society, without respect to the immorality of them; yet as such actions are immoral, so the sense which men have of the immorality of them, very greatly contributes, in different ways, to bring offenders to justice, and that entire absence of all crime and guilt in the moral sense, when plainly appearing, will almost of course procure, and circumstances of aggravated guilt prevent, a remission of the penalties annexed to civil crimes, in many cases though by no means in all" (Vol. I, p. 63).

Punishment varies from capital to less drastic forms. The principle envolved is the same: that one's duty to society is a greater obligation than his duty to another single individual. Capital punishment is justifiable, says Butler in his Sermon on the Forgiveness of Injuries, because the life of the criminal "is inconsistent with the quiet and happiness of the world: that is, a general and more enlarged obligation necessarily destroys a particular and more confined one of the same kind, inconsistent with it" (Vol. II, p. 134). Less drastic forms of punishment instance the same principle. The pain that society inflicts serves to remind us that the moral order of society must be protected and preserved.

How should punishment be administered? This question must bear in mind that man should conform to the demands and requirements of society. If it achieves this result the punishment is wisely administered. By creating the fear of punishment in the mind of the potential criminal, it sets up a defense against the committing of crime. Many individuals will refrain from ill-doing for fear of detection and the consequences for them if caught. If the individual reflects upon the reasons why he has been punished, he may be won over to the dislike of falsehood, injustice and cruelty, seeing in these vices the ultimate damage to

---

[5] *Vide* Vol. II, p. 260: "But still it is to be remembered, that every man's behaviour is his own concern, for every one must give account of his own works."

human nature. Punishment tends to bring about a warning to the innocent by way of example (Vol. II, p. 264).

Butler considers some of the specific ways in which such punishment is best brought about. He says: "And whether it be not a thing practicable, and what would contribute somewhat towards it, to exclude utterly all sorts of revel-mirth from places where offenders are confined, to separate the young from the old, and force them both, in solitude, with labour and low diet, to make the experiment, how far their natural strength of mind can support them under guilt and shame and poverty; this may deserve consideration. Then again, some religious instruction particularly adapted to their condition would as properly accompany those punishments which are intended to reform, as it does capital ones" (Vol. II, p. 264).

Basis of Political Obligation. All government is founded upon God. And this is ultimately the basis of its authority. Government can be spoken of as the orderly direction of society under the self-conscious wisdom of its rulers. As representing the voice of society the rulers stand invested with the authority of its expression. Through them society arises to its own self-consciousness. To obey the rulers is to pay one's deference to society. Is then the basis of society or the rulers merely an ultimate, or can one seek further for the rational basis of obedience? Why should the subjects obey the rulers? This means: why should an individual conform to society? Two answers can be offered here: (1) that in obeying society one is obeying his ideal self, i.e., his nature as implying its ultimate perfection; (2) that obedience to society is subjection to the will of God. These are not contrary, both of them are implied in Butler's writings.

As to (1), we have seen that society arises *immediately* from man's system of impulses, at first unconsciously realized, and then consciously organized and redirected. But man, from whose nature society proceeds, is himself not ultimate, but the handiwork of God. Hence society, arising through man's nature, can be viewed as an expression in a later stage of a divine history in which both it and man are fragmentary parts. The truer explanation of society is to be found in ordination by God. It is a phenomenon arranged for by him and arising through the instrumentality of man. Decreed to be what it is in the divine scheme of things, it exhibits the rationality of its ultimate origin in the expression of its laws. Obedience to these laws means a conformance to the demands that God makes through a society aiming at its fullest fruition.

Its divine foundation is the reason why subjects are enjoined to respect its magistrates and to obey their laws. "Civil government," Butler says, "is that part of God's government over the world, which he exercises by the instrumentality of men, wherein that which is oppression, injustice, cruelty, as coming from them, is, under his direction, necessary discipline, and just punishment" (Vol. II, p. 305). The relations in which man stands to God make it incumbent upon him to observe God's will and intentions. Loyalty to civil government is loyalty to God's expressed wishes. Obedience to law is obedience to what God commands through the instrumentality of his agents. "*Submit yourselves,*" Butler tells us, "*to every ordinance of man for the Lord's sake: whether it be to the king, as supreme; or unto governors, as unto them that are sent by him*" (Vol. II, p. 271). And further on he repeats the same thought by saying: "this reverence and submission (to civil authorities) will at best be very precarious, if it be not founded upon a sense of authority being God's ordinance, and the subordinations in life of providential appointment of things" (Vol. II, pp. 281; cp. also pp. 225, 285).

Let us briefly sum up the main points we have been emphasizing concerning the political aspect of the state, for then we shall be better prepared to appreciate the duties that follow as a consequence from the place of government in society; and see the necessity of these duties in the moral life of the individual citizens.

Society exists for the expression of man's moral life, but there can be no society without a government under which it is organized. Within the government there exists from the standpoint of its administration a hierarchy of magistrates. These magistrates are so arranged that they point to or terminate in a king or a supreme ruler. But even at this level there is the reference of the government to God (Vol. II, p. 312), so that the whole structure of government is an argued defence for the divine right of kings.

Such a government is none the less a free one because there is manifest within its structure a respect for the personality of the various ranks into which the subjects naturally fall. Both rich and poor are equal before the law in the sense that the

lower classes are not repressed by the upper classes. The freedom seems to consist in the perpetuation of the inferior ranks
into which the subjects are born. The poor are under the super-
intendence and patronage of the rich, and their minds are formed
by providence for the reception of their superior guidance.
Moreover the education of the poor should be of such a nature
as not to put them beyond their class (*Vide*, SS. IV, *in toto*, pp.
286-303, esp. p. 297), but "to make them good, and useful, and
contented, whatever their particular station be" (Vol. II, p. 297).
And when their education is completed, they are to be placed out
into the service of society in those employments in which they
can be most serviceable and "which are most suitable to their
ranks" (Vol. II, p. 302). The laws of the country afford to the
rank and file of the people the privilege and opportunity of
continuing in their station of life, without oppression from those
in authority.

Besides this equality of civil law, we further observed the
benefits of a pure and undefiled religion, free from the super-
stitions of alien religions, and in harmonious accord with the
government. Consequently, there results freedom for the individual to conduct himself in the light of its religious teachings.
These teachings according to Butler persuade them to the profession of religion through a rational conviction (Vol. II, p. 311).

Lastly we noted that the deficiencies of any government could
be repaired by a proper sense of liberty exerted in the interest
of a gradual reform. A conservative attitude was better than one
of radical subversion of government, because destruction undermined all sense of authority, and removed the long standing customs on which man morally depends. *Ad hoc* reformation at
least preserves intact the larger benefits that have been accumu-
lating; whereas the period of restoration that would follow upon
the destruction of a free government rests insecurely upon a
thousand future contingencies (Vol. II, p. 278).

DUTIES IN AN ORGANIZED STATE

We are now prepared to note the character of the obligations
that rigidly follow from the unquestioned acceptance of an order
such as we have summarily outlined above, pointing out the class
aspects that they necessarily assume. Let us first recall that virtue consists in the pursuit of nature. The nature to be followed is
preeminently social. That is, its greater reality lies within an

organized society or community. The community within which it lives is more comprehensive than the actual individual self, for in the first place it is the precondition of the moral life, and secondly it is the sphere within which a plurality of social natures meet and communicate. Presumably the ranks of society spring from the natural differences in the individual natures that compose it. Into a genetic account of society Butler does not enter, but we have had good reason to believe that some such account would have been given had he become more explicit on this point. What we must accept is that once society is acknowledged as a real objective factor in the scheme of the universe, its reality assumes in relation to the constituting individuals a commanding importance.

Presumably traceable to human tendencies and deficiencies, society is at any one time superior to its extant members. Discernible within its nature are laws of its own being that must be respected and fulfilled once we have granted to society its right to exist. Though at first the expression of man's moral nature, it later turns out to be his moral teacher pointing out to him the way he must traverse if he wishes to live virtuously.

Some virtues, namely justice, veracity and regard to common good, appear to belong to society as a whole. Of veracity, Butler says very little. In his Second Dissertation he sees a difficulty involved when man attempts to use it as a guiding rule to life (Vol. I, p. 338), for the interest of men, which is often confined to their particular ranks and employments, makes it impossible for them to understand the intentions of others. Benevolence, which would be the root virtue for the preservation of society, is expressed according to the class within which one finds himself. Hence it will be conceivably different in its specific manifestations. Benevolence in a superior man will be of such a nature as to "make dependence, inferiority, and even servitude easy," with the result that "a good or charitable man of superior rank in wisdom, fortune, authority, is a common blessing to the place he lives in" (Vol. II, p. 186). But as the expression of an inferior individual "this good principle . . . would discover itself in paying respect, gratitude, obedience, as due" (*ibid.*). As to the virtue of justice, we have already noted that in legal matters, at least, it stands for equality of laws "by which the great are disabled from oppressing those below them" (Vol. II, p. 314).

Within society men are engaged in specific pursuits in life

and fall into definite spheres of action. As such, they become members of classes that stand in relationship to each other. Since these classes are natural, the obligations incumbent upon their members are to preserve them intact. There can be few specific obligations within society at least, that are common to all men in virtue of their humanity, but instead there are specific obligations that follow as a result of class participation.

Within the state man finds himself in a particular class of society to which he owes a degree of loyalty and support. His main obligation here is to perpetuate the orders of the society that he finds himself a member of, by according to them obedience and reverence. Definite moral attitudes become his obligations. For instance, the important virtues in inferiors will be gratitude, respect and obedience to those who are above them (Vol. II, p. 186). On the other hand those of superior rank should exhibit kindness to the poor and distressed; they should endeavor to make their dependence, inferiority, and state of servitude easy to bear (Vol. II, p. 186).

The rich should aid the poor by educating them in the principles of religion, and instructing them to be economically self-sufficient (Vol. II, p. 259). When unemployed through no fault of their own, they are to be aided, and their miseries alleviated (Vol. II, pp. 330, 332). When guilty of misdemeanors, the poor are to be morally corrected (Vol. II, p. 263). Since the rich are usually regarded as the leaders of society, whose conduct sets the moral tone for the other members, it behoves them to comport themselves with dignity (Vol. II, pp. 295, 266), to refrain from covetousness, debauchery and other vices (Vol. II, p. 259).

The poor have their class of duties to society as well. Some of the more general would be not to imitate the rich in their vicious ways,—to observe strict economy, and be frugal and diligent.[6] The practice of these latter virtues, which should be observed by the middle classes as well, will make for the preservation of trade and industry, without which no well-organized society is possible. This will make for an excess of riches which can be used for the material benefits of the necessitous (Vol. II, p. 329).

---

[6] Cp. Vol. II, p. 260: "The lower people are very greatly to blame in yielding to any ill influence, particularly following the ill example of their superiors; though these are more to blame in setting them such an example."

Butler also mentions the duties that confront the clergy. These duties are treated at great length in his Durham Charge. As enumerated by him, they vary from the most important, such as the fostering and preserving a sense of religion, to the minor ones, such as repair of buildings. We shall not attempt to present in detail the minutiae of duties that are here in evidence, but shall content ourselves with one quotation.

"Your standing business, and which requires constant attention," says Butler to his clergy in his Durham Charge, "is with the body of the people; to revive in them the spirit of religion, which is so much declining. And it may seem, that whatever reason there be for caution as to entering into an argumentative defence of religion in *common conversation*, yet that it is necessary to do this *from the pulpit*, in order to guard the people against being corrupted, however in some places. But then surely it should be done in a manner as little controversial as possible. For though such as are capable of seeing the force of objections are capable also of seeing the force of the answers which are given to them; yet the truth is, the people will not competently attend to either. But it is easy to see which they will attend to most. And to hear religion treated of as what many deny, and which has much said against it as well as for it; this cannot but have a tendency to give them ill impressions at any time; and seems particularly improper for all persons at a time of devotion; even for such as are arrived at the most settled state of piety: I say at a time of devotion, when we are assembled to yield ourselves up to the full influence of the divine presence, and to call forth into actual exercise every pious affection of heart. For it is to be repeated, that the heart and course of affections may be disturbed when there is no alteration of judgment" (Vol. II, p. 339).

It is needless for us to pursue further the varieties of duties that are incumbent upon the members of society to follow. The general duties that we have enumerated show that Butler had in mind English society as he knew it. We must again remind ourselves here that even for Butler society is in the process of growth. New changes will require us to discover new moral duties. We have no right to believe however that the future will mean a supersession of the old. What mankind has labored to establish as morally good will persist and be recognized as fundamental.

Fundamental moral duties will be reinforced; and besides them new duties will take their place.[7]

[7] Butler has brought man's social duties under no one classification. At times he refers to them in terms of their subjective origin, e.g., as self-love, benevolence, conscience, etc., and at other times he mentions them in terms of their objective status and representation in society. His failure to classify arises largely, I believe from the inordinate difficulty of the task, but more probably from the belief that each individual in society is apprised of his duty, through the witness of his conscience and the knowledge of his position. As he becomes more conscious of his place and position he becomes more apprised of what he should do to maintain himself there as a human individual.

20

MORAL ASPECT OF SOCIETY

SOCIETY is based upon moral ideals; for it enjoins men to live morally (Vol. I, p. 328; Vol. II, pp. 272, 275, 301). Being man's self writ large, it displays the same moral tendencies that are discoverable within his nature, approving or condemning respectively what his enlightened conscience would approve or condemn (Vol. II, pp. 282, 305). Between the exhortations of society and the moral practice of man there exists a mutual give and take. Man's nature is edified by its moral teachings; and on the other hand, society receives man's moral decisions as part of its fabric.

Society may express its moral nature in many ways. Through its fundamental constitutional laws it may make known that it stands for justice, veracity and regard for common good (Vol. I, p. 328); that it forbids treachery, injustice and cruelty (Vol. II, p. 272). In its system of punishments it will enforce the observance of its fundamental laws, and tend to bring the individual into line with its ideal. But that is not all. Quite apart from the state's concern for its laws, there is the social attitude towards morality, which can be expressed in at least two ways. The first is a general unorganized social expression, and the second is through an educational preparation. Let us examine what each stands for.

MORAL EXPRESSION OF SOCIETY

Society exhibits its interest in morality by approving of good deeds, and disapproving of unvirtuous ones. In the course of things a virtuous man will be rewarded, and a vicious man will be shunned and ostracized. If a man is publicly known to be good, favors and good offices will be heaped upon him. Honest and good men will befriend their kind. Upon the patriot will fall applause and rewards; and eminent justice, fidelity and charity will be revered. But if it is known that a man is vicious, all sorts of measures will be taken against him, even death will be inflicted if it is necessary (Vol. I, p. 62).

So strong within society is this deep-seated moral concern that it is necessary for evildoers to disguise their evil intentions,

by first making them appear as good.[1] Even those individuals
who make little headway in their evil doings must profess the
cause of morality in order to make themselves heard.[2]

This moral attitude, which is so evident in society at large,
extends itself to the family. Correction of children takes place
upon the lines of virtue and vice. Children are brought up to
despise falsehood, injustice and ill behavior (Vol. I, p. 63), and
are rewarded for veracity, justice, and right behavior.

Again: if we regard the events of history, we shall see there
that the underlying motives in their larger movements are moral.
Take the case of revolutions. Many of them have been inspired
by individuals who refused to submit any longer to the injustice
and oppression of tyranny. Were their motives utilitarian, they
would not have openly invited the personal inconveniences that
always attend such upheavals; but being moral instead, their
resentment was directed towards the immoral practices of those
in power, disregarding their personal feelings.[3]

Although society approves of virtue and condemns vice, yet
it may be ignorant of what either consists in. Individuals may
have good intentions in their approval of others, and be honest
with themselves, and yet fail to do the right thing. It is important
for the individual to be clear about the nature of virtue, so that
good intentions may coincide with true moral results. How can
this be brought about, other than through an organized effort
to know what is right and what is wrong? To be assured that

1 Vol. II, p. 271; also p. 272: "God has constituted our nature, and the
nature of society, after such a manner, that, generally speaking, men cannot
encourage or support themselves in wickedness upon the foot of there being
no difference between right and wrong, or by a direct avowal of wrong; but by
disguising it, and endeavouring to spread over it some colours of right."

2 Vol. II, p. 275: "The history of all ages and all countries will show, what
has been really going forward over the face of the earth, to be very different
from what has been always pretended; and that virtue has been everywhere
professed much more than it has been any where practised; nor could society,
from the very nature of its constitution, subsist without some general public
profession of it. Thus the fact and appearance which the world has in all times
put on, for the ease and ornament of life, and in pursuit of further ends, is the
justest satire upon what has in all times been carrying on under it; and ill
men are destined, by the condition of their being as social creatures, always to
bear about with them, and, in different degrees, to profess, that law of virtue,
by which they shall finally be judged and condemned."

3 Vol. I, p. 62: "For it is plain, men resent injuries as implying faultiness,
and retaliate, not merely under the notion of having received harm, but of
having received wrong; and they have this resentment in behalf of others, as
well as of themselves."

their moral judgments are correct, individuals must be correctly informed, or be taught to discover moral truths for themselves. Such should be the deeper underlying purpose of education as Butler sees it. We shall now examine the role it should play within society.

EDUCATION IN A MORAL SOCIETY

I have included Butler's treatment of education under the moral aspect of society, largely because he conceives it to be the instrument of moral and religious instruction (Cp. Vol. II, pp. 303, 33). Education is a public institution in the sense that it aims at the good of the individual in so far as he is a member of society; but primarily it aims at preserving society, seeing that it cannot be continued without a respect on the part of the people for its functions and the arrangement of its classes and ranks.

Butler had no well-thought-out scheme of education. His views on this subject, which are confined to his fourth Public Sermon (Vol. II, pp. 286-303), are limited here to the poorer classes of people. Whatever views he had on education for the rich, he does not express, but presumably he held its objects to be the same as for the poor, namely the advancement of religion and morality, and the preservation of society.

The restriction of his explicit attention to the education of the poor was incidental, for the sermon in which his educational views are expressed was preached in the interest of charity schools.[4] He saw that the condition of the poor was distressing, and that they had no means of rising beyond it. The rich on the other hand have every advantage for the improvement of their children; with their wealth, they can send them away to school (Vol. II, p. 298). The poor have no such advantages. They lack

---

[4] Education represents for Butler a moral *training,* i.e., the way in which the poorer people *should go* (Vol. II, pp. 286-7). Butler has mentioned the vices of the age, which he sees to be present in the lower and upper classes (Vol. II, p. 254). But the danger of the lower classes is presumably a greater one. Their unruliness is apt to prove a greater disaster to the society in which they live, for it can upset the established tradition of wealth and influence (Vol. II, p. 329). In pleading for the supported education of the lower classes, Butler had in mind the preservation of society with its ranks and classes (Vol. II, p. 290). Butler does not defend the *status quo* in morality of the upper classes, for he sees too the need for them to reform their ways. But the poor do not possess the means for education, as do the rich; they are apt to become a more dangerous class in their profession of vice than the rich. Their problem hence is one of more pressing importance.

the personal means to pay for the education of their children; neither do they possess any education themselves that they can give them. When the parents of the poor are dissolute in habit there is grave danger for the child, for he is a direct eye and ear witness to all that goes on. There is no opportunity here, as in the case of the rich, to remove him from direct contact with his parents, unless this is provided for by some contributing means (Vol. II, p. 299).

The tendency in children to form habits leads them on to imitate what they observe about them, and to base their own conduct upon what they see and hear without ever submitting this observation to scrutiny or criticism. When their parents are immoral there exists no constructive attempt on their part to overcome their immoral living by inculcating good teachings. In fact, if there is any training at all in homes of this kind, it is more likely to be in the way of crime; the "poor children will have their characters formed to vice, by those whose business it is to restrain them from it. They will be disciplined and trained up to it" (Vol. II, p. 299).

Aim of Educational Training.   Education is a social instrument. Its main purpose is to preserve society along the lines of classes and ranks, for it conceives the perpetuation of these classes and ranks to be natural and good.

In doing this, education endorses society, which it recognizes as a natural phenomenon. It sees that society possesses a determinate nature and structure which is based upon wealth and its influence. Likewise it must recognize the divine sanction of its rulers; the hierarchy of officialdom in its varying degrees of dignity that interprets and executes the law, and finally the masses which contribute through their labor the economic sustenance of the whole. Education will foster a united society composed of rich and poor, in which the superior classes and inferior masses mutually support each other. Class status will be based on birth rather than ability (Vol. II, pp. 256, 293). Classes and their participants will possess obligations that they are bound to discharge. Some duties will be common ones, such as patriotic support; other duties will depend upon the relative position of the classes in society as a whole.[5]

---

[5] *Vide* Butler's Second Sermon on Benevolence, Vol. II, p. 176, *et passim.,* and as another instance, SS. VI, p. 328: "As economy is the duty of all persons, without exception, frugality and diligence are duties which *particularly* belong to the middle as well as lower ranks of men."

Such is the scheme of society that educational training must bear in mind, if it is to be effective. In fostering this social structure, it sees that each member fits individually into his place and class. Education becomes at once a training that is religious, moral and vocational. To make the individual serviceable to society, useful and contented in his particular station and respectful of authority, both human and divine, is the end that education must seek to express.

Fortunately Providence has happily arranged this scheme. It has taken care to fashion the mind of the poor so that they will be receptive to the teachings and charities of the masters; at the same time it has endowed the superior members with the abilities to influence, direct and relieve them. This arrangement indicates that the poor are under the patronage and protection of the rich.

In this general aim, education has a moral tendency: to instil virtue so that it becomes a working principle in one's life. As Butler tells us: "It is endeavouring to form such truths into practical principles in the mind, so as to render them of habitual good influence upon the temper and actions, in all the various occurrences of life. And this is not done by bare instruction; but by that, together with admonishing them frequently as occasion offers; restraining them from what is evil, and exercising them in what is good" (Vol. II, pp. 288-9). In its particular application to the individual, education must aim specifically at putting him in the right frame of mind, and "right habits of living, in every relation and every capacity . . ." (*ibid.*).

Habit Mechanism as an Educational Instrument. To carry out this ideal, education must take the nature of the individual into account. Is he so fashioned that he can respond to this ideal and profit by it? To what aspect of human nature must it make its appeal?

Psychologically viewed, education must address itself to the retentive quality of one's mind, which is instanced in one's propensity to form habits (Vol. II, pp. 286-7; *Analogy*, Part I, Ch. V). It sees that all impressions made upon us tend to persist, and to influence future learning, so that what a person's character is results largely from the store of habits he has acquired. The earlier the habits, the more deeply embedded they become and the more lasting is their effect. Long before we reach adulthood habits produce their permanent effect upon our nature, binding

us to a general routine of behavior. After our habits become in-
grained little in the way of drastic change can be accomplished;
the mind becomes inelastic and natural authority ceases. The
individual himself becomes more assertive, less willing to heed,
and less deferential to authority (Vol. II, p. 289; also p. 287).
In view of this, the sphere of education belongs properly to
youth, for it is in application to that age that it can achieve its
best results.

Besides the innate tendency for individuals to form habits, is
the correlated tendency for them to be open-minded and receptive to instruction from others. At first they exhibit a naïve confidence, believing what they are told. Children have a "natural
deference to grown people, whom they find here settled in a world
where they themselves are strangers; and to whom they have
recourse for advice, as readily as for protection; which deference
is still greater towards those who are placed over them: these
things give the justest grounds to expect that they may receive
such impressions, and be influenced to such a course of behaviour,
as will produce lasting good habits . . ." (Vol. II, p. 287).

How can the mechanism of training take advantage of these
psychological traits? By appealing to one's open-mindedness,
and propensity to retain what one is told, education can instill
its ideals for the perpetuation of society and the place of the
individual in it. Working through the medium of habit, it can
institute desirable types of behavior, fashioning them to meet
its end. If children are left to themselves, or if they rely upon
companions of their own choice, falling indifferently in with
their associates, their first impressions are apt to be bad (Vol. II,
p. 286), for at that age youth lacks discretion and judgment.
His choices will be made upon the impulses of the moment. But if
moral training seizes upon these tendencies early and fashions
them towards its conceived goal, all that will be avoided, and the
greatest benefit to the individual and society will be the result.
"Thus if (children) are not trained up in the way they *should go*,
they will certainly be trained up in the way they *should not go;*
and in all probability will persevere in it, and become miserable
themselves, and mischievous to society: which, in event, is worse,
upon account of both, than if they had been exposed to perish
in their infancy" (Vol. II, p. 287).

Method of Educational Training. How in particular shall
the ideals of educational training be carried out, how shall it set

about availing itself of our propensities to form habits? We can either set examples in our own persons to those whose behavior we wish to influence, or we can institute this training by means of a school system. We must act virtuously, admonish others for their misdeeds, restrain their impetuosities and prevent evil whenever we can. This course of behavior devolves in particular upon the upper classes.[6]

In default of this educational training, the individual will become useless to himself and to society. His entire childhood will be wasted in the haphazard accumulation of habits; or passed away in idleness or loitering (Vol. II, p. 298). In later years, he will be unable to adapt himself to the requirements of society; the early habits formed upon fancy, with no effort to direct them towards future utility, will obstinately stand in the way of his improvement and correction. They will create within him an aversion "not only to the restraints of religion, but to those which any particular calling, and even the nature of society require" (Vol. II, p. 298). Possessing no proper security for acting a right part in society, his nature will break down and become corrupt (Vol. II, p. 290). Victimized by contrary habits, the individual will alienate himself from God, scorning the means that God has placed for his recovery, until he sinks into irreclaimable corruption (Vol. II, p. 290).

Education as Public Responsibility. Educating the young where the parents lack the means themselves, should be regarded as a public duty. "Children," says Butler, "have as much right to some proper education, as to have their lives preserved; and that when this is not given them by their parents, the care of it devolves upon all persons, it becomes the duty of all, who are capable of contributing to it, and whose help is wanted" (Vol. II, p. 288). The duty to contribute is a moral one, to improve the accepted order of what is right, to bring up children in order, virtue and religion (Vol. II, p. 301). "There can be no reason," Butler says, "why we should not endeavour, by the likeliest methods we can, to better the world, or keep it from growing worse" (Vol. II, p. 300).

No one would question the right of the public to preserve

[6] Butler has in mind the charity schools of his day. He would delegate to them the task of religious instruction and the preparation of the children for the rank of society in which they are born. At a suitable age they must be placed out in employment, and care must be taken "to do it in a manner which does not set them above their rank . . ." (Vol. II, p. 297; cp. also pp. 229, 302).

the lives of its children. But a mere biological existence is less than human. Preservation of life is preliminary to the way in which that life should be conducted; life has its qualitative aspects, its potential moral features. Rationally viewed, preservation of life must also admit as essential the means whereby this qualitative aspect can be expressed (Vol. II, pp. 288, 300). Such, however, is the aim of education: to supply these means.[7]

What opposition can be raised against this scheme of educating the poor? Some people maintain that the poor will make a perverse use of their learning; others, that they will attempt to raise themselves above their class (Vol. II, pp. 294-5). Both believe that greater ignorance will render the poor more dutiful and will keep them in greater subjection. But such objections as these are ill-founded.

There is no danger that the educated poor will make a more perverse use of their knowledge than the rich, who have greater opportunities for doing so. In their position of influence the rich can do far more wrong and damage (Vol. II, p. 294). Neither can we take seriously the charge that the poor will be dissatisfied with their own class or tend to rise above it. Until the last century or two the classes of society were all nearly on the same level in respect to education, yet the ignorance which they shared did not prevent their natural distinction of rank. We have no right to believe that this class relationship will change if the poor now learn to read. Not to educate them would do them an injustice, for ignorance would tend to lower them from the ranks that they once enjoyed; it would put them at a greater disadvantage. In this state of ignorance they would be less equipped to take their part in the conditions of a changed society (Vol. II, p. 295). Can we not also say that if learning has proved to be a blessing to the rich, it will prove to be a blessing to the poor as well?

---

[7] To insist upon education as a public duty falling upon the shoulders of those who can pay, is to remind us that Butler's view of society was one in which the rich and the influential were naturally in patronage over the poor (See above, Chs. 18, 19, 20, Pt. Four, present work). This relationship we have seen is of long standing, and for Butler was an indication that Providence had intended it to be so. No temporal change can weaken the ties of this obligation. The care of the poor, and their instruction in the matters of religion and morality, was originally the duty of the heads of families (Vol. II, p. 258); the circumstance of economic change does not lessen the nature of this basic obligation. Today we should say that the relationship is in actual evidence between the rich and the poor (Vol. II, p. 330).

21

RELIGIOUS ASPECT OF SOCIETY

"A CONSTITUTION of civil government without any religious establishment is a chimerical project, of which there is no example" (Vol. II, p. 308). These words express for Butler that civilized society cannot endure without its organized church. Without a religion a civilized community sinks to the level of superstition. Under the influence of superstition the morality and unity of society is threatened, for the members become prey of opportunists whose intended work, not being based upon the common good, leads the country into irrecoverable ruin (Vol. II, p. 245). The immediate results of irreligion are atheism and a scorn for all things divine; both of these lead insensibly into the undermining of the political and civil life.

Butler regards religion as the stabilizing force in society. Its teachings keep up a bond of union among the people in their intercourse with each other, and it makes for the security of civil government. It preserves the bonds of human relationship by basing its principles of morality upon the authority of God, and it makes for the security of the civil government by proclaiming the divinity of kinship. Neither civil government nor social intercourse could rest without their deeper setting and foundation. Morality would lose its ultimate significance if not related to the will of God, and respect for authority would cease were one not certain of the divine order of government. To see how this is borne out for Butler, let us briefly indicate what the force of religion in society is, and how it influences people and governments in the affairs of life.

The doctrine of religion teaches us "that all things are under the direction of one righteous Governor" (Vol. II, p. 235). Society and man, it holds, are creations of God; both of them show the nature of their divine source within their structure. In man the presence of conscience attests God's presence; its announcements are his proclamations. Society too shows its divine origin, which is instanced in the persons of its rulers. Likewise it is within society that man learns the existence of the religious order, the particular place of society within that scheme; also the relation of himself to God and to society. He further sees that it is his duty to ascertain these truths and pass them on to others so that they too can find their complete moral expression in deference to the diviner law of religion (*Vide, Analogy,* introd.; also Pt. II, ch. I). As a member of society it becomes his duty to regather the teachings of religion, preserve them in communities, and spread the knowledge of them to his fellow beings at home and abroad.

In Butler's sermons on the importance of religion we gather that the age to which he addressed himself was one in which the increasing neglect of religion was in great evidence. In his Durham Charge we hear that "the number of those who profess themselves unbelievers, increases, and with their numbers their zeal" (Vol. II, p. 334).[1]

The preservation of religion at home, to prevent its falling into decay, devolves as a general duty upon all Christians, more particularly though upon the professed clergy (Vol. II, pp. 334-351). To pray at home, while valuable in itself, is not sufficient, for it leads to the neglect of church attendance, and inevitably towards the dissolution of all Christian communities (Vol. II, p. 238). Through these organized communities men learn in detail the relation in which they stand to God, and the obligations of obedience, resignation and love they owe to him (Vol. II, p. 241). In the absence of these communities many individuals would be deprived of that important knowledge. It is the only source through which they can become informed.[2]

From religious institutions one learns what God has revealed to other individuals. The fact that this knowledge has been imparted by revelation should indicate to us the peculiar importance and sacredness of the message we should learn.[3] If we conform

[1] "It is impossible for me, to forbear lamenting with you the general decay of religion in this nation; which is now observed by every one, and has been for some time the complaint of all serious persons" (*ibid.*); also pp. 335, 339, 340; *Analogy,* p. 1. "It is come, I know not how, to be taken for granted, by many persons, that Christianity is not so much as a subject of inquiry; but that it is, now at length, discovered to be fictitious." Also in his Public Sermons, Butler comments upon the irreligiousness of the times, cp. p. 248: "In every view of things, and upon all accounts, irreligion is at present our chief danger." Also p. 267: "And indeed amidst the dark prospect before us, from that profligateness of manners, and scorn of religion, which so generally abound." Also, pp. 295, 297; Vol. I, p. 53.

[2] We should not raise such questions as why God did not impart these religious truths immediately to each and every man; we must accept the fact of the situation that he did not, and avail ourselves of the best way we know how to remedy the situation.

[3] "Revelation therefore, as it demands to be received with a regard and reverence peculiar to itself; so it lays us under obligations, of a like peculiar sort, to

to the external form of religion, e.g., by attending church services, we shall gradually appreciate the deeper value that it indicates and the reality that it stands for.[4] We cannot be certain that to all men appealed to will come this deeper discernment, but at least a few will experience its influence upon their heart and their actions (Vol. II, p. 246).

Church attendance is not the only means of preserving religion within the community or of making its value known to others. In the face of professed irreligion discreet silence is often of value (Vol. II, p. 328); if retorts must be made they should be made with caution and reserve, so as to indicate the difficulty of the subject matter and the impossibility of establishing to any one's satisfaction a complete exposition of proof.[5] To enter into disputation may lead to a misunderstanding, especially as some "people are too apt inconsiderately to take for granted, that things are really questionable, because they hear them often disputed" (Vol. II, p. 336).[6]

To the generality of people religion must be presented in a positive manner, for their minds are not trained in argument. Lengthy proofs, while convincing to some of them, will strike others as wearying and tedious. Those minds that had no doubts

communicate the light of it" (Vol. II, p. 242), and that "Christianity is very particularly to be considered as a trust, deposited with us in behalf of others, in behalf of mankind, as well as for our own instruction" (*ibid.*).

[4] *Vide* Vol. II, p. 244: "It is a serious call upon men to attend to the natural and the revealed doctrine of religion. It is a standing publication of the gospel, and renders it a *witness* to them: and by this means the purposes of Providence are carrying on, with regard to remote ages, as well as to the present."

[5] Cp. also Vol. II, p. 337: "Now a man may be fully convinced of the truth of a matter, and upon the strongest reasons, and yet not be able to answer all the difficulties which may be raised upon it." Also "The general evidence of religion is complex and various. It consists of a long series of things, one preparatory to and confirming another, from the very beginning of the world to the present time. And it is easy to see how impossible it must be, in a cursory conversation, to unite all this into one argument, and represent it as it ought; and, could it be done, how utterly indisposed people would be to attend to it—I say in a cursory conversation" (*ibid.*).

[6] Butler points out that no one in all earnest can believe that the dogmas of religion have been proved false once and for all. Even the most biased of man must admit the subject matter to be doubtful. But to admit its doubtfulness is to allow the possibility of its being true. In his state of suspense, man can avail himself of the practical benefits that religion has and promises (Vol. II, p. 337). As Butler says: "For would it not be madness for a man to forsake a safe road, and prefer to it one in which he acknowledges there is an even chance he should lose his life, though there were an even chance likewise of his getting safe through it?" (Vol. II, p. 337).

before the proofs of religion were pressed into its service will now begin to have an ill impression of its truth.

To present religion in its positive aspects, freed from the disquieting affects of controversy, is not all that should be done. The value of religion is also practical.[7] Hence religion should be imparted to men in the same way as moral education to children, namely by practical illustration in our own lives. In this way decency and reverence in our lives towards the teachings and precepts of religion will tend to beget the same attitude in others.

Our conscious daily exercise of religion must be reinforced by as many helpful devices as we can resort to. A tranquil faith in its truth must be kept alive; and our attitude reassured through its external forms and ceremonials, such as the upkeep of the churches, family prayers and grace before meals; not neglecting religious teaching to the young. By dropping constantly into one's conversation a few words about God and religion, we are bound to leave religious impressions upon the hearer, that in time to come will advance him to states of religious consciousness (Vol. II, p. 347).

The central purpose of positive instruction is to focus religion within our lives and to make of it a dominant and practical force. To understand the services and rituals that we observe will make for this attitude, for it will emphasize our place in society and our obligations to it.

Religion must not be regarded as the exclusive property of any one creed or people.[8] To spread a knowledge of his religion

---

[7] Vol. II, p. 340: "Our chief business therefore is to endeavor to beget a practical sense of it upon their hearts, as what they acknowledge their belief of, and profess they ought to conform themselves to."

[8] It is true that Butler identifies it with Protestant Christianity and does not allow the legitimacy of the rival claims of other religions. But he explains his attitude by observing that a religion must allow basically for the responsible exercise of our conscience, which, as he maintains, is denied by the rival religion of Roman Catholicism. "The salvation of every man," he says, "cannot but depend upon his behaviour, and therefore cannot but depend upon himself; and is necessarily his own concern, in a sense in which it cannot be another's" (Vol. II, p. 240). In a later sermon he repeats in different words the same thought by warning us that "every man's behaviour is his own concern, for every one must give account of his own works . . ." (Vol. II, p. 260). But only in Protestant Christianity is the mind of the individual allowed freely to study the scriptures and so acquaint himself with the knowledge of natural religion. Under an arrangement of that sort, religion will prevail in its purity, and the mind is enabled to study, understand, transmit, and yet to worship according to his own conscience, to an extent that is not encouraged or allowed by Christian religions of rival claims (Vol. II, p. 247).

abroad, to the uncivilized as well as to the civilized peoples, becomes the further religious duty of man. Uncivilized people belong to the race of mankind, as much as the civilized; the privileges of the latter should be granted to them so that they too can live more like men and less like brutes, and qualify themselves as well for a higher state in the life to come (Vol. II, p. 243). Among other means of bringing this about should be those of commerce and navigation, which "should be consecrated to the service of religion, by being made the means of propagating it in every country, with which we have any intercourse" (Vol. II, p. 243). Then the civilized world could look forward to the time when the whole world would submit itself to the teachings of Christianity, and become one state (Vol. II, p. 250).

Society can be looked upon as only one phase through which man will live; it is a period of trial and probation, but it cannot be considered as the only or the ultimate phase (*Vide Analogy*, Chs. IV, V). The immortality of human nature indicates endless realms through which he will pass. Society, too, is not without its wider aspects. We have seen in our present chapter that through the doctrine of religion we are afforded a glimpse of the wider universe within which society has its stated place. If we view more fully the nature of society, we observe that its roots are an aspect of an intended design that reflects a deeper spiritual purpose. The laws of society will also be seen as an indication of God's purpose. In the long run man must adjust his life to this comprehensive scheme, and live in society in full consciousness of its cosmic origins.

To take account of society in its deeper origins leads us beyond the fourfold aspect of society that we have discussed in the past four chapters. Completely to understand the laws of society, we must seek their origin beyond themselves; to ascertain the wherefore of society, and our obligations to obey them, must take us beyond our own immediate nature as its cause of explanation. The complete discussion of this will be attempted in the following chapters.

PART FIVE

THE NATURE OF THE UNIVERSE

22

THE UNIVERSE AS IDEAL

OUR attempt to answer the question what morality consists in led us first to investigate the nature of man. From this we were led to investigate the nature and order of society within which man's nature falls. To be human, we learned, is to be social. But the nature of society showed it to rest upon factors other than itself. It is but one phenomenon among many in the scheme of things, and within its moral and religious basis are reflected the deeper origins from which it arises. No final answer can be afforded us concerning the nature of morality until we have made known to ourselves the nature of the universe at large.

What is the universe? What is the place within it of the particular objects and persons we see? Is it a loose assemblage of objects, persons, and events; or does it reveal a structure and order of which the plurality of observed things are lesser aspects? If the universe is more inclusive than its observed parts, we must see the place of the parts within the structure of the whole. These are some of the important questions that Butler raises and tries to answer.

We are now prepared to indicate the order of our exposition. We shall first discuss the universe as an ideal system of systems. In our attempt to explain the nature of the disconnected objects with which we are surrounded, we shall be led to acknowledge its ideal unity which reflects perfect rationality and goodness. We shall also see that there exist in our immediate experience things and persons that we cannot readily observe, but which are as real as those that we can. Whole portions of the universe remain hidden from our view. We shall refer to this aspect of it as the invisible universe; and of the aspect that we can observe as its visible aspect. To describe the nature of the universe fully and impartially, we must pay attention to each of these two aspects, to show that both of them are ultimately to be understood in terms of one final ideal which they imply. Our second

chapter will be concerned with the universe in its spiritual
origins, for ultimately viewed, the universe as an ideal system
of systems points to a divine source. In the third chapter we
shall discuss the proofs for the existence of God, as well as his
relation to the world and to man. Our fourth and fifth chapters
will take us back to the place and task of man in the universe
as we now understand it. These chapters will discuss the reign
of law in human nature, together with the cosmic significance it
implies. We shall see that man is not unaware of the part that he
is to play within the scheme of things; for in its communication
of pleasure and pain it informs him that it requires for its progressive unification the unremitting moral contributions of man.

LOGICAL STRUCTURE OF A SYSTEM

As preliminary to the present part of our work, we shall
find it necessary to bring to a focus the various meanings of a
system that run throughout Butler's philosophy.

If we sum up the various formal characteristics of a system
or constitution as Butler conceives it, we can make several judgments concerning it. (1) A system is either actual or ideal; i.e.,
objects may exist as actual systems or as potential systems. But
since Butler holds that "every work both of nature and of art
is a system" (Vol. II, p. 7), we must say that those objects that
become systems exhibit in their stages of ideal approximation a
systematic structure in various stages of incompleteness. In
drawing this distinction between actual systems and ideal, we do
not intend to imply all absence of relation between them. An ideal
system is immanent within its actual instance, and as such is
capable of attainment or realization. (2) All systems, whether
actual or ideal, are either animate or purely mechanical. An
instance of the latter would be a machine (Vol. II, p. 58); of
the former would be a plant or a man (*ibid.*). Butler would probably classify civic bodies, etc., under the former heading. Then
again, we can make another subdivision of animate systems by
pointing out that some systems are self-controlled; the constitution and governance being put into their own power. The only
instance that Butler will allow of this is man (Vol. II, p. 9). (3)
A system is composed of parts and relations. It is in virtue of the
relations, that an object of conceivably divisible parts can be
considered as a whole (Vol. II, p. 7; also pp. 221, 224, 226).
That the relations are internal, and so establish the systematic

structure, can be gathered from Butler's remarks in the preface to his Sermons. To paraphrase him: an object cannot be considered as a system until one takes into account the relations and respects that the parts bear to each other (Vol. II, p. 8). In regard to a watch, he says that if the parts are brought together in a random way, be the union ever so close, they will not resemble that object. This leads us to observe further (4) that a system exhibits an internal teleology (Vol. II, pp. 59, 127). By this is meant that each part is so intimately related to other parts of the system, that it is only in reference to the other parts of the system, that our selected part is to be understood. Another way of stating this would be to say that external to any part of our system is an end or object to which that part tends or points, and that this objective end and the factor that is conducive to it are both internally included within the system. But though this inner teleology is not brought out clearly by Butler in his instance of the watch, tree, or civic institution, it is implied in the latter and is directly affirmed in regard to the nature of man. (5) Every system exists for some use or purpose "out of and beyond itself" (Vol. II, p. 7; cp. also p. 44). We can thus characterize a system by saying that it also exhibits an external teleology. But since each system taken as a whole is conducive to an end beyond itself to which it is intimately related, it must follow that the system so related must internally exhibit (6) an hierarchical unity (Vol. II, pp. 10, 179), in which some of the parts are evidently superior to other parts. (7), Lastly, all systems are ideal or spiritual, in the sense that they owe their reality to a conceiving mind, whether or not such a mind be that of man or God. This enables us to see more clearly the relation between any actual system and its ideal counterpart. Any actual system implies its ideal to which it can approximate, only because the ideal goal or counterpart was the pattern in terms of which the actual system was fashioned. The ideal is immanent within the particular because the former is the prior condition of the latter. But the ideal counterpart could not be unless there exists some mind that conceives it in its imagination and executes it.

We can expect to find the above characteristics of a system in the world as it actually exists, and its ideal counterpart as a scheme conceived in the mind of God and man. In the present chapter, we are concerned with the nature and description of the

actually existent systems as made by man, and the physical
world as made by God. In a later chapter we shall be concerned
with the ideal scheme or counterpart as it exists in the minds of
God and man.

THE VISIBLE UNIVERSE

As we become aware of our environment, we fancy that we
are surrounded by a multiplicity of unrelated objects, but as we
examine more closely our field of surrounding objects, we see
that no object stands alone. Each object is intimately related to
other objects with which it forms a system. The multiplicity
of objects that we first observed is apparent only; their seeming
isolation breaks down, they manifest individually less self-suffi-
ciency, and imply a dependence upon objects other than themselves.

What is the nature of this relationship that carries us from
one object to another; how does it affect the object as we first
know it? The relationship is one of causal reference. Each object
points beyond itself to a cause of its condition. But no one cause
can satisfy us; we are led on from this cause to seek its prior
conditions in the medium of space and time. Every object is
related to its past conditions, as well as to other objects of the
contemporaneous present. Nor is this all, for the unexamined
future lies before it. Let us suppose that we could succeed in
tracing the causal origins of an object throughout the distant
past, as well as the present, even then the object would be imperfectly known to us. As the object endures through time it
receives new associations and gives rise to new consequences.
Every changed aspect of its nature will modify what we believed
to be its original nature. The present moment from which we
start is but one instance in a stage of continuous development.
No final stage can be contemplated because the universe within
which they grow is everlasting in duration.

From this interrelation of one object with another emerges
a system of objects, throughout which can be traced multiple
paths of connection. Within its structure one event does not
merely give way to another event. Single objects fall into inclusive systems, and these systems themselves imply further ones.
In their relation to each other these higher systems point to an
ultimate one which is the universe itself.

In its most inclusive aspect the universe is an actual system of systems, progressively enriching itself in time. Like a particular object whose nature awaits future development and association before it can be declared complete, the universe too endures in the medium of time awaiting the unborn contributions of the future. Incomplete at any one instant of time, it implies a potential completion. Each stage can successively advance it and register in comparison with its precedent stage a higher approximation, but no stage ever achieves it. In like respect the universe is good and perfect. The chaos of the moment points to a possible cosmos, and the evil indicates a good that can cancel its smirch. Nothing can be actually predicted as to its outcome, for nothing is actually predetermined.

In those aspects of the universe that owe their reality to the contributions of man, senseless change may occur, for what man does depends upon the degree of intelligence he uses. If he conducts himself under the banner of conscience, his life-span will exhibit a progressive moral advancement in which each subsequent phase of his life will morally eclipse its former. To his moral life the universe will be receptive. But if he follows his instincts, his deeds will bear no particular reference to what has gone before; consequently his life will be a meaningless series of unrelated changes and events. As qualifying the universe these unrelated deeds will divert it from the course of unitary goodness that the universe implies.

Viewed from its inner aspects, no part of the universe is superfluous, and no part is without meaning. The whole is sustained through the agency of the parts and the parts contribute progressively to the whole. They meet within its developing unity, partake of its purpose and share in its significance. Objective events that appear insignificant to some play their important parts within the universe, could their wider setting be known. Waste and extravagance in the order of nature may be but a pronouncement of human ignorance. Events unfavorable to our plans or that make for our destruction might reveal elements of good if they could be seen in their cosmic setting. The indication of perfection and good is imperfectly revealed within all its parts.

How do these particular objects fit into the universe; how do they exhibit within their own nature its systematic aspects? The answer to these questions will occupy us for the rest of the chapter. To answer the questions that we have just raised requires us first to recognize a distinction that runs throughout Butler's thought between the visible and invisible aspects of the universe. The former are directly accessible through the senses of man, the latter are ascertainable by his reason. Under the former we can place manufactured objects, human societies and natural objects. The latter comprises individual minds, underlying substances of physical objects, God's mind, etc. In the present section we shall be concerned only with the visible aspect of the universe, taking up in turn: objects manufactured by man, then human societies, and lastly the objects of the physical or natural world. We shall see that in each case the objects falling within each group are apparent only; that to be completely understood they imply the unity and perfection of the universe.

Man-Made Objects. The objects that man manufactures are related to each other, and form in their interrelation a system of objects in reference to which each individual object becomes intelligible. Thus, both food and drink are instances of economic commodities. As such they fall into the system of economic products and exhibit the laws of economic activity.

But even in this setting this system of man-made products is not completely intelligible until it is further viewed in reference to man's nature. As economic objects they are capable of satisfying his instinctive drives of hunger and thirst. But as systematic they represent the objective organization of his impulses which makes it possible for them to be realized. Their essential reality is more truly known only when seen as the means whereby human purposes are satisfied. Food and drink make it possible for man to survive. What meaning could we attribute to them in the absence of this utility? If not considered in reference to man, they become mere things or objects, and less intelligible; likewise would the economic realms of which they form a part. But if seen in their relation to man, they become meaningful, their significance is conferred by their setting within a system of impulses that they outwardly represent and seek to satisfy.

Not only food and drink become intelligible when seen as instruments of human desire, but other objects as well. All that man utilizes satisfies some drive within his nature. These objects, too, acquire a systematic character as their relationship to man is seen. But the characteristic of the human self is its subordination of claims to conscience, the constant unifying of its affections in terms of the virtuous quality of its highest principle. The genuine self is potentially unitary if it consciously lives up to its nature. But this unitary character must be also true of the objects that the self is concerned with. They too acquire unity as they are appreciated and utilized by a self that is thoroughly self-conscious. With the aspect of unity is conferred the quality of good.

We shall now see that the unity of manufactured objects is ideal and not actual. Ideally the objects that man manufactures tend to express the unitariness of his nature. Actually they do not. If man's mind were thoroughly rational, i.e., rationally expressed so that his products were forged in exemplification of his highest purposes, the environment within which he lives would be likewise rational and equally unified. Every product of his environment would be harmoniously related to his self-conscious life, and reflect its unity. As the ideal unity of his life is a moral unity, i.e., one that is expressed through the sanction of his conscience, the world within which he lives would be unified in terms of his highest purpose and would be correspondingly moral. The products he makes would be moral objects, for they would be the expression of a moral nature.

But no one man is thoroughly rational. Although he may work under the ideal of his own interests, he is not always aware which interests are genuinely good, or what they should ultimately be. The objects that he seeks, the products he makes, the life he experiences may all satisfy in their outward form inner subjective drives that in themselves have not been previously related or coordinated into a genuine purpose. The individual may pander to unworthy designs and motives. The objects that he seeks in the fulfilment of his spurious longings will fall into systems, it is true, but the systems in which they partake will objectively represent an inner array of unrelated motives. Hence they will be unrelated to other systematic groupings of objects in the same environment. There will be no actual systematic relationship between them. Hence these groups of systematic objects will be mutually exclusive, for the impulses that they represent will themselves be many and as such unrelated to each other. In the actual world of the partly moral man the objects he uses will be aspects of systems but these systems will be mutually exclusive and as many in kind and number as are the unrelated inner impulses from which they spring and which they aim at expressing.

Such then is the actual world of man, the world that he observes, experiences and makes. It is partly unified and partly rational. No man nor object actually stands alone; they fall into groups or systems. The systems within which they fall are mutually exclusive because man has fashioned their products in terms of no one moral ideal. His world is pluralistic, chaotic and irrational. But the ideal tendency of all man-made objects is to be inclusively systematic, i.e., to form a perfectly coherent system. Their detached plurality implies a monism that is at once rational and moral. Each object implies an ideal purpose for which it is made. The purpose that guided its construction is man's idea, but it is an idea that he believes to contain an aspect of his highest good. Although imperfectly formulated, this ideal implies the unity of a moral self-consciousness that could, if it were allowed or favored, relate all of his ideals to a common law of virtue. Taken in their most real sense, i.e., for what they imply or tend to express, the nature of man-made objects would fall into harmonious systems, ideally unitary and good.

Human Societies. Are human societies and groups an exception to this systematic aspect of things, or do they ideally point to a unity of structure instancing a common law? At first glance we seem to be surrounded by a multiplicity of unrelated groups and societies. Petty dislikes as well as deeper issues separate and divide mankind; the prevalence of party spirit prevents the attainment of man's life as it should be (Vol. II, pp. 186-7). In the world of actual government and societies men are banded together by interests that are largely instinctive and unrational. If men were self-conscious, they would become aware of the instinctive basis upon which their societies are formed and proceed to rationalize them, but until they do so the groups within which they live are founded solely upon instinctive or emotional ties, the worth of which has never been examined or evaluated. As a consequence there exist side by side groups and societies that are outgrowths of unexamined impulses, and as such are unrelated to other impulses in the same nature.

Since men never practise an ideal law of virtue they are never at unity with themselves; their immediate social worlds are unrelated, and as numerous as are the aims that they selfishly pursue.

Yet despite this actual discordance and separateness of aims and policies, human societies point to an ideal unity, to a structure that is systematic, rational, and good. If all mankind were equally rational, they would unify their societies in terms of a common virtue under which their own nature would be best expressed. The application of the moral law by each individual would draw him into an intimate relation with his neighbor. Their interests would become common interests. Instinctive compassion guided by an enlightened benevolence would forge a bond of sympathy, and the society within which they live would express a singularity of aim and the goodness of a common moral purpose. Consistently expressed in all communities, the law of morality would insensibly draw them together until the manifold groups and societies became lesser aspects of one social world. These lesser social groups would advance in an orderly way into the future, progressively expressing the ideals of mankind, through which they would become unified.

Actual Physical Universe. Besides the actual world of man and society both of which imply an ideal structure, there exists also the domain of the physical world. This realm of nature includes such material objects as stones, plants, etc., i.e., non-human and non-social products. Do these natural objects also imply an ideal system of law that explains them more intelligibly, or are these objects a loose array of mutually exclusive things?

Like man-made objects and social groups the objects of the natural world exist in an apparent isolation only. A deeper inspection reveals them to be instances of more general laws. "We know indeed several of the general laws of matter: and a great part of the natural behaviour of living agents is reducible to general laws" (Vol. I, p. 203), says Butler. But of many laws we remain in ignorance, for there are many natural objects whose nature we do not fully understand. Yet there is no doubt that if we could discover the laws of these seeming exceptions, we should see them to be instances of more general laws, for "there cannot, in reality, be any such thing as chance" (Vol. I, p. 203). This is true of the whole world of nature, all of its objects and events are related. In the natural world, Butler tells us, there is no event "which we are acquainted with, so single and unconnected, as not to have a respect to some other actions and events. And things seemingly the most insignificant imaginable are perpetually observed to be necessary conditions to other things of the greatest importance: so that any one thing whatever may, for ought we know to the contrary, be a necessary condition to any other" (Vol. I, p. 134).

Butler has very little to say in detail about the physical order of nature. What we know about his views can be gathered indirectly from his remarks on other subjects (Vol. I, pp. 25-6; 202-3; Vol. II, pp. 219, 220). Inanimate objects are material in their structure, i.e., they are ultimately composed of solid particles of matter. The gross objects themselves undergo change (Vol. I, p. 27) and dissolution, being transferred from one system to another; but the elementary particles cannot. These are indestructible. But the atoms of which the grosser objects are formed fall into systems and arrangements that manifest laws of their own (Vol. I, p. 28). As to their place in the human body, we learn that "every man in his physical nature is one individual single agent" (Vol. II, p. 58, footnote). The elementary physical particles pass from one system of matter to another, and yet the grosser physical unity of the living agent is preserved.

Plants and animals too can be regarded as systems of matter (Vol. I, pp. 59, 318). Animals and plants fall into species the characteristics of which they individually bear. "In this great scheme of the natural world, individuals have various peculiar relations to other individuals of their own species. And whole species are, we find, variously related to other species, upon this earth" (Vol. I, p. 133). The species are so related that the vegetable world subserves the animal world; both subserve man. And between the world of organized bodies and minds we have already had occasion to show that the body of man exists for the use and control of his mind. In other words it is the instrument through which he comes into contact with the physical world, and the means whereby he can exert his nature. The natural world forms then one system; to be expressed in terms of one end or purpose, i.e., one general law.

To a great extent the unity of nature is actual, for the multiplicity of natural objects do not depend upon the actions of men before they become instances of a common law. But in another way the unity is ideal, for the undeveloped future lies before it in which new objects and associations will spring into being. Implied as effects in the causal nature of the actual objects, they are necessary to the completion of the present physical system. These future objects will have to abide their time before they fall into the systematic structure of the present and add to its unity. Although actually implicit, this future state of affairs must always appear as ideal from the standpoint of an unfinished present.

What relation if any exists between this ideal system of nature and the ideal system of human objects and societies? Do they too imply a higher purpose common to both, just as each system singly implies within its particular members a centrality of aim? To Butler's mind there is no doubt that these two worlds are ideally united and form a higher system. "Indeed the natural and moral constitution and government of the world are so connected, as to make up together but one scheme" (Vol. I, p. 135). How this is achieved, we do not exactly know, for there is a great deal of which we are ignorant. Between the outer world of nature and the nature of man, we can observe instances of correspondence or attunement.

In an important sense, Nature exists for the convenience of man, affording to him the means through which he can achieve a higher self-expression.[1] His various instincts imply the existence in the outer world of objects to satisfy them. Thus the pangs of hunger imply food, and the feeling of thirst implies drink. In this instance man's nature is dependent upon the offerings of nature; without the actual presence of possible sustenance he could not survive. Biologically viewed his physical nature is completed in its contact with these necessary objects.

We must be on our guard, however, in our teleological interpretation of nature. The physical world does not exist for the sole utility of man; it is not to be characterized or evaluated in terms of its subservience to his merely human needs, and yet the laws of its nature express a moral purpose.

The principles of morality to which the laws of the physical are ultimately subordinated are not merely human laws, even though they are expressed through human nature and for human good. In their deliverance by conscience they indicate a course of behavior that his actual nature should follow. As such they are supra-human, and represent a higher order than that of man's arbitrary contrivance. Their origin is cosmic, not human. It is to the moral order understood as compulsory to man and the rest

---

[1] Cp. Vol. II, p. 92: "There is a much more exact correspondence between the natural and moral world, than we are apt to take notice of. The inward frame of man does in a peculiar manner answer to the external condition and circumstances of life, in which he is placed" (also Vol. I, p. 89).

of creation that the physical world is subordinated. Subordinated to these cosmic laws of morality, man's nature and objects of the physical world assume their systematic aspect.

Butler appears to have borrowed his views on the nature of the physical world from the scientific thought of his day. Everything is viewed under the category of substance, of which there are two kinds: matter and mind. Under the former are subsumed individual physical objects; under the latter, the minds of persons living and dead, as well as the mind of God. Events are expressions of substances in space or time. Strongly contrasted with this pluralistic realism, is his insistence that the universe is one, systematic and ideal. As this view gains ascendency in his mind, the earlier substantialist metaphysics becomes unconsciously abandoned. He is forced to recast his categories of mental substance, physical substance, time and space. Since the natural world is placed in subordination to the moral world, the characteristics of the latter take precedence over the former. The category of substance is no longer sufficient. Personality, organicity, temporal creativity take its place and become dominant categories. Individuals can no longer be viewed as mental substances, atomic and separate. For Butler they are in the process of becoming, their unity is in the making, their nature bears a growing social implication.

To complete our account of the universe, there remains for consideration its invisible aspect; that which is ascertainable to man only through his reason.

THE INVISIBLE UNIVERSE

Our direct acquaintance with the universe is limited to a very small area. What we actually know is infinitesimal compared to what we do not know. As Butler tells us: man "could not but be sensible, that there must be innumerable things, in the dispensations of Providence past, in the invisible government over the world at present carrying on, and in what is to come; of which he was wholly ignorant, and which could not be discovered without revelation. Whether the scheme of nature be, in the strictest sense, infinite or not; it is evidently vast, even beyond all possible imagination. And doubtless that part of it, which is opened to our view, is but as a point, in comparison of the whole plan of Providence, reaching throughout eternity past and future; in comparison of what is even now going on in the remote parts of the boundless universe; nay in comparison of the whole scheme of this world" (Vol. I, pp. 174-5). Let us consider for instance the nature of a physical object, or of our minds.

We say that both of these are known to us directly, yet how much of each do we really know? In regard to a physical object we speak of its elemental constituent parts, the indestructible particles whose effects we know in sensation. Yet even here we are unacquainted with this causal nature. Of any physical object we know but its effects. The substantial nature of physical things remains forever hidden. "It is indeed in general no more than effects, that the most knowing are acquainted with: for as to causes, they are as entirely in the dark as the most ignorant. What are the laws by which matter acts upon matter, but certain effects; which some, having observed to be frequently repeated, have reduced to general rules? The real nature and essence of beings likewise is what we are altogether ignorant of. All these things are so entirely out of our reach, that we have not the least glimpse of them" (Vol. II, p. 219; Cp. also p. 213). In all we can observe and know we are limited to a system of effects. We can trace one effect to another effect and unite both within systems of which they are a part, but we are never able to penetrate to the underlying substances, which act as direct physical causes.

According to the way in which we are equipped to know the world, there is no reason to believe that we can ever repair this deficiency, for according to Butler, to know is not the proper business of man (Vol. II, p. 227). We can expand the scope of our knowledge but since the expansion will proceed along the level of observed effects, our knowledge will never be complete. Nor can we hope to complete it; for "our senses give us but an imperfect knowledge of things: effects themselves, if we knew them thoroughly, would give us but imperfect notions of wisdom and power" (Vol. II, p. 213). In extending our knowledge, we have at the same time extended our ignorance.

Nor is the nature of mind known to us. Even here, it is only the effects that we perceive, feel and come in contact with. About ourselves we know as little as we do of the world about us; of "how we were made, how our being is continued and preserved, what the faculties of our minds are, and upon what the power of exercising them depends" (Vol. II, pp. 219-220), we remain in the utmost ignorance.[2]

The inner recesses of consciousness are unknown. We are aware that the mind exercises a control over the body, and that it organizes it and directs its growth. The influence of the mind is further seen in the fact that it makes the unity of the body possible. How it does so, we cannot know, but the way in which it is brought about is traceable to the hidden powers and capacities that the mind has and that it exercises (*Vide* our chapter on Self-Identity; also *Analogy*, Part I, Ch. II). Another way in which the mind affects the body is in volition, the laws of which are unknown. Equally mysterious are its laws of association and memory. How association and memory are controlled we do not know; for the laws that we formulate concerning them are merely a recorded observation that these mental processes take place, without informing us how or why they take place. The laws themselves are expressions of factual situations that are still open to explanation. Could we penetrate into the hidden sources that give rise to the visible effects that we observe, they could be completely accounted for.[3]

We have stated that the area of our knowledge is small and that even events and objects that we immediately observe are unknown to us in their inner recesses. But as we have already pointed out there exist infinite stretches of the past and future that cannot be explored by us. These too contain objects and

[2] Since the substantial nature of things is unknown, there are many things that take place in the visible world that cannot be explained, but must nevertheless be accredited as being logically plausible. For instance in the realm of nature we witness the inordinate waste of life, seen in the many seeds that never ripen, and in the mutilated and misshapen instances of those that do. Besides this one observes untimely deaths, tempests and famines that have no regard for human life or settlements in the course of their fury (Vol. I, p. 203). All of this seems to indicate at first sight an evil, or the work of a blundering stupidity, but this is only because we are unacquainted with all the factors of the case. To understand these seemingly irregular events, we should have to be acquainted with the inner substantial nature of objects and of minds.

[3] Cp. *Analogy*, Pt. I, p. 203: "But we know in a manner nothing, by what laws, storms and tempests, earthquakes, famine, pestilence, become the instruments of destruction to mankind. And the laws, by which persons born into the world at such a time and place are of such capacities, geniuses, tempers; the laws, by which thoughts come into our mind, in a multitude of cases; and by which innumerable things happen, of the greatest influence upon the affairs and state of the world; these laws are so wholly unknown to us, that we call the events which come to pass by them, accidental; though all reasonable men know certainly, that there cannot, in reality, be any such thing as chance. . . ."

events that fall within the universe and contribute to it in part
the systematic nature that we know it to bear. Let us consider
here one instance that Butler has in mind; the reality of the dead.
What is their status in the universe?

History bears testimony to the past existence of other people
and societies; we know that generations of people succeed each
other, pass on, and give way to the future. As past, they are no
longer revealed to us in actual observation, but does this mean
that they are no longer real, that they no longer exist? An account of the universe that pretends to be adequate must have its
say about these.

Under our discussion of personal immortality, we have learned
that man is immortal. Death, as Butler believes, is not the end
of life, but the dating within our own lives of a physical change
that has been noted in the lives of others. It is the indication
to us that the consciousness of man has passed on to new types
of expression and new kinds of association. For us who observe
the change is a drastic one, for all contacts and associations have
been broken. The broken contact, or decay of the physical body,
should not be taken as a sign that the person whom we refer to
as dead has ceased in any way to be, but only that we are unable
to fit into his associations or to come into contact with him.

But if man is immortal, so are the societies and groups that
spring out of human associations. These must endure with him.
It is true that societies and nations as recorded by history do
not exist now in the same way as they did then. Neither does
ancestral man. But human survival must *ipso facto* imply the
survival of society. Just as man in his post-mortal existence is
not in sensory communication with us, neither are his social
groups. We shall let Butler speak for himself. "And thus, when
we go out of this world, we may pass into new scenes, and a new
state of life and action, just as naturally as we came into the
present. And this new state may naturally be a social one. And
the advantages of it, advantages of every kind, may naturally
be bestowed, according to some fixed general laws of wisdom,
upon every one in proportion to the degrees of his virtue. And
though the advantages of that future natural state should not
be bestowed, as these of the present in some measure are, by the
will of the society; but entirely by his more immediate action,
upon whom the whole frame of nature depends: yet this distribution may be just as natural, as their being distributed here by

the instrumentality of men. And indeed, though one were to allow any confused undetermined sense, which people please to put upon the word *natural*, it would be a shortness of thought scarce credible to imagine, that no system or course of things can be so, but only what we see at present . . ." (Vol. I, pp. 38-9).[4]

Butler opens up to our imagination a universe which teems with life, humanity, and societies. Nothing is lost. Human life endures, not in isolation but in societies. The laws of its nature and of society under which it lives are much the same, for all we know, as for the societies we actually observe or that are known to us through history. The conditions under which life progresses there may be more favorable to the expression of human designs; the obstacles may be fewer, instinctive nature may be less of an inroad, and reason may be clearer and sounder. The desire to live virtuously, i.e., in terms of one's highest ideals, may have a greater chance to realize itself. The weakness and frailties that existed in their mortal life may still exist in their post-mortal life, but with less persistence and with fewer obstacles; to overcome all of them may require an eternity, and throughout this eternity there may be required many changes through which the will of man must exert itself anew. In comparison to the vast generations of life the world of visible men and societies is small, indeed.

In its visible and invisible aspects the universe finds its completion as a system of systems. But this completion is ideal or potential. Actually there is no relationship between the mortal and post-mortal societies. They are united by no bond of virtue. The threads of connection are remote and recondite. In their attempt to live virtuously they are bringing to bear in concrete realization the unity of a common purpose. Infinite stretches of time lie before them for this accomplishment, but from any instant of human expression these principles are ideal, not actual.

---

[4] Cp. also *Analogy*, p. 98: "Nothing which we at present see would lead us to the thought of a solitary unactive state hereafter: but, if we judge at all from the analogy of nature, we must suppose, according to the scripture account of it, that it will be a community. And there is no shadow of any thing unreasonable in conceiving, though there be no analogy for it, that this community will be, as the scripture represents it, under the more immediate, or, if such an expression may be used, the more sensible government of God. Nor is our ignorance, what will be the employments of this happy community, nor our consequent ignorance, what particular scope or occasion there will be for the exercise of veracity, justice, and charity, amongst the members of it with regard to each other; any proof, that there will be no sphere of exercise for those virtues."

23

THE UNIVERSE AS SPIRITUAL

IN THE present chapter we shall complete our account of the nature of the universe, bringing together in a summary conclusion the results that we arrived at in our last chapter. In doing so, we shall try to express from a somewhat different angle the importance of those results.

To our questions: what is the universe, what relations, if any, do the myriad of objects that we perceive around us bear to each other? we replied that in many instances their mutually exclusive singularity was apparent only. A closer inspection revealed to us that man-made objects and physical objects implied unities of law within which their apparent multiplicity was resolved.

Examining in detail how this was borne out, we considered each class of object separately. Man-made objects implied the ideality of human plans. A familiar instance of this implicit ideal would be a table and a chair. In their deeper aspects these are not two separate objects. If we view them as things, and read no further meaning into them, their separateness is an undeniable fact. But they are more truly known when regarded as instances of furniture, than when they are regarded as separate physical things. Viewed as instances of furniture, their individual unity is forfeited, for in their new relationship they are seen to be more intimately part of one another, and of a system of desires that has given rise to them. As concrete presentations, they have been wrought as the effects of prior causes. Their actual coming to be has depended upon the workman who has fashioned them, and upon the individuals by whom they will be used. In this newly discovered network of relations they are seen to be inextricably bound. Intrinsically and inseparably related to their causes, they could not exist without them. Trying to comprehend their nature thoroughly, we find we must renounce our superficial views of their independence and now regard them as members of a system.

This is no less true of natural objects. Composed of simpler constituent parts of matter, they exhibit in some degree the laws of their unknowable substrata. They are alike in sharing a common substance. But viewing them in regard to their more knowable aspects, we soon see the need of referring them to prior conditions, of looking upon them as effects, the further intelligibility of which can be acquired by seeking the causes that give rise to them. In this interrelation of cause and effect greater unity is achieved; the observed singularity of the objects in the physical world disappears in the higher unity of physical law. We can extend the process further, and each step that we advance reveals less and less of the initially observed plurality, and more of the unity of law that runs throughout their field. We pointed out that in each step one's intelligence was progressively satisfied; the accumulation of prior effects and prior causes in the physical world did not result in a mere addition to what was known, but in a further understanding of them. The causal regress followed is neither blind nor infinite; each step adds in meaning to what was already known, later stages modify earlier stages of established knowledge; the area of accumulated knowledge shows its contents to be interrelated in many ways and to imply an ideal systematic unity of which they were lesser parts.

The unity that is progressively revealed to our minds is a unity that we discover, but do not make. Between the world of nature and the knowing mind there exists a correspondence. The demands of one are fulfilled in the subsequent yieldings of the other. What the mind expects, it finds. The unity of law that it seeks is objective to its nature and independent to its discovery. The promised unity of the material world is objectively structural, and this ideality is the potential development that it now possesses for the future expression of this unity. All of this is transparent to the mind of man, but not constituted by it.

Within this ideally implied system of physical objects there exist many lesser systems that instance characteristics of their own, and these lesser systems reveal specific laws in addition to the more general laws that unite them. The construction of species, their relation to one another, are instances at hand; the structure of the human body gives evidence of its being a systematic unity, with laws that are different from the laws of their constituent material particles. We cannot believe however that these lesser systems are ultimate or mutually exclusive any more than the material particles of which they are composed; neither can we believe that they violate the laws of their material nature. Both types are interrelated. Moreover, further investigation would show that these lesser systems transcend themselves, when we attempt to take them as ultimate. Each in turn must be re-

garded as an effect of prior causal conditions, until the completion of all investigation reveals an ideal system of systems. Established through the methodology of cause and effect, the nature of
our completed objects is seen to be a totality, best understood
in terms of teleology or, as Butler puts it, final causes. For
Butler blind mechanism is unintelligible and irrational.

But the two classes of man-made objects and physical objects
do not stand alone, isolated and cut off from each other. The laws
of one enter into and interpenetrate with the laws of the other.
The manufactured articles cannot violate the physical laws of
the material from which they are made; the physical materials
lend themselves to the service of human needs and human wants.
Many of the natural objects subserve human purposes directly;
the food we eat, the water we drink enter into associations with
the human body. The loss or growth of the latter can be described
by laws which are on the border line between the two realms.
A fuller account of the human body would force us to recognize
the laws of physical particles out of which it is made; likewise
a complete understanding of the physical nature would demand
an account of the many associations that its lesser material particles formed, and of the newly acquired laws describing these
various formations.

The world of mind is related to the world of nature through
its body to which it is allied and over which it has control in
acts of volition. We have considered in our chapter on Self-
Identity that the systematic character that the body assumes
may be accounted for (were all the facts of the case known!)
in reference to the soul that animates it and makes it one; that
the identity of the body as a whole may be accounted for, despite
the inner replacement of its physical particles, by the mind that
dominated it for purposes of its own. In this observed relationship in which the mind assumes a superior partnership, the
physical and mental realms were seen to be further united.

This further interconnection of the apparent manifold is
borne out more clearly in the nature of man's affections in their
reference to the physical world. The ends that the affections
seek lie external to themselves viewed as psychological springs of
action. In many cases they point to an end that is external to
the immediate body of their agent. But since the affection can be
known only in terms of the object it seeks, we must grant that the
object that satisfies it must be viewed as intrinsic to its completed

nature. In separation from its object the propension would have no meaning. Through contact with its object the propension is intimately related to the outer world, as well as is the agent who bears it. The food in its natural state that the individual seeks is a further instance of a system in which physical nature and human nature meet. Neither member can be considered as real in abstraction from the other; if the end of hunger is food, then one of the aspects of food is its edibility for man and animal.

Just as one physical object is related to another physical object so that both together form a system, likewise one individual mind forms in its contact with another mind a system of which they are both inseparable members. We have already shown that man's instinctive drives carry him over into the realm of physical nature, by insisting that the object of the instinct was inseparably connected with it. We have had occasion to observe that in a similar way man is drawn over into companionship with his fellow beings. The more instinctive bonds of affection make him at first blindly sympathetic; but later their development into rational principles of self-love and benevolence makes for the various orders of society that history tells us about. These are indispensable to man's nature, for in intimate relationship with his fellow beings he rises to a greater consciousness of himself and is enabled thereby to achieve the full expression of his moral and religious nature.

Such were some of the ways in which the observed plurality of objects was seen to be united. No one object is truly single, and no one object can stand alone. Through the application of cause and effect they were all seen to imply a systematic grouping within which all were united. Some of the relationships were direct and immediate, others were reconditely united. Within the system they imply are observable levels of distinctions which show the lesser systems to be hierarchically arranged. Certain groupings of matter are superior to other groupings, mind is superior to body, aspects within the mind are superior to other aspects. As Butler says: "the natural and moral constitution and government of the world are so connected, as to make up together but one scheme: and it is highly probable, that the first is formed and carried on merely in subserviency to the latter; as the vegetable world is for the animal, and organized bodies for minds" (*Analogy*, p. 135).

But within the realm of mind we have had occasion to observe that some principles of action deserve a higher approbation than others. "It were ridiculous to assert," says Butler, "that a man upon reflection hath the same kind of approbation of the appetite of hunger, or the passion of fear, as he hath of good will to his fellow-creatures" (Sermon XIII, p. 197). And likewise society, which allows for the protection, advancement and expression of the particular individual, is superior to his individual and finite nature. And so the laws of human society are superior to the laws of nature; and in turn the laws of morality are superior to the laws of actual societies. Finally superior to them all are the laws of religion, for these latter are the direct expression of God.

Within these levels of distinction there is, as we have pointed out, no forfeiture of the levels inferior to them. Mind does not ignore body, but works through it, and utilizes its laws for its own ends. In the first part of our work where we discussed the psychology of the moral self, we pointed out that in the realm of mind the admittedly higher principles took over the contributions of the lesser propensions, so that it was indifferent whether we spoke of the principles as the propensions idealized, conscious of themselves, or not. Although superior to the particular propensions upon which they depend, the principles themselves are powerless to work without them. In their conscious control of them the principles were seen to direct the particular propensions to the end they unconsciously implied, so that they neither rose too high nor fell too low. In society too we pointed out that there should be no neglect of the individual. The laws of the state were laws in the interest of individuals and before them, all had equal claim to develop uninterruptedly and morally in their station of life. And so each higher level within any system is seen to have a directive claim over the lower, yet it cannot violate the laws and structure of the lower from which it emerges.

In our actual observation it was seen that many of the objects appeared to fall outside of their assigned systems. They do not at first sight appear to fulfil the function for which they were made. But concerning their isolation, or refusal to fall into actual systems, we can say that the failure on the part of some to do so is epistemological and not ontological; resting with man himself. If we possessed greater knowledge we could see that they must fall into systematic groupings as do the more regular and familiar instances. Our success in explaining things by final causes would prove to be successful in their case too. If we abandoned teleology as a category for ultimate reality we should reduce to confusion those realms of partial knowledge that we now understand so well. In our rejection of this category, we should lose everything; in its retention we have everything to gain, for there remains the intellectual hope to sustain us that those instances that now stand out against us will in time become more intelligible and less recalcitrant. This is one reason that Butler gives to account for exceptional instances. If we ask him for the guarantee of the teleological method (i.e., of final causes), he replies that it is borne out by the repeatedly observed instances of experience, and moreover experience affords us no other method (*Vide* esp. Introd. to *Analogy*).

But there is another reason that can account for the fact why many actual objects appear to stand outside of systems: and this reason is that the universe is a temporally growing and progressive affair. Accepting this as such, it would mean that the systematic contents of the world are still in the making, i.e., in the act of systematic formation. What appear to us now to be exceptional instances standing out against our known system of objects, are not. These merely require a longer period of time, actually to grow and develop. At the completion of their history they will be seen to take on a systematic relationship as truly as many of the more regular instances that are observed today.

Having seen that the universe is implicitly ideal, we must now see that it is spiritual as well, being the creation of a divine mind that expresses progressively in time an ideal scheme that He entertains. The universe which we have spoken of as a system of systems ideally expressing unity, goodness, reason and perfection, will now be seen to imply deeper origins for its completion of purpose. We shall see that it exists only in relation to the mind of God who has conceived it in ideal, and who is executing it in fact. That we are led to this conclusion arises from our further understanding of the nature of a system.

THE SPIRITUAL ORIGIN OF THE UNIVERSE

All systems indicate a design or purpose, and design or purpose indicates a mind for whom the design exists. Let us view this first in regard to man.

Our emphasis here has been on the fact that the objects that surround man and that suffice for human purpose have come into existence because of the prior demand for them in human nature. Manufactured objects supply a human need; they are called into existence to satisfy the primary instincts concerned with human desires. We can admit that in the first instances when these objects came into existence there was no directed endeavor upon the part of man consciously to seek objects to satisfy his demands; presumably he was fortunate in discovering what he needed. But as his wits became sharpened and as his alertness grew, he became aware of his wants and needs, and sought consciously to satisfy them. When he could not discover objects to satisfy his needs, he was forced to create objects and refashion in terms of human utility the raw and available material he could find. All of this refinement of search and satisfaction led to a conceptualizing of the situation in which he found himself. He became aware both of his nature and of the objects he needed for its satisfaction; as a consequence he bethought himself of the proper means.

Were one to examine the field of man-made objects, with the sole purpose of understanding their nature fully and completely, one would first see that they implied a unity which was ideal, but that this ideal unity revealed the purpose and demands of human needs that were articulated through the light of reason into a plan whose sole purpose was efficiently to satisfy these demands. And so in this way the manufactured objects of man reveal their human origin. Likewise with human society.

The forms and institutions of religion and government, as well as the lesser sectional divisions of neighborhood associations, all reveal as their ultimate origin the deeper human needs of benevolence, self-love and conscience from which they spring. Their apparent mutual exclusiveness reveals to a more penetrating inspection the unity of an ideal. The ideal is then seen to be a plan, and the plan is then observed to be a conscious endeavor on the part of man to provide for the satisfaction of human wants and desires. Were one to object, by pointing out that the origin of man's institutions lies in primitive obscurity, maintaining that at the time of their inception they did not come into being under the rational guidance of consciousness, Butler would nevertheless point out that they responded to human desires; whether their establishment was purblind or haphazard, or rationally arranged for, makes no difference to the truth of their origin. In either case the social institutions are explicable upon the ground that they meet and answer human needs.

We can now see that a system reveals design and order; design and order, as we have shown in reference to the realm of human products and society, reveal human nature, making its demands felt and striving concretely to realize them. We have also indicated that the more enlightened man is concerning his wants and needs, the more completely will this rationality be expressed in the world of outer objects. The more perfect, i.e., rational, any examined system is, whether it be one of manufactured objects, or of societies, the more advanced is the human source from which it arises. Hence, the more perfect the examined system, the more enlightened or rational is man. In proportion to its extent, precise interrelation of parts, and subordination of these parts to a common end, a system indicates a source whose intelligence must be at least causally equal to these revealed effects.

Let us carry our exposition a stage further. We have a right to say, according to Butler, that the presence of design indicates a designer, and that the more extensive and complicated the observed design, the more rational is the intelligence that conceived it. Applying this method of approach and interpretation to other objects of the universe, we must now examine and account for human nature itself, as a system thought out and sustained by a designer; and then the world of physical objects, in reference to the mind that conceived it.

In regard to human nature we see that we are in the presence of a system, which is complicated, neatly and exactly interrelated in the assemblage of its parts. As a system, it is observed to consist of an array of propensions and principles, so contrived that they imply each other; propensions and principles mutually imply each other and themselves. Secondly, we have pointed out that they also instance a logical and orderly progression: the particular propensions lead into the principles of self-love and benevolence, and these lesser principles lead into conscience or principles of reflection. Compassion offsets resentment; resentment and compassion judiciously exercised under the guidance of conscience advance the entire nature of man and the moral order. But the system of human nature must imply an intelligence by whom it was designed, and the nature of this intelligence must be at least equal to the system it conceived.

But since human nature is a fragmentary aspect of his society, the completion of the human constitution must take into account the societies man implies. Societies grow and advance in time; each stage is related to what goes before it and what follows. Man himself is immortal, and hence a creature of growth and development. He is presumably adapted to the various societies and groupings within which he happens to find himself. He knows that wherever he is, there are available for his utilization objects that can serve him. The objects available for his use, the societies for his advancement and exercise, the potentiality of both for infinite expansion into time, all give evidence of a system of extraordinary complexity. The adequate cause of this scheme can be no less than God.

That his intelligence is unsurpassable is evidenced in the enormity of the scheme, so arranged for beforehand that every aspect of its constitution implies a mutual dependence upon every other part. Part falls into part; both imply a more comprehensive unity; the unity they imply has been foreseen and arranged for, before its concrete actualization has come to be. All this implies foresight and intelligence. But as the scheme is of such a nature that in its everlasting advancement into time there has been arranged for beforehand the possibility of present parts fitting into and expressing future parts, the intelligence that has conceived this in advance of the fact staggers the imagination of man when he tries to picture it (Vol. II, p. 217). Just as man is superior to the objects of his creation and manufacture, likewise is God superior to man. The vastness of His scheme gives us an insight into the transcendence of His wisdom and power, but leaves unrevealed the essential nature of His mind within which the scheme was conceived.

As with human nature and the scheme that it entails, so with physical nature. This too is a scheme of great complexity. As a scheme it implies as its designer the same God and creator as does the system of man and society. The reign of physical law implies a law-giver; the inevitability of effect that follows from the cause indicates His steadiness of purpose and unswerving aim. The biological aspect is one in which species implies species. Foresight is instanced in this arrangement. Inanimate nature subserves animate nature, plants furnish to animals their necessary food. Both plants and animals are utilized by man for his own physical sustenance and preservation of life. In this arrange-

ment intelligence is seen; in this indication of systematic structure intelligent preference has gone before. The system of physical nature meets the system of human nature, and forms a part
of it. The work of God is seen throughout all. The extent of the
universe correspondingly implies a profoundly creative imagination that conceived it; the possibility for the parts to grow into
each other, and for both to imply higher parts of the same scheme
within which they grow, gives evidence of God's unfathomable
wisdom, for He foresaw in advance of the actual accomplishment the need that each part had for the other and arranged for
the possibility.

Having shown that the universe of actual appearance is spiritual as well as ideal, and that its spiritual basis lies in the mind
of God, we shall consider now, more in accordance with Butler's
procedure, the arguments that establish for him the existence and
nature of God. After this we shall interest ourselves more particularly in the relation of God to the world, and to man. This
will necessitate our considering God both under the aspect of
creator and under that of governor. This will be our task in the
next chapter.

24

GOD: HIS RELATION TO MAN

BUTLER never doubts the existence of God and never considers that his readers will. The *Analogy*, within which the problems of religion rise to the foreground, was, according to Mark Pattison, an answer to the Deists, meeting them upon their own grounds and presuppositions. Assuming this to be so, there is no doubt that Butler's main interest was to argue for the validity of Christianity and the Scriptures. He maintained that one could not deny the divinity of the scriptures, any more than one could deny that the system of nature proceeded from God. Yet many who accepted the divine authorship of nature refused to accept the divine authority and inspiration of the Scriptures, giving as their reason of disbelief the admitted presence of many insuperable difficulties. It was Butler's aim to point out that similar troubles were to be found in our acceptance of the world as created by God. In the system of nature, the difficulties are equally great, and yet we do not deny God's authorship; indeed we should have just as much right to do so here, as we have in the case of the Scriptures; but likewise we have as much right to accept His presence in both cases. Such is the issue that Butler himself brings up in the Introduction to his *Analogy* (Vol. I, pp. 8, 9). It never occurs to him that we may have in the observed difficulties of nature added arguments for the rejection of our belief in God's existence and nature.

It is not our aim to discuss the polemics of the *Analogy* nor to view it as a record in the controversy of deism, but rather to lay bare, in the metaphysics it implies, the nature of God and His relation to the universe and to man. We have already noted that for Butler the intelligent Author of nature and natural governor of the world can be accepted as proved (Vol. I, p. 10; also p. 115).

EXISTENCE OF GOD

Should one venture to ascertain for himself the nature and number of proofs for the existence of God, he could, from a review of the accumulated evidence, reduce them to four headings: analogy and final causes, abstract reasoning, ancient tradition and testimony, and general consent of mankind (Vol. I,

p. 10). The first plays by far the most important place in Butler's thought and is continually referred to, throughout his religious and ethical writings. It also has the merit of fitting in with the general framework of his thought, and illustrates *par excellence* the teleological method. As it will occupy the greater part of our attention, we shall refer to it later after we have first dismissed the other proofs.

Since Butler mentions that God's existence has been established through ancient tradition and the general consent of mankind, and says no more about them, we need not dwell upon these two sources. About the establishment of God's existence through abstract reasoning he also has very little to say. We shall discuss this first.

The argument based upon abstract reason appears, as far as I have been able to discover, in two references only. In his earlier correspondence with Clarke, when his friend Secker played the faithful postman for him, Butler after some uneasiness declares himself convinced by the abstract reasonings of Clarke on the nature and existence of God. And then no more is said. In his Ethical Sermons the argument based on reason is neither referred to nor repeated. It appears however in a later chapter of the *Analogy* in a new form (Vol. I, p. 116). We shall repeat it *verbatim*.

"We ascribe to God a necessary existence, uncaused by any agent. For we find within ourselves the idea of infinity, i.e., immensity and eternity, impossible, even in imagination, to be removed out of being. We seem to discern intuitively, that there must, and cannot but be somewhat, external to ourselves, answering this idea, or the archetype of it." The legitimacy for us of passing from the idea to the reality itself lies in the truth that every abstract (idea?) implies its concrete (object?); "this abstract as much as any other" (*ibid.*). Such is the abstract argument.

It is difficult for us to bring this argument under any of the three classical forms that were later made popular by Kant. It is not strictly speaking ontological (although it comes near to this type) for this reason: the idea of an infinite being that we entertain is not guaranteed as implying a concrete reality to which it refers, upon the basis that it is most clear, non-contradictory, or all-inclusive, but upon the principle announced by Butler that an abstract implies a concrete (*ibid.*). This idea of God in its logical status evidently belongs to a class of abstract ideas that in being abstract imply their concrete counterpart. Unlike the idea of God which is referred to in the ontological argument, our idea of God does not imply its objective reality upon the basis of being the most perfect idea that we can think of, out of many. Neither can this argument of Butler's be reduced to the Cartesian argument that sees implicated in the idea of God an objective cause that must be adequate to the idea entertained, so that God must be postulated as the real cause.

The proof of God's existence from analogy and final causes takes on many aspects. There is no attempt even here by Butler consciously to prove God's existence, for all the arguments that we are now presenting do not appear in Butler's writings as a conscious attempt on his part to add to the extant proofs. They rather appear in his writing in the nature of *obiter dicta* when he discusses other issues, such as Love of God, or Ignorance of Man, or Moral Government of God. They should all be regarded as instances of the way in which Butler's thought moved, and the general direction in which he would have gone, had he found it necessary to argue against sceptics for the existence of God.

Under this class of arguments can be placed the causal argument. The existence of the world as an effect proves God to be its cause, for there is no effect without its cause. The world shares, in common with other facts that we observe, a dependence upon prior conditions; when examined it leads us beyond itself to its intelligent cause (Vol. II, p. 219). This is the cosmological argument in its most undisguised form, and appears only once in Butler's writings, and then most sketchily stated. Even in its presentation, it is out of harmony with Butler's statement, for while he maintains that every effect has its cause, he does not say that the cause of an observed effect must unconditionally be a person or a mind. In the second place, he maintains that it is only effects that we are acquainted with. Causes, he holds, elude us; about them we are strictly in the dark (*ibid.*). Were he to adhere to this position, he could not postulate or rest in any one thing or person as an adequate cause; neither in God as the intelligent cause of the universe, nor in matter as the lesser and intermediate cause of man's knowledge of matter (Vol. II, p. 219). Yet Butler allows that in created nature there exist unknown physical substrata (presumably in the Lockian sense) whose nature has some causal relation to the physical laws we observe. For Butler to assume the existence of minds or bodies as causes of their observed effect would be, upon the basis of his statement, a gratuitous assumption. Hence we should be cautious against taking Butler's statements too literally or too seriously. As usual, his insight into the nature of the universe with its spiritual basis in the mind of God is more certain and more real to him than any arguments that lead to its establishment for us. It is this undercurrent of vision that Butler never doubts or forsakes.

The second argument that can be brought under the class of teleological proofs bases itself upon the appearance of design in the interrelated totality of objective nature (Vol. I, pp. 53, 146; Vol. II, p. 213). For Butler it was an obvious truth that designs implied designers, and the illustrations to which he constantly refers are a watch, civil constitution, or building; objects within which human workmanship is discernible, and about whose authorship there can be little doubt. It was an easy matter for Butler to make the transition from human designs to a belief in a cosmic designer, especially as he could derive support for his belief from his theory of probability and analogy. Upon the theory of analogy, he had every reason to believe that the designs we observed without the associated presence of a designer nevertheless implied a designer as necessary; for, being akin to those designs that had designers, they could not differ from them in having no designers themselves. To take the opposite view, namely that the appearance in experience of designs without designers was a genuine fact, would mean for Butler the rejection of all that probability stood for. But since most designs were patently explicable upon the assumption of a designer, it was highly probable that all designs were instances of the same principle. Exceptions to this rule could be accounted for by our ignorance. Since the only basis upon which we have to go is that of observed experience, we must remember that the majority of objects which we are surrounded with are objects that are directly traceable to designers. To assume then that the objects of physical nature, as well as their systematic interrelation with the realm of manufactured objects, are best accounted for by referring them to a cosmic designer, is borne out for us by an overwhelming probability. Moreover it is reasonable as well, for in terms of a cosmic designer we can give a more intelligible interpretation to the existent scheme of things.

The teleological argument for God has its other aspects. It does not rely solely upon the observance of design in the world of outer objects. It is more particularly instanced in human nature itself, not merely in the sense that we have already presented, i.e., that the human constitution implies a designer, but rather in the immediate factor of consciousness itself, and the proclamations that it makes (*Vide* Sermon XIII, esp. pp. 194-5). Butler has so well expressed the substance of this argument himself, that I shall take the liberty of quoting it somewhat fully.

"Let us then suppose a man entirely disengaged from business and pleasure, sitting down alone and at leisure, to reflect upon himself and his own condition of being. He would immediately feel that he was by no means complete of himself, but totally insufficient for his own happiness. One may venture to affirm that every man hath felt this, whether he hath again reflected upon it or not. It is feeling this deficiency, that they are unsatisfied with themselves, which makes men look out for assistance from abroad; and which has given rise to various kinds of amusements, altogether needless any otherwise than as they serve to fill up the blank spaces of time, and so hinder their feeling this deficiency, and being uneasy with themselves. Now, if these external things we take up with were really an adequate supply to this deficiency of human nature, if by their means our capacities and desires were all satisfied and filled up; then it might be truly said, that we had found out the proper happiness of man; and so might sit down satisfied, and be at rest in the enjoyment of it. But if it appears, that the amusements, which men usually pass their time in, are so far from coming up to or answering our notions and desires of happiness, or good, that they are really no more than what they are commonly called, somewhat to pass away the time; i.e., somewhat which serves to turn us aside from, and prevent our attending to, this our internal poverty and want; if they serve only, or chiefly, to suspend, instead of satisfying our conceptions and desires of happiness; if the want remains, and we have found out little more than barely the means of making it less sensible, then are we still to seek for somewhat to be an adequate supply to it. It is plain that there is a capacity in the nature of man, which neither riches, nor honours, nor sensual gratifications, nor any thing in this world can perfectly fill up, or satisfy: there is a deeper and more essential want, than any of these things can be the supply of."

"Yet surely there is a possibility of somewhat, which may fill up all our capacities of happiness; somewhat, in which our souls may find rest; somewhat, which may be to us that satisfactory good we are inquiring after. But it cannot be any thing which is valuable only as it tends to some further end. . . . Since the supreme Mind, the Author and Cause of all things, is the highest possible object to himself he may be an adequate supply to all the faculties of our souls; a subject to our understanding, and an object to our affections" (Vol. II, pp. 209-11; cp. also pp. 202, 215, 216).

This yearning for God is a yearning for a somewhat to complete our nature. The nature of God is a personality that man seeks. On the subjective side of human nature is the pre-existent drive towards its object. Now Butler's professed belief, one that is never directly expressed however, but reappears throughout his writings, is that the desire that man possesses for companionship or experience with a perfect self, is an undeniable proof that such a self does truly exist. "It is plain," says Butler, "that the nature of man is so constituted, as to feel certain affections upon the sight or contemplation of certain objects. Now the very notion of affection implies resting in its object as an end" (Vol. II, p. 194). And further on he again remarks that the "very nature of affection consists in tending towards, and resting in, its objects as an end" (Vol. II, p. 195). In other words, we are able to know that the objects of our affections exist merely from the knowledge that we desire them. Since man's nature is ideally one, we are assured that the objects sought by the enlightened self of man, in the enjoyment of which man's nature is completed and realized, must somehow exist. God is more intimately present to us than any one object can be (Vol. II, p. 25). He speaks to us through the voice of conscience (Vol. II, p. 98); the rules of it are the laws of God (Vol. I, p. 123). He is not sensibly present (Vol. II, p. 201), but presence through the sense is merely an accidental circumstance (*ibid.*). Since the objects of the higher principles of man are more assuredly real than those implied by the particular propensions, the ideals of perfect goodness, wisdom, and truth must be viewed as the expression of a divine mind within which they reside. Granting the existence in man of the several affec-

tions such as love, reverence, fear and desire of approbation (Vol.
II, p. 214), there must correspond to them the objects that they
seek. The perfections of God's nature are the only real objects
that will satisfy them (Vol. II, p. 25). In other words the existence of God's nature is assured us through our desire for him.

NATURE AND ATTRIBUTES OF GOD

We are now prepared to speak of the nature and attributes
of God, as far as Butler's expression on the subject will allow.
We have been cautioned by Butler to refrain from speaking with
too much conviction as to the nature of God (Vol. I, pp. 55, 125).
There are certain qualities that we should not ascribe to him.
For instance he is not moved by appetite or passion, as we are;
neither does he see, hear, or perceive with any sense like ours,
but in a manner infinitely more perfect (Vol. II, p. 84). Unlike
the objects of our perception he is not sensibly present (Vol. II,
p. 204). What then can we say specifically of his nature and
being?

We must first realize that there is much more in his nature
than we can fathom or ever find out. Our direct acquaintance
with his nature is gathered from the effects we observe about us.
But the cause from which these effects spring is infinitely superior to the effects we see (Vol. II, p. 213). An infinitely higher
exercise of our understanding would be required to view it as a
plan in the mind of God, before its actual foundations were
laid (*Analogy*, p. 116). But even were we capable of this exercise of mind, there would remain unexplored and hidden from
our view the infinite understanding, imagination, and wisdom of
God himself, whose sovereign mind gave birth to the universe
(Vol. II, p. 214). Yet these qualities that we attribute to the
Divine Mind do not cover God's quintessential nature. He is wise
and powerful, but wisdom and power are not God. The causes
which center themselves in God's nature are never completely
given in their effects, "this is no more than saying, that the
Creator is superior to the work of his hands. For observe," says
Butler, "the contemplation of that principle, faculty, or power
which produced any effect, must be an higher exercise of the
understanding, than the contemplation of the effect itself. The
cause must be an higher object to the mind than the effect"
(Vol. II, pp. 213, 214).

We do know however that God is one, simple and uniform,

"forever the same without *variableness or shadow of turning*" (Vol. II, p. 204). Yet, infinitely replete in perfect wisdom and goodness, he can only be known to minds like ours in partial and different views (*ibid.*). From the world that he has created, we can gather that he is not indifferent to vice and virtue (*Analogy*, p. 73). The fact that he favors virtue and discountenances vice can be observed in the moral government of the universe in the particular acts of enlightened man and society. His attributes of benevolence, justice and veracity furnish the foundations of religion (*Analogy*, p. 121). He has further indicated that virtue and right shall finally prevail over fraud and reckless force (*Analogy*, p. 74). And furthermore he can only approve of what is right, fit, and just (Vol. I, p. 335).

We have spoken of the attributes of God, and have pointed out that he favors the virtues of truth and goodness. Our insistence upon the virtues of the divine nature might indicate to some individuals that God's nature is determined by ends outside and beyond himself. Butler says in his Sermon Upon the Love of God (Vol. II, p. 214) that the moral attributes of God consist in their conformance to the law of truth. He did not consider until many years later the implications of determinism that this might involve for man and God.

In expressing himself more expansively upon the position, in regard to God, Butler tells us: "I am far from intending to deny, that the will of God is determined, by what is fit, by the right and reason of the case. . . . But if it be intelligible to say, that *it is fit and reasonable for every one to consult his own happiness*, then *fitness of action, or the right and reason of the case*, is an intelligible manner of speaking. And it seems as inconceivable, to suppose God to approve one course of action, or one end, preferably to another, which yet his acting at all from design implies that he does, without supposing somewhat prior in that end, to be the ground of the preference; as to suppose him to discern an abstract proposition to be true, without supposing somewhat prior in it, to be the ground of the discernment. It doth not therefore appear, that moral right is any more relative to perception, than abstract truth is: or that it is any more improper, to speak of the fitness and rightness of actions and ends, as founded in the nature of things, than to speak of abstract truth, as thus founded" (Vol. I, p. 125, footnote).

Yet notwithstanding the conformance of God to whatever is

good, it cannot be said that in God as well as in man, this necessity excludes "deliberation, choice, preference, and acting from certain principles, and to certain ends: because all this is matter of undoubted experience, acknowledged by all, and what every man may, every moment, be conscious of" (Vol. I, p. 115). In regard to the existence of God himself we are bound to affirm it as necessary, and uncaused by any agent (Vol. I, p. 116). It cannot be accounted for by reference to anything beyond itself. But admitting the necessity of God's existence, and the necessity of his acting always in the interest of what is right and fit, we cannot exclude from him either intelligence or design. Presumably God can imagine and conceive, and yet deny in the moment of conception the alternate modes of behavior, seeing in these latter courses a less good and less perfect means of operation.

GOD AS CREATOR

We have pointed out in a former section that the actual universe implies an ideal unity; we have also shown that the ideal unity exhibits a systematic order or plan the reality of which is to be understood only in reference to God's mind. Merely to view the universe as a scheme in God's mind is not sufficient however to account for its spiritual basis, any more than it would be to state that plans in the mind of man are spiritual merely because they exist conceptually for his mind. To appreciate the spiritual basis of the universe we must understand that it serves a deeper purpose for God's nature. If we ask what purpose it serves, or why the universe has come into being, we are told that "perfect goodness in the Deity is the principle from whence the universe was brought into being, and by which it is preserved; and . . . general benevolence is the great law of the whole moral creation" (Vol. II, p. 115).

Although the universe was conceived as a plan in the mind of God in which all things were laid out beforehand (*Analogy*, p. 207), the execution of the universe was not carried out at the moment of ideal conception. So perfectly has it been conceived that its coming to be requires an everlasting extent of time, before the ends that have been arranged for can be attained (*Analogy*, p. 206). The means that are conducive to the ends must await their time and order.

In the world of inanimate nature the reign of law is slow and deliberate; plants and animals grow up by degrees to their states of maturity. And man is no exception. He is equipped with adaptability to make his way, and provided with the means of habit-formation, so that he can accumulate and store up experience in the interest of virtuous living (*Analogy*, Pt. I, Ch. V). To conquer his own passions and to unify his own nature requires a length of time necessary to establish this result (Vol. I, p. 68). And particularly in the life of the moral individual, "there must be sufficient length of time; for the complete success of virtue, as of reason, cannot, from the nature of the thing, be otherwise than gradual: there must be, as one may speak, a fair field of trial, a stage large and extensive enough, proper occasions and opportunities, for the virtuous to join together, to exert themselves against lawless force, and to reap the fruit of united labours" (*Analogy*, p. 70; also p. 135). Butler realizes that in a timeless or eternal universe the moral life must prove to be illusory. But he also sees that nothing short of an everlasting duration in time is necessary for the coming to be of a perfect universe and the creation of man.

Besides being everlasting the universe is a progressive scheme. It is not a mere senseless unrolling in time, in which any one stage of its existence is potentially the same as any other stage, or in which future and past would reveal to a mind more comprehensive than ours a compresence of homogeneous events. A universe in which time were the mere unravelling of events that in comparison with each other were neither better nor worse, more perfect or less perfect, would be a universe in which time was ineffectual and a mockery. The value for Butler in the temporal aspect of the universe consists precisely in the fact that the later stages exhibit from the standpoint of the earlier stages a potential advancement of ideal unity and moral purposiveness.

There is offered to the universe at any one stage of its being the possibility for subsequent improvement. The actual universe, we must recall, is chaotic, or at best a partial unity. The universe as it should be is ideal and unitary. To expand from the lesser stages of incompletion demands a period of time in which assurance is granted for the progressive establishment of the implicit ends. The medium of time makes possible the fact of its growing completion. Each later period of time will mean the accumulation and preservation of what has gone before. It is not a new instance nor a fresh start that is unrelated to precedent events. In its accumulation of past stores it represents an ad-

vance upon the earlier stages, for it has gathered unto itself
the contributions of the earlier stages and the successful establishment of partial unity that they have achieved.

To accomplish the fulness and perfection of the indicated
plan, as it exists in the mind of God, requires an everlasting
period of time in which the ideal is gradually and progressively
realized. The time required is everlasting in the sense that at
no one instant will the ideal be completely established, but the
time is not a meaningless succession of events, for at any one
later period of time an appreciable advancement over an earlier
period of time can be observed.

MAN IN THE DIVINE SCHEME

We must now examine from the standpoint of our ideal
scheme the place and position of man, and the *role* that God intended that he should play. Man is one object among many in
the universe planned by God. Like the objects of physical nature
he owes his origin to God. Yet man is the acknowledged governing animal upon the earth (*Analogy*, p. 67). As one creature
among many he falls as one factor within the cosmic scheme.
His future is laid out beforehand, and what he is supposed to
do and become is already indicated in the ideal scheme of the
universe as entertained by God. Being immortal, his enduring
reality is everlasting. As a member of a progressive universe,
his future should partake in the superior and more advanced
stages of its development. He should share in its completer reality, and as a developing factor himself he should contribute
to it.

But man differs from the other creatures of God's scheme by
possessing choice, freedom, and deliberation. In his possession
of moral reflection he can know the nature of the scheme of
which he is a part, and he can know the part that he is supposed
to play. Likewise he has the choice of accepting the nature of the
revealed scheme, and the means to adapt himself to it and to
advance it as God intended it to be. "Our constitution is put
in our own power," Butler tells us (Vol. II, p. 9). Man is not
necessary but free (*Analogy*, pp. 120, 129, 130). "From our
original constitution, and that of the world which we inhabit,
we are naturally trusted with ourselves; with our own conduct
and our own interest" (*Analogy*, p. 149; cp. also p. 120).

What does this freedom imply? Does it mean that whatever

man believes to be true and right is cosmically and objectively so? Not at all. For we have been told that the scheme of the universe has been laid out beforehand, and man being part of that scheme has had his future path preordained. The freedom of man consists solely in the fact that he can accept this indicated plan or not; not that he can excogitate moral plans of his own to follow, that he can put in place of God's plan as being preferable. His acceptance of God's plan together with his putting it into practice will be rewarded by God, but his rejection in theory or practice will meet with punishment. "Consciousness of a rule or guide of action," says Butler, "in creatures who are capable of considering it as given them by their Maker, not only raises immediately a sense of duty, but also a sense of security in following it, and of danger in deviating from it. . . . But then the sense or perception of good and ill desert, which is contained in the moral discernment, renders the sanction explicit, and makes it appear, as one may say, expressed. For since his method of government is to reward and punish actions, his having annexed to some actions an inseparable sense of good desert, and to others of ill, this surely amounts to declaring, upon whom his punishments shall be inflicted, and his rewards be bestowed. For he must have given us this discernment and sense of things, as a presentiment of what is to be hereafter: that is, by way of information beforehand, what we are finally to expect in his world" (*Analogy*, pp. 123, 124).

We are now enabled to see that there is no inevitableness or necessity of events that can be predicted in regard to the future of the world, or of man's place in it. The scheme as God intends it is laid out in advance, but not its actual coming to be. Creating man his most important product, and endowing him with freedom of will, God has deputied to man a share in his everlasting creation. Upon the enlightened will of man rests the realization of the progressive universe. Indicated to him in terms of rewards and punishments are God's commands. But it is for man himself to decide whether or not he will heed them. If man lives according to the dictates of moral consciousness, he will advance in his own nature that share of the creation that was assigned to him. But if he becomes a victim of his passions, if he ignores the commands of conscience, he will leave unfulfilled the aims and desires of God. Whether or not the universe will actually become in time what God has arranged in his own mind for it to be rests in a large part with man himself.

GOD AS GOVERNOR

In creating the universe, God does not, as we have pointed out, execute it in the perfection of his ideal. He has left to man a large share of the work. This requires that man be instructed and guided in what he is supposed to do, be rewarded for his efficient cooperation or punished for his indifference or defection. The constant supervision of God over his universe, and especially over man's activities in it, reveals God to us in the further light of governor as well as creator. In the realm of inanimate nature the reign of law represents the reign of God, for he is the lawgiver. In the realm of human societies the same authority of divine law holds. The difference between the two classes of law does not consist in their authority, but in the conformance to the former of inanimate objects, and the respect to the latter that man may or may not pay. The fact that a moral intention of God for man may not be observed does not constitute that which is avoided to be any less of a law.

As a governor of the world, God presumably is more concerned with man than with any other of his creatures. The true notion or conception of the Author of Nature, says Butler, "is that of a master or governor, prior to the consideration of his moral attributes. The fact of our case, which we find by experience, is, that he actually exercises dominion or government over us at present, by rewarding and punishing us for our actions, in as strict and proper a sense of these words and even in the same sense, as children, servants, subjects, are rewarded and punished by those who govern them" (*Analogy*, p. 46). And further on we are told that "God exercises the same kind of government over us, with that, which a father exercises over his children, and a civil magistrate over his subjects" (*Analogy*, p. 122).

We are not left in ignorance as to what is right or wrong, for the dictates of our conscience are the laws of God (Vol. II, p. 98; *Analogy*, p. 123). Since we are not uninformed as to our task in life, or as to the duties we should fulfil, Butler holds that it is only fitting that we should be judged by what we do. We can expect that everyone shall be dealt with according to his deserts (*Analogy*, p. 126).

How does God communicate to man the moral path that he should traverse? How is the government of God made known to man and appreciated by him? These are questions that we must now consider, in order to understand more completely the means whereby man himself is informed as to God's intentions. The answers to these shall occupy us in our next chapter.

25

REIGN OF LAW IN HUMAN NATURE

AS DO aspects of the universe, so human nature too exhibits its laws of regular behavior. Viewed in their broader aspects, they are indications, in God's scheme, of ways in which we should conduct our lives. Since these laws are compulsory upon human nature, their origin more properly viewed is cosmic, not human. As such, their presence is an intimation that God exercises his government over man.

Human laws are of two kinds, natural and moral; the former are concerned with those deeds of man that are strictly utilitarian or biological, the latter are the laws of conscience. But in both instances they are commands of God to man. Natural law must be considered as preliminary to moral law, for since all human behavior must come ultimately under the direction of conscience all commands issued to it must refer themselves to this source of scrutiny. Natural law can prove to be no exception. Hence the examination of moral law must engage the greater part of our attention.

We have already pointed out that the universe properly understood favors a life which exhibits progressive development rather than mere change, we have seen that the moral endeavors of man are harmoniously received in its tissue of events; likewise we have shown that the moral acts of man add to the universe and actually complete the moral ideals that they imply. But this is not all. We must now see that the universe is so fashioned that it *commands* man to conduct his life according to the ideas dictated to him by his enlightened conscience. But since the deliverances of conscience come from God's scheme for man, this inner exhortation must now be regarded as an evidence that the universe is itself moral. In other words the universe gives instances of moral laws, just as in the physical domain it gives instances of physical laws. Man's duty in one case as in the other is to apprise himself of their respective natures so that he can conform to them. Our discussion of moral law will show in detail that the objective universe is governed upon the basis of moral law, that it communicates this fact to man in the form of pleasure and pain, as he respectively conforms or disobeys; and lastly, that the pleasure experienced by him is an indication to follow that action that produced it, just as the pain is a warning to him to desist from its repetition.

In speaking of law, we must be clear as to the meanings involved. Law, as used in connection with human nature, may mean inexorable happenings, over which man has no control, such as the growth of his body, the workings of his digestive system, the laws of memory, or the factors present in his mental make-up that allow for the expression of his powers and capacities in the way in which they do actually operate. Or law may indicate those norms of behavior over which man has control and to which he can conform. The former use of the term law indicates actual happenings; the second use of the term indicates an ideal. It is this second use of the term law that Butler is concerned with in his account of natural law and moral law. The first type of law may be more properly termed physical or physiological, and will not concern us in this chapter. What all of these usages have in common is this: that from the presence of an actual factor a designate effect must eventually follow. This inexorableness of cause and effect is Butler's understanding of law; not the inability to vary the causes, but the inevitable consequent of effect once the cause has come into being.

Let us now become clearer as to the distinctions between natural law and moral law before we examine each one on its own account. For Butler these laws govern different types of action in human nature. Natural law is applied to those human events that have no moral significance as such, although they can contribute in the long run to the moral life. Moral law on the other hand applies to those acts that are professedly moral, about which we can say that they are good or bad. They represent events about which we can make moral judgments. It is also Butler's interest to show that moral and natural laws are in their own way as much worthy of the name of law as is physical law. Natural and moral law, like physical law, are characterized by an inexorableness of cause and effect; they also have a teleological significance. Both indicate an intended purpose, the nature of which man should learn so that he can conform to it.

NATURAL LAW

As living creatures we possess the capacity for pleasure and pain; for both of these are the attendants and outcome (i.e., the effects) of all our actions (Vol. I, p. 41). Presumably it is through experience that we learn which of our innumerable actions bring us pleasure and which of them bring us pain. This is particularly true in the realm of physical objects and our experience with them. Some food is edible and some is not; if poisonous, we experience discomfort or even great pain. Hot liquids scald us, hot objects burn us. In light too strong for our eyes, our eyes smart, etc. These are the various instances that Butler has in mind when he speaks of natural law and our capacity for pleasure and pain. Physical and psychological aspects are intimately bound up with each other.

If our contact with objects were not registered in the form of pleasure or pain, we could not tell in advance those objects we should re-experience or those that we should avoid. The bare knowledge of physical events would be of little avail to us if we could not know the effect of physical objects upon our bodies. If in our experience we felt no degree of pleasure, or none of pain, we could not tell whether the object was beneficial in advancing our life or its purposes, or was harmful. We must grant that there exists between the realm of nature and man a delicate economy in which the needs of the latter are adjusted to the former. To discover this economy or arrangement becomes in a sense man's duty. Long before the advent of his reasoning he works instinctively in this direction, for in the pursuit of his instinctive life he is satisfying blindly the demands made by his nature, by seeking in his outer world those objects that have brought him pleasure in the past. Man is so contrived that he can become consciously aware of those objects whose presence is harmful and which he should avoid. Without this prior capacity for sentience man would be at a loss in the universe and quickly exterminated.

How should we interpret these feelings of pleasure and pain that man experiences in his contact with objects? To Butler at least the interpretation is obvious. Man seeks his natural happiness and views those objects that he can enjoy as constituting his natural good. At this stage of consciousness he further believes that the consequence of pain on certain actions, and of pleasure to others, is an indication of the existence of cosmic laws, that certain courses of behavior are approved for man to follow, whereas others are to be avoided. Viewing the situation from the side of our persons, we can feel assured that the pleasure that is experienced is an indication that we are acting according to the intended design of our nature, while if we experience pain we know that we have violated our nature. From the side of the object it means that if the object affords us pleasure it is fashioned to suit our needs; if not, it indicates that it is detrimental.

Besides the capacities we have for pleasure and pain, we have the ability within our power to live in accordance with our nature or not. Thus we can arrange our behavior so as to seek pleasure-giving objects, and to avoid those that bring us pain. So much then for the observed facts in the case. "And in general," says Butler, "we foresee, that the external things, which are the objects of our various passions, can neither be obtained nor enjoyed, without exerting ourselves in such and such manners; but by thus exerting ourselves, we obtain and enjoy these objects, in which our natural good consists" (Vol. I, p. 41).

It is futile for us to raise questions as to why the factors of human nature are not arranged otherwise or why within the scheme of things happiness should not be the natural consequence of all our actions, so that there would be no need for us to exert ourselves for the attainment of what brings pleasure. To answer such questions would require an insight into the scheme of things that we do not at present possess; or the assistance of revelation. Yet according to Butler we can appreciate even now that the divine plan may be disposed in other ways without at the same time being unfair or less good. It may happen that it is the wish of God to make only the virtuous man happy, or to require that man behave suitably to the nature God has given him (Vol. I, p. 43).

Natural Law as Beneficial. Thus it follows that actions are bound up with pleasurable and painful consequences and that man has it within his power to foresee these consequences, and know that they are inexorably united with the action; that he has it within his power to avoid the act if it is painful or delight in it if it is pleasurable. Butler now insists that those objects that bring us pleasure are biologically good, while those that do not are bad.

We must be on our guard against believing that every action that brings pleasure with it is necessarily a good act. It is not Butler's intention to say that in such a pursuit of pleasure we can find an infallible guide to our physical well-being. He insists that foresight is an intrinsic part of the process. The act may be immediately pleasurable but in the long run it may prove to be connected with painful consequences. The case of the glutton or the libertine is one at hand; the consequences of his immoderateness and intemperance may be far removed in the distance.[1] Even in actions that concern our most material interests there is the reference of consequence to consequence so that a degree of insight, calculation and reason is strictly necessary to inform us of the advisability of the act. While in some respects we are handicapped from knowing exactly what the consequences of any act will be, yet we are not completely without assistance. Nevertheless in the long run, it is the promised returns of well-being that will decide for us the pursuit of particular acts, and not the *immediate* promise of pleasure (Vol. I, p. 44).

Natural Government. The degree of pleasure or pain that attaches itself to natural acts indicates for Butler the existence of a natural government. This government is under the dominion of God, for it represents part of the divine scheme that he is projecting and bringing to realization. Butler sees implicated in these exhibitions of pleasure or pain an intention on the part of God to approve or admonish, just as much as if the spoken word were uttered. But furthermore, Butler sees there a warning as to what type of action we should select. The existence of pleasures or pains in the normal course of actions establishes a system of natural duties. We are enjoined to follow the pleasure-giving actions and are warned away from those that bring us pain.

We must look upon the consequence of pleasure and pain in the same way as we should upon the spoken word of approval or disapproval. But not only does pleasure indicate approval, it likewise indicates reward. In the same way, pain means disapproval and consequently punishment. All this must be granted if we allow for the reality of final causes, and ultimately the existence of God as the contriver of the scheme who is expressing his wishes through it. As Butler tells us: "if God annexes delight to some actions, and uneasiness to others, with an apparent design to induce us to act so and so; then he not only dispenses happiness and misery, but also rewards and punishes actions. If, for example, the pain which we feel, upon doing what tends to

---

[1] Cp. Vol. I, p. 134. "Things seemingly the most insignificant imaginable are perpetually observed to be necessary conditions to other things of the greatest importance: so that any one thing whatever may, for ought we know to the contrary, be a necessary condition to any other."

the destruction of our bodies, suppose upon too near approaches
to fire, or upon wounding ourselves, be appointed by the Author
of nature to prevent our doing what thus tends to our destruction; this is altogether as much an instance of his punishing our
actions, and consequently of our being under his government, as
declaring by a voice from heaven, that if we acted so, he would
inflict such pain upon us, and inflicting it, whether it be greater
or less" (Vol. I, p. 46).[2]

This natural scheme of pleasures and pains (or natural rewards and punishments) is an inexorable one that knows no
exception in an ideally actual practice, for there is the tendency
within an object of the pleasure-giving class always to produce
in the experient its degree of pleasure. The pleasure may not
always be immediate, it may be naturally delayed; or the pleasure
may be naturally immediate but unnaturally delayed. But none
the less there is afforded us every reason to believe that the
pleasure is intended, just as there is every reason to believe that
the pain is intended in the other class of objects.

Let us view now what at first sight appear to be exceptions
to this rule, namely that class of actions that should result in
painful consequences but do not do so, at least immediately.
They would be immoderateness in eating, drinking, loss of sleep,
etc. On the contrary, these acts, according to Butler, are often
attended with the highest degree of pleasure. But over a given
period of time, painful consequences are certain to come, and
when they do come, they are often excessive in amount, such as
sickness or untimely death. If we measure their immediate consequences against their far-reaching effects, i.e., their modicum
of pleasure against their subsequently entailed pain, they are
seen to be undesirable. The natural punishment may be so long
delayed that when it does come the agent may have forgotten

<hr />

[2] We must be cautious here against reading into Butler more than he means
to say, or to see conflicts where no conflicts really exist. In this section he is
speaking only of natural law and not moral law; he is not considering whether
morally many of the acts that are naturally beneficial would be approved of by
conscience. Granting then that it is a good thing for us to preserve our lives,
what can we further say? Butler makes at least six distinct statements. (1) As
a matter of fact some actions are pleasure-giving. (2) Pleasure-giving actions
are beneficial to the system of man. (3) Man seeks those objects that bring him
pleasure. (4) Pleasure-giving objects are signs of approval that those objects
should be sought by man. (5) The pleasure that attaches itself to an object is
man's natural reward for selecting the object. (6) Man *should seek* those objects
that afford him pleasure. This latter injunction must be accepted as an hypothetical imperative, as a guide to action at the level of prudence or self-love.

the original act that is responsible for it. In many actions of this kind in which the painful consequences are far removed from the original cause the agent is apt to consider the original act as one of exception, in the performance of which he is escaping the consequential punishment, but "things," according to Butler, "take their destined course, and the misery inevitably follows at its appointed time, in very many of the these cases" (Vol. I, p. 48).

In our youth we often contract unnatural habits for which we may be ready to excuse ourselves and others, on the ground that youth is rash or impetuous. Nevertheless these habits make for ruinous consequences that are often disastrous in their completed course. Upon the formation of habits our characters are formed, and an entire lifetime may take its unfortunate turn from early deeds of folly, or inattention to sound advice. Also by turning our minds to folly in early youth, we may miss opportunities of available benefits that may never come again (Vol. I, p. 49). "If the husbandman lets his seedtime pass without sowing, the whole year is lost to him beyond recovery. In like manner, though after men have been guilty of folly and extravagance *up to a certain degree*, it is often in their power, for instance, to retrieve their affairs, to recover their health and character; at least in told measure; yet real reformation is, in many cases, of no avail at all towards preventing the miseries, poverty, sickness, infamy, naturally annexed to folly and extravagance *exceeding that degree*" (Vol. I, p. 49).

Critical Appraisal. I will now consider critically Butler's remarks on the inexorableness of natural punishment, and his assertions that pleasure and pain are guides to natural actions.

In regard to the inexorableness of natural punishment Butler points out that many natural acts are not *immediately* followed by painful consequences; he does not say that they always will be, but only that there is the tendency for harmful actions to bring discomfort, and that feelings of discomfort are the natural indications that our bodily system has been abused. "Misery," Butler assures us, "inevitably follows at its appointed time" (Vol. I, p. 48). For Butler, the truth of this remark consists in the many empirical instances that he has observed; the probability, he would argue, lies in the direction of natural punishment. From this he goes on to say that the observed exceptions to this rule are apparent only; that if we could follow up the history of the act, we should arrive at a stage when the punishment so long delayed would announce the unnaturalness of the original act.[3]

Now arises a genuine difficulty concerning the desirability of those natural acts that would terminate in the death of the agent. This raises the whole question of whether man's temporal existence should be preserved as long as possible. Since man's natural life should contribute to, and at the same time subserve, his moral life, the actions of the former should be guided by the decisions of the latter. According to Butler "death may immediately, in the natural course of things, put us into a higher and more enlarged state of life, as our birth does; a state in which our capacities, and sphere of perception and of action, may be much greater than at present" (Vol. I, pp. 36-7). But if the action that brought about the death of the individual were to be classified with those of painful consequences,—which according to Butler should have been avoided,—yet it might turn out in the long run to be good just because it allows the person to rise to a higher state of living. All those acts that in the long run eventuate in death may for all we know be good.

To consider such questions as these belongs more truly to the discussion of *moral* law and exercise of conscience. We have assumed in our present section that to preserve one's physical life is a good thing. By way of anticipation: Butler would hold that our present life affords us the exercise and development of our moral faculties, that to be deprived of life in our earlier stages would leave us unprepared for the trials and demands imposed by the later, i.e., post-mortal stages. (Cp. *Analogy*, Pt. I, Ch. V; esp. sects. 5, 13, 15, 16, 17, 18.)

We must do all that we can to live and to live well; and this demands the biological conditions upon which moral education can depend.

---

[3] In maintaining that the exceptions to this rule are apparent, Butler has in mind (a) that they exhibit no independent law of their own that could be formulated on a basis other than the rule of natural punishment, (b) that we may be ignorant of the sense in which they are exceptions, (c) that in the possession of more knowledge we could see the reducibility of these apparent exceptions to the general law. In maintaining that the general law is a genuine law, Butler would hold (i) that it explains the facts, by answering to the end for which they were designed, (ii) whereas to deny the general law would not enable us to explain the so-called exceptions but throw us into confusion concerning the totality of presented facts. (For further understanding of Butler's views here, see his *Analogy*, Introd., also Pt. II, Chs. IV, VIII.)

MORAL GOVERNMENT

In our section on natural government we saw that our natural actions were bound up with feelings of pleasure or pain. These feelings of pleasure and pain according to Butler could be taken as indications as to how man should conduct himself in the normal course of living. They should represent for him ideal courses of behavior (sanctioned and instituted by God), as rigorous and as compelling as any physical law. They differ from physical laws in the possibility of their being violated or ignored just as we wished; if we do not conform, we pay the natural penalties of pain that were enacted. The pain that we experience is to be interpreted as a punishment for a wrong course of behavior and also as a warning that such a course of behavior should be avoided in the future.

In the present section we are raising a similar query, but of a more extended scope and also of greater importance. Man is a moral creature as well as a natural creature; and his moral nature is pre-eminently superior, for it is the source of the judgments concerning his natural activities, as well as the source of moral distinctions. Can we discover in the mutual affairs of men within society an instance of moral law, as we did of natural law? Are there any indications in the scheme of things that moral actions are a necessary aspect of humanity that draw our attention to them and compel our recognition? Do they too stand for a reign of law to which we must conform or pay the consequences of inobservance? Butler believes that there are such laws. We shall state his arguments and evidence for this position.

Moral activity unlike physical action is bound up with the self-expression of a conscious and rational being who evaluates the ends he proposes to follow. The existence within the universe of human nature means the constant expression of a moral nature. But in the universe itself within which man lives and exercises his nature are signs of moral workmanship, for the universe we have shown to be the constant expression of God's nature. As moral, the universe is disposed in a friendly way to the moral advances of men. We shall discern in the rest of this chapter the moral nature of the universe, and reserve for the next chapter the existence within it of the moral law. Under the moral nature of the universe we shall present the observed instances of moral law as they are implicit in the nature of man, in the nature of God, and lastly in the structure and behavior of society.

Morality in the Nature of Man. Since the moral quality of the universe is derived both from the presence within it of man and from the effect of God's workmanship, to show that the universe is necessarily moral, now that we have admitted the existence of God and man, is to show that morality logically follows from the nature of man and from the nature of God. From our survey of man's nature we observe that morality is an implied attribute. The proof of this was offered in the first part of our work. We attempted to show there that according to Butler to be a man is to be *ipso facto* moral. The distinctions that one makes between right and wrong have their origin in the constitution of man. To appraise persons for their deeds is the natural attitude that man assumes when he is conscious of himself and of other people. When his judgment is directed towards his fellow beings, he is announcing their moral nature, for he criticizes or praises them for their deeds or motives. But at the same time he is admitting the fact of his own moral nature, for in passing moral judgments upon his fellow beings, he is showing that he himself is a moral being.

The highest expression of man is activity in terms of his reason, and this is a moral activity. Man is so constituted that if he follows his reason he cannot gainsay his moral nature; this rule, says Butler, is never inverted (Vol. I, p. 64). He informs us: "there can be nothing on the side of vice, to answer this; because there is nothing in the human mind contradictory, as the logicians speak, to virtue . . . there is surely no such thing, as a like natural regard to falsehood, injustice, cruelty" (Vol. I, p. 65). Butler does not mean here that vice cannot be countenanced by man, but only that when it is so countenanced, it is in opposition to his natural law of virtue, for it is the obscuring of his moral sense by the dominance of passion.

Moral Expressions of God. Morality is also implied in the very nature of God with even greater certainty than in the nature of man. The law of virtue that man lives under when he allows his conscience to govern his actions is the law of God. The law of virtue is the condition of man's living as a moral being. This law lies outside of his particular finite nature; it is compulsory upon him and hence not directly of his own making. Existing as part of the universe, as the ideal for its highest intelligent members, it owes its reality to the same cause as the universe, which is God. The law of virtue that governs man's nature, and is fundamental to his society, is the law of God.

Moral Aspect of Society.   We have stated above that both man and God are moral beings; that the fact of their morality consists in their constitution as intelligent and rational beings. We shall now indicate that the moral nature both of God and of man is reflected in the societies in which man lives.

That society is moral is impressed upon us when we consider what is implied in its nature as well as in its pronounced attitude upon the moral and immoral deeds of its members. Morality is implied in the nature of society, for it affords to man the necessary conditions whereby he can live more fully, develop his interests, and unify his nature. The only intelligible meaning that we can assign to society is that it exists for the development of man's moral nature. Its sole reality consists in this: to show to man the way to achieve the moral life. Human beings manifest their moral nature by endorsing what is right and reasonable, by countenancing and supporting veracity, justice, and charity in themselves (Vol. I, p. 65), and also in others. Being attuned to each other so that sorrows and joys are shared in common, we as human beings are sensitive to rebukes, and feel in our own nature the shame of the ill-doing that is committed by others, as actively as if we had done it ourselves and as if our own consciences had borne us witness. This control over the happiness of others follows inevitably from the fact of our being moral agents, for it is in virtue of the exercise of conscience that approval or disapproval brings its consequent train of happiness or unhappiness.

Society actively takes an interest in the moral deeds of its members; for it favors virtue and discountenances evil. The practice of virtue, according to Butler, brings its external advantages to man. He points out that in the wise management of our own affairs we reap the benefits that we strive for. But when we are wilfully profligate, rash, or negligent, we do not. If we act unwisely, i.e., without being guided by conscience, we pay the penalty for our folly in many ways. The good man is publicly honored and trusted. Likewise he is rewarded by others for being virtuous. If known to be sincerely just, he will be offered posts of responsibility, and be acclaimed by the public. But if he is known to be villainous at heart, he will be shunned and punished. If he is known to be indifferent to moral distinctions, never allowing himself to be governed by principles of fair conduct, he will be avoided; no work of importance will be trusted to him. Besides this, the immoral man will be at odds with himself, as well as at odds with society. Internally he will be ill at ease or completely unhappy in the pursuit of what is wrong. On the other hand the good man will be at peace with himself and in harmonious accord with his fellow beings. These are the outstanding instances that Butler announces in his insistence that society is genuinely moral at heart.

We can admit, says Butler, that many actions that are really good at heart are punished by society, while ill and mischievous actions are sometimes rewarded. In answer to this he replies that good acts are never punished under the belief or knowledge that they are good. Likewise, mischievous acts are not rewarded under the belief that they are evil in their intentions. The fault lies here with society (i.e., those who administer its policy), and not with the intrinsic nature of the act itself. The fact that society rewards an evil act under the guise of its being good is unfortunate, but even in doing so it is seen that society is fundamentally interested in morality as such, and in the external recognition and reward of moral deeds. Were society a truly moral society it would admittedly not have made that mistake, for if it were more truly self-conscious it would detect the shortcomings of its judgments. But we cannot use as evidence in favor of the non-morality of society the fact that it cannot always detect the truly good and distinguish it from the truly evil.[4]

We can admit that virtue is not always recognized, but only because it is mistaken as vice by those who prevent its establishment, not because vice is openly countenanced. If the instance that is misunderstood by society and punished is a genuine moral principle, it will the inner tendency to succeed, and the motive to persist (*Vide* Vol. I, p. 72). If all the external hindrances were removed, virtue would proceed to establish itself. Given the right conditions, good deeds would thrive. But this is not true of vice, for it does not flourish in the open. Were all external obstacles removed, vice would tend to discredit itself and perish;

---

[4] "Reward," Butler says, "is in no sort necessary, and consequently not natural, in the sense in which it is necessary, and therefore natural, that ill or mischievous actions should be punished" (Vol. I, p. 6).

for vice is a principle of disruption. Such in brief are Butler's replies to the charge that virtue is not always rewarded.

Another counter-objection calls our attention to the fact that injustice often escapes the eye of the civil government. There are known instances of wicked people prospering, and also of the righteous suffering affliction (Vol. I, p. 66). These are facts that Butler readily admits; but he maintains that they afford no particular denial of the law that virtue is intended to be encouraged and vice to be discouraged. One can admit actually that in the natural course of things "happiness and misery appear to be distributed by other rules, than only the personal merit and demerit of characters" (Vol. I, pp. 65-66). But for this arrangement there may be the best of reasons. Unhappiness may be assigned in the interest of discipline, or the world may be governed by a set of laws from which "such promiscuous distribution perhaps must follow" (*ibid.*). Such is the situation as Butler sees it and the type of reply he offers. It would not follow, for him at least, that the escape of injustice or the material advancement of the wicked indicated any contrary evidence, that good deeds were not favored. He resorts here in support of his position to the nature of providence itself "plainly declaring itself for virtue, by way of distinction from vice, and preference to it" (*ibid.*). The fact that many individuals who deserve punishment do not receive it is no evidence that those individuals are favored by society.

There exists in society, especially in civil government, the tendency to bring all of its malefactors to justice. The fact that many of them escape the punishment that they deserve is incidental to the situation. It cannot be offered as an argument that the civil state connives at injustice, but only that the punishment of injustice has eluded its vigilance. If we take these circumstances into account we cannot maintain that the escape of injustice should be construed as evidence that vice is favored in the scheme of things (Vol. I, p. 67). "Good and bad men would be much more rewarded and punished as such," says Butler, "were it not, that justice is often artificially eluded, that characters are not known, and many, who would thus favour virtue and discourage vice, are hindered from doing so by accidental causes" (*ibid.*).

26

OBJECTIVITY OF MORAL LAW

THE evidence for the existence of moral law is instanced in the nature of man himself, in his experiencing pleasure in the performance of moral acts, and suffering pain when his deeds are wrong. In the constitution of conscience can be seen the most important indication that man exists under a law of virtue, whose precepts he is urged to discover and put into practice.

Just as in his non-moral activities man is apprised of the existence of natural law that he should follow if he is to preserve his life and health, likewise is he instructed in moral behavior. There exists here a similar intimation that man is subject to a type of law that it is incumbent on him to follow. In other words there is a demand made upon the nature of man for him to pursue a life of virtue. For Butler this demand is an evidence that the universe not only is receptive to the moral advances of man, but insists upon man's conducting himself according to its law of virtue, which is as objective and compulsory to him as are the natural or physical laws. It emphasizes at the same time that in its completer reality the universe is much more than a framework for physical and natural law. To be truly known it must be viewed as moral and religious as well. We shall now present and consider in detail Butler's arguments for the stated moral law of the universe; after that, we shall indicate the relation that exists between natural and moral law.

MORAL LAW

That there exists in the universe a type of moral law is seen in the fact that pleasure or pain is the invariant accompaniment of our moral deeds. If my thoughts or deeds are moral, I feel happy; if they are bred in vice, I feel miserable or unhappy. It follows then that pleasure and pain are necessarily intrinsic to the moral act as such. We have stated in the last chapter that it is the tendency of virtue in society to be externally rewarded, and of vice to be externally punished, quite apart from the feelings of the man that are also involved. Butler is calling our attention now to the inner subjective feelings that accompany the planning or the outcome of a moral act. He is not concerned with the fact that society sometimes punishes an innocent man, or that a guilty man often escapes civil punishment; but rather with the feelings of an innocent man who is wrongly punished, or of a guilty man who escapes the vigilance of the law. He is concerned here with the same problem that concerned Plato in the first part of his Republic, when he makes Glaucon and Adeimantus urge Socrates to defend the intrinsic nature of virtue in opposition to the claims of Thrasymachus.

In both of the instances of this latter case Butler maintains that the innocent man experiences the pleasure of having done the right thing, while a guilty man, if self-conscious as to his deed, experiences the emotional pain of having done wrong. Thus a virtuous man is happy quite apart from the fact that his virtuous acts are recognized and rewarded externally. Society may condemn an individual as being vicious, but if he is truly moral he will experience an inner satisfaction and complacency of mind. On the other hand a vicious individual will be ill at ease with himself, even though his viciousness be hidden from others, or rewarded by them under the belief that it is virtue.

What interpretations can be placed upon this admission? The invariable association of pleasure with a virtuous act and of pain with an immoral act shows the presence of an inexorable law. It further indicates that virtuous deeds are the intended course of behavior that man should follow, and that vicious deeds are those from which he should refrain. It likewise shows that the accompanying pleasure is an aspect of reward, and the ensuing pain, if the deed is vicious, a form of punishment. Lastly, it assumes that man seeks as a matter of course whatever will bring him pleasure, and avoids whatever will cause him pain; that in the absence of the feelings of pleasure and pain he, would be at loss to know what deeds or courses of action were sanctioned and what were not. Man possesses insight into what is virtuous and has at the same time the means of pursuing it. He can learn those acts that are intrinsically virtuous and that bring him pleasure and those acts that do not and that never will. He can then adjust himself in all of his conduct so as to identify himself with what is good, and experience the pleasure that is consequent on good deeds. Having learnt in the past what acts are virtuous, he can expect to re-experience them in the future and to enjoy the complacency of mind that is natural to them. To avoid the pangs of conscience lies within his control as well. The misery entailed by a career of vice can be cut down to the barest minimum, or completely avoided, just as he wishes.

To understand the relationship between pleasure and virtue, and vice and pain, we must observe here that as in the case of natural pleasure and pain, the appropriate feelings of moral deeds may be delayed, or temporarily miscarry. It is not contended that a vicious act or plan may not be immediately pleasant, for many times it is, but the painful consequences that are intrinsic to vice may be delayed. But we should not accept this delay of punishment as an instance that the deed we are contemplating is one to be favored; that in our immediate experience of pleasure it is to be sanctioned as good. We have every reason to believe that the expected pain will invariably follow in its due time and order. We are told that in the course of time, after the act has run its history, the painful effects will be forthcoming. And since man is immortal, there remains stretched before him an endless expanse of time, in which he has opportunity to arrive at greater self-consciousness, and to experience the delayed effects of earlier deeds, even though these deeds were originally committed during his moral life. His earlier vices will tend to transmit their influence to these subsequent stages of his life. At some time during this future stage, one may experience the full consequence of his earlier follies and fall at last victim to the pangs of his conscience. But he has everything to gain from having lived in accordance to virtue.

We may grant here that the pleasure that is intrinsic to virtue may likewise be delayed, and that a virtuous life may be one which is irksome, as long as we are on earth, and as long as we are not fully rational or self-conscious. The fuller blossoming of a virtuous life may be delayed until long after the original events have ceased to be, until long after the man has passed to his other life. But the tendency of virtue to reap its full reward should sustain the individual in his hopes and influence his life here on earth.

Having made clear to ourselves the fact that virtue tends inevitably to bring about its reward to its author and vice its degree of pain, we must now take care not to confuse this class of feeling with another class of emotions that is experienced by the individual at the same time. For the sake of convenience we shall refer to this second class as the natural emotions, and to the first class, i.e., those we have just discussed, as the moral emotions. We shall find it necessary to consider this class of natural emotions in detail; together with its bearing upon the class of moral emotions.

NATURAL AND MORAL EMOTIONS

Natural Emotions. Every act of man has its psychological precondition, for it is the outcome or expression of an affection which is part of man's natural equipment. Viewed from its psychological side, each act is the fulfilment of a tendency to act. We dwelt upon this phase of action at great length in the earlier chapters of the present work. Each act of man is the bringing to completion of a tendency in the direction of its outward expression. Until it is expressed in overt behavior, the urge to act is restless, and is experienced by us as a dissatisfied craving. When we are in the presence of an object that we know will satisfy this inner tendency, we can arrange for the affection to be released, and direct its course so that it will terminate within the object. When we have done so, we become emotionally appeased. The dissatisfied craving is then quieted, and the ensuing emotional tone is pleasant. Hence all acts are the outward expression of tendencies within the nature of the individual which we have already referred to and termed "affections." These affections can be viewed as nervous arrangements or conditions, capable of activity, and tensely set for outward expression. Their release into nervous activity brings its consequent relief; the tendency is appeased because satisfied. This is a psychological account of every act we perform. If the felt dissatisfaction is hunger, we are emotionally appeased in the consumption of food.

It is none the less true of deliberative acts, i.e., the use of our reason, or of altruistic acts, i.e., the devotion of ourselves to other people. In regard to the latter, we can psychologically explain our altruistic acts by the prior possession of altruistic impulses, called benevolence, that restlessly seek outer expression. The presence of other individuals affords us the opportunity to give vent to this psychological principle. In the performance of our benevolent act we are satisfying according to Butler the underlying affection that preconditions it. As a result we experience a feeling of satisfaction, largely because our psychological predisposition towards benevolence has been exercised and quieted.

Our moral actions are no exception to this rule. We act morally because of an inner drive to do so. From the standpoint of our psychological equipment, conscience is but one affection among many. As a psychological precondition, it tends to an outward expression, for only in its outward course can it complete its nature. From the standpoint of the body there is experienced the consequent feeling of contentment in its release.

But what is true of our strictly virtuous acts, holds likewise for our unvirtuous acts. These too are based upon psychological preconditions. They differ from the virtuous acts in this: the psychological impulse that preconditions their activity is not native, but acquired; the impulses that precondition the activity of virtuous acts are part of man's original constitution. But, even though the "mechanism" for one's unvirtuous mode of behavior has been acquired, the emotional effect that accompanies its expression is not different from the emotional effect that follows in the expression of a virtuous act. From the standpoint of psychological feeling we experience in both cases a feeling of contentment that a course of action has discharged and completed itself. Viewing our unvirtuous acts from their psychological aspects only, we experience a feeling of satisfaction when these acts have been actively expressed in accordance with the plans that conceived them.

Some individual might readily grant that the more instinctive impulses such as hunger, thirst, or the mechanisms of habit exhibit this law of emotional contentment that comes into operation after they are discharged; but they are ready to deny that in the case of the more conscious principle this feeling of emotional contentment is likewise experienced. In answer to them we must again refer to the earlier part of our work wherein we discussed the relation between the principles and the particular propensions. We pointed out there, how the principles are materially dependent upon the particular propensions for the medium through which to work. We showed that the proper expression of the principles occurred only when they utilized the pre-existent particular propensions. We said that the principles could be viewed as the particular propensions illuminated by consciousness of the ideal ends they remotely implied. Since we grant to the particular propensions the psychological contentment consequent upon their active expression, we cannot deny to the principle, which is in one respect the propensions idealized, a similar emotional concomitant.[1]

Moral Emotions. Having called our attention to the existence within man of this natural class of emotions, we are now aware that at the level of man's conscious life there exist two types of emotions, the natural and the moral. The recognition of their separate origins enables us to distinguish more clearly between those feelings that are merely natural and those that are essentially moral. Thus for instance, if a man of vicious tendency experiences no uneasiness, but on the contrary experiences a feeling of satisfaction over what he has accomplished, we are enabled to account for his feeling of ease and enjoyment and to see at the same time how foreign and unconnected that feeling is to the act when it is viewed in its moral aspect. The pleasure that follows is not to be accepted as a sign that the act has been morally sanctioned, but only that an "acquired mechanism" has been released and expressed.

On no account are the moral feelings to be confused with the natural feelings. The moral feelings of complacency are not to be identified with the natural feelings of psychological well-being. They are distinct in genus. The moral feelings like the natural feelings are registered in the mind; both are experienced as psychological data. The former are intrinsic to the act as good or bad. They are the halo that crowns the goodness of the act, or the misery that follows from the act's being vicious. Although these feelings are distinct in their origin, they are nevertheless both present to the mind of the agent in the course of his virtuous acts; whether immediately or not, Butler does not say. The moral feeling may not always immediately follow the virtuous act, for in many cases it is created or brought to light by our reflecting subsequently upon the intrinsic worth of the committed deed.

1 As Butler tells us: "the gratification itself of every natural passion must be attended with delight. . . .An action then, by which any natural passion is gratified . . . procures delight or advantage; abstracted from all consideration of the morality of such action. Consequently, the pleasure or advantage in this case, is gained by the action itself, not by the morality, the virtuousness or the viciousness of it; though it be, perhaps, virtuous or vicious. Thus, to say such an action or course of behaviour, procured such pleasure or advantage, or brought on such inconvenience and pain, is quite a different thing from saying, that such good or bad effect was owing to the virtue or vice of such action or behaviour. In one case, an action abstracted from all moral consideration, produced its effect; in the other case, for it will appear that there are such cases, the morality of the action, the action under a moral consideration, i.e., the virtuousness or viciousness of it, produced the effect" (Vol. I, pp. 60-61).

Thus it is probable that it occurs later in time than the natural feeling, for this latter would be experienced as soon as the act had completed itself, since it is the psychological announcement of a satisfied affection.

Butler is more explicit about the unvirtuous acts and the feelings consequent on our experiencing them. In the commission of a vicious act, about which the individual has become reflective, there are present in his mind two kinds of feeling, i.e., the natural feeling of pleasure or pain, and the moral feeling of uneasiness. If the act is naturally detrimental to the self, because founded upon an unnatural impulse, the natural feeling will be one of harm and sense of loss. Even here a distinction is to be drawn between the natural feeling of harm and the moral feeling of disquietude. As Butler tells us: "That inward feeling, which, respecting lesser matters, and in familiar speech, we call being vexed with oneself, and in matters of importance and in more serious language, remorse; is an uneasiness naturally arising from an act of man's own, reflected upon by himself as wrong, unreasonable, faulty, i.e., vicious in greater or less degrees: and this manifestly is a different feeling from that uneasiness, which arises from a sense of mere loss or harm" (Vol. I, p. 61).

Critical Appraisal. We have already stated that Butler distinguishes between moral feelings and natural feelings so that he can satisfactorily account for the emotional tone of pleasure that often accompanies unvirtuous acts. Having assumed that man is always attracted to what is emotionally pleasant, he wants to point out that there are instances when man should not repeat in the future those acts that brought him pleasure in the past; and that these instances are to be seen in those unvirtuous acts whose outlet is naturally satisfying. But when Butler distinguishes as he does between these two types of feeling, he is in danger of forfeiting the criterion whereby moral acts can be distinguished.

Let us grant with Butler that the ordinary individual is swayed in his conduct by the alluring happiness to be experienced by him through the moral feelings. There arises here a difficulty for the individual in discriminating between the natural feelings and the moral feelings that both attend an act of conscience. As feelings they are both registered in the same consciousness, both are experienced as states of mind. As such they are on the same level. But we have reason to believe from what

Butler explicitly tells us, as well as from the general tenor of his thought, that the moral feelings, since they are the results of reflection, will come about later than the natural feelings that are immediately felt at the completion of the act; for the moral feelings cannot come until the individual is convinced at heart that the act he has performed is a good act. But at this point a complication arises for us, because to arrive at this moral appraisement requires at the same time an exercise of his mind that from the standpoint of his natural equipment presupposes a natural affection. This natural affection will give rise to a feeling of pleasure in its very exercise of appraising the committed deed. Hence at the completion of man's moral reflection there should be present in his mind two classes of feelings, the natural and the moral. The moral feeling is the complacency of mind in having done well. The natural feeling is the experience of psychological satisfaction that the affection upon which the course of reasoning is founded has completed itself in an outward course of action.

Let us consider this first. Suppose one were to deny the presence of this natural feeling? In this case he would be presupposing that the subsequent act of moral reflection either rests upon no psychological precondition, i.e., on no affection, as do the active principles, or that there is experienced from the psychological standpoint no feeling of ease or satisfaction brought about by the overt exercise of this affection. But since it is Butler who makes the distinction in the first place between the moral feelings and the natural feelings, for one to say that the act of virtuous reflection is without its psychological aspect of natural feeling would be nothing less than an arbitrary assumption. Hence we have every right, in accordance with the principle of natural and moral feelings that he lays down, to believe that no act of moral reflection is ever without its accompanying natural feeling.

Having granted that these two types of feelings are both present to the mind of the agent, we are at this point confronted with an insuperable difficulty. The attempt on Butler's part to distinguish between moral and natural feelings for the sake of a theory is unsuccessful, for on what basis shall we distinguish between them and assign them each to their proper origin? Since these both classes of feelings are contemporaneous or in close succession, how can we tell accurately whether the experienced feeling of pleasure was natural or moral? Suppose we grant that a vicious act brings its degree of uneasiness, yet we must also admit that the subsequent reflection of settling its moral status brings its natural pleasure; in this case we should find it difficult to assign the feelings to their proper sources or ever to know whether the feeling of pleasure were moral or the feeling of pain natural.

But the mere failure on our part to distinguish these feelings and to evaluate them does not constitute all the difficulty. It is a common occurrence that when acts of vice are reflected upon, especially by the penitent man, the resulting feeling is often relief in the acknowledgment of his wrong. This is especially true in cases of prayer and acts of confession. There is mental ease in divulgement. In considering a case like this it would be difficult to read any particular significance into Butler's statements, for he assumes that men will avoid the feelings of pain that accompany immoral acts. But if a particular act which is vicious is closely allied with the feeling of relief in its divulgement or confession, there ensues for the person who faces this situation for the second time a foresight of assuagement. His expectancy of this later consequence would not act as a deterrent to his repeating the morally vicious act. In fact, we could easily picture to ourselves instances when it would be an incentive, especially to those religious fanatics who commit sins for the joy of penance. A less extreme but more common case would be seen reflected in those who willingly martyrize themselves for the pleasure of self-commiseration. If we only assume that the pleasure or pain of an act is an inducement or deterrent respectively to the performance or the avoidance of the act, it might often happen in the practice of this natural rule that the virtuous act would come out the loser, for the promised pleasure which would act as an inducement for the agent to repeat the act would now fall into that class of feeling that Butler terms natural.

There is a further point of criticism that I will raise here. Let us grant the distinction between the moral and natural feelings, and allow that each can be fully accounted for and assigned to its proper source. My inducement to perform a moral act would, according to Butler, be influenced by the pure joy of heart in doing what was right. But suppose, since one is granting the influence of pleasure as an inducement, that the promised natural pleasure is of greater degree or more appealing than the promised moral pleasure, how then would one decide between them? If the natural pleasure were more intense, should I forswear the moral deed because in comparison of intensity the moral pleasure, although we allow it to be superior in quality, is of a lower degree? Or if I forswear the natural pleasure and pursue the moral pleasure, then in respects to quantity I am following a lesser pleasure, or a pain? But if I allow to the moral pleasure a superiority of worth because of the pleasure's being moral, then I am clearly not swayed by considerations of pleasure at all, but by inducements of value. Then for Butler to develop as he does a doctrine of moral pleasure and pain, and to hold up the latter as an undesirable consequence of wrong-doing, losses all its meaning. He must make his appeal frankly upon the intrinsic desirability of the virtuous act itself, and refuse to sell it under a guise.

We should not press any further a point of criticism that would force Butler to admissions he did not make, or intends to make. If we take in abstraction from the general tenor of his doctrine his remarks upon the moral government of God, he comes dangerously near the identification of his position with an ethics of hedonism. But such a goal is not his aim. In his Dissertation on Virtue, Butler tells his reader that man is "constituted so as to condemn falsehood, unprovoked violence, injustice, and to approve of benevolence to some preferably to others, abstracted from all consideration, which conduct is likeliest to produce an over-balance of happiness or misery . . . Were the author (i.e., God) to propose nothing to himself as an end but the production of happiness . . . yet ours is not so" (Vol. I, p. 335).

Virtue is clearly to be pursued for its own sake, but whenever the deed is genuinely virtuous, it is at the same time productive of moral feeling, such as contentment, ease, or even the sense of sublimity. We can say, if we wish, that man would not pursue virtue if he gained nothing in its pursuit, i.e., if no happiness were to be gained from it, for he is a sentient as well as an intellectual being; but we cannot say that it is pure feeling (if such a state is possible for man), abstracted from its object, that he is concerned in realizing. It is always a moral feeling that man genuinely desires, and a moral feeling is one that has been made through moral ideals and values that have entered into its nature and endowed it with its unique feeling-tone. Happiness and virtue, Butler holds, cannot be divorced, but the happiness sought is the happiness of virtue, belonging to it and colored by it. As such it enters into the very constitution of conscience and forms, as we have already pointed out in our section on conscience, one of its inseparable features.

It may happen that in the course of his life the individual may not experience the joy of having performed a genuine moral act; or that he may be misled in what he thinks is a moral act and a moral feeling. Butler would not hold that the individual should repeat in the future such an act as in the past brought him pleasure, if in the meantime the individual has discovered that the act was not one of pure virtue. Virtue, and not happiness in abstraction from it, is to be his guide. It is for this reason, i.e., the possibility of being misled by private feelings and mis-estimations, that Butler puts the recognizability of the moral act in its intellectual setting rather than in the subjective and private feeling of virtuous happiness, without denying however that a virtuous act is blissful, and that in the absence of its sentient quality it could have no appeal for man.

In fairness to the critical reader of Butler one must admit however that his remarks on happiness and virtue are not always free from ambiguities.[2] Instead of showing clearly that virtue brings its own reward to the virtuous man in the inner knowledge and bliss of having done well, he makes it appear that external rewards, e.g., public honor, or the gifts of heaven, are part and parcel of one's moral merit. The general tenor, however, of his doctrine is in favor of intrinsic happiness rather than extrinsic; he does not exclude the latter, though its presence may be regarded as gratuitous, so that its absence in an unjust society is not sufficient to detract from the intrinsic worthiness of a moral life.

INTERCONNECTION OF NATURAL AND MORAL LAW

We are now prepared to indicate the relation for man between the realm of natural and moral law. Both types of law issue their imperatives, but no conflict is involved nor can be. Natural law legislates for the instinctive or non-rational self, while moral law

---

[2] Cp. esp. Vol. I, p. 336: "Moral government must consist in rendering them happy and unhappy, in rewarding and punishing them, as they follow, neglect, or depart from, the moral rule of action interwoven in their nature, or suggested and enforced by this moral faculty: in rewarding and punishing them *upon account of their so doing.*" (Italics mine.)

commands the conscience. But since man's conscience is his organ of unity that legislates for his lesser principles and propensions, moral law is at the same time an imperative to them. When man is fully conscious about himself, the natural laws do not cease to be, any more than the propensions or lesser principles to which they refer; on the other hand they continue to operate as before, but receive in the light of man's understanding a moral quality, for they are now seen to be necessary and conducive to man's moral life. Without them, i.e., without recognizing their subservient worth, man could not live, just as without his array of propensions and lesser principles conscience or the moral life would cease to be.

The natural law enters into the body of the moral law and forms part of its contents; in its absence the moral law would be so much poorer, that it is doubtful whether it could recognizably survive. Moral law receives as part of its expression, much in the same way as we have seen that self-love includes benevolence, the contributions made to it by the dicta of natural law. Although moral law contains much more than the contents of natural law, yet in its possession of its contents the individual is better informed, and more capable of fulfilling the requirements of morality, and of his own nature.

SUMMARY AND TRANSITION

We can now bring to a completion the contributions of our past five chapters. Our aim has been to characterize the nature of the universe. To do this it has been necessary to draw distinctions between the universe as it actually is in any stage of its progress, and as an ideal that should be realized. Viewing the universe under the former aspect we have had occasion to note that at any one stage of its existence it is actually many in its contents, unrelated in many of its parts, ununited and unorganized. In contrast to the ideal universe the actual universe instances incompletion, absence of unity, and partial rationality. Viewing the universe under its latter aspect, we have seen it to be a system of systems, within which every object tends to fall harmoniously with precision and nicety. This ideal aspect of the universe is the goal implicit in every one of its actual contents. It is not real, in the sense that things or events are actual, or predetermined. The ideality may or may not come to be actual. This is especially true of perfect selfhood or society, to take these as instances. Much depends upon the intelligent activity of man.

The relation of the actual universe and the ideal presupposes the presence of minds, i.e., of God and man. In relation to them the universe was seen to be spiritually grounded, and through their activity the actual universe and the ideal universe become mediated. No longer static, the actual universe now progressively develops towards its ideal in time, in which each stage exhibits potentially (and sometimes actually) an advance on the precedent stage. Nothing is specifically predetermined about the actual future of the states; we have no guarantee that the ideal of unity, perfection or goodness will come to be. Since the advancement of the actual towards its ideal rests upon the activity of mind, the actual accomplishment depends upon the wisdom of the mind concerned. There is God's province and man's province to take into account. Wherever God directly operates, his wisdom is instanced: more particularly in the realm of inanimate nature. Hence it is possible for us to predict here that the actual laws of inanimate nature are expressing their ideal, that they are being progressively realized over an endless period of time; but we are denied this assurance in those provinces where man is concerned. Less rational and less moral than God, he works faithfully and consistently to no principle; there is no indication that the fields of his interest will eventually express the ideality they imply. Consequently, his future may instance no more of the ideal plan than has already been instanced in the past. In fact, its future stages may instance aspects of retrogression. Were man completely wise and good, we could be equally assured in this field also that the ideal scheme implicit in the nature of things would be concretely realized. The cosmic significance of the moral law now becomes more apparent, for it commands man to recognize the desired ideality of the universe in his province, and to bring this plan into execution. In doing this, man is at the same time religious, for he is furthering the plans of God. In being attentive to the moral law man furthers in his own nature the actual coming to be of the cosmic scheme. In proportion to man's moral expression the chaotic unrelated universe of actual contents and events become systematic and moral.

Man's actual self likewise implies its ideal. His ideal should be regarded as the goal that his actual self should strive to realize. In realizing this ideal of selfhood he is at the same time advancing the plans that God has in mind for him, for ontologically the ideal of perfect selfhood is part of the cosmic scheme that God is concerned in concretely projecting as a system and in bringing to realization. Whereas the ideality that is being progressively realized in nature is the direct work of God himself, the ideality of human nature has been left for man to realize concretely for himself. To him alone has been entrusted the responsibility of completing his own nature (*Vide* Pt. I, Ch. V, *Analogy*, esp. p. 96), his entire constitution instances this fact in its faculty of conscience and reason through which he acquires knowledge, as well as in his propensity to form habits whereby he can adapt himself effortlessly to moral practice, and engage himself in new directions. As Butler informs us: "It is as plainly a general law of nature, that we should, with regard to our temporal interest, form and cultivate practical principles within us, by attention, use, and discipline, as any thing whatever is a natural law; chiefly in the beginning of life, but also throughout the whole course of it. And the alternative is left to our choice: either to improve ourselves, and better our condition; or, in default of such improvement, to remain deficient and wretched" (Vol. I, pp. 112-113; cp. also, Vol. I, pp. 78, 79, 80, 87).

For man to complete his nature means for him to unify it in terms of moral values announced through his conscience. In the course of self-development he is brought into immediate intimacy with his environment, learning the degree to which he is dependent upon it. Its manifold of features and aspects must be wrought into a unity, for the unity of his nature rests in part upon the unity of his environment. To the extent that his immediate world is unorganized, his own nature fails to be consistent, and virtuous. If he fails to unify his nature, his deeds remain unrelated to each other; blunders and stupidities of all sorts are committed. If he lives viciously, he brings into his immediate environment elements of discordance and disruption. If not corrected they will continue as features openly opposed to the unity that is ideally implied in man's nature, and openly preventive of man's happiness. But if he lives virtuously, all of this is open to correction. A promise is thus held open to us that vice is not irretrievably irremediable. But until this promise is fulfilled by ourselves, the contradictory and irrational nature of the committed vice will prevail, human nature will con-

tinue to be a congeries of unvirtuous motives and conflicting
emotions, and the environment within which he lives will be a
discordant many.

We are now better prepared to indicate the next stage of our
discussion. In the present part of our thesis we have ascertained
that the deliverances of conscience are cosmic, and issue to man
the principles he must observe if he is to further his own nature
as God intended it, as well as that part of the scheme that comes
directly under his province. We have shown that whatever morality is, it is objective, universal and binding upon the nature
of individual men. We have not however discussed the precise
nature of the moral principles and practices that conscience
delivers to man to follow. Neither have we shown in detail the
precise nature of the moral scheme that man is to realize. It will
be the purpose of the next part of the present work to take up
this subject somewhat fully. In this part we shall bring to completion the answer to our original question: what is the nature
of virtue?

PART SIX

THE MORAL LIFE

27

DOCTRINE OF VIRTUE

VIRTUE, maintains Butler, consists in following the nature of man, and vice in deviating from it (Vol. II, pp. 5, 9, 46, 57). In making this statement Butler has fortified his position against those who would argue different meanings into "nature," or who demand to know what part of our nature we should follow. For admittedly, if man's nature forms a system in which conscience is the unifying principle, then to follow one's nature would be to express oneself according to the dictates of conscience. One could not follow his nature in any other sense.

Some readers of Butler have maintained that man's moral nature consists in his principles of self-love, benevolence, or a partnership of both, but none of those replies sees its own short-sightedness. Others have asserted that conscience alone, in separation from man's instinctive desires, is the sole source of moral distinctions. Butler's final position, which is best represented in his Sermon On Compassion, is that man's *entire* nature must form the contents of virtue (Cp. also Vol. II, S. III).

Neither conscience, self-love, nor benevolence, taken singly or in combination, is the principle that man should follow, for he cannot ignore the participation in the moral sphere of the remaining particular propensions. "Reason," Butler informs us, "alone, whatever any one may wish, is not in reality a sufficient motive of virtue in such a creature as man" (Vol. II, p. 83). Also, later on when he refers to self-love and the need for its intimate cooperation with the particular propensions, he tells us (Vol. II, p. 87): "The private interest of the individual would not be sufficiently provided for by reasonable and cool self-love alone; therefore the appetites and passions are placed within as a guard and further security, and without which it would not be taken due care of. It is manifest our life would be neglected, were it not for the calls of hunger, and thirst, and weariness; notwithstanding that without them reason would assure us, that the recruits of food and sleep are the necessary means of our preservation." In regard to benevolence he reiterates the need of co-operation between that principle and the particular propensions over which it has sway. "Is it possible any can in earnest think, that a public spirit, i.e., a settled reasonable principle of benevolence to mankind, is so prevalent and strong in the species, as that we may venture to throw off the under affections, which are its assistants, carry it forward and mark out particular courses for it; family, friends, neighbourhood, the distressed, our country?" (Vol. II, p. 87).

No sound view of morality can dismiss the claims of the particular propensions. Do they not also form part of man's nature; is their activity not to be provided for? Butler answers these questions in his fifth Sermon. It is here that he is eager to show the place of compassion as a particular propension within the scheme of virtue, and in view of this he anticipates an objection that may be raised. He imagines his opponent as saying (Vol. II, p. 83): "Does not passion and affection of every kind perpetually mislead us? Nay, is not passion and affection itself a weakness, and what a perfect being must be entirely free from?" As against this point of view, Butler contends that our passions form as integral a part of our constitution as our senses. We learn that both our senses and our passions are a supply to the imperfection of our nature; as such they are required by us; the bare exercise of them would lead to the good and happiness of the world (Vol. II, p. 84 *et. passim*).

The harmonization of the particular propensions, although Butler is arguing specifically for the place of compassion, is achieved through the medium of reason. This is indicated in the same section where Butler says (Vol. II, p. 83) that when the particular propensions are allowed scope to exercise themselves under the strict government and direction of reason, we act suitably to our nature and to the circumstances God has placed us in. That Butler's final position is one that favors the entire nature of man in its array of principles and propensions, can be further gathered from his repeated references to self-love as expressive of man's whole range of impulses and desires. In his Sermon Upon Forgiveness of Injuries (Vol. II, p. 128), we are told that "we cannot but have a greater sensibility to what concerns ourselves." [1] Even in his Sermon on the Love of our Neighbour, where he has in mind the principle of benevolence and its place within the scheme of human life, a sermon in which one would expect to hear an overemphasis on benevolence, Butler never for one instant loses sight of the importance of the self in its complete possession of propensions and principles. In this respect he says, "Suppose a person to have the same settled regard to others, as to himself; that in every deliberate scheme or pursuit he took their interest into account in the same degree as his own, so far as an equality of affection would produce this: yet he would in fact, and ought to be much more taken up and employed about himself, and his own concerns, than about others and their interests" (Vol. II, p. 183). [2]

Some of Butler's critics have accused him of arguing in a circle. They interpret his position as saying: Virtue lies in following human nature; to follow human nature is to follow conscience; but to follow conscience is to follow human nature. This interpretation must be rejected as one that does not square with the facts of the case, for it considers Butler's doctrine of morality in isolation from the more positive contents of the Analogy. The plausibility of this alleged interpretation could only be upheld if the self were limited to a reflection upon its actual impulses; and if it could do no more than to release one or the other in the presense of its suitable object. It is an interpretation that falsely sees too great an influence upon Butler's thought of Lockian psychology, where reason is reduced to a discursive level, and where its function is limited to the combination of material afforded to it by the senses. [3]

That Butler was aware of this view of human nature is made clear to us in his second sermon when he discusses the various meanings in which the term "nature" can be used (*Vide*, Vol. II,

[1] Cp. also in his Sermon upon Self-Deceit, where Butler brings out the same thought when he is describing the fallacies of actual human nature (Vol. II, p. 152, etc.).

[2] Cp. also Vol. II, S. XI, p. 173; S. II, p. 53; S. II, pp. 63, 64, 65; S. VI, p. 99; S. IX, p. 134; S. XII, p. 184; S. XIII, p. 203, also pp. 119-20, 122, 128. We have already said that in his use of the term "self-love," Butler opens himself to a considerable amount of ambiguity; for there are evidences in the sermons of Butler that the term is sometimes used in a very narrow sense while in other passages it is used in a much broader sense, being equated with the self-conscious unity of the entire self. We have maintained throughout our discussion that this broader use of the term is the true use. *Vide* Ch. *13.*

[3] As an instance of distorted interpretation, see account of Butler by T. H. Green, *Works,* Vol. III, pp. 101 et seq.

pp. 47-50). But he mentions these views only to prevent their being confounded with the view that he had in mind. The proper interpretation of conscience is one that sees it to be revelatory of standards and principles of action that make their demands upon the self for recognition and fulfilment. In possession of these guiding principles the self becomes enabled to unify its nature and advance it towards the ideal of perfect and moral selfhood that it implies.[4]

Not to release uncritically in the presence of its suitable stimulus any propension or principle, but to judge beforehand whether it shall affirm or not the act contemplated by the individual, is to see that conscience operates in the presence of a standard; for how can conscience distinguish between internal principles of the heart unless there is a standard implied in terms of which the distinction takes place? Likewise how can it approve or disapprove unless that which approves is other than that which is approved of? We must accept as Butler's intended position on this point the view which maintains conscience to be legislative, as opposed to the Lockian standpoint, which sees reason to be discursive. Hence there is no circularity involved in Butler's position. To say that self-development forms the content of conscience is to establish as the standard of judgment the *ideal* nature of the self and not its actual nature.

Realm of Moral Standards. Having shown that morality means the ruling of man's entire nature by his conscience, we must now pursue our enquiry into the nature of virtue one step further. What are the ideal principles or standards that conscience commands the self to follow? In the first place they are objective, in the sense that they are independent of individual desire; secondly they are disinterested, in that they do not favor the self in its narrower aspects.

---

[4] That Butler himself favors this point of view is to be explicitly gathered from the remarks on conscience that follow immediately upon his disapproval of the other views of nature. "There is a superior principle of reflection or conscience in every man," he says (Vol. II, p. 51), "which distinguishes between the internal principles of his heart, as well as his external action; which passes judgment upon himself and them; pronounces determinately some actions to be in themselves just, right, good; others to be in themselves evil, wrong, unjust: which, without being consulted, without being advised with, magisterially exerts itself, and approves or condemns him the doer of them accordingly; and which, if not forcibly stopped, naturally and always of course goes on to anticipate a higher and more effectual sentence, which shall hereafter second and affirm its own."

We are told (Vol. I, p. 328) that there is a universally acknowledged standard of virtue, publicly professed by all ages and countries, and observed in all the fundamental laws of civil institutions. All countries and governments agree that justice, veracity and common good are the principles of virtuous action for themselves and their citizens. As individuals looking for guidance in this matter, we are to accept these ideals as standards that our conscience would approve of. These ideals serve the interests of the entire self and not exclusively its lesser aspects. Through it neither self-love nor benevolence is favored as opposed to the other. And so when Butler tells us in the preface (Vol. II, p. 22) that "we may judge and determine, that an action is morally good or evil, before we so much as consider, whether it be interested or disinterested," he is but drawing our attention to the fact that the moral ideals do not exclusively favor either self-interest conceived as distinct from benevolence, or benevolence itself, but the higher organized self which is common to both and which has emerged from the partnership of both to its fuller self-consciousness.[5]

Having seen that conscience requires a standard in terms of which it makes its moral judgments, our next task will be to examine more in detail the nature of its standard. Once we know what conscience approves of and what it forbids, we shall be enabled to know morally what our duty consists in, i.e., what we are obliged to do if we are to live a moral life and express ourselves according to nature.

Our chapter on society has shown the type of society that man should endorse if he follows his conscience and devotes him-

---

[5] Cp. here Vol. II, pp. 190-1: "There are certain dispositions of mind, and certain actions, which are in themselves approved or disapproved by mankind, abstracted from the consideration of their tendency to the happiness or misery of the world; approved or disapproved by reflection, by that principle within, which is the guide of life, the judge of right and wrong . . . this much however is certain, that the things now instanced in and numberless others, are approved or disapproved by mankind in general, in quite another view than as conducive to the happiness or misery of the world."

It may seem upon first appearance that such virtues as fidelity, honor, strict justice, have no connection with the particular propensions, or principles, but closer scrutiny would reveal that the ideally completed self is somehow constituted by the convergence of the actual affections to them as a common aim. The ideal nature of the self is such as to demand their realization. As such, they would properly represent the fulfilment of the self as implied in its equipment of component factors, and thus would truly represent the end of these affections remotely considered (Cp. also Vol. II, p. 112).

self to the moral life. It has also shown that society is divine in its origins, for it reflects the laws of God in its constitution. To live the completely moral life, man must go beyond the exterior forms and laws of society to the origins themselves upon which it is built. In doing this he will not be ignoring society, but understanding its nature further; he will be acquainting himself with the *raison d'être* of its commands. To conform himself to society in this sense is to live religiously.

But what religion should man resort to? There is revealed religion and natural religion. Within the former group may be brought the Christian religions and the non-Christian. Even within the class of Christian religions, there is a difference of opinion between the claims of the Protestant and the Catholic. Which of these furnishes to man the standards he must follow? This question takes us into the enquiry: which religion is the true one? Only after we settle this question can we ask what are the standards we are urged to follow.

Our following chapters will attempt to answer these inquiries so as to do justice to Butler's thought. We shall take up in turn the doctrine of religion in its two broadest aspects, natural religion and revealed religion, seeing that the claims of the latter as a guide for man's moral life are as indisputable as the claims of the former. But the self whose nature is to be satisfied through religion is also rational and appetitive. Since these too form part of the self's nature, they must also be satisfied; and to their satisfaction religion must prove adequate. It will be our task to show how religion provides in its pronouncements for the respective satisfaction of reason and the appetites; how by following the dictates of religion man can morally express these other drives. After this the place of reason and the lesser affections in the moral life will occupy our attention.

28

NATURAL RELIGION

IN OUR account of Butler's metaphysics we saw that the universe reduces itself to a creation of God's mind upon which it is ultimately dependent. The knowledge that the universe and its contents are a creation of God becomes for man a body of truth that may be called religious. It furnishes to him an insight into the being and attributes of God, as well as into the relation of God to the universe and his creatures. At the same time this knowledge enables man to learn particularly his place in the universe and the part he is expected to play.

Man's knowledge of the universe viewed as an ultimate theistic system is obtained in different ways. He may reason about experience and learn therefrom that the course and constitution of nature impart important truths as to its fuller nature, its hidden aspects, and its origin in God; or he may be more directly informed by a written account such as the Scriptures which contain virtually the same contents that experience would inform him of. The first means of understanding the nature of the world, its relation to God and the law of God's creation establishes Natural Religion. The second channel of information, whereby the Scriptures of Christianity furnish him more directly and with less effort on his part with the same truths, establishes the core and substance of Revealed Religion. In the present chapter we shall be concerned with the first aspect, and the duties they enjoin upon man to follow.

GENERAL ASPECTS OF NATURAL RELIGION

Only a few people are capable of learning for themselves the ultimate nature of the universe; even they cannot apprise themselves completely of its nature. They can however gather from a sufficient study of its lesser features and aspects an insight as to its essential structure, the purpose it displays and the reasons that called it into being. They can see reflected in the activities of its lesser aspects the laws that govern its nature, and can learn therefrom the part designed for them as human beings; likewise they can gather the attitude that should characterize their behavior to themselves, other human beings, society and God himself. When they act towards others in full recognition that they owe their origin to God and reflect his will and his workmanship, their actions are truly religious. In this sense all human behavior should be religious, and the highest of human relationships, whether towards oneself or others, is religious to the extent that it is conscious of its divine origin and manifests a true reverence for all of God's creation.

Religious obligations arise from religious knowledge, and religious knowledge is knowledge of the highest realities. What can we say more particularly about it? We have already considered in detail Butler's metaphysical views of the universe, and have shown that the universe is a system that is actually and at any one time of its history incomplete. But the scheme or plan guiding its construction has been arranged for, and is laid out in advance in the mind of God. The laws of nature are the laws of this plan and indicate the way that God has decreed things and objects to behave. From a survey of its parts we can be assured that the scheme has been conceived in infinite wisdom; from a study of its laws we learn that the scheme manifests righteousness and justice. There are many things that man cannot understand, for being a creature of limited and imperfect faculties, there remain hidden from his view vast areas of reality the knowledge of which would require more perfect beings than we are at present. Likewise, we are ignorant of events to come; for since the universe is still in the process of creation, there exist in the mind of God plans and intentions of which we have not the slightest intimation. Were our faculties adequate to a knowledge of all existent reality as it has so far come to be, were we completely acquainted with its endless past states, there would still remain for our further exploration all the states of the universe that are to come; but for this we have not at present the adequate means. To do so would demand an insight into the hidden recesses of God's mind, and for that we are not equipped (Vol. II, p. 213).

As a consequence of our imperfect knowledge, we can expect to meet in the scheme of nature a great many difficulties, some of which will appear as insuperable obstacles. But these difficulties cannot in themselves belittle the scheme of things, show the universe to be defective or the ways of God open to reproach. Whatever appears to be irregular or subversive of our ideals should cause us to reflect that the difficulties lie within us and not in the scheme we are contemplating and looking towards as a pattern for our lives.

Granting that ignorance and knowledge both exist side by side, how can we tell what is right and intended, and what is wrong; especially when we are repeatedly told that our faculties are imperfect, that they reveal only the fragments of a scheme and not its total reality? How can we be assured that what we know is genuine knowledge, when whatever is revealed is so organically related to what is not revealed that in the light of further knowledge our small but positive field of knowledge is apt to become transformed? For Butler himself tells us that "no part (*of the universe*) can be thoroughly understood, without taking in its reference and respect to the whole; and this is what we have not faculties for" (Vol. II, p. 221). To answer this question fully would take us beyond the intentions of our present chapter, for it involves an investigation of Butler's epistemological theories, and a consideration of his doctrines of probability and analogy. But we can say at present that for Butler right appearances endure through further knowledge. In their more exact reference to unknown parts it would be seen that their rightness was strengthened and reinforced in other ways (Vol. II, p. 227). But wrong appearances would not. In the light of further knowledge there would be the tendency for them to become transformed and finally destroyed. We shall let Butler speak briefly for himself.

"Now suppose a spectator of that work or constitution was in a great measure ignorant of such various reference to the general end, whatever that end be; and that, upon a very slight and partial view which he had of the work, several things appeared to his eye disproportionate and wrong; others, just and beautiful: what would he gather from these appearances? He would immediately conclude there was a probability, if he could see the whole reference of the parts appearing wrong to the general design, that this would destroy the appearance of wrongness and disproportion: But there is no probability, that the reference would destroy the particular right appearances, though that reference might show the things already appearing just, to be so likewise in a higher degree of another manner. There is a probability, that the right appearances were intended: there is no probability, that the wrong appearances were. We cannot suspect irregularity and disorder to be designed. The pillars of a building appear beautiful; but their being likewise its support does not destroy that beauty: there still remains a reason to believe that the architect intended the beautiful appearance, after we have found out the reference, support. It would be reasonable for a man of himself to think thus, upon the first piece of architecture he ever saw" (Vol. II, pp. 226-7).

If we now raise the question what determines an appearance to be right, and what authorizes us to reject other appearances as wrong, we are informed through a study of a method that Butler effectively handles throughout his writings, but especially in his *Analogy*, that the guarantee of a right explanation is to be found in the application of the teleological method. To state this briefly and abstractedly, we can say that if A implies B so that A is understood rationally when its nature is seen to be completed by B, and at the same the nature of B is seen to rest upon A, then the stated relationship of A to B is a correct one. Further investigation may reveal B to be conducive to C, but such an investigation will not destroy the lesser one, but will show it to be further reinforced. But if A is seen at other times to imply non-B that runs counter to B, we can rest assured that non-B is not intended as the *nisus* of A, and that furthermore it is a perversion of it. We require however a vast assemblage of instances in which both cases are involved before we can arrive at this conclusion, and before we can definitely know what factors A does imply and which it does not. But when we finally judge, e.g., non-B to be a perversion, we have in a sense brought it as an instance under the principle of A's truly implying B; for whereas the principle that A implies B explains these two factors, and can at the same time account for non-B as a single perversion, the principle "A implies non-B" could neither explain itself, nor explain the appearance that A implies B. Hence upon the basis of repeated observation and the application of the teleological principle as a mode of explanation, we are enabled to explain the apparent unrelatedness of our world, and to observe further that some appearances are right and other appearances are wrong.[1]

Let us now turn our attention to the scheme of things, for from a further investigation of right appearances in its parts we can tell what is implied in the whole scheme. Just as right appearances exhibit the teleological method as the effective principle of metaphysical explanation, the universe likewise can

[1] For an extended treatment of Butler's theory of knowledge, see Chapter 31 of the present work.

be understood in the same way. As wrong appearances or perversions furnish no impediment to the exercise of the teleological principle but in a sense come under it, we can likewise expect to discover in the universe at large the same persistence of factors whose rationality we cannot encompass. Furthermore the progressive discovery of designs shows a designer to be implied, and that the wisdom of the designer is indicated in his work. As the universe is further explored by man he becomes more and more certain of unshakeable truths, but the most important for him is that the universe, which is the work of God, must indicate the perfect qualities of God's mind. Whatever he fails to understand can be accepted as indicative of a purpose that is greater than he can know and wiser than he can understand. Hence his corresponding attitude should be one of compliance and ready acceptance, not unmingled however with awe and reverence for what is so mysterious, recondite and transcendent.

Man's interest in the gathering of knowledge is never merely speculative. His province, says Butler, "is virtue and religion, life and manners; the science of improving the temper, and making the heart better. This is the field assigned us to cultivate" (Vol. II, p. 229). Let us first consider the reason why man is concerned with the discovery of the rule of life before we ask what this rule is.

Of all of God's creatures man is presumably the only one who possesses a free will; moreover he is in a position to exercise this will or not in the direction of whatever interests he sees fit. But the possession of a will indicates a use or a principle for which it exists. The presence of this will in man indicates that man's nature, which is incomplete and fragmentary, should be advanced and unified by it, and that man himself is entrusted with this work. It is of the utmost importance that in order to fulfil his destiny man should ascertain the laws of the universe that God has set down for his guidance. He must see that he is a part of the universe and that like the other aspects of the universe his reality is in the making and requires for its completion an unending period of time. Man must also see that, just as for the other objects of creation, there exists in the mind of God a pattern or scheme in terms of which his own perfection is to be fashioned, for this too is laid out beforehand. The difference between himself and the other objects of creation consists in this, that whereas other objects are under the direct control of God, the task of bringing to perfect completion the nature of man rests with man himself. To him directly is assigned the task of completing the nature that God started him with. Upon him falls the responsibility of this fulfilment. To carry this out successfully requires that he discover exactly whatever he is supposed to do and be, i.e., God's plans concerning his nature. His persistent search for this knowledge is a religious search, and the results of his findings constitute the corpus of natural religion.

That man is committed to this task and that he knows the necessity of carrying it out is indicated in the emotional consequences that accompany his acts. We have shown in a previous chapter that pleasure or pain attends all that man does; that the pleasure he experiences indicates that his course of behavior is a proper one, while the experience of pain shows him to have performed a wrong deed. Thus, his experience of pain reveals that he is violating a law of his nature; or in other words, a course of behavior that God has set down in the scheme of things for him to follow. He cannot choose at random his course in life. He cannot decide in advance of experience what he will decide to do. It is true that he can do within limits whatever he likes, but if it is not in accordance with what he should do, he will be punished through the infliction of pain. It is in these earlier emotional experiences that man first learns that there is a course of behavior to which he is bound; it is later on through the application of reason that he is able to discriminate between true and false pleasures, and learn to value those pleasures that are higher and of more permanent value. It is at the highest expression of his nature that he learns that the correct actions are those actions that conform to God's prearranged scheme and that virtue consists in the overt respect he pays to it in thought or in action.

We are now prepared to indicate the scheme of God as far as it affects man himself. We shall then proceed to indicate the duties he is obliged to perform in consequence. Man's relations to God and his consequent duties to him are of two kinds. There are the more general ones: those that dictate the conformance of man's behavior to God and to the laws of his creatures, and secondly, the more particular relations that man bears to God in respect to man's being man. These latter involve the conformance of this actual self to the laws and nature of his own being as God decrees them to be. Although these two types of relations and duties are not unrelated, nevertheless for the sake of clear exposition we can consider them separately as if they were. We shall take up the more particular relations of man to God first.

TENETS OF NATURAL RELIGION

From the course and constitution of nature man learns his status and the place he must fill. He learns that he is appointed to live in a future state. Hence he must realize that his temporal life is only one stage of an immortal existence. His greater interest and duty demand that he bear in mind the inevitability of that future existence and that he conduct his life on earth accordingly. Were he to study the nature of his temporal life, he would see that it is one of trial and probation for the life to come. His life span shows that the preparation for the future life depends upon his own efforts. And towards this end he is sufficiently and adequately equipped. He possesses faculties that enable him to meet the circumstances of life. At his earlier stages of life his faculties are unformed and undeveloped, but in the accumulation of knowledge he is enabled to repair the deficiencies. Thus his state of deficiency teaches man that he should develop himself to the utmost degree of his capacities. But the presence of these capacities points out that their development is not to take place as an end in themselves. There is indicated even in their state of undevelopment the fact that man's future temporal life is such as to demand their maturity and readiness for activity. Man is thus apprised that his future will be different from the present, and that it will demand the exercise of faculties other than those he is at present exercising. But he also knows that he possesses the equipment for this future exercise. To achieve the perfection of that future state, there is much he must endure, and many disappointments he will have to live through. Each stage of life will present its difficulties and each stage will be a test for the stage that is to come. No one stage of his life is final; at no one time can he rest assured that he has completely expressed and developed his nature.

Convinced of his immortal existence, he can expect that the quality of that life will not be unlike his present temporal life. Just as each stage of his temporal existence is a preparation for the stage to come, his entire life span must be similarly regarded as a stage of his immortal life. Just as in matters of practical affairs on earth man is confronted by many difficulties that must be overcome to achieve his end, likewise in preparation for the life to come there will be previously experienced difficulties of a similar kind. As trial and patience characterize his endeavors on earth for the accomplishment of tasks that he undertakes to perform, likewise he must expect, throughout the course of his temporal life regarded as preparatory for the life to come, to experience a similar state of trial and exercise an equal if not a higher degree of patience. Many things will appear unnecessary, and disappointments will weaken his ardor, but all of this must be accepted in the course of things. To accept the disappointments without forfeiting his belief in life eternal is his duty; and to persevere even when his ardor is lessened and his credulity is imposed upon is what he must set himself to do.

Besides the knowledge that he is appointed to live in a future state, and that he must expect to encounter difficulties in the present life regarded as preparatory to the life to come, man is aware of the quality of his immortal life. This he learns from the present life, which indicates in the main the nature of the life to come. We have already pointed out that man experiences the reign of natural and moral law during the course of his temporal life. There is pleasure and pain inseparably affixed to right and wrong actions. We can speak of this experience of pleasure and pain as the reign of law, but the more correct explanation of it sees it to be the direct government of God over man. Ultimately viewed, pleasure is really reward, and pain is truly punishment. But these rewards and punishments are not indifferently conferred. Closer survey reveals to us the fact that they follow a definitely indicated course of action. There is the tendency of virtuous actions to be rewarded by feelings of inner elation and joy, and externally by the approval of others, and by the bestowal of honors upon them by all right-thinking men of the community. And concerning vicious actions, there is a corresponding tendency to feeling abashed, ashamed, overwhelmed, or degraded, depending of course upon the nature of the unvirtuous deed. And similarly there is the external tendency in society for it to punish the malefactor; and in virtuous individuals to discourage, disapprove and severely condemn what they believe to be vicious in deeds and thoughts of their fellow-brethren. All of this must be accepted as an instance of divine government and of the fact that God has made up his mind, in advance of the fact, what is right and what is wrong, and that he has laid down a course of action for mankind to follow.

To Butler's mind there is no injustice in this dispensation of providence, but only the exhibition of righteousness and fair-mindedness. Mankind cannot understand the ways of God, but in its knowledge that God is wise and perfectly good can have faith in the divine goodness of God. An instance of his goodness and sense of justice is seen in the fact that God announces in no uncertain tones what man is to do; for he approves of virtuous actions and disapproves of unvirtuous. We can admit that to man's mind much of this remains wrapped in mystery and that there is much that he personally cannot understand. Nevertheless God has indicated to him what is right and what is wrong; consequently it is man's duty to have faith and obey, and so to order his life that his constant endeavor will be a growing consciousness of God's commands and an effort progressively to realize them in the course of his life.

The constant sense of being under the law of God is brought home to man throughout the course of his temporal life. But more than that: man begins to appreciate that his immortal life will not be unlike his present one. There will be exhibited there the same tendency for virtuous acts to be rewarded and unvirtuous acts punished. But presumably the reward and punishment will be less of a tendency and more of a realization, for in our immortal life we shall be more under the direct and sensible government of God (Vol. I, p. 98), and the absence of our bodily senses may readily be the means of removing the hindrances to clearer thinking and finer sensitivity. And so we can expect a more ready responsiveness to God's laws of virtue, and an immediate experience of the consequences of our ill-doing, or the rewards of our virtues.

If we appreciate however that our immortal life is intrinsically connected with our present life, in the same respect as a later consequence in our temporal life is related to an earlier stage, we can recognize that the tendencies of one life are carried over into the other. Since temporal life and immortal life are two inseparable aspects of one continuous existence, they both partake in the same continuous law of virtue. In other words: the rewards for virtue and the punishments of vice have no one time during which their settlements are made. Virtuous reward may be delayed long beyond the death of the virtuous man; likewise the vicious man may live his entire life free from the disturbing qualms of conscience. But since it is the tendency for virtue to be rewarded and for vice to be punished, and thus for God's government to proceed uninterruptedly during the whole course of man's temporal and immortal life, it is to man's interest to conduct his life on earth with the full appreciation of God's unintermittent reign.

DUTIES OF NATURAL RELIGION

We are now prepared to consider the more general relations of man to God, and of man to the products of God's creation. Both of these relations are religious: the first comprise those owed to God directly, and the second comprise those owed to God indirectly.

Man's immediate duties to God arise from the consciousness of his dependence in origin on him. When man considers the nature of his self, he knows that his very being, all of his faculties, as well as the means of exerting them, belong to Almighty God and not to himself (Vol II, p. 316). His first thought must therefore be of God and not of himself. In thought he must gain a sense of his dependence upon God, coupled with the correlative feeling for God's authority over him. In full consciousness of this he will see that there is no will apart from God's and no purpose that should be expressed that runs counter to his. "We should, with joy, gratitude, reverence, love, trust, and dependence, appropriate the character, as what we had a right in; and make our boast in such our relation to it. And the conclusion of the whole would be, that we should refer ourselves implicitly to him, and cast ourselves entirely upon him. As the whole attention of life should be to obey his commands; so the highest enjoyment of it must arise from the contemplation of this character, and our relation to it, from a consciousness of his favor and approbation, and from the exercise of those affections towards him which could not but be raised from his presence" (Vol. II, p. 200; vide also p. 207).

As a consequence our one untiring aim should be to obey God's commands. In our life of practice we should entertain no aim that he does not endorse, and no one thought that he does not approve of. The full consciousness of God's reality should mean the resignation and submission of our entire self to his law and his commands (Vol. II, pp. 207, 222). The conclusion of this is "that in all lowliness of mind we set lightly by ourselves: that we form our temper to an implicit submission to the Divine

Majesty; beget within ourselves an absolute resignation to all the methods of his providence, and in his dealings with the children of men: that, in the deepest humility of our souls, we prostrate ourselves before him" (Vol. II, p. 231).

Religious obligation does not mean our withdrawal from the activities of temporal life; to substitute in its stead a constant contemplation of God's being. Butler reminds us in his last sermon (Vol. II, p. 224) that we were designed to be inhabitants of this earth; in his sermon, Upon the Love of God, he tells us that we should keep alive a sense of God's meaning and authority so that in contact with our fellow beings we can profit in our daily relationship (*Vide* also Vol. II, p. 127). The final point of view that we must adopt is one that enjoins mankind to a course of behavior measurable in terms of the highest divine goodness. To lose our will in God's will, we must interpret as the identification of the human with the divine aim, so that in our daily lives the nature of God is brought to a more complete realization on earth. (Yet cp.; Vol. II, p. 84; Second Diss., Vol. I, pp. 335-6.)

The relation of religion to ethics is one that sees in the former the ultimate values upon which the latter should draw so that in terms of them each act of human nature will become illuminated by a transcendent good. The principles and propensions whose aims are manifestly external objects, and whose immediate purpose is the temporal activity and relations of the self, are not in any sense decried; their activity though still guided by conscience is now endowed with and directed by the values of religion that conscience endorses because it recognizes their divine origin. The self, whose nature is to be determined by religious obligations, does not deny the expression of its lesser affections. They are in no sense obliterated, but become more conscious in the light of man's relation to God, of the aim they are destined to express. Neither does the self in its religious enlightenment cease to be self-conscious. In its most exalted moments when it is sensitively aware of the presence of God and the principles of goodness emanating from him, it never loses its sense of private individuality, nor forgets that its aims and expressions are such as redound to its own development. Self-love, the term that Butler uses to express this intimacy of immediate and private individuality, becomes furnished with more determinate and more precise contents. In regard to it,

Butler says, " 'Must we then, forgetting our own interest, as it were go out of ourselves, and love God for his own sake?' No more forget your own interest, no more go out of yourselves, than when you prefer one place, one prospect, the conversation of one man to that of another" (Vol. II, p. 203).[2]

We shall now indicate that in Butler's final point of view, i.e., that man should follow the teachings of religion, there is no violation of his initial statement that man should follow his own nature. "As we cannot remove from this earth, or change our general business on it, so neither can we alter our real nature. Therefore no exercise of the mind can be recommended, but only the exercise of those faculties you are conscious of. Religion does not demand new affections, but only claims the direction of those you already have, those affections you daily feel; though un-happily confined to objects, not altogether unsuitable, but alto-gether unequal to them. We only represent to you the higher, the adequate objects of those very faculties and affections" (Vol. II, p. 202). Introspection would reveal them to consist in "those affections of mind which are due immediately to him from such a creature as man, and which rest in him as their end" (Vol. II, p. 194). Specifically they are known as love, reverence, fear, desire of approbation (Vol. II, p. 204).

We shall not develop in detail man's indirect obligations to God. We shall indicate what they are and how they should be regarded by man. We have already shown that all things owe their origin to God, and that they fulfil the plans that God entertains for them. The laws of their being, ultimately viewed, are the laws of God. In this sense all natural laws are a species of religious laws. As religious laws, they are more genuinely known than as natural laws. But to view them as religious laws is not to controvert their nature, but to see them more intelligibly, and to appreciate the part they are fulfilling in the divine scheme of things. This religious basis of natural law is not only char-acteristic of inanimate nature, it likewise holds for the world of

---

[2] Cp. also Vol. II, p. 173: "It may be allowed, without any prejudice to the cause of virtue and religion, that our ideas of happiness and misery (i.e., self-love) are of all our ideas the nearest and most important to us." And above: "religion . . . far from disowning the principle of self-love . . . often addresses itself to that very principle, and always to the mind in that state when reason presides; and there can no access be had to the understanding, but by convincing men, that the course of life we would persuade them to is not contrary to their interest" (Cp. also Vol. II, pp. 119, 120).

man and human society. Our attitude to our brethren, to society, and to government is substantiated in religion; for human groups, societies, and states, are the products of God,—the laws of their structure, formation, and growth are the laws of God. In following their course they are fulfilling the designs that God has laid down for them.

In the possession of his religious enlightenment man becomes conscious of his relation to these objects of experience, and the duties he is obliged to perform. In our relations with our brethren we should treat them not as ends in themselves but as beings created by God. We have seen that each man must view himself as belonging to God; in a similar way must he view every other agent. Beneficence really means furthering the will of God. In deeds of charity, God's will is being realized. "To relieve the poor *for God's sake*," says Butler, "is to do it in conformity to the order of nature, and to his will, and his example, who is the Author and Governor of it; and in thankful remembrance, that all we have is from his bounty. It is to do it in his behalf, and as to him" (Vol. II, p. 267).

The knowledge of God's interest makes the obligation more binding than if we acted solely in the knowledge that we are aiding man for his own sake. Were we to aid man for his own sake rather than for God's, there might arise opportunities when we should consider charity unwise, when it is not. There would always exist the possibility of self-deceit in this instance, for the chances of our not aiding our fellow beings when they truly deserved it would be greater if the burden of ultimate choice rested with us than not. But to do things when God commands them, even when we do not fully see the reasons for them, guarantees that more individuals are aided than would otherwise be aided. It likewise means that although many unworthy people will be aided, yet the worthy will not be neglected. Were charitable giving to rest upon our private judgment, it might follow that some unworthy people would still be aided, but also that many worthy beings would not.

This sense of God's authority in all that we do should be uppermost in our minds. We have seen in our discussion of government how man's exacted obedience to the laws and institutions of his country are species of a religious obligation. "Submit yourselves," says Butler, "to every ordinance of man for the Lord's sake: whether it be to the king, as supreme; or unto governors, as unto them that are sent by him" (Vol. II, p. 271). Even our sense of freedom is one that is significant only as we see that it means a coincidence of our will with God's. For Butler this is absolute freedom in the most literal and absolute sense (Vol. II, p. 270). These are only some of the instances that Butler has in mind when he speaks of man's obligations as being ultimately religious. He does not mean that man should desert the sphere of social activity, by conforming himself to objects that are religious in a devotional sense. Quite the contrary. He holds that man should submit and resign himself to the laws of God's created objects. Since societies and states are God's products just as much as the objects of inanimate nature, it is man's duty to find out their laws, and conform to them, as he comes into contact with them.

There may be much in the course of man's social life that he will not understand. But, in enjoining his religious attitude here, and in urging man to view the objects of his social life as instances of God's will, Butler is pointing out the need to submit where we have no cause to question or rebel. The peculiar force of insisting upon the religious basis of things in our life of everyday affairs consists then is this. If we take things as entities in themselves, we are apt to ignore the demands they make upon us, especially when we cannot comprehend their demands as rational claims. But on the other hand, if we know that these demands reflect the will of God, then our duty here will be to submit, for while in expressing God's will they will stand for much more than we can comprehend, nevertheless we may rest assured that what they demand is ultimately good, just because they emanate from the authority of God. We also know that in respect to things divine, our duty is always to submit, and God's products can afford us no exception to this rule.

29

REVEALED RELIGION

OUR account of Natural Religion has shown it to comprise a body of knowledge that states the relations existing between God and man, together with the duties that man owes to God as his Maker. We have also pointed out that this knowledge, apart from the actual practice that follows from it, is metaphysical in substance, for it furnishes us with an insight into the nature of the universe, the status of man, and the relation of both to God, who is the contriver and projecter of the scheme that is being progressively reflected and realized in man and the universe. We have also mentioned that a self-informed knowledge of this scheme is accessible only to a few individuals, for it requires a persistency in reasoning from the course and constitution of nature that is denied most individuals whose reasoning capacity is limited. But since the purpose of knowledge, as Butler holds throughout his writings, is for the moral self-expression of the individual who requires a principle to govern his life and action, very few individuals would be capable of expressing themselves to any degree of happiness. Only the privileged few that had superlative and unerring reasoning powers would be moral beings. But fortunately the scheme of the universe has been imparted as knowledge in more than one way. Not only is it attainable to those who reason by the "light of nature," but also to those many individuals who do not reason at all, and have not the capacity for it. The provision for their instruction and edification has been made through a body of writings called the Scriptures, i.e., through the Old and New Testaments of the Christian Bible. In these written accounts we can find transmitted for our benefit a scheme of the universe that is virtually the same as that which is discernible by "natural reason." Revealed religion not only reaffirms natural religion, but also adds to it valuable knowledge that can be ascertained in no other way.

A difficulty arises as to the authenticity of revealed religion. To men of reason there is not afforded in its contents the same degree of certainty as is afforded by the light of reason which informs us of natural religion. Revelation which revealed religion asks us to accept has not the same degree of appeal or cogency. Thus some individuals are all too ready to reject the accounts of revealed religion without first examining its claims or apprising themselves of its contents. Since revealed religion contains more than a mere republication of natural religion, by claiming to afford additional knowledge for the practical life of the individual, those who reject its material deprive themselves of the benefits of its important announcements. There is a consequent need to substantiate the claims of its defenders. Accordingly our mode of procedure in the present and the following chapter will be to present the aims and positive contents of revealed religion, in which we shall also note the relation of revealed religion to natural religion; to expound the arguments that Butler urges in support of its acceptance, and lastly to consider the duties that are obligatory upon man in reference to revealed religion, i.e., that are equally obligatory upon him, whether he believes in revealed religion or does not.

GENERAL ASPECTS OF REVEALED RELIGION

Revealed Religion may be regarded as endorsing the claims of natural religion. We have already discussed in full the contents of natural religion; the Scriptures repeat the same announcements. They too claim that there is one God who is the maker and proprietor of his world; that all his creatures are under the domain of his government, which is conducted in the spirit of righteousness according to the law of virtue; and that mankind shall be rewarded or punished hereafter as they obey or disobey God's law on earth (Vol I, pp. 270, 276). This repetition has had its great value, for it has made possible the religious enlightenment of primitive communities in which reason was too weak for the individuals to gather these truths for themselves by evolving a natural religion (Vol. I, p. 153). Although one is not absolutely certain that no individual in earlier times could not have reasoned out the system of natural religion free from superstition, yet it is quite certain that the majority of individuals could not.

Butler takes into account the possibility of discrepancy between natural religion and revealed religion, especially in those instances where there is a conflict of duties, presumably from the same authorities enjoining different courses of behavior. What course of duty shall we observe in these cases?

In no uncertain terms Butler gives precedence in authority to "natural reason," which is the only faculty we have for judging anything, even revelation itself (Vol. I, p. 183). As he tells us: "Reason is able to judge, and must, of the evidence of revelation, and of the objections urged against that evidence. . . ." (Vol I, p. 198).[1]

In this can be seen the reason for his stated preference in favor of reason, for reason works directly in the interest of moral duties, whereas revelation is more concerned with positive duties, i.e., those that are externally commanded by God, the reason of which may not be always apparent to its reader. Hence if we are confronted with two sorts of duties, both purporting to be moral, one of which we see the reason of upon examination, and the other of which we do not, "it is indisputable that our obligations are to obey the former; because there is an apparent reason for this preference, and none against it" (Vol. I, p. 169). Butler goes so far as to say that if "in revelation there be found any passages, the seeming meaning of which is contrary to natural religion; we may most certainly conclude, such seeming meaning not to be the real one" (Vol. I, p. 172).

Besides announcing the truths of natural religion to mankind, revealed religion supplies the deficiencies of its reports by informing us more extensively of God's scheme of things. What are these additional reports?

In the first place revealed religion and Christianity are synonymous, so that in speaking of revealed religion Butler has in mind the teachings of organized Christianity as they are spoken of in the Old and New Testaments of the Bible. But revealed religion is much more than a body of teachings; the written account that is reflected there is but one aspect of its nature. Its greater reality is reflected in and completed by the external institutions in society that are recorded by history. Just as natural religion comprises the scheme of the universe as it is intellectually apprehended as well as the course of recorded history that is actually exhibited in the affairs of men and human societies, Christianity too has its external aspect. And upon a closer

---

[1] And with greater emphasis in an earlier passage he announces: "Reason can, and it ought to judge, not only of the meaning, but also of the morality and the evidence, or revelation. First, It is the province of reason to judge of the morality of the scripture: i.e., not whether it contains things different from what we should have expected from a wise, just, and good Being; for objections from hence have been now obviated; but whether it contains things plainly contradictory to wisdom, justice, or goodness; to what the light of nature teaches us of God" (Vol. I, p. 196).

observation the parallel between natural religion and revealed religion shows them to be much more alike.

Like natural religion Christianity is a scheme quite beyond our comprehension (Vol. I, p. 200). It contains aspects that are only partly evident to a scrutinizing mind; it contains much more than mankind can hope to understand. Consequently some of the duties that it imposes upon man will be quite beyond his comprehension. Hence he should be chary about rejecting the entire account because of his failure to understand the parts. Only if he could comprehend the entire scheme could he clear up the difficulties of the lesser parts that now remain opaque to his understanding. As a scheme, Christianity consists of parts in relation to other parts. The prophecies of Christ, e.g., are remotely but inevitably connected with the advance and progress of Christian teachings as they influence the lives of later men and nations. Its economy is as mysterious as that of the universe; means are made use of, some of which seem roundabout and extravagant.

Recognizing that Christianity forms a system of systems, the thorough comprehension of whose parts presupposes a full comprehension of the entire scheme, we can as a matter of course expect to meet with obstacles in the details of its lesser aspects. Like the scheme of natural religion that of revealed Christianity is a system self-expressing without end. Although starting with the teachings of Christ, its establishment is not yet complete. Its growth which is steady and its influence which is still on the increase have been in course of development for several hundred years. And there appears to be no end to its possible influence. Objectively organized into churches which act as the repositories of its teachings, the intended aim of revealed religion is to spread over the entire extent of mankind; not merely to see established there institutions for instruction in it, but to keep alive in the hearts of succeeding generations the stimulus of its teachings and to equip them with a working principle of life. It is in such a sense that the scheme of Christianity must be regarded as an unending system.

Besides being an unending system of steady and progressive growth, Christianity is likewise a particular scheme that comes under the more comprehensive scheme of Natural religion (Vol. I, pp. 200-1). As a part of this more comprehensive scheme it is connected with it in many ways. For instance it completes its teachings by adding to it, for the edification of man, the further dispensations of God in his relations to mankind. Its complete comprehension would carry thought over into the plan that God entertains for the course of the universe. Likewise as a system objectively expressed, it is of one piece with the events of mankind that run antecedent to its initial establishment (Vol. I, pp. 278-80). The earlier ignorance of mankind concerning its relation to God, the low degree of prevalent morality, the need for enlightenment, have been subsequently met and provided for in the advent of Christianity. Although its initial establishment is dated at the birth of Christ, the history of the Christian scheme carries it far beyond its period of birth and makes it of one piece with the events of secular history that preceded it (Vol. I, Pt. II, Ch. VIII, *et passim*).

POSITIVE CONTENTS OF REVEALED RELIGION

So much for the general aspects of Christianity. What can we say now of its positive contents: of those reports which purport to supplement the teachings of natural religion? In the first place it states that the world exists in apostacy and ruin (Vol. I, pp. 15, 194), and that mankind stands in need of special assistance in the form of a mediator or divine redeemer who will bear to it a message, that if heeded will lead to its salvation. Only a very few of us are able to conduct our lives in accordance with the unerring predictions of our conscience. And even those who are able to do so are not always clear as to the standards that this conscience should embrace. Although some individuals believe themselves to be unbiased and free from superstition, yet self-deceit and unrecognized prejudice often play a large part in warping the inerrancy of the reports of conscience (*Vide* Vol. II, Sermons on Balaam and Self-Deceit). These individuals too stand in need of external assistance, and require a clear announcement as to the proper course of life (Vol. I, p. 184).

In the course of their lives men experience the consequences of their misdoings. They learn that punishment inevitably follows in the wake of their misdemeanors. Although this knowledge may have a salutary effect, in preventing the repetition of the same course of action in the face of future temptation, yet the disastrous consequences of their earlier deeds may descend upon them with devastating effects. Repentance for what they have done may appear unavailing; slowly, steadily, and with unmerciful inevitability can the future punishment be foreseen.

Thus to those individuals whose knowledge of God and his moral law is gathered only by the light of reason, the experience of God's ways will intimate an austerity that is hard, rigid, and unyielding. To repent for what has been done would be to indulge oneself in what is futile and ineffectual. The moral law will be stern, for it will afford man no mitigation.

As to his immortal life: if man is convinced of the truth of a continuous post-physical existence, and if he is aware that the tendencies towards punishments for wrongs committed on earth are more likely to be fulfilled in that existence, he will be faced with the terrors of its inevitability against which a life of repentance, and one remodeled upon the strict observance of the law of virtue, will be powerless and unavailing. To such individuals will be denied the knowledge that God is compassionate, and that his system of government is less rigid than it appears. But in the communication of scriptural knowledge mankind learns that God tempers his justice with mercy. More particularly he learns that "the moral government of the universe was not so rigid, but that there was room for an interposition, to avert the fatal consequences of vice; which therefore, by this means, does admit of pardon. Revelation teaches us, that the unknown laws of God's more general government, no less than the particular laws by which we experience he governs us at present, are compassionate, as well as good in the more general notion of goodness: and that he hath mercifully provided, that there should be an interposition to prevent the destruction of human kind; whatever that destruction unprevented would have been" (Vol. I, pp. 214-15).

The means of bringing about this tempering was through his incarnate presence in the person of Christ. Through this "he interposed in such a manner as was necessary and effectual to prevent that execution of justice upon sinners, which God had appointed should otherwise have been executed upon them: or in such a manner, as to prevent that punishment from actually following, which, according to the general laws of divine government, must have followed the sins of the world, had it not been for such interposition (Vol. I, p. 215).

In the role of a mediator are revealed the nature and services of Christ. First, he is to be regarded as a prophet, who declares to mankind the will of God. In this office he declared anew God's law of virtue that had fallen into desuetude. His purpose here was to awaken mankind to its sense of duty, to authorize them to live *"soberly, righteously, and godly in this present world,* in expectation of the future judgment of God" (Vol. I, pp. 219-220).

Secondly, he founded on earth a kingdom that was dedicated to the realization of his aims. To carry out his teachings, he established as an external means a church which was to be regarded as a memorial of this aim, and as an invitation for all men to join it (Vol. I, p. 220; Vol. II, SS. I). Without this provision, Christianity "must have been, in a great degree, sunk and forgot in a very few ages. To prevent this, appears to have been one reason why a visible church was instituted: to be, like a city upon an hill, a standing memorial to the world of the duty which we owe our Maker: to call men continually, both by example and instruction, to attend to it, and, by the form of religion, ever before their eyes, remind them of the reality: to be the repository of the oracles of God: to hold up the light of revelation in aid to that of nature, and propagate it throughout all generations to the end of the world—the light of revelation, considered here in no other view, than as designed to enforce natural religion" (Vol. I, p. 159; also SS. Vol. II, p. 237). Over this church, God exercises through his spirit an invisible government (Vol. I, pp. 200, 174), conducted according to explicit laws for the discipline and spiritualization of its members.

PROOFS OF REVEALED RELIGION

We have outlined above in the most general terms the contents of revealed religion, and then only to the extent that this knowledge bears upon the moral life of man. To live according to one's conscience requires that conscience be provided with a rule for action. We have tried to make clear how revealed religion supplies this rule by republishing the truths of natural religion, and by providing at the same time supplementary truths of its own that it behoves mankind to follow. To live according to one's conscience is to live as a Christian, to follow Christian rules, and to conform to the requirements and rituals of Christian teachings. As Butler tells us, natural religion points out the relations that exist between man and God conceived as father; revealed religion not only endorses these but further indicates the relations that exist between man and God conceived as Son and Spirit (Vol. I, p. 163).

There are however certain misgivings in the minds of men as to the truth of this scheme of revealed Christianity. Its importance for men is of such consequence, that every attempt should be made to make clear and substantiate its claims to legitimacy. We shall expound in the present section the various arguments and types of evidence that Butler considers effectively to establish its truth.[2]

Before one produces positive arguments in favor of the truth of revealed Christianity, one finds oneself confronted by a whole series of objections that are levelled against its truth. Some of these arguments are raised against the plausibility of revelation in general, others are more directly aimed against the pretensions of the Christian scheme in particular. These two lines of attacks have a traditional standing, and in their union they present a bulwark of opposition that must be weakened before one can proceed to gain a hearing for the arguments on the other side. Consequently Butler finds it necessary to meet these counter arguments first, before presenting the arguments in favor of the truth of the Christian scheme. He considers them under two headings, and we shall follow him in his arrangement.

Credibility of Revealed Religion. Because the contents of revealed religion are not immediately intelligible upon examination, there is a tendency for many to reject it as being false. But if it is clear that there are of necessity many things in the course of experience that we do not understand, and yet do not reject because of our ignorance, we cannot in all fair-mindedness reject the presented scheme of revelation for the same deficiencies that the scheme of nature shows. Also, if we know in advance that there are many things that we cannot understand, we shall be prepared for the particular difficulties as we come upon them.

[2] Our purpose in this present section is not directed towards the verification of revealed religion as Butler believed it, or to summarize its arguments for the reader; rather it is to show the argumentative skill with which Butler fortifies his position. In no part of his writings does he show himself to be more of a master of criticism than he does here, i.e., *Analogy*, Pt. II, Chs. II-VII. With consummate skill he calls to his aid every possibility of logical reasoning in his effort first to show the credibility of revealed Christianity, and secondly to supply positive arguments for its truth. We shall proceed to present his arguments under two aspects: first, those arguments that he levels against the incredibility of the scheme of revealed religion, and secondly, those arguments which he feels establish its positive proof, once the arguments against its credibility have been successfully disposed of. The first aspect will concern us for the rest of the present chapter, the second will be presented in the following chapter.

But rejection of the entire scheme is not a reasonable attitude. If we reject revelation, the rejection must be based upon other grounds.

Another type of objection raised against revelation in general points out that there exists in nature no counterpart to what it asserts: there is no corresponding likeness to support its claims. In the first place, according to Butler, this assertion is ambiguous. If it means that revelation in general is unsupported by facts of experience, the assertion is false, for there is a great deal that revelation professes that is borne out by experience. But if the objection implies that the specific contributions made by revealed religion, i.e., those aspects of it that are to be regarded as supplementary to the contents of natural religion, are unlike the announcements of natural religion, then the objection is true. But as an objection, it is beside the point. For granting that there is no likeness between the specific communications of revealed religion and those of natural religion, yet this unlikeness cannot warrant our rejecting revealed religion as false. In the course of experience itself we are acquainted with many instances that are unlike each other and yet are aware that they are members of the same system; likewise with the alleged reports of revealed religion, mere unlikeness between them and the contents of natural religion is no presumption of the falsity of the former.

A third type of objection raised against the plausibility of revealed religion is directed against the alleged reports of its miracles. In the first place they are denied as factual occurrences; in the second place they are attacked as being incredible. As to their being factual occurrences, Butler points out that they are reported as such by tradition in the same way as many other facts of the past of which we were not immediate eyewitnesses. If reports of tradition are to be accepted for the occurrence of secular facts, its reports of the occurrence of religious happenings are not to be denied. The reports of tradition must be accepted as respectable in both instances.

Other individuals maintain, however, that miracles are incredible. History may report their occurrence, but the nature of what is reported is said to be a sham. If internally examined they are seen to be pretentious and impossible. The reason that these individuals offer in support of their judgments concerning the incredibility of miracles is that miracles report a course of

nature different from what we know it to be today. To their
position Butler points out that the course of nature as revealed
by miracles might very well be admitted to be different from
that reported by contemporaneous observation, without however
our accepting the consequence that miracles are necessarily false
because of this difference. The peculiar moral conditions of the
earlier times might have made the use of miraculous powers necessary, so as to attract to the new teachings an entire class of individuals who could be attracted in no other way. But while
admitting the apparent differences between the course of nature
today, and the course of nature at the time when miracles were
actual occurrences, to be as great as they are, yet a credibility is
gained for the acceptance of miracles if we compare them not to
ordinary events of nature but to the extraordinary ones.

Butler next draws our attention to the fact that if we are
going to argue for the credibility or incredibility of miracles,
we must be acquainted with parallel instances in our own world
or in a world similar to ours. This means of verification however
is denied us. One or a few instances would be infinitely precarious (Vol. I, p. 178). Let us even grant further that there are
extant many facts that run counter to the plausibility of miracles,
yet as mere brute facts, being irrationally opposed to a set of
facts explicable by theory, they would be ineffectual. When
unallied to theory or unillumined by explanation, facts are un-
informative. When these unmarshalled facts, whose common denominator consists in what they deny rather than what they
affirm, are considered side by side for human acceptance with
those facts whose common denominator consists in what they
affirm, there is according to Butler greater probability that the
latter set of organized facts is true and that the unorganized sets
of facts are false, even though from the standpoint of number the
unorganized facts are infinitely greater. Upon such an argument
Butler would reject those instances that deny the credibility of
miracles after these latter have been reported by history. Finally,
to uphold his argument Butler maintains that the instances of
miraculous happenings accord perfectly with the admitted moral
scheme of the universe. As he says: "Take in the consideration
of religion, or the moral system of the world, and then we see
distinct particular reasons for miracles: to afford mankind instruction additional to that of nature, and to attest the truth of
it. And this gives a real credibility to the supposition, that it

might be part of the original plan of things, that there should be miraculous interposition" (Vol. I, p. 180).

Credibility of the Christian Scheme in Particular. When we argue against the supposed truth of a statement or a theory, we must possess, to argue effectively, a goodly store of information beforehand; we must be certain of our ground and position, in terms of which the theory or statement we are opposing is found to be defective. In other words we must first be assured of a prior truth before we can advance our criticism to an actual situation. This is no less true of our attitude towards revelation. In this particular instance we are apt to be illogical and presumptuous, for to argue against the particular communications of revealed religion such as the advent of a redeemer and his office as mediator between God and man is to assume, in advance of this particular communication, that God is not revealing what he should reveal. Butler's pronouncements on this point are so clear and concise that I shall let him speak for himself.

He tells us: "As we are in no sort judges beforehand, by what laws or rules, in what degree, or by what means, it were to have been expected, that God would naturally instruct us: so upon supposition of his affording us light and instruction by revelation, additional to what he has afforded us by reason and experience, we are in no sort judges, by what methods, and in what proportion, it were to be expected, that this supernatural light and instruction would be afforded us. We know not beforehand, what degree or kind of natural information, it were to be expected God would afford men, each by his own reason and experience: nor how far he would enable and effectually dispose them to communicate it, whatever it should be, to each other: nor whether the evidence of it would be certain, highly probable, or doubtful: nor whether it would be given with equal clearness and conviction to all. Nor could we guess, upon any good ground I mean, whether natural knowledge, or even the faculty itself, by which we are capable of attaining it, reason, would be given us at once, or gradually. In like manner, we are wholly ignorant, what degree of new knowledge, it were to be expected, God would give mankind by revelation, upon supposition of his affording one: or how far, or in what way, he would interpose miraculously, to qualify them, to whom he should originally make the revelation, for communicating the knowledge given by it; and to secure their doing it to the age in which they should live; and to secure its being transmitted to posterity" (Vol. I, pp. 185-186).

Furthermore we cannot judge what is expedient and necessary in a scheme of revelation or not. Admitting the plausibility of revelation, i.e., of the fact that it is communicated to man as a message of God, and also granting that we cannot judge beforehand the particular nature of these communications, we cannot according to Butler even judge *a posteriori* that the revealed contents are unnecessary, or maintain the means in which the religious scheme is established, to be extravagant or unintelligible (Vol. I, p. 225). To do so would be again to argue upon our conception of things. For "though it is highly right, and the most pious exercise of our understanding, to inquire with due reverence into the ends and reason of God's dispensations: yet when those reasons are concealed, to argue from our ignorance, that such dispensations cannot be from God, is infinitely absurd" (Vol. I, p. 225).

Having shown that we cannot raise *a priori* objections against the contents of the revealed scheme in general, we shall now show that we cannot raise any objections against any of its detailed contents considered singly. The positive contents of revealed religion, as we have pointed out above, maintained that God carries on his system of government through the mediation of a divine person; that this dispensation of providence is proved by miracles; and that the communication of this providential dispensation is not made to all men with an equal degree of clearness or cogency. Objections are raised by the opponents of revealed religion to the plausibility of these three statements. Let us examine each opposition in turn and present Butler's reply.

First as to the statement of revealed religion that God's government on earth is carried on through the mediation of a redeemer through whom God works compassionately. To this it is objected that God is represented as attaining through intricate means what his nature should be able to achieve immediately, and that it presupposes the necessity of voluntary sacrifice in order to bring about good ends. But these objections, maintains Butler, are ineffectual, as there can be found in the course and constitution of nature which is admittedly the work of God corresponding instances. Let us see how.

The promise that God makes to man through his revealed teachings is that sincere repentance is efficacious. As a consequence of genuine contrition, it is promised to man that the ordinarily expected punishment that is supposed to follow from a vicious act can be averted or lessened. In other words it is possible to appeal to the compassion of God, and gain a remission for one's sins. There is nothing unplausible about this claim of revealed religion and nothing in nature that runs contrary to it. On the other hand it is endorsed by similar occurrences in nature, which show that in support of its truth there is available analogical evidence. Individuals exhibit the same behavior to each other, for to act so arises from the fundamental constitution of their nature. As Butler tells us in his Sermon on Compassion (Vol. II, p. 96), that "compassion is a call, a demand of nature, to relieve the unhappy; as hunger is a natural call for food." The compassion of God is also instanced in the arrangements and disposals of inanimate nature in its bearing upon human life. Often through inadvertence or rashness, or even deliberate self-will, man brings upon himself the consequence of disease with all the uneasiness and pain that this entails. Yet in these cases God has "provided reliefs, and in many cases perfect remedies for it, after some pains and difficulties: reliefs and remedies even for that evil, which is the fruit of our own misconduct; and which, in the course of nature, would have continued, and ended in our destruction, but for such remedies. And this is an instance both of severity and of indulgence, in the constitution of nature. Thus all the bad consequences, now mentioned, of a man's trifling upon a precipice, might be prevented. And though all were not, yet some of them might, by proper interposition, if not rejected: by another's coming to the rash man's relief, with his own laying hold on that relief, in such sort as the case required" (Vol. I, p. 210).

There are also discoverable in nature corresponding instances when a series of intricate means are made use of in establishing a desired end. But upon this point we shall allow Butler to speak for himself. "The whole analogy of nature removes all imagined presumption against the general notion of *a mediator between God and man.* For we find all living creatures are brought into the world, and their life in infancy is preserved, by the instrumentality of others: and every satisfaction of it, some way or other, is bestowed by the like means. So that the visible government, which God exercises over the world, is by the instrumentality and mediation of others. . . . There is then no sort of objection, from the light of nature, against the general notion of a mediator between God and man, considered as a doctrine of Christianity, or as an appointment in this dispensation: since we find by experience, that God does appoint mediators, to be the instruments of good and evil to us; the instruments of his justice and his mercy" (Vol. I, pp. 207, 8).

Lastly an objection is made against the notion of voluntary sacrifice that was instanced in the life of the redeemer. But even this is not without its parallel in the course of nature. We are told that many individuals can be aided in their troubles and relieved from their difficulties only through the voluntary assistance of other individuals. Often this assistance cannot be rendered without much suffering, labor, and pains to ourselves (Vol. I, p. 224). To reason against the plausibility of God's religious scheme as it is revealed is to forget that vicarious suffering is an everyday occurrence, or to ignore that the course of nature is at the bottom God's own scheme. What actually takes place in one aspect of God's scheme cannot be denounced as unplausible when it is spoken of in the other.

We shall now consider the objections that are brought against the credibility of miracles in the Christian scheme. We have already urged in this connection that the objections against miracles in general offer no serious argument, for miracles are reported by tradition, and they do not run counter to the more comprehensive scheme of natural religion. In the present instance we shall consider however a different type of objection. The type of objection that now advances itself maintains that the miraculous powers that were evinced by some of the converts to Christianity were exercised in a highly irregular and disorderly way (Vol. I, p. 191); and that the recognition of this fact is sufficient indication that they were not really miraculous.

Butler's reply is that all powers, faculties or gifts are to be understood by the purpose for which they were designed, i.e., the tendency they naturally point to, and not to be judged by their perversions (Vol. I, pp. 16, 192). If we compare the existence of miraculous powers with unusual gifts in nature, such as extraordinary talents, we can note especially in regard to the latter that these are misuses of the same. But the misuse is no denial of the reality of the talent or of the value of the use it was originally intended for. "Consider," says Butler, "a person endued with any of these gifts; for instance, that of tongues: it is to be supposed, that he had the same power over this miraculous gift, as he would have had over it, had it been the effect of habit, of study and use, as it ordinarily is; or the same power over it, as he had over any other natural endowment. Consequently, he would use it in the same manner he did any other; either regularly, and upon proper occasions only, or irregularly, and upon improper ones: according to his sense of decency, and his character of prudence. Where then is the objection?" (Vol. I, p. 192).

Another objection that is raised against miracles in the Christian scheme is that they are not instances of general laws by which the scheme of nature appears to be conducted (Vol. I, p. 204). It is not understood why miraculous interventions should occur when or where they do: nor why they should take place with regard to some individuals rather than to others. When they do occur the course of nature which has up till then been carried on in a regular fashion receives a new direction. But those objections cannot be seriously considered, for in the course of nature itself, not every event is governed by general law. We are ignorant of the laws whereby famines, earthquakes, tempests, come to be instruments of destruction to man; also we are still unacquainted with the laws of individual minds, their temperaments, capacities, and genius (Vol. I, p. 203). But we do not deny their reality, nor do we believe them to be so irregular in kind that they cannot, if our revelation were sufficient, be reduced to the more general laws of nature. Likewise with the occurrence of miracles. Comparable to the more extraordinary events in nature, they should share with them an equal claim to recognition and acceptance. And for all we know, they too are reducible to the more general laws of God's government, were it possible for us to comprehend it in its entirety.

We shall now consider the final objection that is often raised against the claims of revelation. This objection complains of the want of universality in the Christian scheme (Vol. I, p. 227). It is neither universally known nor imparted to every one of its adherents with an equal degree of cogency. But according to Butler, this cannot be offered as a serious objection against the truth of it. If we look to the analogy of nature in search of similar instances, we find that in regard to matters other than those of revelation, men are differently favored. Indeed God "appears to bestow all his gifts with the most promiscuous variety among creatures of the same species: health and strength, capacities of

prudence and of knowledge, means of improvement, riches, and
all external advantages. And as there are not any two men found,
of exactly like shape and features: so it is probable there are not
any two, of an exactly like constitution, temper and situation,
with regard to the goods and evils of life" (Vol. I, p. 229). Also
in the examples of other religions there is an equal want of universality, and likewise there are varying degrees of evidence in
support of them. If we reflect upon the great variety of human
beings and the varying range of their capacity for specific knowledge, common understanding, or animal faith, we shall readily
observe that the same religious truths could not be received by
all with equal belief (Vol. I, p. 233). Hence it is quite possible
that God's government is such as to require this complexity of
human nature, and that it is not necessary for all of us to be
equally informed. Although this may be so, yet "Providence's
designing to place some in greater darkness with respect to religious knowledge, is no more a reason why they should not
endeavour to get out of that darkness, and others to bring them
out of it; than why ignorant and slow people in matters of other
knowledge should not endeavour to learn, or should not be instructed" (Vol. I, p. 232).

We cannot object to the scheme as unfair because in the
nature of things it cannot be universally known. Since God is
aware that the degree of comprehension varies from man to man,
he has undoubtedly taken into account these differences of natural ability and has allowed for a proportional compensation
when the final reckoning comes about. At the same time it is
conceivably possible that men have been put into a state of religious probation, that they have been subjected to the necessity
of patience and endurance in what they cannot fully comprehend; that furthermore they are on actual trial to probe into the
religious evidence to instruct themselves in its claims. As Butler
says: "Thus, that religion is not intuitively true, but a matter
of deduction and inference; that a conviction of its truth is not
forced upon every one, but left to be, by some, collected with
heedful attention to premises; this as much constitutes religious probation, as much affords sphere, scope, opportunity, for
right and wrong behaviour, as any thing whatever does" (Vol.
I, p. 234).

30

REVEALED RELIGION

POSITIVE EVIDENCE FOR REVEALED RELIGION

OUR last section in the previous chapter presented and considered those arguments that were raised against the credibility of revelation in general and Christian revelation in particular. The examination of these arguments showed their claims against the plausibility of revealed religion to be unfounded. But the counter-arguments of Butler aimed at showing no more than that the opponents of revealed religion have no serious claims; he did believe however that with all objections against this scheme swept aside it would be possible to offer positive arguments in support of the truth of revealed religion. He was under no illusion as to the simplicity of his task. Both in his *Analogy* and in his *Durham Charge* he maintains that the evidences of Christianity depend upon "a long series of things, reaching, as it seems, from the beginning of the world to the present time, of great variety and compass, taking in both the direct, and also the collateral, proofs; and making up, all of them together, one argument: the conviction arising from which kind of proof may be compared to what they call *the effect* in architecture of other works of art; a result from a great number of things so and so disposed, and taken into one view" (Vol. I, p. 248; Cp. also *Dur. Charge*, Vol. II, p. 337).

To unite this evidence into one argument is a Herculean task; not an impossible one, but still one that affords a difficulty to those who have not the sustained patience for apprising themselves of its contents or working up the argument for themselves. Butler himself announces that he will not supply this evidence in detail, for his main interest has been to show that the difficulties raised against the credibility and claims of Christianity are ill-founded. He indicates briefly, however, the lines of procedure that such positive argument in defence of Christianity must sustainedly follow. In our present chapter we shall indicate the lines of this evidence that Butler has pointed out but with even greater brevity than he does himself.[1]

[1] The material from which this present chapter has been taken will be found in the *Analogy*, Pt. One, Ch. VII. There the reader can see worked out with greater elaborateness the arguments that we are paraphrasing. The arrangement

The particular evidence for Christianity can be considered under three headings: upon the claims of miracles, upon the acceptance of prophecies, and, from what Butler terms "direct and circumstantial evidence" (Vol. I, pp. 268-9, 288). In what respect each affords evidence for Christianity we shall now see.

All presumption against the credibility of miracles having been removed, the outstanding question becomes an historical one, namely, did they take place as are asserted, and did they achieve what they claimed to achieve? In regard to miracles their claims to actual occurrence are based upon the same reports of history as are the claims of secular events. "The facts, both miraculous and natural, in scripture, are related in plain unadorned narratives: and both of them appear, in all respects, to stand upon the same foot of historical evidence" (Vol. I, p. 250). Even making allowances for the bias of human nature and the enthusiasm that is apt to over-merit the evidence of observed miraculous facts (for such enthusiasm colors reports of secular events as well), yet we should allow that "scripture-history in general is to be admitted as an authentic genuine history, till somewhat positive be alleged sufficient to invalidate it" (Vol. I, p. 251). To denounce it as purely fictitious requires much more positive evidence against it, than we have at present.

There is also the independent evidence of Paul to be gathered from his epistles to the Corinthians, as well as from the letters he wrote to other individuals and churches. Accepting their authenticity (Vol. I, pp. 251-52), there is no reason for denying the contents of their reports; but in accepting their evidence we are afforded a proof of Christianity detached from all others and of weight in itself (Vol. I, p. 252). From them (i.e., from the Epistles to the Corinthians) we gather that Paul "received the gospel in general, and the institution of the communion in particular, not from the rest of the apostles, or jointly together with them, but alone, from Christ himself; whom he declares likewise, conformably to the history in the Acts, that he saw after his ascension" (Vol. I, p. 252). Paul also speaks of his powers of working miracles and of the miraculous gifts possessed by the churches to which he was writing. He enjoins them to use their powers with decency and propriety, and for the purposes for which they were endowed. Butler holds that this incidental

of Butler's arguments in the present thesis has been made to suit the purpose it is interested in advancing, i.e., the place of religion in the moral life.

mentioning of miracles on the part of Paul "in the manner any one would speak to another of a thing which was as familiar and as much known in common to them both, as any thing in the world" (Vol. I, p. 252), is an additional proof of miraculous occurrences.

We mentioned above that the question of miracles was primarily a question of fact, but they also involve the question of doctrinal truth, since they claim to give testamentary evidence to the truth of Christian teachings. Upon this latter claim they were received and recognized as genuine by the people at the time of their occurrence. That they were accepted in this light is borne out by the number of conversions that was effected both among the primitive Christians and among the martyrs of a later age (Vol. I, p. 256). And if it is objected to that the peoples at those times were strongly biased by the outcome of a belief that would be greatly to their advantage, Butler replies that they also had much to lose from the standpoint of conveniences (Vol. I, p. 254). For them to renounce voluntarily their accustomed scheme of living indicates that they must have been really convinced of the truths of these miracles. "And it will, I suppose, readily be acknowledged, that the generality of the first converts to Christianity must have believed them: that as by becoming Christians they declared to the world, they were satisfied of the truth of those miracles; so this declaration was to be credited" (Vol. I, p. 254). Also it must be borne in mind that this wholesale conversion took place during an age that was averse, from the standpoint of education, prejudice, and authority, to all that Christianity claimed to be (Vol. I, p. 255). And as to the martyrs of a later age, their actions too must be accepted as a further evidence for the claims of miracles. Although they themselves were not eyewitnesses to them, yet it is presumably certain that these martyrs had opportunities to inform themselves whether or not the miracles had occurred (Vol. I, p. 256).

We must recognize that without doubt many of the reports of miraculous happenings were false, but the admission of this does not commit us to the conclusion that none were true. As Butler says: "To argue, that because there is, if there were, like evidence from testimony, for miracles acknowledged false, as for those in attestation of Christianity, therefore the evidence in the latter case is not to be credited; this is the same as to argue, that if two men of equally good reputation had given evidence in different cases no way connected, and one of them had been convicted of perjury, this confuted the testimony of the other" (Vol. I, p. 260).

The acceptance of prophecies affords another piece of valuable evidence in favor of revealed Christianity. But in opposition to their being accepted as such, definite objections are raised. For instance, it is contended by the opponents of prophecies that much of their content is unintelligible or at the best obscure (Vol. I, p. 262).

To this charge Butler points out that "the obscurity or unintelligibleness of one part of a prophecy does not, in any degree, invalidate the proof of foresight, arising from the appearing completion of those other parts which are understood" (Vol. I, p. 262). Things are to be judged by the explanation that can be given to the known parts, rather than to be rejected *in toto* because some parts are wanting in explanation.

There is another objection that is raised against the acceptance of prophecies. As to those parts of prophecies that are intelligible and that point in this intelligible aspect to the particular events to which they were applied by Christians, it is again maintained, that such later application was not originally intended by the utterers of them. In short their intention, if such there originally be, was probably in reference to other events unknown to us; hence they are not to be interpreted as affirming the coming to be, e.g., of a Christ as Messiah (Vol. I, p. 263). Such is the substance of the second objection.

The proof of this objection, i.e., that prophecies are not applicable to the Christian scheme, lies with those who make it; it is not the duty of the professors of the Christian scheme first to show that this counter-assertion is false before they advance their own explanation and use of them. In their interpretation of prophecies Christians are at least advancing a principle that explains them, whereas those who deny the legitimacy of this interpretation have none to offer themselves. Butler points out that the Christian interpretation of miracles is one that is fortified in many ways. He says: "if a long series of prophecy is applicable to the present state of the church, and to the political situations of the kingdoms of the world, some thousand years after these prophecies were delivered, and a long series of prophecy delivered before the coming of Christ is applicable to him;

these things are in themselves a proof, that the prophetic history was intended of him, and of those events: in proportion as the general turn of it is capable of such application and to the number and variety of particular prophecies capable of it" (Vol. I, p. 264).

With these preliminary objections removed we can now appreciate the part that prophecies play in the substantiation of revealed Christianity. In the first place they predict a course of events that has been fulfilled, and secondly they instance in their completion a proof of foresight more than human. Taken by themselves they are insufficient to bear the entire burden of proof, but in conjunction with miracles and other circumstances they lend considerable weight. We are now brought to our final consideration of positive evidence in support of revealed Christianity: this evidence Butler terms circumstantial.

Circumstantial Evidence. Under this heading can be brought such evidence as the joint influence of miracles and revelation, that taken together in their mutual support make for greater certainty than either taken singly (Vol. I, p. 269). Under the same heading can be brought the accounts of the Old and New Testaments. Thus this type of evidence is mainly historical. Butler holds this third type of evidence to be of the greatest importance, for it comprises a variety of circumstances whose force of conviction is brought about by the convergence of these several things considered in respect to each other.

When we first made clear the nature of revealed religion, we said that it was to be considered above all as a republication of natural religion. If both natural and revealed religion are considered from the standpoint of their common claims they are seen to differ only in the ways whereby knowledge of each is acquired. Thus natural religion is known or can be known through reason, independently thought out. As Butler says concerning it: "It is to be remembered, that how much soever the establishment of natural religion in the world is owing to the scripture-revelation, this does not destroy the proof of religion from reason; any more than the proof of Euclid's Elements is destroyed, by a man's knowing or thinking, that he should never have seen the truth of the several propositions contained in it, nor had those propositions come into his thoughts, but for that mathematician" (Vol. I, p. 277).

The main channel for one's knowledge of revealed religion

lies through the scriptural accounts. All that we require to know for the proper conduct of our lives is to be found within it. It contains, besides, an account of the world as God's world (Vol. I, p. 270), i.e., as his creation, subject to his laws and commands; in it can be found a description of religion and its professors during the world's state of wickedness, etc. (Vol. I, p. 271). The scripture covers a period of the world's history of nearly 6,000 years (Vol. I, p. 272). In its later account it includes prophetic history and the particular dispensation of Christianity (Vol. I, p. 273). Thus the promises in the Old Testament of the coming of a redeemer were fulfilled. Likewise was the foretelling fulfilled that this Messiah would be rejected by the nation to whom he had been promised (Vol. I, p. 275). The consequent details can be furnished by oneself: such as the account that the Messiah should be Savior of the Gentiles and that he performed miracles (Vol. I, p. 275). To this can be added that he endued his followers with the same miraculous powers as "proof of the truth of that religion, which he commissioned them to publish: that, invested with this authority and power, they made numerous converts in the remotest countries, and settled and established his religion in the world; to the end of which, the scripture professes to give a prophetic account of the state of this religion amongst mankind" (Vol. I, p. 276).

The presumption to truth of the scriptural accounts is reinforced as we learn that "its chronology, its account of the time when the earth, and the several parts of it, were first peopled with human creatures, is no way contradicted, but is really confirmed, by the natural and civil history of the world, collected from common historians, from the state of the earth, and from the late inventions of arts and sciences" (Vol. I, pp. 277-8). Thus as the accounts of civil and political events mentioned in the Bible are substantiated through independent sources, it is highly probable that in its account of miraculous and prophetic events it is equally trustworthy and acceptable. Upon the congruence of lay history as narrated by the Bible and as gathered from independent sources rests the probability that those portions of the Bible that have little or no independent verification are themselves no less true.

Summing up this situation, Butler remarks: "A history, claiming to commence from the creation, and extending in one continued series, through so great a length of time, and variety

of events, should have such appearances of reality and truth in
its whole contexture, is surely a very remarkable circumstance
in its favour. And as all this is applicable to the common history
of the New Testament, so there is a further credibility, and a
very high one, given to it by profane authors: many of these
writing of the same times, and confirming the truth of customs
and events which are incidentally as well as more purposely mentioned in it. And this credibility of the common scripture-history,
gives some credibility to its miraculous history: especially as
this is interwoven with the common, so as that they imply each
other, and both together make up one relation" (Vol. I, pp. 279-
80). Since the claims of revealed religion are of such importance
that they should not be dismissed until there is available a sufficiency of weighty evidence against it, we should neither be
hasty, nor attempt a task that might be beyond our individual
powers. Hence, Butler urges that we should put store upon the
reports of authorities. They are men who have examined the
varieties of extant evidence and have been satisfied with the
results of their findings.

DUTIES ENJOINED BY REVEALED RELIGION

On individuals already convinced of the truth of revealed religion are imposed duties of the most exacting sort for their observance and practice. But likewise are there imposed duties of investigation and action on those who are not convinced of its
truth.

The asserted claims of the Christian scheme, says Butler, are
such as to command the attention of unbelievers and the doubtful.
Considering the influence it has had for the past several hundred
years, we cannot reject this scheme without more extensive
examination. We are obliged to consider carefully the claims that
it makes. If we are doubtful about its truth we should investigate
for ourselves the available evidence, and consider the positive
arguments that can be asserted in its favor. But in our failure
to work towards or achieve an intellectual conviction our duty
in the meantime is not to act in thought or deed as if the claims
of revealed religion were admittedly false. In the light of this
we are commanded to refrain from trivial or derogatory conversation concerning it. And in our practice we are urged to pay
a conscientious regard to the moral virtue that religion advocates.
To observe this latter injunction is highly important, for it is a

commonplace fact that our behavior influences, rightly or wrongly, the behavior of others. As Butler points out: "From a character of understanding, or a situation of influence in the world, some persons have it in their power to do infinitely more harm or good, by setting an example of profaneness and avowed disregard to all religion, or, on the contrary, of a serious, though perhaps doubting, apprehension of its truth, and of a reverent regard to it under this doubtfulness; than they can do, by acting well or ill in all the common intercourses amongst mankind. And consequently they are most highly accountable for a behaviour, which, they may easily foresee, is of such importance, and in which there is most plainly a right and a wrong; even admitting the evidence of religion to be as doubtful as is pretended" (Vol. I, pp. 236-237).

The belief in revealed religion carries with it a system of duties that are immediately deducible from the assumed nature of its general truths; they are consequently obligatory upon all who profess an adherence to the claims of revealed religion. The more general nature of many of these duties has been treated by us in our section on natural religion. The coincidence of the duties of revealed religion with those of natural religion is owing to the fact that revealed religion is a republication of natural religion. As such both proclaim God to be author of the scheme of things which we see objectively expressing itself in, through, and around us, according to the laws of his wisdom.

Both types of religion reveal one and the same message, and demand fundamentally the same kind of duty. We are to love God and honor him, observe his laws, as his commands, and resign ourselves in reverence, awe, dependence and trust to his ways (Vol. I, p. 123; Vol. II, Sec. XIII, *et passim*). Since we are to regard all things as having been created by God and as owing their present existence to him, we are to consider our more particular obligations, whether they be to the service of man, or society, as religious obligations at bottom. When we cannot understand the *raison d'être* of the obligations we are pledged to, we should be ready to attribute the shortcomings to ourselves rather than to the institutions; to them we should pay the same sort of reverence that we should pay to God who has created them. Such is the general kind of obligation that we are committed to upon the acceptance of religion, whether it is natural or revealed. But as believers in revealed religion, we are bound

in the observance and practice of other duties besides. These
additional duties are implicit in the difference between the two
types of religion. The emphasis that revealed religion places
upon the scripture binds us to its perusal to see what God really
commands, and to the consequent duty of carrying out his commands that are mentioned in them. More particularly in this
respect we are apprised of his truer reality, i.e., of his manifestation as spirit and son, in the accounts of revealed religion.
From this announcement other duties arise. As an example, Butler informs us that baptism is to be conducted in the name of
the three persons of God.

Very little individual judgment is required of us to decide
for ourselves what we should do in general or along what lines
we should conduct our lives; but only an effort to discover this
rule for ourselves and submit in obedience to it. In the broader
affairs of our conduct we should base our lives upon the model of
the Saviour, imitating him in his examples of goodness, love and
charity (Vol. II, p. 174); loving our enemies and forgiving injuries committed against us. As a consequence we should endeav-
or to be sincere in all our dealings (Vol. II, p. 269), and live
in accordance with honesty and fairness of mind (*ibid.*, p. 163).

Besides acquainting ourselves with the contents of the scriptures we are also bound to the observance of another general
type of duty: this is the preservation of revealed religion, its
transmission to others, and enforcement upon ourselves, through
an established church.

We shall not consider any further the minutiae of duties that
follow from the acceptance of and belief in revealed religion,
such as the support to be given by the congregation for the
propagation of the Gospel abroad, or the need of the clergy to
pay greater attention to the ritual and to the repair of their
churches. It is plain that in all of these Butler has in mind the
duties that are connected with the Church of England, rather
than the principles of Church organization. His intolerance to
other forms of Christianity is undisguised. The Roman Catholic
Religion is openly spoken of as the corruption of Christianity,
for Butler sees in it the "usurpation of all human and divine
authority" (Vol. II, p. 309). In a conversation that Butler had
with Wesley it is reported that he was out of sympathy with the
work of the Methodists. He differed from them on many points
of doctrine, and urged Wesley to leave the diocese of Bristol

(Vol. II, pp. 366-7). As to the Jewish religion he believed it to be fulfilled and completed in the Christian religion.

In discussing the meaning of religion both natural and revealed, and its place within the moral life of the individual, it has been our aim to show that both systems prescribed to the conscience of the individual the course of behavior he is to follow. The most important virtues are already announced for him in the scriptural accounts; for the type of life he is to follow is exemplified in the life of the Redeemer. Thus there is little left for his own conscience to act independently upon. In cases of every day affairs his duty is to find the general principle under which the actions will come, and to bring this law into his daily life. There are conceivable occasions when it will be necessary for him to act upon his own judgment, but these will be few indeed, and when they do arise, the individual can intuitively see for himself the proper course of action to follow (Vol. II, p. 112).

AUTHORITY OF RELIGION AND AUTHORITY OF CONSCIENCE

Our account of revealed religion and the duties it imposes upon the individual may suggest that conscience is being overridden in authority, instead of being allowed to judge for itself what is right and desirable. Is the supremacy of conscience subordinated to religion or is it not?

Butler's consistent thesis has been the supremacy of conscience as a guide to man's moral life. He has insisted that it is the ultimate authority to which we can and should appeal in moments of difficulty. He further states that each man himself possesses conscience as a law of his own nature. In moments of doubt he can consult it and profit by its decisions; the urgency to abide by its decisions is moreover self-imposed. Our account of natural and revealed religion seems upon first sight to be a violation of this moral thesis. In being commanded to observe the prescriptions of religion, we seem to be neglecting the calls of conscience or supplying to it *ab extra* a course of behavior that ignores its rightful authority to judge for itself what it conceives to be right or wrong. For, if I am urged to live a life of goodness, charity, veracity or justice, it must appear at first sight that the supremacy that is claimed for my conscience has been conveniently set aside or ignored. Yet this is not so. Peremptory as are the exhortations of revealed religion for me to live a life of virtue already conceived and laid down in advance, yet my conscience is neither quietly ignored nor overtly dethroned from its place of lawful authority. How this is so we shall now try to make clear.

Natural religion, we have pointed out, is much more than a metaphysical account of the universe. It is an endorsement of a discovered scheme to which man can turn for guidance. When morally reflected upon by man, it entails obligations. Thus understood man's metaphysical knowledge turns into an ethics and a religion. Only when man carries his reflection to its *ne plus ultra* does he arrive at the realm of religious and moral values. But once he has arrived there, it is incumbent on him to heed and to carry into overt activity what he has discovered to be true; for the discovery has been attained and completed not merely as a result of his reflectiveness, but ultimately through this procedure of reflectiveness, turned moral. Thus, far from natural religion making impositions upon man's conscience, it is possible for man only because of his possession of a conscience.

To make this point still clearer: let us grant that I raise to myself the question why I should observe the commands of revealed religion. I am told that the truths of its teachings can be discovered by closely observing the course and constitution of nature. Let us grant that I do so. Limited to an exercise of speculative reason that is capable of affording me an account of nature that is highly probable, I gather little by little that it is created by God, that man is moral, that his life is one of trial and probation, that he is part of God's scheme, etc. Were I to stop my enquiries at this stage, I should possess a philosophy of the universe, or a system of metaphysics which would be of speculative interest, but certainly no more. But since I, as an investigating being, am primarily moral and secondarily speculative, I am forced through an inner impetus of my nature to evaluate morally the metaphysical system, the knowledge of which I have previously gathered. In other words, I now complete my account of the universe by affirming it to be good, and by endorsing what it reveals to me in relation to myself as necessary. But this evalution and endorsement are the expressions of my conscience, without which no natural religion would have been possible. We can now see that although revealed religion commands men, its commands are justified only because they can be based upon the reports of natural religion. The obligations to follow its teachings are fundamentally the same as our obligations to follow the teachings of natural religion. But we have just seen that the obligations of natural religion, far from overriding the authority of conscience, and neglecting its claims to supremacy, are possible only to the extent that conscience actively endorses and evaluates the findings of speculative reason in its reflection upon the course and constitution of experience.

Reflection and conscience work hand in hand. Although the latter is superior to the former in so far that it completes its work, none the less it is impotent without its assistance. The truer view of conscience, as we have already urged at length in the first part of our discussion, is the view that sees it to be reflective as well as moral: rational as well as axiological; i.e., as inseparably both. Since conscience is inextricably allied to reflection, it borrows from the latter the degree of objectivity that it professes. To the extent that reason establishes for us the existence of an objective scheme of things dependent on God, it follows that the contents of natural religion claim a similar objectivity; for Butler assumes that even in the moral aspect of reasoning there will be no less objectivity than is proclaimed in its solely rational aspect. Just as all men are capable (provided that native capacities are present) of agreeing as to the discoveries of reasoning, in an equal measure are they capable of attaining to the same moral decisions and enforcing upon themselves the same type of behavior. It is presumably for this reason that in laying down for one's fellow-creatures a system of duties that they are enjoined to follow, there is committed no inroad upon their moral nature, which claims for itself the supremacy of its conscience. Butler would hold that were they capable of exerting themselves to the same degree of moral understanding as do their more enlightened brethren, they too would see the universe in the same way and endorse as desirable the same type of action. To insist that they follow a moral order is not to ignore their conscience. It is to recognize that this conscience is undeveloped and is not to be trusted if it engages itself to think independently upon matters for which it is defective or not trained. But to bring home to them the fact that they are not capable of thinking independently for themselves and that they should rely upon the moral decisions of their wiser brethren is to make an appeal to them that is basically moral, for it is addressed to their conscience: as such it is commensurate with the degree of activity that conscience at that stage of development is capable of showing.

In concluding this point we can say that there is no conflict between natural religion and conscience, but we must likewise insist that conscience is neither arbitrary, capricious nor individual. In its operations it is dictated to by the laws of its own structure; for in discovering through its rational aspect that the nature of the universe is what it is, conscience before approving or disapproving these reported results, has come in contact with a scheme that is not of its own making. Just as in its rational aspect it discovers an objective universe, and reports its condition to man, conscience likewise in its moral aspect assents to what it conceives to be necessary. In doing this it is recognizing that its approvals are directed towards what is objectively good. It is for this reason that Butler speaks of conscience as the voice of God, or the candle of the Lord within us. Thus conscience that must approve of the scheme of things before it acquires for the individual a moral significance and the status of a natural religion is itself part of the scheme that it is evaluating; as such, it works according to a law that is characteristic of itself, but a law that none the less betokens a structure that owes its origin and being as do other things in the universe to God. Thus we can admit the necessity of conscience in natural religion, and yet affirm that its autonomy consists in the fact that man is privileged to assent morally to a scheme of things already laid down and which he discovers through reason; or to dissent, but to recognize in his dissension that God's disapproval of this act of conscience is instanced in the natural and moral punishments that man receives on earth.

Granted that reflection and conscience are inseparable and that in their cooperative activity they establish for us an objective scheme of natural religion, we must now point out the fact that religion as the highest virtue contains within itself all the lesser virtues; that within its contents can be found all demands that are made by the self in its aspects of benevolence, self-love, and the particular propensions. To do so, it is only necessary to remind ourselves that when the self has reached the level of moral expression, it has already evolved from the lesser principles and the particular propensions. But in evolving from these lesser affections it has taken over into its own nature all their contributions as its particular contents.

In our discussion of the self we have pointed out that the lesser principles can be spoken of as the particular propensions emerging into self-consciousness of their common ends; that whether we speak of the lesser principles as the particular propensions rationalized, or speak of the particular propensions as incomplete aspects of self-love, or benevolence, we are viewing the same situation in two ways. It will also be recalled that the lesser principles of self-love and benevolence are themselves incomplete aspects of the supreme principle of conscience; that when we become thoroughly conscious of our native tendencies towards benevolence or self-love, we have insensibly passed over into a realm of moral reflectiveness that is common to both of them and that completes their nature. And thus there can be no moral expression of the self that does not contain concretely the drives of the lesser principles. But since the lesser principles themselves contain the particular propensions, it follows that whenever the completed self works in accordance with its highest interests, it carries out in speculation and deed the totality of its parts in every phase of its expression.

A satisfactory religion is one that must pay respect to the self in its variety of lesser parts. It must prescribe for its active display of benevolence in deeds of charity, obedience, patriotism, and good fellowship. And it must also provide for the exercise of one's particular propensions, such as the expression of compassion and the proper use and limits of resentment. To the extent that it provides for this manifold of tendencies religion is truly living up to the purposes that called it forth. All these elements, we have found, take their place in the schemes both of natural and of revealed religion.

31

REASON IN THE MORAL LIFE

OUR analysis of human nature did not reveal reason as one of its fundamental drives. For Butler at least the desire to know is not fundamental, but derivative. Man does not desire knowledge for its own sake, but as a means for virtuous living. Speculative reason merely explores what is actual and extant in the scheme of things; as a principle for the guidance of life it is barren and uncreative. If expressed for its own sake, it tends to pass over into the exercise of conscience. Although reason is not a fundamental drive of man, it tends to become so. Hence it is important to examine its nature and claims so that its place in the moral life can be determined. With some individuals reason tends to become an end in itself. What then is its place in the nature of man? It will be the purpose of the present chapter to show the origin and nature of reason, and then to determine from the standpoint of the moral life the degree of expression that it should be allowed.

When we examine the nature of speculative reason as a drive in human nature, we see that it reveals itself as being an intrinsic aspect of the moral principles, contributing to conscience, self-love, and benevolence the speculative function of their expression. Examining reason more closely, we can ascribe to it at least three functions. First, it is the faculty of general awareness whereby man ascertains in the light of his self-consciousness the objects that his affections seek. "It is by reason that we get the ideas of several objects of our affections" (Vol. II, p. 195). Secondly, reason is discursive, or instrumental. Accepting the presence of drives in human nature, being aware of their nature, and the kinds of objects that will satisfy them, reason proceeds to establish in the most efficient way the means that will result in the overt expression of these drives. In this function reason does not question the ends that are set to it to follow, but only the means that are conducive to it. Thirdly, reason may be viewed as a method for the discovery of objective reality, i.e., the structure and laws of the outer world, and its dependence upon God. This latter aspect of reason is the most important, hence we shall consider it further.

Our reason is limited and the knowledge it supplies is neces-

sarily incomplete. It is small because our observation is limited
to those facts that we immediately and directly experience; our
knowledge is incomplete because we are never in touch with the
source of our incoming sensations. Owing to the constitution of
our nature, there remain hidden from our experience the unknown causes of these sensations, such as matter or mind from
which the effects we observe in experience arise. As to our objective world, all that we can intimately know is a congeries of
effects, wrought into the variety of interdependent systems. Apparently there is no completion to these systems, for there is
always more to be added, and always more that eludes our observation. The increase of knowledge makes us keenly aware of the
vast extent of the universe: of whose "infinite stores . . . poured
forth throughout the immensity of creation," we know but the
merest fragment (Vol. II, p. 221). "Every secret which is dis-
closed, every discovery which is made, every new effect which is
brought to view, serves to convince us of numberless more which
remain concealed, and which we had before no suspicion of"
(Vol. II, p.220). Were it possible for man to have a complete
knowledge of the entire scheme of creation, he would see that many
of the parts that are now present and familiar would appear in
a totally different light. Since all the facts of the universe
whether known or unknown are intimately related to each other,
it follows that "no part (of the universe) can be thoroughly understood, without taking in its reference and respect to the whole"
(Vol. II, p. 221). The consequence of this "should convince us,
that we are much less competent judges of the very small part
which comes under our notice in this world, than we are apt to
imagine" (Vol. II, pp. 220-1).

We can now readily appreciate that reason is inadequate to
a total and complete comprehension of the universe. Beyond its
reach lie regions of reality that it can never grasp.[1]

---

[1] We must be on our guard against rejecting *in toto* its reports as "mere
appearance." While it is true that a knowledge of the whole would altogether
alter our knowledge of the lesser parts, it would not alter the nature of *all*
these parts in any radical way. Many parts of the universe that we know now,
would be further reinforced, as we have already pointed out in a previous chapter. Also the fact that reason is not in touch with the causes of our incoming
sensations, does not lessen the value for us of the reported effects, or the systems
into which they fall. There is perceivable here a strong influence of Lockian epistemology in which the term "reality" is reserved for the unknown substances, but
Butler escapes from the consequences that such a position would logically imply,
through his heuristic logic of probability and analogy. By means of this method-

Yet, when we seek a knowledge of the world about us, we are dependent upon our reasoning powers. In no other way can we be informed as to the nature of the universe, or the place of man in it. In the field of natural religion reason is itself indispensable. Nor is it less important in the field of revealed religion. In those cases of discrepancy that arise between the claims of natural and those of revealed religion, it is the function of reason to step in and adjudicate the differences. And in the field of natural religion the body of its tenets can be established only through the reports of speculative reason. How could we know, for instance, that man is immortal, that our temporal life is but a preparation for the life to come, or that we are at present in a state of trial and probation? Barring revelation, which we have seen is dependent in a certain sense upon natural religion, this knowledge is available to us through the exercise of our rational powers. Strictly speaking, they are not known by conscience, if by conscience we mean an instrument that approves and commands. We cannot approve of rightness, goodness, or even the truth of things until we first know what the things are, about which we are making judgments of value. Hence it is important for us to examine in greater detail the nature of reason in itself, and then to see the relation of it to the field of religion, for all the facts of the latter are dependent upon no other source for being known than upon reason.

Our problem then is briefly this. How can we gain an insight into the scheme of things by means of reason? Butler's answer to this is given in his account of probability and analogy, which, as a canon for the correct use of reason, lays down the path that reason must follow if it is to function both truthfully and usefully.

PROBABILITY AND ANALOGY

All knowledge is based upon experience; and experience, for Butler, is whatever is reported by the senses. Thus the basis of reason is empirical. Without the facts of experience we cannot reason, and we cannot know (*Vide* Sermons on Ignorance of Man). But the certainty and the truth of reason's reports depend upon the character and frequency of one's observation. The

ology, Butler evolves—unconscious perhaps of his Lockian position—a unique theory of truth and reality. We shall treat of this more fully later on in the present chapter.

number of times which the facts of experience are reported, taken
with the comparison and relations of these facts to other facts,
give rise to degrees of certainty or probability. Our present interest is concerned with the nature and meaning of probable
evidence.

Probable evidence is first to be distinguished from demonstrative in that the former admits of degrees of certainty whereas
the latter does not. Concerning the former: The continual observation of two or more events in their relation to each other
increases the presumption that the observed relation is a true
one. It does not however establish with any degree of undeniable
certainty that the relations are absolutely true, but only a heightened probability that they are. According to the logic of probability, we cannot say that a series of events is absolutely true,
but we can maintain that the certainty of its being so increases
with each additional observation. As Butler tells us: "a man's
having observed the ebb and flow of the tide to-day, affords some
sort of presumption, though the lowest imaginable, that it may
happen again to-morrow: but the observation of this event for
so many days, and months, and ages together, as it has been
observed by mankind, gives us a full assurance that it will" (Vol.
I, p. 3). Although the logic of probability may be deemed to be
unsatisfactory when viewed from the standpoint of finality or
completeness, nevertheless it is the only method that we actually
possess in our course of acquiring knowledge. To God, or to beings more perfect than man, a more direct and certain knowledge
may be possible, but to man, whose capacities are limited, probable evidence remains his only guide to knowledge and to life
(Vol. I, p. 5).

The method of probability is not completely explained by
stating that it consists in repeated observations, or that repeated
observations bring about higher degrees of certainty. In the first
place it presupposes a prior mental disposition on the part of
the observer, not to give undue prominence to those instances
that are really exceptions rather than the usual rule (Vol. I, p.
4). In the second place it demands a careful comparison with
other instances, different in kind and circumstance, to make sure
that the instances at hand are pure and not just exceptions that
we are erecting into a general rule. Resorting to a terminology of
a later date, we can say that probability is an instance of induc-
tion in which both the method of agreement and that of differ-

ence are used. To argue that water never congeals, solely from the fact that the observer living in a warm climate has never seen it freeze, would be an instance of incomplete observation, largely because other varieties of water under different conditions have not been taken into account (Vol. I, p. 4).

Besides taking positive instances into account the degree of probable instances depends upon its comparison with contrary evidence. To the extent that contrary evidence is strong, our asserted evidence can gain very little acceptance as true. On the other hand if the contrary evidence is weak, the probable truth of our asserted evidence is correspondingly high (Vol. I, p. 6).

Closely bound up with the logic of probability in our search for truth is the logic of analogy. Butler holds that both are inseparable. "When we determine a thing to be probably true, suppose that an event has or will come to pass, it is from the mind's remarking in it a likeness to some other event, which we have observed has come to pass" (Vol. I, p. 4).

But apart from this inseparable aspect of probability, analogy can be employed as a method of its own. Let us suppose that we have no means of establishing directly the truth of an instance that we nevertheless believe to be true. If we can show that this instance is essentially like another instance whose credibility has been established for us through probability, then our disputed instance gains a degree of credibility for itself, that it could not have acquired in any other way. Likewise we can avail ourselves of "probability" here in our use of the analogical method, for the degree of truth that we can gain for our disputed instance will increase in certainty as we observe that its structure shares a common quality with other instances that have been already accepted as true. An instance at hand is Butler's accepted belief in immortality. Repeated observation of life in all its forms and varieties, he believes is an argument in favor of its continuance. The fact that no known instance of death—for death is not to be confused with physical decay—has been recorded, supplies us with a negative instance in our application of probability. Thus, through probability we arrive at a high degree of certainty that human beings are immortal.

Let us now consider an instance of "analogy." Granted that human beings are immortal, then the only kind of existence that it is conceivable for us to grant them is that which is analogous to temporal life as we know it. In other words, future life will

probably be a community in which the essential nature of its
members will be a moral one and in which their highest interest
will be the expression of their virtuous character as well as the
unification of their selves. Although this latter instance is primarily one that illustrates Butler's method of analogy, it is not
without its aspect of probability.

Through the application of analogy we can arrive at a degree
of truth that may not be ascertainable by any other means. But
analogy as applied by Butler has another use; one that is not
committed solely to the discovery of probable truth, but to the
undermining of stated beliefs that run contrary to his own. This
rhetorical use of analogy does not seek to establish what is true
or real, but to expose the impertinence of arguments that believe themselves to be destructive of Butler's own position. By
removing the sting of these counter-arguments, in showing that
they have no bearing upon his views, Butler succeeds in throwing
open the possibility for the future substantiation of his own
views.[2]

The destructive or critical use of analogy and probability
proceeds as follows: It first makes a comparison between the
doubtful instances, i.e., those that have been assailed by their
opponents, and other instances, the alleged truth of which has
been admitted by the same opponents. By doing so, it points out
the irrelevance of the attack. In this way it removes arguments
that have hitherto been brought against the acceptance of a
disputed fact. Thus, it succeeds in preparing the way for more
positive arguments. Instances of this critical use of analogy occur
more frequently in the second part of the *Analogy* when Butler,
in his discussion of miracles and in his attempts to gain for them
a respectful hearing, points out that there is nothing absurd in
their claims, and that the charges that are seriously brought
against them can be likewise brought against known instances
in nature. If we accept the latter to be plausible, we cannot in
all fairness denounce the former as unlikely.

There are some readers of Butler who affirm that this use of
analogy is a two-sided sword that cuts both ways. They main-

---

[2] It is not to be supposed that Butler granted the future proof of his views
to be establishable through means other than that of analogy and probability
used constructively. He recognized in his logic of analogy and probability a twofold function, *viz.* the negative or destructive, and the positive or constructive.
The first prepared the way for the second, while the second established what the
first had made possible.

tain that you do not gain plausibility for your disputed facts by showing that they are like undisputed facts; instead, you show that the arguments of your opponents are effective in more fields than one, and that the undisputed facts now become as doubtful as the disputed ones. This line of thought fails to consider the positive or constructive use to which the logic of analogy is put. It also overlooks the fact that the accepted instances that are referred to, have been (i) admitted by Butler's opponents, i.e., the Deists, as being true, (ii) that their truth has been or can be guaranteed by the constructive use of 'analogy'; (iii) that the instances from which suspicion has now been removed are open to positive proof through the constructive use of the logic of analogy. (*Vide* Butler's remarks in *Analogy*, Pt. II, Ch. VIII.)

This critical use of analogy is most extensively exercised by Butler to show that revealed religion is not unplausible, for in the admitted course of nature there are equal difficulties to be found. Butler tells us in reference to Origen that "he who believes the scripture to have proceeded from him who is the Author of Nature, may well expect to find the same sort of difficulties in it, as are found in the constitution of nature. And in a like way of reflection it may be added, that he who denies the scripture to have been from God upon account of these difficulties, may, for the very same reason, deny the world to have been formed by him. On the other hand, if there be an analogy or likeness between that system of things and dispensation of Providence, which revelation informs us of, and that system of things and dispensation of Providence, which experience together with reason informs us of, i.e., the known course of nature; this is a presumption, that they have both the same author and cause; at least so far as to answer objections against the former's being from God, drawn from any thing which is analogical or similar to what is in the latter, which is acknowledged to be from him; for an Author of nature is here supposed" (Vol. I, pp. 8, 9).[3]

[3] Revealed religion contains more than natural religion. It announces religious truths *not* to be found in the latter. Strictly speaking, the use of "analogy" here in its negative aspect is quite beside the point. To the extent that revealed religion republishes the truths of natural religion, there can be no dispute of the tenets of the former, but to the extent that it makes extra claims, the counterpart of which is not discoverable *in rerum natura*, critical analogy cannot be applied to defend the plausibility of these extra claims. Butler himself is aware of this difficulty and limitation in application of critical analogy, for when he comes to grips with the asserted truths of the doctrines of revealed religion that are peculiar to itself, in contradistinction to those of natural religion, he is forced to

Let us now turn our attention more particularly to the way in which analogy and probability work. Through their joint application we are enabled to arrive at an understanding of the objective world, of its laws, as exhibited in societies, and in human nature; and to acquaint ourselves with the fact that the objective world as it is progressively known reveals itself as a system of systems. The teleological principle which is implicit in this view of nature as a system of systems, must be accepted as a report of probability and analogy, as it studies the objective order. Its claims as a true interpretive principle rest upon the innumerable evidences gathered by man.

OTHER ASPECTS OF REASON

Our discussion of analogy and probability was motivated by the fact that Butler explicitly recognizes this logic as a means whereby we can become acquainted with the existent order of things in its teleological and systematic set-up. It is represented as the canon of correct reasoning for man, the way in which speculative reason must work if it is to express its nature truly. It is basically empirical, for it is confined to facts reported through sensory observation. But for Butler reason can take other forms. He does not grant to them the same overt recognition as he does to analogy and probability, but implicitly and indirectly he accords to them a logical status, for through their operation access to what is true and real can be had.

One of these methods is formal, abstract, deductive and nonempirical. In the preface to his Sermons, Butler informs us that "there are two ways in which the subject of morals may be treated. One begins from inquiring into the abstract relations of things; the other from a matter of fact, namely, what the particular nature of man is, its several parts, their economy or constitution; from when it proceeds to determine what course of life it is, which is correspondent to this whole nature. In the former method the conclusions is expressed thus, that vice is contrary to the nature and reason of things: in the latter, that it is a violation or breaking in upon our own nature. Thus they both lead us to the same thing, our obligations to the practice

have recourse to consistency, i.e., what he calls "circumstantial evidence." It consists briefly in this: the unique doctrines of revealed religion are consistent with those doctrines that are the same as natural religion. Hence the truth of these disputed doctrines is established through consistency. We have raised this point for consideration at the end of the present chapter.

of virtue; and thus they exceedingly strengthen and enforce each other. The first seems the most direct formal proof, and in some respects the least liable to cavil and dispute: the latter is in a peculiar manner adapted to satisfy a fair mind: and is more easily applicable to the several particular relations and circumstances in life" (Vol. II, p. 5).

In this passage we have the contrast of the two methods, the empirical (i.e., probability and analogy), and the rational or deductive. Butler commits himself to the use of the former, i.e., the empirical or the matter of fact (Cp. also footnote, Vol. I, p. 32; also p. 227), as over against the formal with which it is contrasted. In making this distinction he recognizes the fact that the formal or abstract method must be characterized by principles of its own, other than those of probability or analogy. What these principles of abstract reasoning are, Butler does not discuss. That he does acknowledge the existence of this abstract mode of reasoning, however, cannot be denied. In the introduction to the *Analogy* (Vol. I, p. 3) he again contrasts the method of probability with that of demonstration, ascribing indirectly to the latter a degree of certainty that the former does not possess. Later on, i.e., page five, he admits that the status of probable knowledge is subjective and human for it belongs to the province of man but not to an infinite intelligence, or to a being superior to man. But Butler does not state even here that man is incapable of abstract, rational, or demonstrative knowledge; only, as far as a guidance to action is concerned, the method of probability should serve man. That is, if man is to act at all, the evidence upon which he does act, and which is endorsed by his conscience (and on which therefore he should act) must be supplied by probability. But nevertheless man is capable of thinking abstractly. This is the type of thinking he engages in when he builds for himself, as did Descartes, the notions of God and the course of the world without reference to experience (Vol. I, pp. 9, 10). That he can think abstractly (but should not) is evidenced in those instances when man fashions through his creative imagination a type of world other than the one in which he is actually living.[4]

I have mentioned in detail the above instances, in order to

4 Vol. I, p. 11. Another reference of the same sort is made later on, Vol. I, p. 172, when Butler cautions us against determining beforehand from reason what the scheme of revelation must be.

show that Butler admitted in man a mode of reason that was demonstrative or abstract, and thus different in kind from that of probability and analogy. Some of the quoted instances indicate that Butler's attitude towards reason of this kind is one that disapproves of its exercise. But on the other hand he expressly allows the legitimacy of its constructive use in the field of moral theory. He refrains from indulging in formal reasoning himself, because of the superior pedagogic value of the empirical method.

Besides the acknowledgement of formal reason, Butler also admits of another aspect, in the type of evidence that he calls "circumstantial." This type of reason which he admits to be logical is exhibited when he argues for the positive truths of revealed religion. It will be recalled that Butler's use of "analogy" in establishing for us the reality of revealed religion was to a great extent critical. In other words it aimed at removing arguments against the presumption of revealed religion's being true, but it did not supply of itself any positive arguments in its favor. Recognizing its shortcomings, Butler resorts to what he calls circumstantial evidence to repair the difficulty.

Concerning its nature, Butler says that "it is the kind of evidence, upon which most questions of difficulty, in common practice, are determined: evidence arising from various coincidences, which support and confirm each other, and in this manner prove, with more or less certainty, the point under consideration" (Vol. I, p. 269). As a proof of revealed religion, consistency considers not only the variety of circumstantial instances each in independence of the other, but also as they are interrelated and joined together. "The proper force of the evidence consists in the result of those several things, considered in their respects to each other, and united into one view" (Vol. I, p. 269). This view of regarding evidence from the standpoint of the fitness and interrelatedness of the facts cannot be brought under the head of either analogy or probability. Since we have already discussed in our chapter on Revealed Religion the reports of this proof, there is no need to repeat them here. Our only concern here is to recognize that Butler's attempt to prove the reality of revealed religion from the congruity of its reported events with the reported events of secular history, gathered from other sources, represents an instance of argumentative persuasion that is neither based on analogy nor on probability.

REASON IN THE MORAL LIFE

We are now prepared to consider more specifically the place of reason, in its various aspects, in the moral life of man. Of the three aspects of speculative reason that have been discussed, namely probability and analogy, formal reason, and consistency, we must admit the validity of consistency, and allow to it a place in man's daily decisions (Vol. I, p. 269). Its main purpose for Butler however consists in its service in establishing the truth of revealed religion. For him it is a type of argument that is used mainly to support men of thoughtful mind by supplementing their conviction already based upon analogy. There appears to be no doubt that Butler would evaluate it, in the scale of logical excellence, lower in importance than the method of probability and analogy. In justice to Butler's intellectual temperament and persistent assertions, the logic of consistency should be regarded as a less fundamental type. His appeal for the acceptance of revealed religion is based upon analogy, and analogy in turn refers us to the asserted truths of natural religion that are arrived at through probability. There is no reason for us to believe that Butler felt the inadequacy of probability and analogy, or though that he had failed to apply this logic successfully in the establishment of revealed religion or its claims.

Concerning the use of formal reason, we can but record Butler's disapproval of the same. He recognizes its legitimate existence in the field of moral demonstration, but even here he disapproves of its being used. We have already referred to those other instances of demonstrative reason that lead man astray when they seek to determine what is real.

It is upon analogy and probability that Butler puts the greatest stress, and his use of this method itself showed the degree to which he favored it. But for the individual man who is faced with the necessity of making practical decisions, analogy is apt to play a less important role—even to the point of negligibility than probability. Pressed into the service of religion, its main function is to remove arguments against its plausibility. The use to which Butler himself puts the logic of analogy is purely intellectual, i.e., to build up for his readers the edifice of revealed religion, to appeal to their understanding for acceptance of its truths. Analogy by itself plays no practical role.

Probability is more important than the logic of analogy for

the practical life of man, for through its constant use man achieves a knowledge of the universe in its broader outlines and fundamental laws; as well as of the particular situations that confront him. Reason used analogically is referred to under a variety of names, such as the light of nature (Vol. I, pp. 153, 172, 193, 195, 309), the law of nature (Vol. I, p. 161), or natural light (Vol. I, p. 194). But since Butler's intention in the use of some of these terms implies a moral connotation as well (especially "faculty of reason," p. 307), it is difficult to say whether Butler was referring to speculative reason, considered apart from its moral connotation, or not. Important as speculative reason is, whether we view its analogical use, or any other of its alleged aspects, it must for Butler fall somewhat short of the perfection of the moral life, and give way to the moral pronouncements of conscience within which speculative reason achieves its own fulfilment.

Speculative reason is a necessary aspect of conscience. Not only does it afford man a knowledge of his environment, and of the immediate situation at hand, but it instrumentally proposes means whereby the ends decided upon in advance can best and most economically be achieved. Were man not possessed of this auxiliary capacity, conscience would be paralyzed, for it would be limited to a *de facto* judgment of moral worth on each and every situation, and be incapable of comparison or of the means of carrying its ideal decisions into overt activity.

But on the other hand conscience is the completion of reason, for it completes what reason speculatively establishes, by passing upon it judgments of moral worth. Reason *per se* merely apprises us of an objective situation, either practical or ideal, but in itself its reports cannot proclaim the system of the universe as being morally good. This moral pronouncement must proceed from a source other than itself, such as conscience.

Reason in its speculative role cannot play the supreme part in the moral life. Limited so completely in what it can report and inform us of, reason cannot in any degree be upheld as an end in itself. As Butler says: "Indeed, if the proper happiness of man consisted in knowledge considered as a possession or treasure, men who are possessed of the largest share would have a very ill time of it; as they would be infinitely more sensible than others of their poverty in this respect. Thus *he who increases knowledge would* eminently *increase sorrow*" (Vol. II, p. 227-8).

But we know that we were designed to be inhabitants of this earth (Vol. II, p. 224), and can feel assured that in our capacity as human beings, we are equipped sufficiently for the end for which we have been designed. Our faculties are suitably disposed towards the furtherance of this end. But "if to acquire knowledge were our proper end, we should indeed be but poorly provided" (Vol. II, p. 224). We can definitely know that we cannot completely know; but to know this is to know that we should not make knowledge an end in itself. To turn reason from a means for the advancement of accepted ends into an end in itself, is to misapply it, and is to deviate from the moral life. Properly expressed it must serve conscience in the sense above described and pass over into the realm of moral pronouncement.

When Butler refers to reason as the candle of the Lord within us (Vol. I, p. 307), or when he tells us that "reason can, and ought to judge . . . the morality of revelation" (Vol. I, p. 196), he has in mind the completion of speculative reason by the moral functions of conscience. The way has been prepared by reason, but the end arrived at has been added to by the moral valuations of conscience. Speculation and moral judgment must be regarded as intrinsically and inseparably joined; while one is incomplete apart from the other, nevertheless in their compresence it is readily seen that conscience plays the higher role.

32

CONCLUSION

THE quest for virtue seems to have led us far afield, but it has not. What must we do, if we are to act as human beings, and as it becomes our nature? To live as human beings is to live as self-reflecting creatures; we must be aware of the situation in which we find ourselves, reflect upon the outcome of any plan of action that we undertake, and force ourselves to bring it about as we judge it to be morally valuable. Such is the course of reflection and action, according to Butler, that man practises when he pursues his normal course of life. By nature man is a moral being. He is endowed with a conscience, just as he is endowed with reason or appetite. The existence within man of the former is an undeniable fact, for experience guarantees its presence and reality.

Merely to assert that man has a conscience is not sufficiently informative, until we know what conscience does, how it acts, and wherefrom it receives the force of its authority. Does it inform man what to do in moments of doubt, can it instruct him in the course of behavior he should conform to? Butler believes that it can. As man reflects upon his nature, he sees to what extent he is bound up in relationship to others; he finds himself a member of society with laws of its own; a society that reflects an inner structure, and one that is continuous with its own past. Into such a medium man is born; on all sides he is surrounded by classes and institutions that are superior to him, for they belong to the natural order of things, and reflect in their structure a wisdom that is greater than his.

Upon this external condition man is capable of reflecting. He sees already laid down for him lines of actions that he should follow, if he is properly to take his place among men. Society has its officials; to them he must pay his respect. The Church imparts to him the word of God; to it he must listen. Throughout the order of society are discernible classes of influence and power; to them he must bow in reverence. Everything indicates its law and proclaims its structure. To find them out, to be clear as to their nature, to further their claims become man's duty. And to this task conscience is an adequate instrument of discovery. Not only does it inform man as to his duty, it commands him as well to ascertain it and follow it.

To adjust himself to his moral environment, it becomes necessary to keep down in his own nature the inner tendency to live heedlessly according to his passions and instincts; to refrain from engaging wilfully upon courses of behavior that violate the respected order of laws. To keep these tendencies in restraint, so that the individual can clearly see and measure in terms of righteousness the tasks and situations that beset him, requires the constant guiding force of conscience. In this role it is the purpose of conscience to exercise control, to play off one tendency against the others, and to counterbalance the undesirable by the worthy. Only through this exercise of self-discipline can the individual hope to achieve his expression as one human being among many. For outward harmony in society inner survey, constraint, and self-imposed commands to refrain, are necessary.

As the outer order of things is not haphazard nor arbitrary, neither is conscience that illuminates it. In the light of his greatest self-consciousness man learns what is and what has been decreed. Societies, classes, institutions have not grown up blindly, or without forethought. So intimately do they exhibit the work of wisdom in their structure and mutual interrelations, that their cause and origin points to a divine creator. Their history indicates the degree to which they have managed to express their original intentions. In learning this man sees that it is his duty to acquaint himself with the plans that his institutions express. He cannot sanction what runs counter to their nature, no matter how dissatisfied he may be as an individual or how incommoded he is. "Things and actions are what they are, and the consequences of them will be what they will be: why then should we desire to be deceived" (Vol. II, p. 114). Throughout all, God's will is instanced, and to obey in love and fear of him leaves man no alternative in his course of duty. The knowledge and sanction of all of this come to man through his conscience.

To assure the proper exercise of conscience requires much more than intellectual insight, or a mandate to perform when the proposed course of action is seen to be right. Reason by itself, we have been told, is no security to the practice of virtuous living (Vol. II, p. 87); reason by itself is ineffectual. For the undertaking of virtue it is necessary that man should experience pleasure in its performance, or suffer the consequences of pain in his

failure to ascertain or heed. Whereas reason may fail to coerce
man in the search and performance of his duties, the experience
of pleasurable and painful emotions does not. In paying attention
to them man often learns what he is intellectually doubtful about
in his moral affairs; and furthermore he becomes aware that he
is under the dominance of a moral law external to himself, the
nature of which he must discover and conform to. In no case
should man act upon what he believes conveniently to be right,
or in ignorance of what should be. External to him is the objective law of what is right or wrong, laid down in advance of his
knowledge and practice. What does it prescribe for him? Its discovery and practice become one of man's highest duties. Obedience to it is enjoined by his conscience, and its practice is God's
way of bringing to fruition through the agency of man the plans
that he entertains for the objects of his creation.

Very few are gifted with a perspicacity sufficiently fine and
unerring for the discovery of God's moral law. But others although deprived of the satisfaction of discovering the rule of life
directly for themselves, need not sink into moral obliquity, for
they too possess a conscience that serves them satisfactorily. In
being attentive to it they learn that some individuals are morally
superior to them, and from these magistrates and teachers, they
can learn the course of life they should follow, the class of society
they naturally fall into, and the duties they should perform. In
learning this they are adequately provided for. And on the emotional side they learn, through the infliction of civic punishment,
the consequences if they fail to conform.

We have said above that conscience is able to inform us
either directly or indirectly of the general course of life we
should follow, such as the station of life that we should naturally
fit into; as well as the virtuous principles that we should observe
such as veracity, justice, honesty, and benevolence. These constitute its primary reports, or its fundamental deliverances. But
besides this it is the task of conscience to pass judgment upon
individual instances and problems as these arise in the course of
life. Within our class in society it often becomes necessary to
apprise ourselves of our duty, and of the rightness or wrongness
of a particular course of action. At other times it becomes important to know whether in the conflict of duties we should be truth-
ful but unkind, or kind but unjust. Or again, in the absence of
all conflict, we may be doubtful whether our contemplated course

of action comes under one of the primary virtues, and of which one it is a particular instance. To meet and solve issues of this sort is likewise the task of conscience.[1]

And to this settlement conscience is fully competent. "In all common ordinary cases," Butler tells us, "we see intuitively at first view what is our duty, what is the honest part" (Vol. II, p. 112).

But whether the rule of life intimates man's station and general course of behavior or passes judgment upon *ad hoc* instances, it is in all cases the expression of a scheme which is superior to man, of God's creation and for his purpose. Nothing should be done for the sake of man, as man, but rather for the sake of man as God's creature, and as God wills him to be. Man contributes to the scheme of things what God has decreed in advance of his coming to be, and in advance of his activity, plans, or expressions. Man can make on his own behalf no unique contribution of personality that is foreign to the will of God. He brings into the realm of things no unique values that have not been decided upon. All exists for the glory of God, and should be enacted with this greater understanding in mind. The constant pursuit of his discoverable purpose, and the enactment of it as revelatory of the divine scheme, constitutes man's moral life.

Although man's course of life is laid down in advance of its actual expression, very little, as we have pointed out in an earlier chapter, is known to him about it. From his point of view the universe is an endless growth, approximating in its outer expression to the design that God entertains for it. Since the universe is known to us as a progressive scheme, we cannot say that we have discovered completely all that human nature represents. Owing to the limitations of human intelligence, there may be

---

1 *Vide* Vol. II, p. 148-9. "Whoever will consider the whole commerce of human life, will see that a great part, perhaps the greatest part, of the intercourse amongst mankind, cannot be reduced to fixed determinate rules. Yet in these cases there is a right and a wrong: a merciful, a liberal, a kind and compassionate behaviour, which surely is our duty; and an unmerciful contracted spirit, an hard and oppressive course of behaviour, which is most certainly immoral and vicious. But who can define precisely, wherein that contracted spirit and hard usage of others consist, as murder and theft may be defined? there is not a word in our language, which expresses more detestable wickedness than *oppression*: yet the nature of this vice cannot be so exactly stated, nor the bounds of it so determinately marked, as that we shall be able to say in all instances, where rigid right and justice ends, and oppression begins. In these cases there is great latitude left, for every one to determine for, and consequently to deceive himself."

extant, in the nature of humanity at large, much that is awaiting
our discovery; or there may evolve in the concrete nature of
humanity itself factors which are not as yet actually present.
As humanity is in the process of change, likewise are its institutions. There can be no final knowledge of human nature, for the
data are not completely known. Consequently there can be no
absolute and binding rules that can be laid down once and for
all in the field of moral relationships. This does not mean that
the scheme of human nature is not eternally present and complete
in the mind of God, or that the knowledge which we now possess
concerning morality is fundamentally faulty; but rather that
our knowledge of humanity is not yet complete. Yet what we know
about it through the endorsement of an unerring conscience can
be accepted as valid, for although much remains for future discovery, we cannot believe that the moral knowledge of tomorrow
will overthrow the accumulated truths of today. Future investigation will confirm us in what we know to be right, besides furnishing us with further instances of moral relationship.

What is of value for us in this moral philosophy of Butler?
What is significant? What has he truly established for us and
proved? These are the questions that I shall try to answer as
far as I can, in the remaining part of this chapter. I shall confine
my remarks almost solely to his theory of conscience.

Butler has proved, at least to my satisfaction, that man possesses a conscience, namely, that each of us is a moral being whenever we reflect about our course of life, or contemplate particular
actions that we plan to undertake. He has shown, I believe, beyond
all dispute that man is led to a moral appraisal of persons, deeds,
and events; that all reasoning in this respect tends to pass into
the realm of moral evaluation. Just as, in our estimation of external things, we tend to interrelate our various fields of observation, to expose the implications involved, and to pass upon
them judgments affirming the truth or falsity of our speculations;
likewise do we tend by nature to judge as good or bad this particular deed, person, or situation. He has shown that the guarantee for ascribing to man a moral sense rests upon the evidences
of experience, i.e., upon the reports of one's mind as it gives
itself to the study of itself and others. His words concerning the
fundamental tendency in man towards benevolent deeds can be

brought in justification of man's moral nature. The importance of this utterance is so considerable that I shall take the liberty of quoting it in full.

"If any person can in earnest doubt, whether there be such a thing as good-will in one man towards another; (for the question is not concerning either the degree or extensiveness of it, but concerning the affection itself:) let it be observed, that *whether man be thus, or otherwise constituted, what is the inward frame in this particular*, is a mere question of fact or natural history, not provable immediately by reason. It is therefore to be judged of and determined in the same way other facts or matters of natural history are: by appealing to the external senses, or inward perceptions, respectively, as the matter under consideration is cognizable by one or the other: by arguing from acknowledged facts and actions; for a great number of actions in the same kind, in different circumstances, and respecting different objects, will prove, to a certainty, what principles they do not, and, to the greatest probability, what principles they do proceed from: and lastly, by the testimony of mankind" (Vol. II, p. 32, footnote).

The non-existence of conscience cannot be shown by arguing that it is fallible, or that it is factitious, not fundamental; for its observable effects in man's conscious nature bear vivid testimony to its reality. Neither can we dismiss it as being a mere product of an evolved self, by pointing to man's anthropoid progenitors as being devoid of it, for in those instances we should be referring to its origin, or to the history of its precedent states, but accepting all along as our point of departure the very thing that we are concerned in disproving. As Butler has shown, a faculty is best understood in terms of its function, i.e., the end it is to serve, rather than the conditions from which it springs.

What more can we believe about it? Conscience not only surveys, but we can likewise believe through inner inspection that it commands the performance of the deed it decides upon favorably. Together with this, we can accept the fact that it exercises a control over one's passions, that it calls our attention to our premeditated excesses, and forbids their outward expression. No less than this it punishes by consequences peculiar to itself, i.e., by the familiarly known pangs or qualms. To the existence of these closely allied qualities, Butler has successfully called our attention. But we shall not dwell any longer upon these admitted aspects.

To admit the existence of a moral faculty within man is one thing, but to claim for it all that Butler does is another. Many of his further protestations in its favor can be questioned, and many of the claims that he dogmatically ascribes to it must be set aside. What are these claims, and how far can they be substantiated?

In the first place Butler maintains that conscience is the chief or supreme principle in the nature of man (Vol. II, p. 173). In upholding this, he is putting the moral faculty of man before all other aspects of his conscious life. That it should be so put, is not clearly evident. If we are consistent to Butler's empirical methodology, through which he establishes for us the existence of this faculty within man, we must likewise maintain that a further exercise of our observation reveals that man evaluates persons, things, and events in more ways than the moral. It is also true that man is concerned with truth, beauty, the useful, and for all we know many more types of valuation. These too, form part of his conscious self-expression, and are operations of his mind that cannot be denied. But in affirming their reality we cannot judge without further evidence, or without resorting to methodological means that Butler does not provide us with, that moral appraisal stands unquestionably superior to man's appraisal of e.g., truth or beauty. To say that man's moral sense—once we have acknowledged its existence—decides this for us, is begging the issue, for it is judging in terms of its own interest a question that requires the assistance of a higher tribunal. Truth and beauty must also be allowed to speak for themselves, and it is quite conceivable that if given the opportunity, they would bear testimony to a different tale.

Butler's insistence that conscience is man's supreme principle of consciousness, rests undoubtedly upon his religious convictions. If the universe were unquestionably the work of a divine mind, fashioned according to the law of goodness as Butler maintains, then it would follow that man's highest and truest predications would be those that would discover it as such; truth would reveal the universe as a moral creation, and beauty would show it to be God's workmanship; in both instances the moral categories would take ascendency over the others. But until we are further

informed as to the nature and origin of the world we must refrain from dogmatic utterances.

Secondly: While establishing for us the existence of conscience
as a phase of man's conscious life, Butler has not succeeded in
showing that it reveals to us a moral universe, created by God
and conducted according to moral law. In stating that it does, he
has divorced his methodology from his metaphysics, instead of
retaining the former as a means for determining what is real.
A consistent application of the logic of probability and analogy
affords us knowledge of the actual and existent facts that we
explore; it furthermore enables us to achieve the unity of their
interrelatedness, and to characterize the laws of their behavior,
but it has failed to show us more than that, for it has not succeeded in showing that the universe is ideal, spiritual, or theistic
in its basis.

Butler's belief that the universe exhibited these latter characteristics rests largely upon the fact that he had previously
accepted without question the status and truth of natural religion; for we must recall here that his Analogy of Religion in
which these issues appear was a polemical work, written for the
purpose of showing that revealed religion had as great a claim
for acceptance by the Deists as natural religion. Since the common ground shared by Butler and the Deists was the field of
natural religion, it was not necessary to lay bare the proofs of
what they both acknowledged. Hence, Butler's metaphysical
views are either inspirational or borrowed from the corpus of
revealed religion. If obtained from the latter source, they are
unworthy of acceptance, for according to Butler's mode of arguing, the validity of the latter can be accepted only after the
truth of natural religion has been previously accepted. But if the
metaphysical views of the theistic universe are asserted to be the
tenets of natural religion, then to them we must demur; for Butler
has not satisfactorily maintained through probability and analogy that the congeries of observed and observable facts are systematically interrelated and grounded in the reality of a divine
intelligence.

Such being the case, then, the realm of moral values, into
which conscience has access, when it passes judgment, may not be
necessarily objective, common to all, or coercive in the sense in
which Butler held. There is no longer imposed upon man's belief
the command to respect society with its inner arrangement of

classes, or to view his social station as inviolably sacred; nor to perpetuate in reverence of its divine origin the structure of society as he discovers it to be; nor to remain content with its social levels of ascending values if he has reason to believe otherwise. Although the divine universe with its immanent moral values may ultimately be endorsed as true by man's investigating intelligence, yet to hail it as such before it has been indubitably affirmed, is to announce the results of investigation before we have begun to examine, and to make of reason a parody.

APPENDIX

BIBLIOGRAPHICAL NOTE

THE number of books written about Butler is small indeed. Despite his influence upon ethics, there is available no more than the work of Bartlett, which can make any claim as original source-material. The works of Collins and Spooner afford no additional information. In Germany and France he is scarcely known. No studies have been devoted to an exposition and interpretation of his complete philosophy. In basing the present study of his philosophy upon his extant Sermons and *Analogy* I have not intended merely to repeat what is generally known about his thoughts, but to lay bare his system of ethics in terms of his more comprehensive religious, epistemological, and metaphysical doctrines. I have endeavored to show that his theory of conscience cannot be completely understood until it is taken in relation to his theory of reality. To what extent Butler himself was aware of this interrelation cannot be known. Certain it is that he never systematized his thoughts upon ethics and religion; had he done so, his readers might have been spared much difficulty about the meaning he ascribed to conscience, or the relation of religion to the moral life.

PUBLISHED WORKS OF BUTLER

Fifteen Sermons, published 1726, second edition, 1729:
    Upon Human Nature (I, II, III)
    Upon the Government of the Tongue (IV)
    Upon Compassion (V, VI)
    Upon the Character of Balaam (VII)
    Upon Resentment (VIII)
    Upon Forgiveness of Injuries (IX)
    Upon Self-Deceit (X)
    Upon the Love of our Neighbour (XI, XII)
    Upon the Love of God (XIII, XIV)
    Upon the Ignorance of Man ((XV)
The Analogy of Religion to the Constitution and Course of Nature, published
    1736.
    Two Brief Dissertations, published 1736, as an appendix to the Analogy of
      Religion:
    I. Of Personal Identity.
    II. Of the Nature of Virtue.
Six Sermons Preached Upon Public Occasions:
    Sermon I, Preached Before the Incorporated Society for the Propagation of
      the Gospel in Foreign Parts, at their Anniversary Meeting in the Parish
      Church of St. Mary-le-Bow, on Friday, February 16, 1738-9.

Sermon II, Preached Before the Right Hon. The Lord Mayor, The Court of Aldermen, The Sheriffs, and The Governors of the Several Hospitals of the City of London, at the Parish Church of St. Bridget, on Monday in Easter-Week, 1740.

Sermon III, Preached Before the House of Lords, in the Abbey-Church of Westminster, on Friday, January 3, 1740-41. Being the Day Appointed to be Observed as the Day of the Martyrdom of King Charles I.

Sermon IV, Preached in the Parish Church of Christ-Church, London, on Thursday, May 9, 1745. Being the Time of the Yearly Meeting of the Children Educated in the Charity-Schools in and About the Cities of London and Westminster.

Sermon V, Preached Before the House of Lords, in the Abbey-Church of Westminster, on Thursday, June 11, 1747. Being the Anniversary of His Majesty's Happy Accession to the Throne.

Sermon VI, Preached Before his Grace Charles Duke of Richmond, President, and the Governors of the London Infirmary, for the Relief of Sick and Diseased Persons, Especially Manufacturers, and Seamen in Merchant-Service, etc., at the Parish Church of St. Lawrence-Jewry, on Thursday, March 31, 1748.

A Charge Delivered to the Clergy at the Primary Visitation of the Diocese of Durham, in the Year MDCCLI.

Correspondence Between Butler and Samuel Clarke.

Literary Fragments of Butler.

SOME BOOKS CONSULTED

ALBEE, *A History of English Utilitarianism,* Macmillan, New York, 1901.

ANGUS, J., *Butler's Analogy and Sermons,* London, Religious Tract Society.

ARISTOTLE, *Nicomachean Ethics,* trans. W. D. Ross, Oxford, Clarendon Press, 1925.

AYER, J. C., *Versuch einer Darstellung der Ethik, Joseph Butler's,* Druck von Kreysling, Leipzig, 1893.

BAGEHOT, W., *Literary Studies* (Miscellaneous Essays), Three vols., Longmans, Green, 1898.

BARTLETT, T., *Memoirs of the Life, Character and Writings of Joseph Butler D.C.L. Late Lord Bishop of Durham,* London: John W. Parker; Cambridge: J. and J. J. Deighton, 1839.

BERNARD, J. H., Article in *Hermathena,* Vol. IX, 1896.

BROAD, C. D., *Five Types of Ethical Theory,* New York, Harcourt, Brace and Co., 1930.

BURTT, E. A., *Metaphysical Foundations of Modern Physical Science,* London, Kegan, Paul, Trench, Trubner, 1925.

CHALMERS, *Posthumous Works,* W. Pickering, London, 1835.

CHURCH, DEAN, *Pascal and Other Sermons,* London, Macmillan, 1895.

CICERO, *De Finibus* (trans.).

COLLINS, W., *Butler,* Blackwood's Philosophical Classics, 1881.

COOK, W., *Ethics of Bishop Butler and Immanuel Kant,* Philosophical Papers of the University of Michigan, 1-2 Series.

Encyclopedia Britannica: Articles: Bishop Butler, Deism, Eleventh Edition.

EPICTETUS, *Works,* trans., W. W. Higginson, T. Nelson and Sons, 1895.

FITE, W., Unpublished Lectures on Ethics of Shaftesbury and Butler.

GEORGE, M. D., *English Social Life in the 18th Century.*

GLADSTONE, *The Works of Joseph Butler D.C.L.,* two vols.; Subsidiary Studies, one vol.; Oxford, Clarendon Press, 1897.

GREEN, T. H., *Works,* Three vols.; 3d edition; espec. Vol. I, pp. 325-8, 331-7; Vol. III, pp. 98-104.

HOBBES, T., *Works,* Molesworth Edition (in part).

———, *Selections by Woodbridge,* Scribner's.

LANGE, F. A. L., *The History of Materialism,* London, Kegan, Paul, Trench, Trubner, 1925.

LAURIE, S. S., *Notes Expository and Critical, on Certain British Theories of Morals,* Edinburgh, Edmonston & Douglas, 1868.

LECKY, W. E. H., *England in the 18th Century,* Two Vols., New York, D. Appleton and Co., 1879.

LEFEVRE, A., "The Significance of Butler's View of Human Nature," *Philosophical Review,* Vol. VIII.

———, "Self-Love and Benevolence in Butler's Ethical System," *Philosophical Review,* Vol. IX.

———, "Conscience and Obligation in Butler's Ethical System," *Philosophical Review,* Vol. IX.

LOCKE, J., *Essay on the Human Understanding,* Bohn Phil. Library.

———, *Selections by S. Lamprecht,* Scribner's.

MACKINTOSH, RIGHT HON. SIR JAS., *Dissertation on the Progress of Ethical Philosophy, Chiefly during the Seventeenth and Eighteenth Centuries,* Phila., Lea & Blanchard, 1845.

PATTISON, MARK, *Essays*—Collected and Arranged by H. Nettleship, Two Vols., Oxford, Clarendon Press, 1889.

RANDALL, J. H., *The Making of the Modern Mind,* Houghton Mifflin, 1926.

ROGERS, A. K., *Morals in Review,* New York, Macmillan, 1927.

SELBY-BIGGE, L. A., *British Moralists,* Two Vols., Oxford, Clarendon Press, 1897.

SIDGWICK, H., *Outline of the History of Ethics,* Macmillan, London, 1893.

SORLEY, W. R., *A History of English Philosophy,* Cambridge, the University Press, 1920.

SPOONER, W. A., *Bishop Butler,* Houghton Mifflin, 1901.

TAYLOR, A. E., "Some Features of Butler's Ethics," *Mind,* July, 1926.

TAYLOR, W. E., *Ethical and Religious Theories of Butler,* 1903, Bryant Press, Ltd., Toronto, Canada.

TULLOCH, J., *Rational Theology and Christian Philosophy in England in the Seventeenth Century,* Edinburgh, 1872, Two Vols., William Blackwood and Sons.

TURBERVILLE, A. S., *English Men and Manners in the 18th Century,* Oxford, Clarendon Press, 1926.

WHEWELL, W., *Lectures on the History of Moral Philosophy in England,* London: John Parker & Son, West Strand, M.DCCC.LII.

WHYTE, A., *Bishop Butler, An Appreciation,* Fleming H. Revell Co., 1906.

WOLLASTON, *Religion of Nature Delineated,* 7th Ed., Glasgow, R. Urie and Co., MDCCXLVI.

INDEX